CW01237897

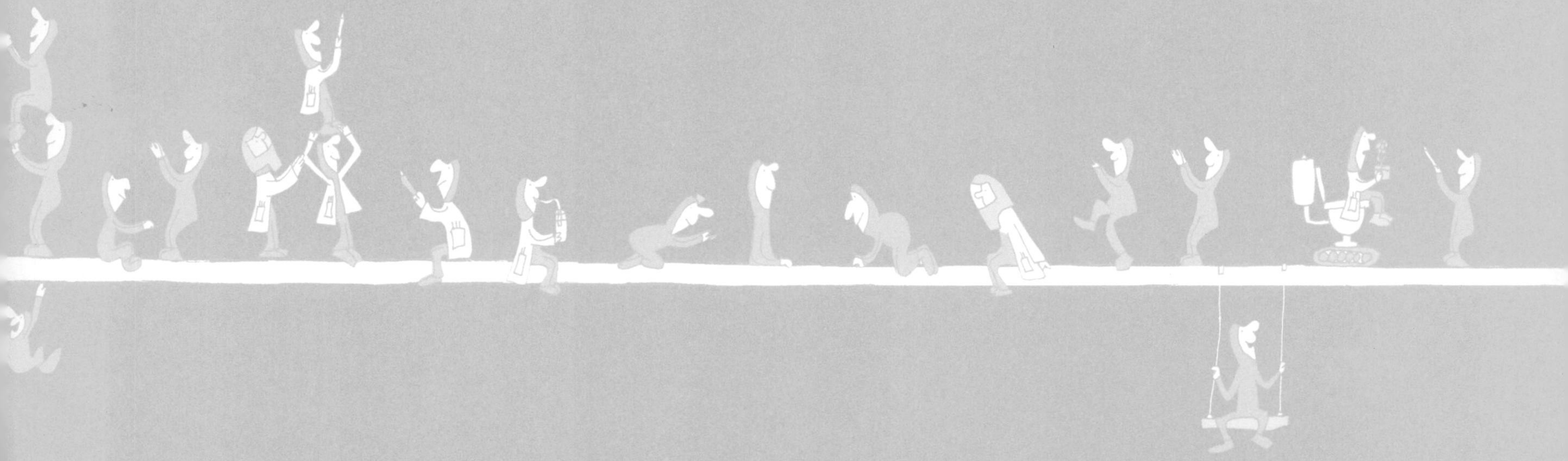

THE MOST EXCITING BOOK OF
SCIENCE, INVENTIONS & SPACE EVER

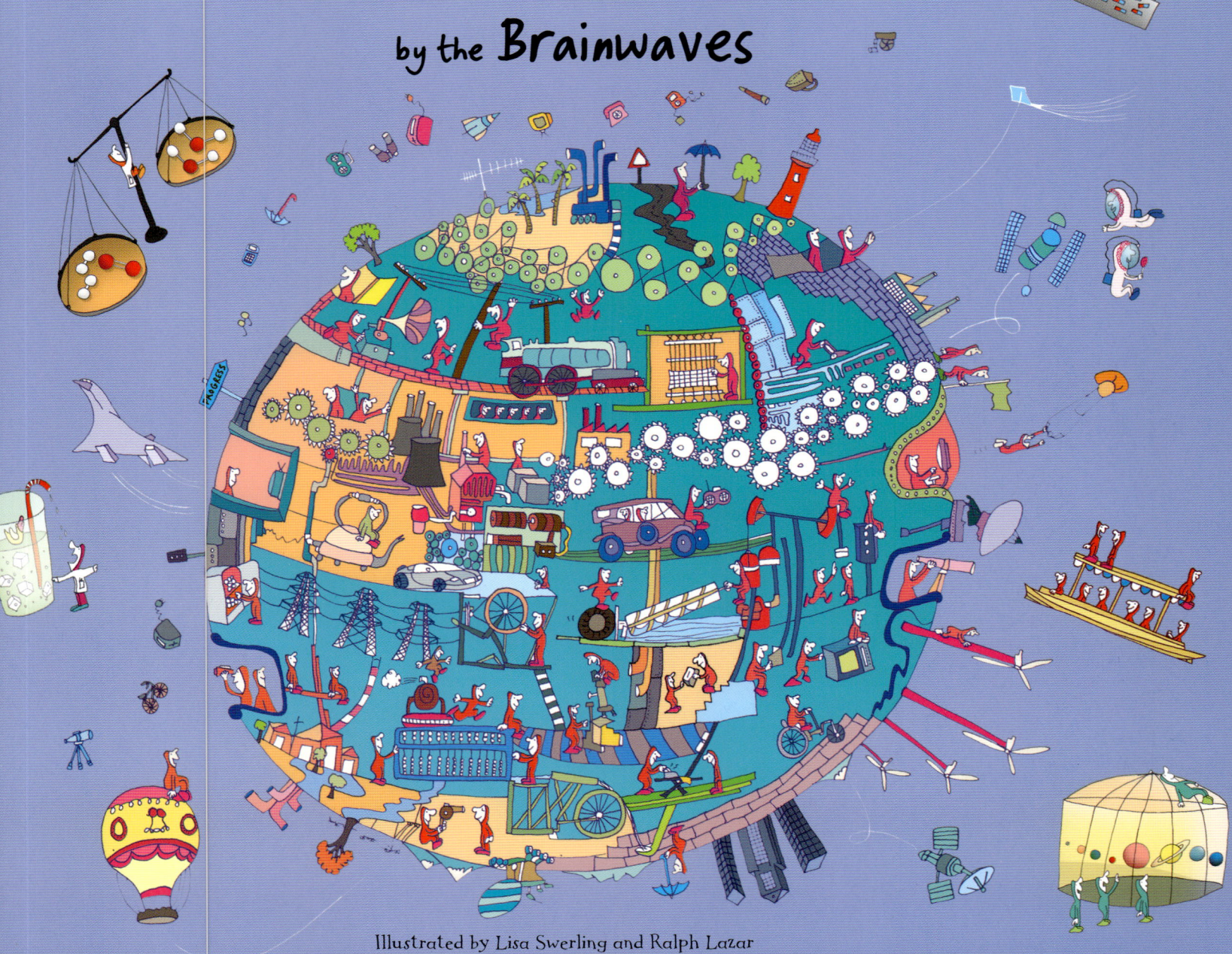

by the Brainwaves

Illustrated by Lisa Swerling and Ralph Lazar
Written by Claire Watts, Jilly MacLeod, Carole Stott, and Richard Walker

CONTENTS

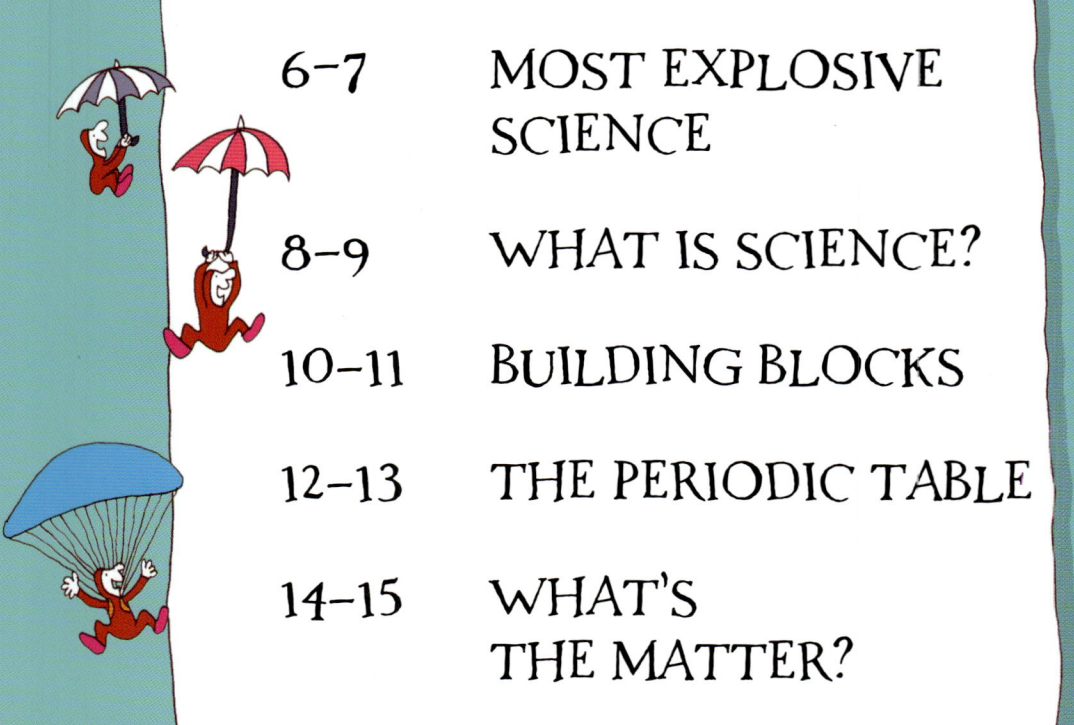

6-7 MOST EXPLOSIVE SCIENCE

8-9 WHAT IS SCIENCE?

10-11 BUILDING BLOCKS

12-13 THE PERIODIC TABLE

14-15 WHAT'S THE MATTER?

16-17 PROPERTIES OF MATTER

18-19 GETTING A REACTION

20-21 BUBBLE, FIZZ, BANG!

22-23 ACIDS AND BASES

24-25 BLUE PLANET

26-27 MIXING IT UP

THIS EDITION

DK LONDON
Senior Editor Fleur Star
Project Art Editor Gregory McCarthy
Jacket Designer Surabhi Wadhwa-Gandhi
Design Development Manager Sophia MTT
Producer Nancy-Jane Maun
Production Editor Gillian Reid
Managing Editor Lindsay Kent
Managing Art Editor Michelle Baxter
Art Director Karen Self
Publisher Andrew Macintyre
Publishing Director Jonathan Metcalf

DK DELHI
Desk Editor Joicy John
Senior Art Editor Nidhi Mehra
Project Art Editor Nehal Verma
Senior DTP Designer Pushpak Tyagi
DTP Designers Satish Gaur, Rakesh Kumar
Managing Editor Saloni Singh
Managing Art Editor Romi Chakraborty

Consultants Penny Johnson (Science),
Simon Adams (Inventions), Dr Jacqueline Mitton (Space),
Dr Kristina Routh (Human Body)

ORIGINAL EDITIONS
Senior Editor Andrea Mills
Editors Steven Carton, Niki Foreman
Senior Art Editors Jim Green
Designer Katie Knutton
Managing Editor Linda Esposito
Managing Art Editor Diane Thistlethwaite
Indexers Lynn Bresler, John Noble
Publishing Managers Andrew Macintyre,
Caroline Buckingham
Category Publisher Laura Buller

Consultants Lisa Burke (Science),
Roger Bridgman (Inventions), Dr Jacqueline Mitton (Space),
Dr Sue Davidson (Human Body)

Content previously published in
The Most Explosive Science Book in the Universe by the Brainwaves
How Nearly Everything Was Invented by the Brainwaves
The Greatest Intergalactic Guide to Space Ever by the Brainwaves
How the Incredible Human Body Works by the Brainwaves

First published in Great Britain in 2023 by
Dorling Kindersley Limited
DK, One Embassy Gardens, 8 Viaduct Gardens,
London, SW11 7BW

The authorised representative in the EEA is
Dorling Kindersley Verlag GmbH. Arnulfstr. 124,
80636 Munich, Germany

Copyright © 2006, 2007, 2009, 2010, 2023
Dorling Kindersley Limited
A Penguin Random House Company
10 9 8 7 6 5 4 3 2 1
001–334052–Mar/2023

All rights reserved.
No part of this publication may be reproduced, stored in or introduced
into a retrieval system, or transmitted, in any form, or by any means
(electronic, mechanical, photocopying, recording, or otherwise),
without the prior written permission of the copyright owner.

A CIP catalogue record for this book
is available from the British Library.
ISBN: 978-0-2416-0167-9

Printed and bound in China

For the curious
www.dk.com

is a trademark of Ralph Lazar and Lisa Swerling
and the subject of Community Registered Design
Applications. All rights reserved.

This book was made with Forest Stewardship Council™ certified paper - one small step in DK's commitment to a sustainable future. For more information go to www.dk.com/our-green-pledge

28–29	WARNING! CHEMISTS AT WORK	52–53	ELECTRIC CHEMISTRY
30–31	ENDLESS ENERGY	54–55	RECIPE FOR LIFE
32–33	GOOD VIBRATIONS	56–57	BURSTS OF IDEAS
34–35	HEAT WAVE	58–59	FUTURE SCIENCE
36–37	LET THERE BE LIGHT!	60–61	HOW NEARLY EVERYTHING WAS INVENTED
38–39	BEYOND THE RAINBOW		
40–41	BRUTE FORCE	62–63	FINDING A BETTER WAY
42–43	HARD AT WORK	64–65	SEEING IS BELIEVING
44–45	IT'S ALL RELATIVE		
46–47	POWERFUL ATTRACTION	66–69	LIGHTS, CAMERA, ACTION!
48–49	SHOCKING BEHAVIOUR	70–71	FAMOUS INVENTORS
50–51	BRIGHT SPARKS	72–73	STEAM MACHINE

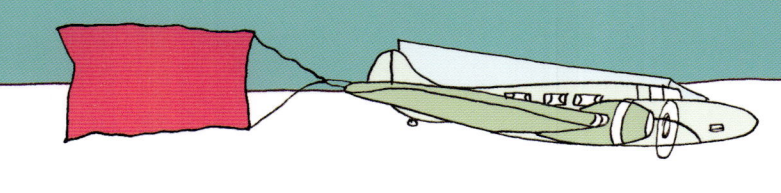

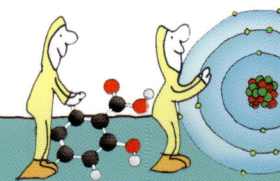

74–77	POWERING A REVOLUTION	104–107	OFF WITH A BANG!
78–79	FANTASTIC INVENTIONS	108–109	TIMELINE
80–81	LEADING LIGHTS	110–111	INTERGALACTIC GUIDE TO SPACE
82–85	POWER TO THE PEOPLE	112–113	COSMIC ZOO
86–87	FASCINATING FIRSTS	114–115	BANG!
88–89	ON THE ROAD	116–117	GLITTERING GALAXIES
90–93	BY LAND, SEA, AND AIR	118–119	ASTRONOMER'S LIFE
94–95	FABULOUS FLOPS	120–121	EYE ON THE UNIVERSE
96–97	SUPER-DUPER COMPUTER	122–123	STARS OF THE SHOW
98–101	LET'S ALL COMMUNICATE	124–125	OUR STAR
102–103	THE FUTURE	126–127	STARRY, STARRY NIGHT

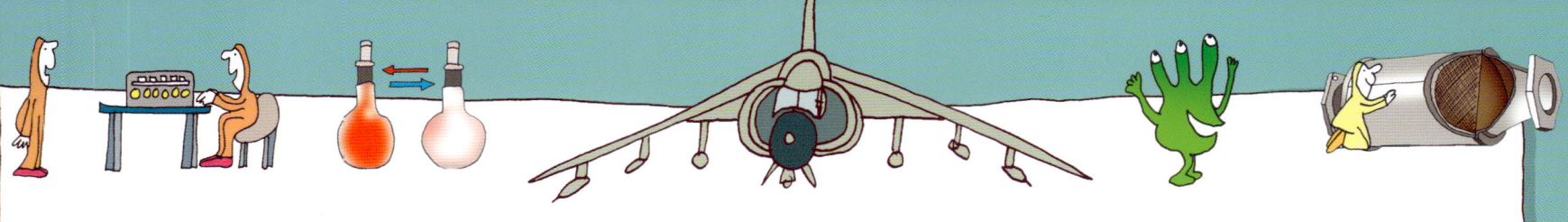

128-129	RECYCLED UNIVERSE	154-155	ANYBODY OUT THERE?
130-131	MEET THE FAMILY	156-157	SPACE SPIN-OFFS
132-133	HOME PLANET	158-159	TIME TRAVELLERS
134-135	BEST MATE MOON	160-161	FUTURE SPACE
136-137	SUN-BAKED WORLDS	162-167	GLOSSARY
138-139	HOLIDAY ON MARS	168-173	INDEX
140-141	RING OF RUBBLE		
142-143	GIANT PLANETS		
144-145	FROZEN WORLDS		
146-147	READY FOR LAUNCH		
148-149	ROBOT EXPLORERS		
150-151	ASTRONAUTS WANTED		
152-153	LIVING IN SPACE		

Look out for us!

Special Brainwaves, and a very hungry Spacehopper, appear in this book. See if you can spot each of them!

Look for me on pages 8-57!

I'm hiding on pages 58-109!

I appear on pages 110-161!

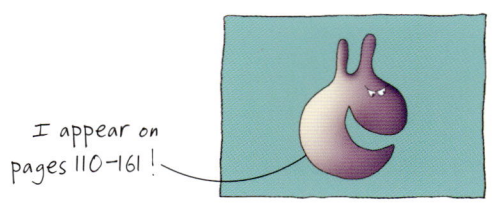

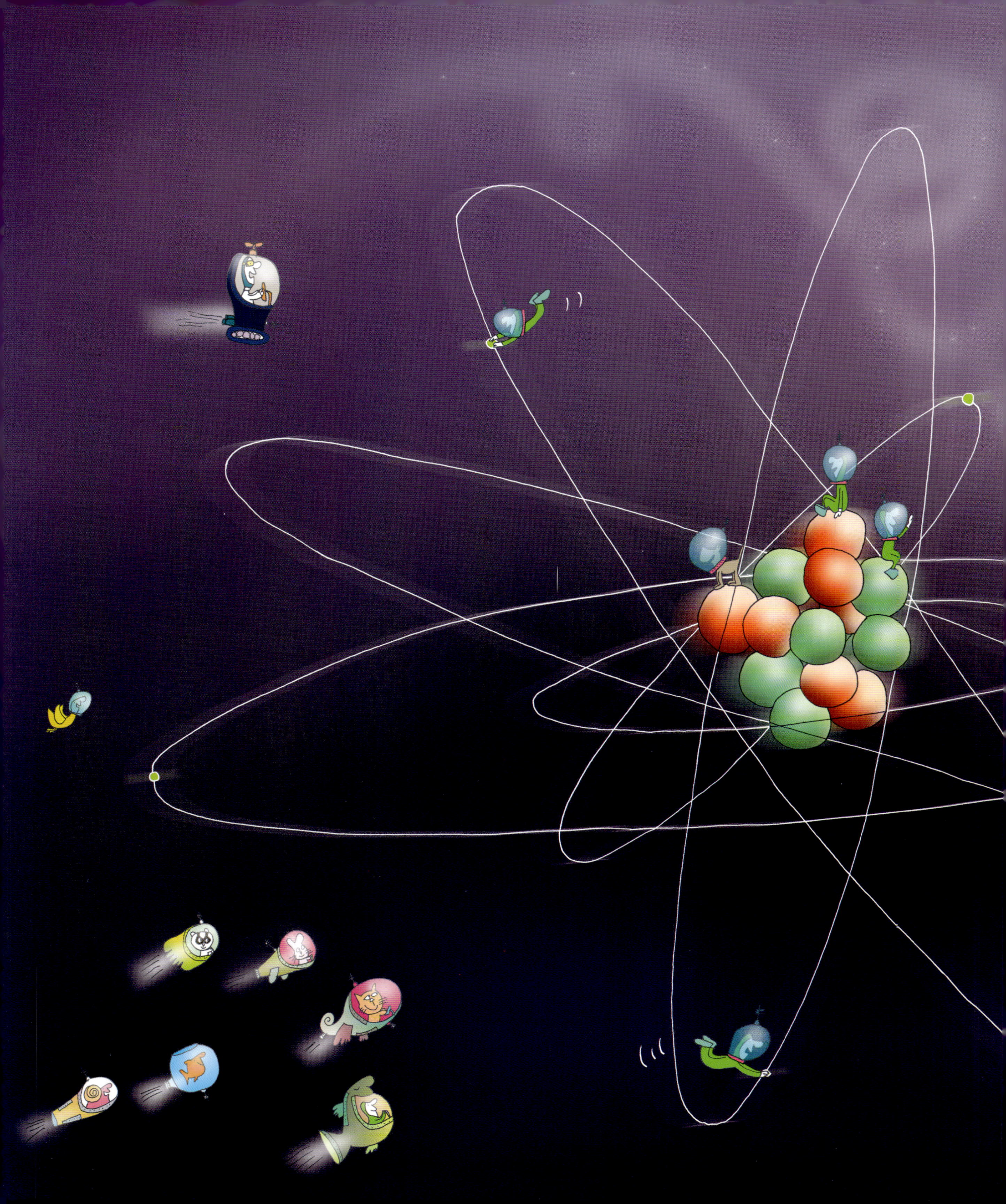

MOST EXPLOSIVE
SCIENCE

WHAT IS SCIENCE?

From the tiny particles that make us to the vast galaxies of the Universe, science is everywhere. This huge body of information explains and describes the structure, properties, and behaviour of all living and non-living things. However, scientists are still learning. There are questions to be asked, experiments to carry out, and discoveries to be made.

Branches of science

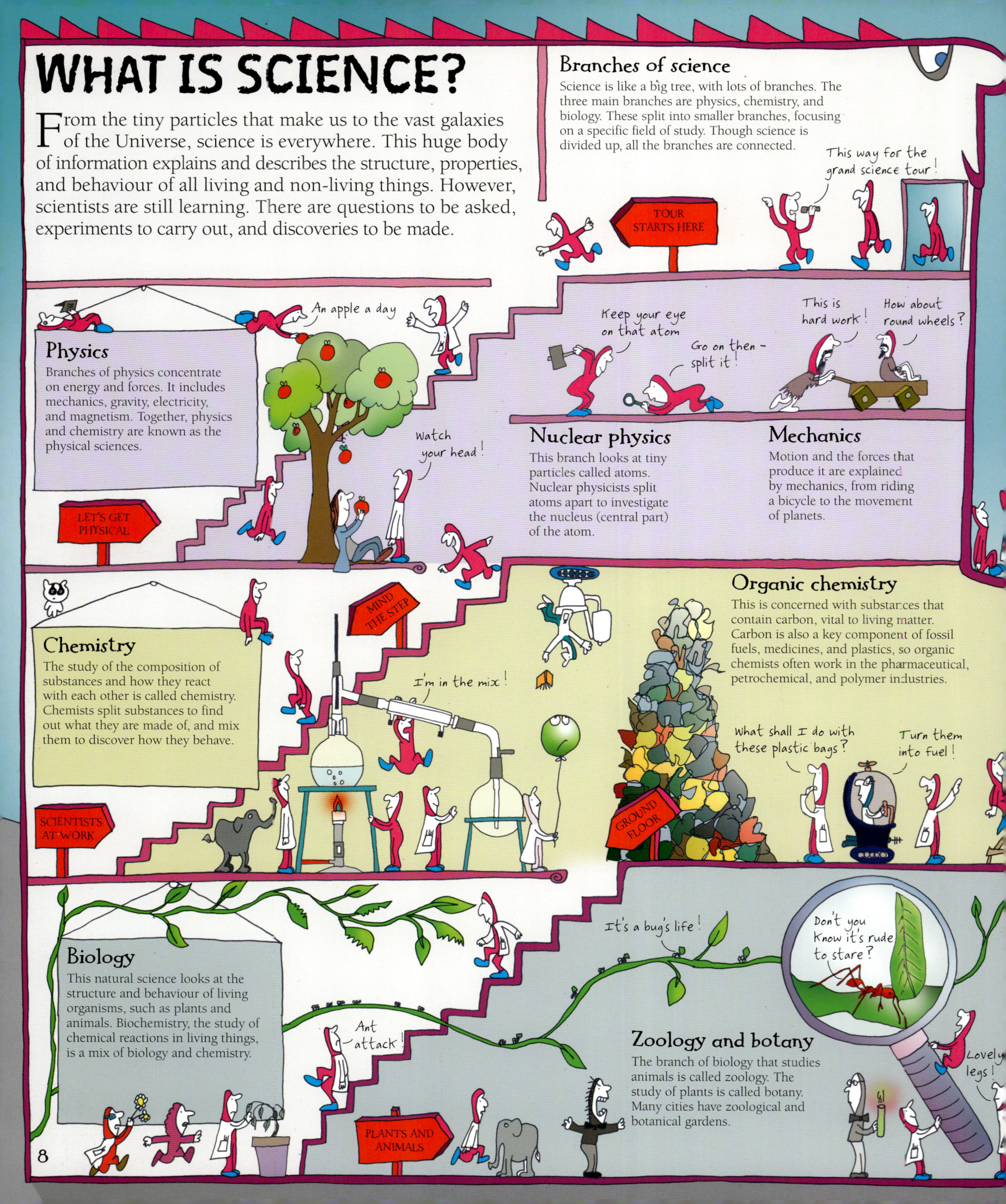

Science is like a big tree, with lots of branches. The three main branches are physics, chemistry, and biology. These split into smaller branches, focusing on a specific field of study. Though science is divided up, all the branches are connected.

Physics

Branches of physics concentrate on energy and forces. It includes mechanics, gravity, electricity, and magnetism. Together, physics and chemistry are known as the physical sciences.

Nuclear physics

This branch looks at tiny particles called atoms. Nuclear physicists split atoms apart to investigate the nucleus (central part) of the atom.

Mechanics

Motion and the forces that produce it are explained by mechanics, from riding a bicycle to the movement of planets.

Chemistry

The study of the composition of substances and how they react with each other is called chemistry. Chemists split substances to find out what they are made of, and mix them to discover how they behave.

Organic chemistry

This is concerned with substances that contain carbon, vital to living matter. Carbon is also a key component of fossil fuels, medicines, and plastics, so organic chemists often work in the pharmaceutical, petrochemical, and polymer industries.

Biology

This natural science looks at the structure and behaviour of living organisms, such as plants and animals. Biochemistry, the study of chemical reactions in living things, is a mix of biology and chemistry.

Zoology and botany

The branch of biology that studies animals is called zoology. The study of plants is called botany. Many cities have zoological and botanical gardens.

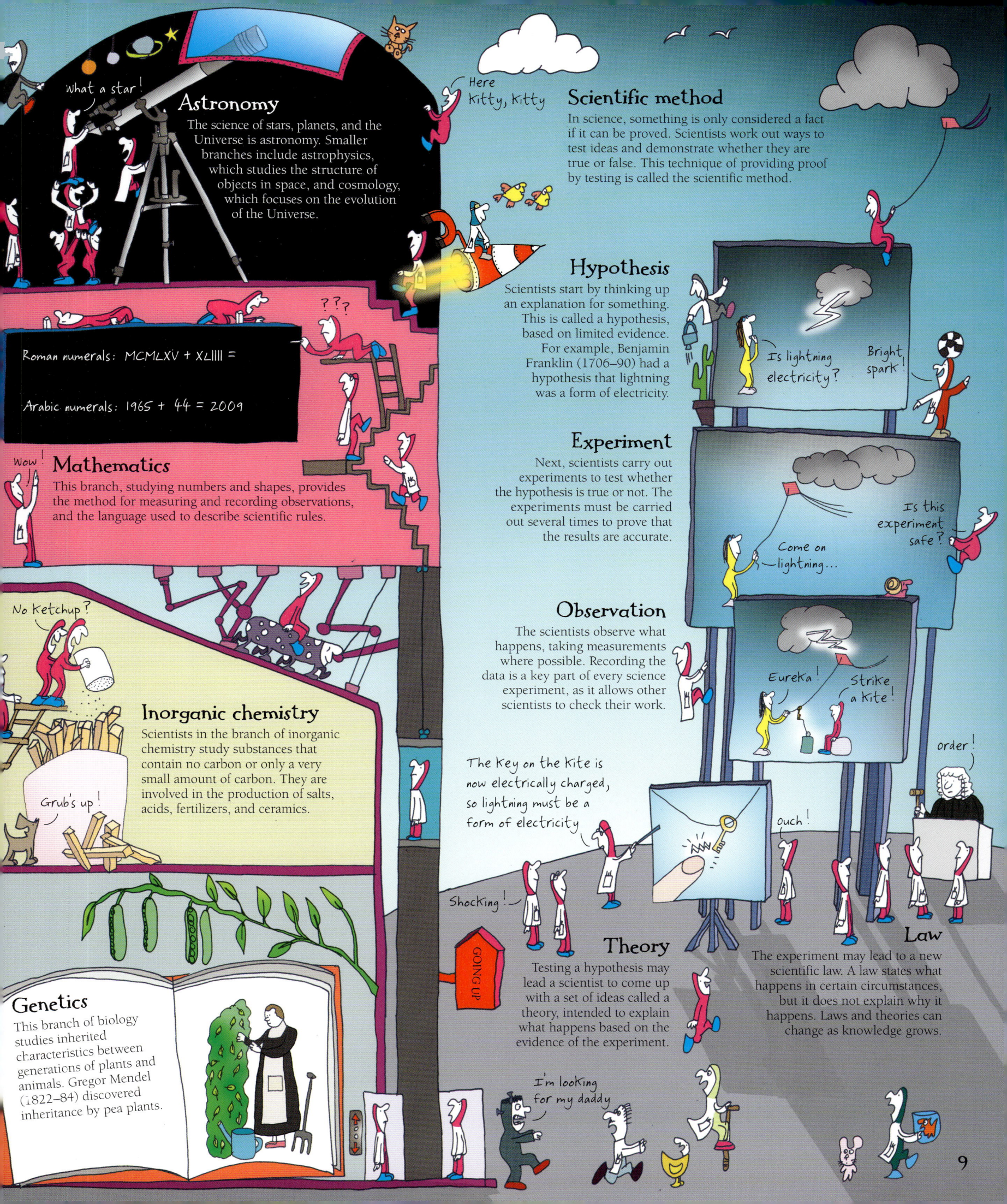

Astronomy
The science of stars, planets, and the Universe is astronomy. Smaller branches include astrophysics, which studies the structure of objects in space, and cosmology, which focuses on the evolution of the Universe.

Mathematics
This branch, studying numbers and shapes, provides the method for measuring and recording observations, and the language used to describe scientific rules.

Roman numerals: MCMLXV + XLIIII =
Arabic numerals: 1965 + 44 = 2009

Inorganic chemistry
Scientists in the branch of inorganic chemistry study substances that contain no carbon or only a very small amount of carbon. They are involved in the production of salts, acids, fertilizers, and ceramics.

Genetics
This branch of biology studies inherited characteristics between generations of plants and animals. Gregor Mendel (1822–84) discovered inheritance by pea plants.

Scientific method
In science, something is only considered a fact if it can be proved. Scientists work out ways to test ideas and demonstrate whether they are true or false. This technique of providing proof by testing is called the scientific method.

Hypothesis
Scientists start by thinking up an explanation for something. This is called a hypothesis, based on limited evidence. For example, Benjamin Franklin (1706–90) had a hypothesis that lightning was a form of electricity.

Experiment
Next, scientists carry out experiments to test whether the hypothesis is true or not. The experiments must be carried out several times to prove that the results are accurate.

Observation
The scientists observe what happens, taking measurements where possible. Recording the data is a key part of every science experiment, as it allows other scientists to check their work.

The key on the kite is now electrically charged, so lightning must be a form of electricity

Theory
Testing a hypothesis may lead a scientist to come up with a set of ideas called a theory, intended to explain what happens based on the evidence of the experiment.

Law
The experiment may lead to a new scientific law. A law states what happens in certain circumstances, but it does not explain why it happens. Laws and theories can change as knowledge grows.

BUILDING BLOCKS

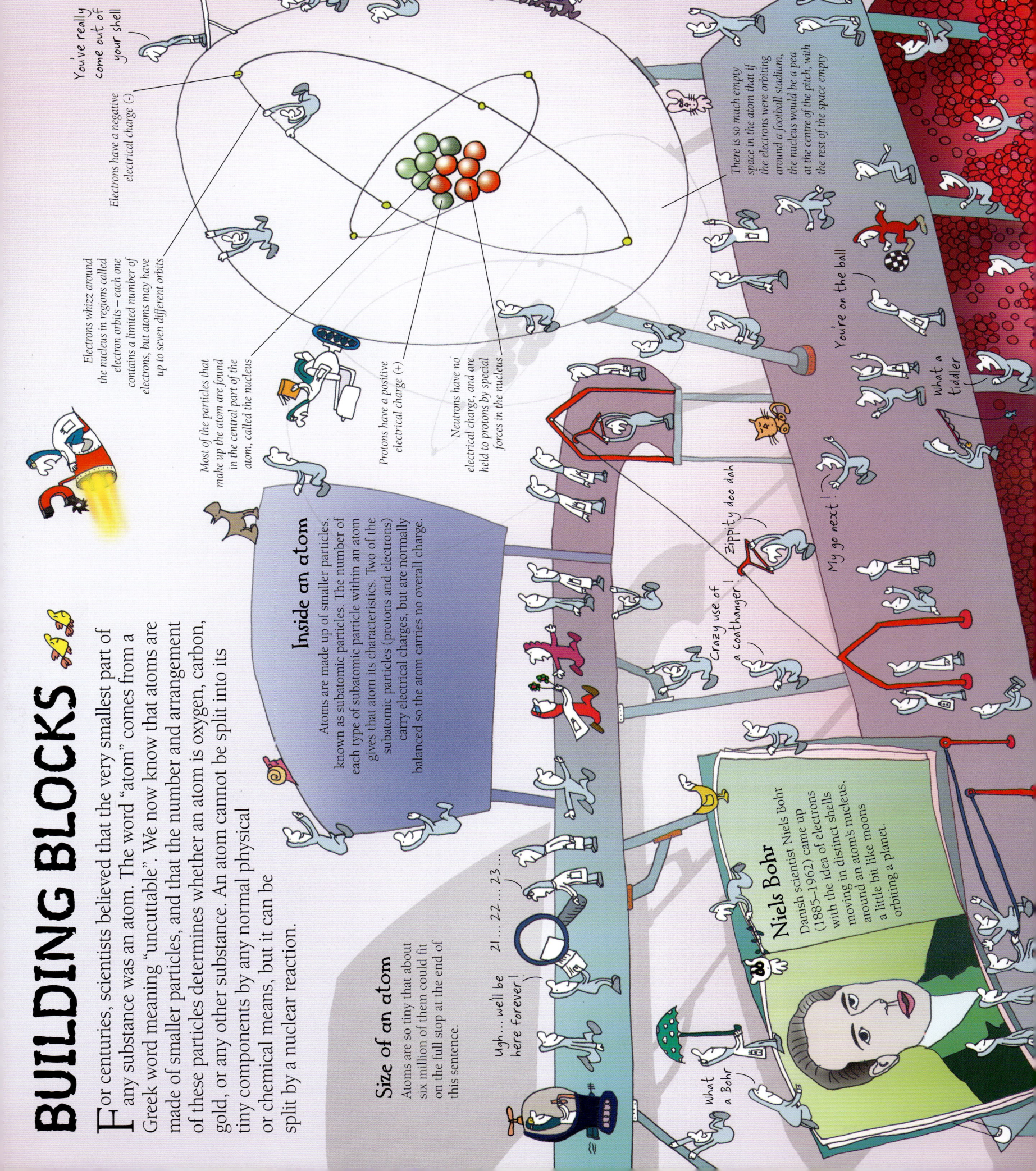

For centuries, scientists believed that the very smallest part of any substance was an atom. The word "atom" comes from a Greek word meaning "uncuttable." We now know that atoms are made of smaller particles, and that the number and arrangement of these particles determines whether an atom is oxygen, carbon, gold, or any other substance. An atom cannot be split into its tiny components by any normal physical or chemical means, but it can be split by a nuclear reaction.

You've really come out of your shell

Electrons have a negative electrical charge (−)

Electrons whizz around the nucleus in regions called electron orbits – each one contains a limited number of electrons, but atoms may have up to seven different orbits

Most of the particles that make up the atom are found in the central part of the atom, called the nucleus

Protons have a positive electrical charge (+)

Neutrons have no electrical charge, and are held to protons by special forces in the nucleus

There is so much empty space in the atom that if the electrons were orbiting around a football stadium, the nucleus would be a pea at the centre of the pitch, with the rest of the space empty

Inside an atom

Atoms are made up of smaller particles, known as subatomic particles. The number of each type of subatomic particle within an atom gives that atom its characteristics. Two of the subatomic particles (protons and electrons) carry electrical charges, but are normally balanced so the atom carries no overall charge.

Size of an atom

Atoms are so tiny that about six million of them could fit on the full stop at the end of this sentence.

Ugh...well be here forever!

21...22...23...

Niels Bohr

Danish scientist Niels Bohr (1885–1962) came up with the idea of electrons moving in distinct shells around an atom's nucleus, a little bit like moons orbiting a planet.

What a Bohr

Crazy use of a coathanger!

Zippity doo dah

My go next

You're on the ball

What a tiddler

Elements

An element is a substance made from only one type of atom. The number of protons in the nucleus determines what type of atom it is. For example, a carbon atom has six protons, and a hydrogen atom has one.

Molecule

Most atoms bond in groups of two or more to form particles called molecules. A single oxygen atom does not have the same characteristics as this oxygen molecule here.

Compound

Molecules made from more than one type of atom are called compounds. Water is one example, as it is made up of two hydrogen atoms bonded to one oxygen atom.

Bonds

Atoms share or exchange electrons with other atoms to gain full outer shells. This forms chemical bonds between the atoms and holds them together as molecules.

Ionic bonds

An ion is an atom with a positive or negative charge. Ionic bonds form when positive and negative atoms join up. In table salt, or sodium chloride, sodium becomes positively charged when it gives one electron to chlorine, which becomes negatively charged. The unlike charges attract, forming an ionic bond between the atoms.

Covalent bonds

When electrons are shared by atoms, a covalent bond is formed. Two oxygen atoms bond to form a molecule by sharing four electrons in their outer shells, so that each atom has a complete outer shell of eight electrons.

Metallic bonds

In metals, all the atoms lose electrons, which flow around freely between the atoms. This mobile sea of electrons can carry heat and electricity quickly and easily from one part of the metal to another, making metals good conductors of heat and electricity.

Linus Pauling

The first person ever to win two undivided Nobel Prizes (for Chemistry in 1954 and Peace in 1962), US scientist Linus Pauling (1901–94) explained how the number of electrons in an atom's outer shell affects the way atoms bond.

Weak bonds

When shared electrons in a molecule are closer to the nucleus of one of the atoms, the electron gives the atom a tiny negative charge and the more distant atoms have a tiny positive charge. The charged ends of each molecule attract the opposite charges of others, holding molecules together weakly, as shown with these ammonia molecules.

THE PERIODIC TABLE

Every element that we know about in the universe is set out in order of the increasing numbers of protons in the nucleus on the periodic table. The elements are arranged in rows and columns that reveal repeating patterns in their structure and properties. Most of these elements exist naturally in the Universe, but some are created artificially. The rows across are called periods and the columns are called groups.

Reading the table
Each element has an atomic number, a symbol, and an atomic mass. This box shows the element germanium, a light grey metal.

Atomic number (32)
The number of protons in the atom's nucleus is shown by the atomic number at the top.

| 32 |
| Ge |
| Germanium |
| 73 |

Chemical symbol (Ge)
Above the element's name is a chemical symbol used to represent the element in chemical equations.

Atomic mass (73)
The number of protons and neutrons in the nucleus is shown by the atomic mass at the bottom.

How the table is arranged
Starting with hydrogen, elements are arranged by atomic number and continue across the rows. Atomic mass usually increases with atomic number, so the elements at the start of the table are light and those at the end are heavy.

Period (rows)
Each row corresponds with the number of electron orbits (also called shells) its atoms have. So, hydrogen in row 1 has one shell, while gold in row 6 has six shells.

Group (columns)
Most elements in a group have the same number of electrons in their outer orbits. Elements become less reactive across the rows, so group 1 elements catch fire in oxygen, while group 18 elements are unreactive gases.

Hydrogen
Element 1 is colourless and odourless, and makes up 88 per cent of all the atoms in the Universe.

Sodium
This soft metal can be cut with a knife, but it explodes if it comes into contact with water.

Silicon
Some people think alien life might be based on silicon, which has similar properties to carbon, the basis of all life on Earth.

I'm top of the table

Stop!!!

1 2 3 4 5 6 7 8 9

	1	2		3	4	5	6	7	8	9
1	1 H Hydrogen 1									
2	3 Li Lithium 7	4 Be Beryllium 9								
3	11 Na Sodium 23	12 Mg Magnesium 24								
4	19 K Potassium 39	20 Ca Calcium 40		21 Sc Scandium 45	22 Ti Titanium 48	23 V Vanadium 51	24 Cr Chromium 52	25 Mg Manganese 55	26 Fe Iron 56	27 Co Cobalt 59
5	37 Rb Rubidium 85	38 Sr Strontium 88		39 Y Yttrium 89	40 Zr Zirconium 91	41 Nb Niobium 93	42 Mo Molybdenum 96	43 Tc Technetium 98	44 Ru Ruthenium 101	45 Rh Rhodium 103
6	55 Cs Caesium 133	56 Ba Barium 137		57–71 (see below)	72 Hf Hafnium 178	73 Ta Tantalum 181	74 W Tungsten 184	75 Re Rhenium 186	76 Os Osmium 190	77 Ir Iridium 192
7	87 Fr Francium 223	88 Ra Radium 226		89–103 (see below)	104 Rf Rutherfordium 261	105 Db Dubnium 262	106 Sg Seaborgium 266	107 Bh Bohrium 264	108 Hs Hassium 277	109 Mt Meitnerium 268

Look, no hands!

Mendeleyev
When Russian chemist Dmitri Mendeleyev (1834–1907) devised the periodic table in 1869, it was so accurate that he even left gaps in the right places for elements that were not yet discovered.

we're not worthy

It's elementary

| 57 La Lanthanum 139 | 58 Ce Cerium 140 | 59 Pr Praseodymium 141 | 60 Nd Neodymium 144 | 61 Pm Promethium 145 | 62 Sm Samarium 150 |
| 89 Ac Actinium 227 | 90 Th Thorium 232 | 91 Pa Protactinium 231 | 92 U Uranium 238 | 93 Np Neptunium 237 | 94 Pu Plutonium 244 |

Uranium
Radioactive element 92 is used as a fuel in nuclear power stations.

we have chemistry

Help me, Helium Superhero!

The coinage metals

Copper Pots and pans are made of copper, because it spreads heat well.

Silver Cutlery and other utensils are sometimes made of silver.

Gold Easy to shape and non-tarnishing, gold is perfect for coins and jewellery.

Key
The elements can be divided into categories with similar properties, such as appearance or behaviour. Each element on this periodic table is colour-coded to match one of the categories in this key.

Alkali metals Silvery solids at room temperature, alkali metals are good conductors of heat and electricity.

Alkaline earth metals These elements combine with many elements in the Earth's crust to form stable compounds.

Transition metals Generally hard, tough, and shiny at room temperature, these metals have high melting points.

Lanthanoids These silvery reactive metals occur only as compounds in nature and are hard to separate.

Actinoids Dangerously radioactive metals, actinoids are usually created synthetically.

Poor metals These are similar to transition metals, but fairly soft and with low melting and boiling points.

Non-metals Poor conductors of electricity and heat, non-metals melt at low temperatures.

Noble gases These elements do not combine readily with others, and are gases at room temperature.

Hydrogen The simplest and lightest of all the elements, hydrogen does not fit into any category.

Nitrogen Vital for building cells in all living things, nitrogen is used in fertilizer to help crops grow.

Carbon Element 6 exists in several forms, from black soot to sparkling diamonds.

Phosphorus Highly reactive, phosphorus glows bright green in the dark, and comes in differently coloured forms.

Helium Lighter than air, helium is used to fill balloons and airships, making them float.

Chlorine Yellow-green element 17 is used to kill bacteria in swimming pools and drinking water supplies.

Mercury A liquid metal at room temperature, mercury was used in hat-making, until it was discovered that it sent people mad!

Natural elements
All matter on Earth is made up of one or more of 94 elements that occur naturally. Some of these elements, such as technetium, are produced when radioactive natural elements disintegrate.

Einsteinium Named after Albert Einstein, this element is produced from plutonium in a nuclear process that takes several years.

Synthetic elements
All the elements heavier than plutonium are made artificially, or synthesized. They have been named after the places they were first created or the first people to create them. Nihonium comes from the Japanese name for Japan. Flerovium is named after the Flerov laboratory. Oganesson is named in honour of Russian nuclear physicist Yuri Oganessian.

10	11	12	13	14	15	16	17	18
			5 B Boron 11	6 C Carbon 12	7 N Nitrogen 14	8 O Oxygen 16	9 F Fluorine 19	2 He Helium 4 / 10 Ne Neon 20
			13 Al Aluminium 27	14 Si Silicon 28	15 P Phosphorus 31	16 S Sulphur 32	17 Cl Chlorine 35	18 Ar Argon 40
28 Ni Nickel 59	29 Cu Copper 64	30 Zn Zinc 65	31 Ga Gallium 70	32 Ge Germanium 73	33 As Arsenic 75	34 Se Selenium 79	35 Br Bromine 80	36 Kr Krypton 84
46 Pd Palladium 103	47 Ag Silver 108	48 Cd Cadmium 112	49 In Indium 115	50 Sn Tin 119	51 Sb Antimony 122	52 Te Tellurium 128	53 I Iodine 127	54 Xe Xenon 131
78 Pt Platinum 192	79 Au Gold 197	80 Hg Mercury 201	81 Tl Thallium 204	82 Pb Lead 207	83 Bi Bismuth 209	84 Po Polonium 209	85 At Astatine 210	86 Rn Radon 222
110 Ds Darmstadtium 271	111 Rg Roentgenium 272	112 Cn Copernicium 285	113 Nh Nihonium 284	114 Fl Flerovium 289	115 Mc Moscovium 288	116 Lv Livermorium 292	117 Ts Tennessine 293	118 Og Oganesson 294

Aluminium Earth's most common metal is used to make aircraft and drinks cans.

63 Eu Europium 152	64 Gd Gadolinium 157	65 Tb Terbium 159	66 Dy Dysprosium 163	67 Ho Holmium 165	68 Er Erbium 167	69 Tm Thulium 169	70 Yb Ytterbium 173	71 Lu Lutetium 175
95 Am Americium 243	96 Cm Curium 247	97 Bk Berkelium 247	98 Cf Californium 251	99 Es Einsteinium 252	100 Fm Fermium 257	101 Md Mendelevium 258	102 No Nobelium 259	103 Lr Lawrencium 262

13

WHAT'S THE MATTER?

Everything in the Universe that is made up of atoms and occupies space is called matter. It is everywhere, in all the animals, objects, and substances that you can see and touch, and in the stars and planets far out in space. Matter is even in the things you can't see, floating around as invisible gases in the air, and as tiny, drifting particles that your nose detects as smells.

Types of matter
Matter is divided into two types: living and non-living matter. Your body is composed of living matter, while objects, such as a metal spoon, are composed of non-living matter.

States of matter
Matter exists in different states, depending on how much energy it contains. The most common states of matter are solid, liquid, and gas. Sometimes matter exists in other states, such as plasmas, which are gases made from parts of atoms.

Solid
Particles in a solid have less energy than those in a liquid or gas. They can vibrate but cannot move around. Solids have a fixed volume, which means they take up a fixed amount of space, and most have a definite shape.

Not much space between particles in solids

Changing states
Matter can change from one state to another by adding or removing energy. For example, water can change from a liquid to solid ice or to a gas, steam. The molecules within ice, water, and steam are identical but they move in different ways.

Heating
Heating a substance gives it more energy, so its particles move faster and further apart. Heating a solid melts it into a liquid, and heating a liquid evaporates it into a gas.

Cooling
Cooling a substance takes away energy, making its particles slow down and move closer together. Cooling a gas condenses it into a liquid, and cooling a liquid freezes it into a solid.

Liquid
Molecules are evenly spread out in liquids

Particles in a liquid have more energy, so they move faster and spread out further from each other. Liquids have a fixed volume, but no definite shape.

14

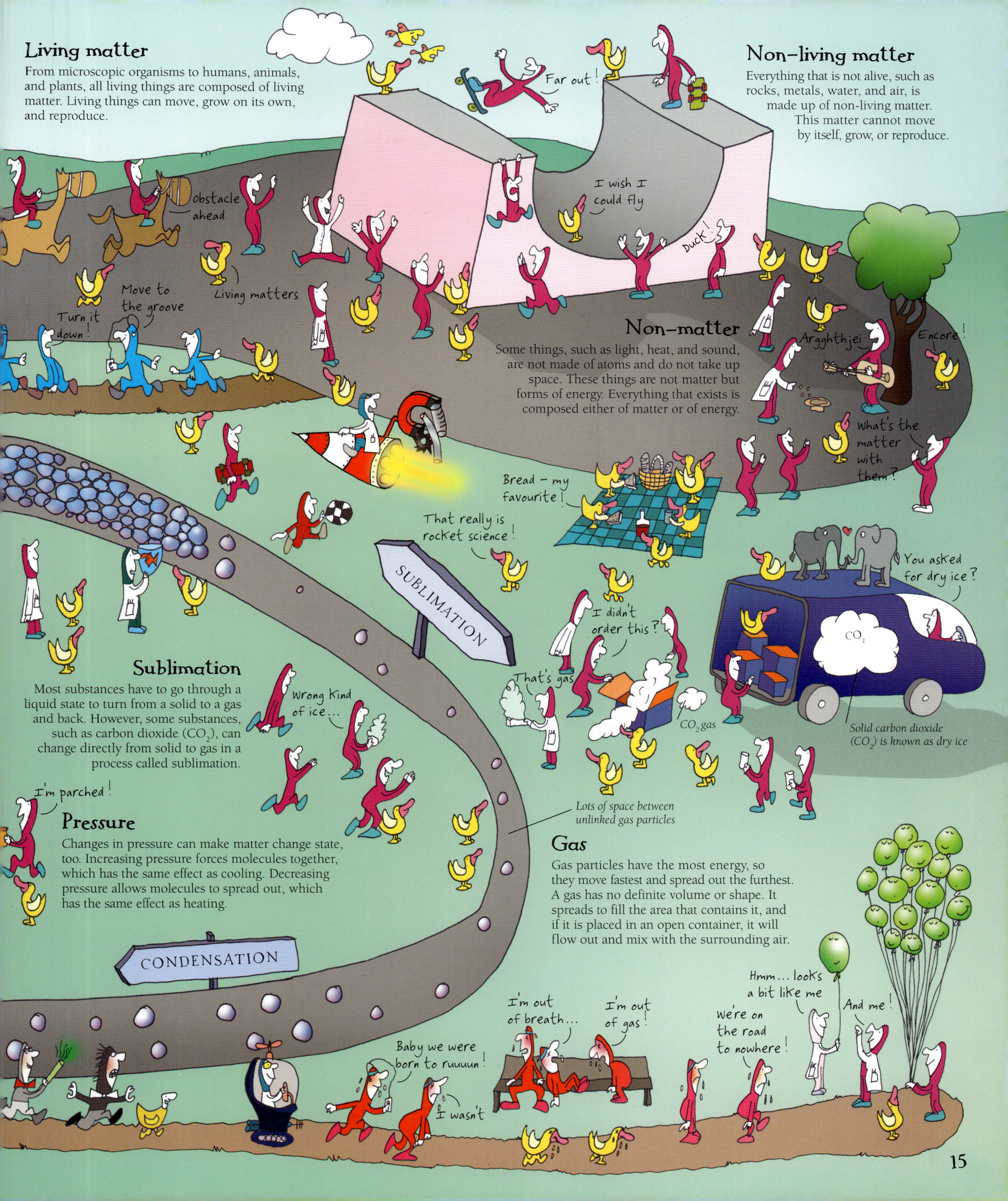

Living matter
From microscopic organisms to humans, animals, and plants, all living things are composed of living matter. Living things can move, grow on its own, and reproduce.

Non-living matter
Everything that is not alive, such as rocks, metals, water, and air, is made up of non-living matter. This matter cannot move by itself, grow, or reproduce.

Non-matter
Some things, such as light, heat, and sound, are not made of atoms and do not take up space. These things are not matter but forms of energy. Everything that exists is composed either of matter or of energy.

Sublimation
Most substances have to go through a liquid state to turn from a solid to a gas and back. However, some substances, such as carbon dioxide (CO_2), can change directly from solid to gas in a process called sublimation.

Pressure
Changes in pressure can make matter change state, too. Increasing pressure forces molecules together, which has the same effect as cooling. Decreasing pressure allows molecules to spread out, which has the same effect as heating.

Gas
Gas particles have the most energy, so they move fastest and spread out the furthest. A gas has no definite volume or shape. It spreads to fill the area that contains it, and if it is placed in an open container, it will flow out and mix with the surrounding air.

Lots of space between unlinked gas particles

Solid carbon dioxide (CO_2) is known as dry ice

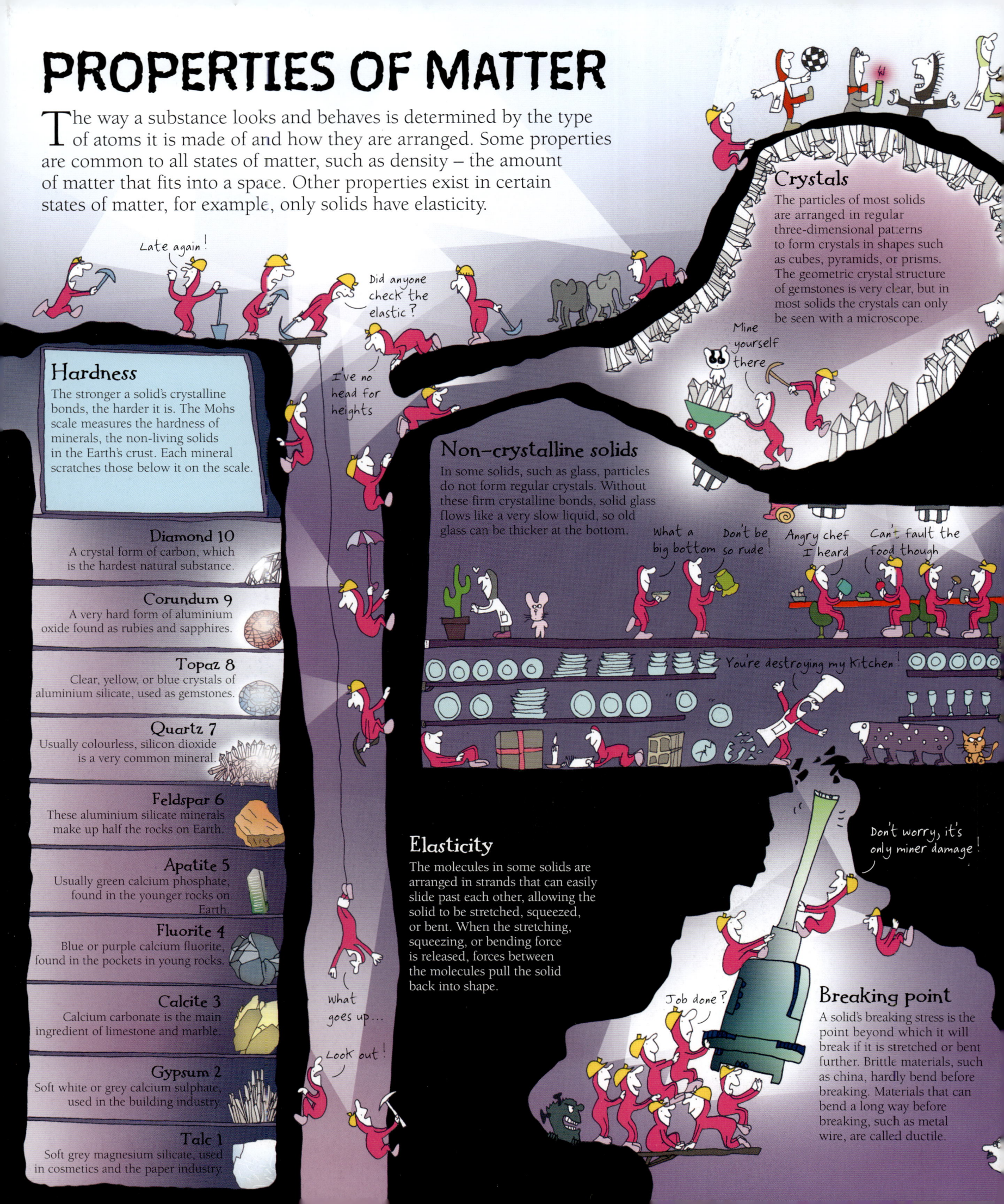

PROPERTIES OF MATTER

The way a substance looks and behaves is determined by the type of atoms it is made of and how they are arranged. Some properties are common to all states of matter, such as density – the amount of matter that fits into a space. Other properties exist in certain states of matter, for example, only solids have elasticity.

Crystals

The particles of most solids are arranged in regular three-dimensional patterns to form crystals in shapes such as cubes, pyramids, or prisms. The geometric crystal structure of gemstones is very clear, but in most solids the crystals can only be seen with a microscope.

Hardness

The stronger a solid's crystalline bonds, the harder it is. The Mohs scale measures the hardness of minerals, the non-living solids in the Earth's crust. Each mineral scratches those below it on the scale.

Diamond 10
A crystal form of carbon, which is the hardest natural substance.

Corundum 9
A very hard form of aluminium oxide found as rubies and sapphires.

Topaz 8
Clear, yellow, or blue crystals of aluminium silicate, used as gemstones.

Quartz 7
Usually colourless, silicon dioxide is a very common mineral.

Feldspar 6
These aluminium silicate minerals make up half the rocks on Earth.

Apatite 5
Usually green calcium phosphate, found in the younger rocks on Earth.

Fluorite 4
Blue or purple calcium fluorite, found in the pockets in young rocks.

Calcite 3
Calcium carbonate is the main ingredient of limestone and marble.

Gypsum 2
Soft white or grey calcium sulphate, used in the building industry.

Talc 1
Soft grey magnesium silicate, used in cosmetics and the paper industry.

Non-crystalline solids

In some solids, such as glass, particles do not form regular crystals. Without these firm crystalline bonds, solid glass flows like a very slow liquid, so old glass can be thicker at the bottom.

Elasticity

The molecules in some solids are arranged in strands that can easily slide past each other, allowing the solid to be stretched, squeezed, or bent. When the stretching, squeezing, or bending force is released, forces between the molecules pull the solid back into shape.

Breaking point

A solid's breaking stress is the point beyond which it will break if it is stretched or bent further. Brittle materials, such as china, hardly bend before breaking. Materials that can bend a long way before breaking, such as metal wire, are called ductile.

Viscosity

The way the particles of a fluid rub against each other affects how easily it will flow. Fluids that resist flowing, such as ketchup, are called viscous, while fluids that flow easily, such as water, have low viscosity.

We're going to need bigger burgers!

Surface tension

Particles at the surface of a liquid are attracted downwards by the liquid particles below, forming an invisible, elastic skin. This effect, called surface tension, enables tiny insects, such as pond-skaters, to walk on water.

Hop on

Up, up, and away!

Room for a small one?

Meniscus

Liquids have a curved surface, called the meniscus, caused by the variation in surface tension where the liquid touches the container. Water molecules are more attracted to the container than to each other, so water's meniscus curves up. But mercury particles are strongly attracted to each other, so the meniscus curves down.

Water — Meniscus
Mercury — Meniscus
Don't fall in!

A flying fish!

Expansion

When matter is heated, the particles move further apart, so the substance expands. As the gas in a hot air balloon is heated, it expands, making the balloon swell. The air inside the balloon is less dense than the air outside, so the balloon rises.

Compression

Gas particles can be compressed to fit into a smaller space. When the pressure is released, the gas expands with great force. Gas dissolved in a liquid under pressure expands into bubbles of fizz when the container is opened, relieving the pressure.

What a fizzer!
Cheers
Yikes!
Burrrp
Congratulations and celebrations
This has popped and all!
Bottoms up!
Dazzling!

17

GETTING A REACTION

Chemical reactions are happening all the time, all around us, and even inside our bodies, as molecules split apart and join together to make new molecules. The substances that are changed by a chemical reaction are called reactants, while the substances that exist after the reaction are called products. Some chemical reactions can split a molecule into pure elements, but they cannot split an atom – that requires a nuclear reaction.

Chemical change
When substances undergo chemical changes, the atoms within them are rearranged to form new substances. One example is when iron is exposed to air. Iron atoms combine with oxygen atoms to form iron oxide or rust.

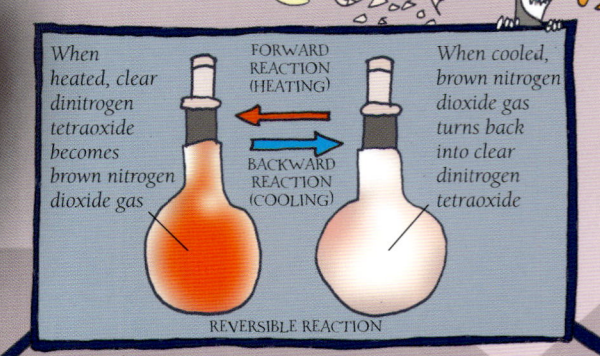

Physical change
Chopping, cutting, crushing, dissolving, and changing state all change the way a substance looks, but does not change the molecules that make up the substance. These are physical changes, not chemical changes.

Non-reversible reaction
In most chemical reactions, it is impossible to change the products back into the reactants. Burning a product makes it react with oxygen in the air to create smoke and ash, which can never be turned back into the original material.

When heated, clear dinitrogen tetraoxide becomes brown nitrogen dioxide gas

FORWARD REACTION (HEATING)
BACKWARD REACTION (COOLING)

When cooled, brown nitrogen dioxide gas turns back into clear dinitrogen tetraoxide

REVERSIBLE REACTION

Reversible reaction
Some chemical reactions can be reversed. The forward reaction changes the reactants into products and the backward reaction changes the products back to reactants.

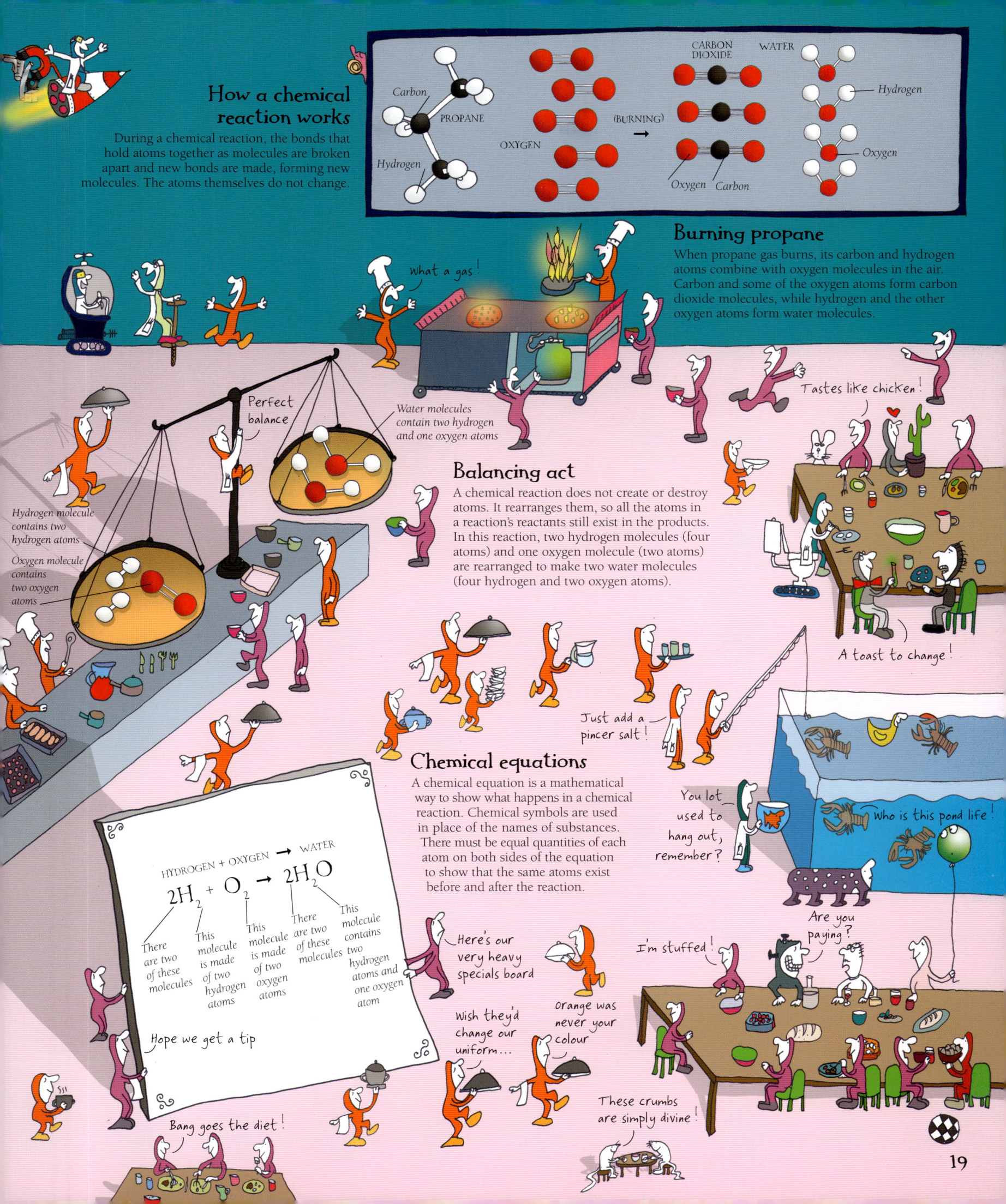

How a chemical reaction works

During a chemical reaction, the bonds that hold atoms together as molecules are broken apart and new bonds are made, forming new molecules. The atoms themselves do not change.

PROPANE — Carbon, Hydrogen
OXYGEN
(BURNING) →
CARBON DIOXIDE — Oxygen, Carbon
WATER — Hydrogen, Oxygen

Burning propane

When propane gas burns, its carbon and hydrogen atoms combine with oxygen molecules in the air. Carbon and some of the oxygen atoms form carbon dioxide molecules, while hydrogen and the other oxygen atoms form water molecules.

Perfect balance

Water molecules contain two hydrogen and one oxygen atoms

Hydrogen molecule contains two hydrogen atoms

Oxygen molecule contains two oxygen atoms

Balancing act

A chemical reaction does not create or destroy atoms. It rearranges them, so all the atoms in a reaction's reactants still exist in the products. In this reaction, two hydrogen molecules (four atoms) and one oxygen molecule (two atoms) are rearranged to make two water molecules (four hydrogen and two oxygen atoms).

Chemical equations

A chemical equation is a mathematical way to show what happens in a chemical reaction. Chemical symbols are used in place of the names of substances. There must be equal quantities of each atom on both sides of the equation to show that the same atoms exist before and after the reaction.

HYDROGEN + OXYGEN → WATER

$$2H_2 + O_2 \rightarrow 2H_2O$$

- *There are two of these molecules*
- *This molecule is made of two hydrogen atoms*
- *This molecule is made of two oxygen atoms*
- *There are two of these molecules*
- *This molecule contains two hydrogen atoms and one oxygen atom*

19

BUBBLE, FIZZ, BANG!

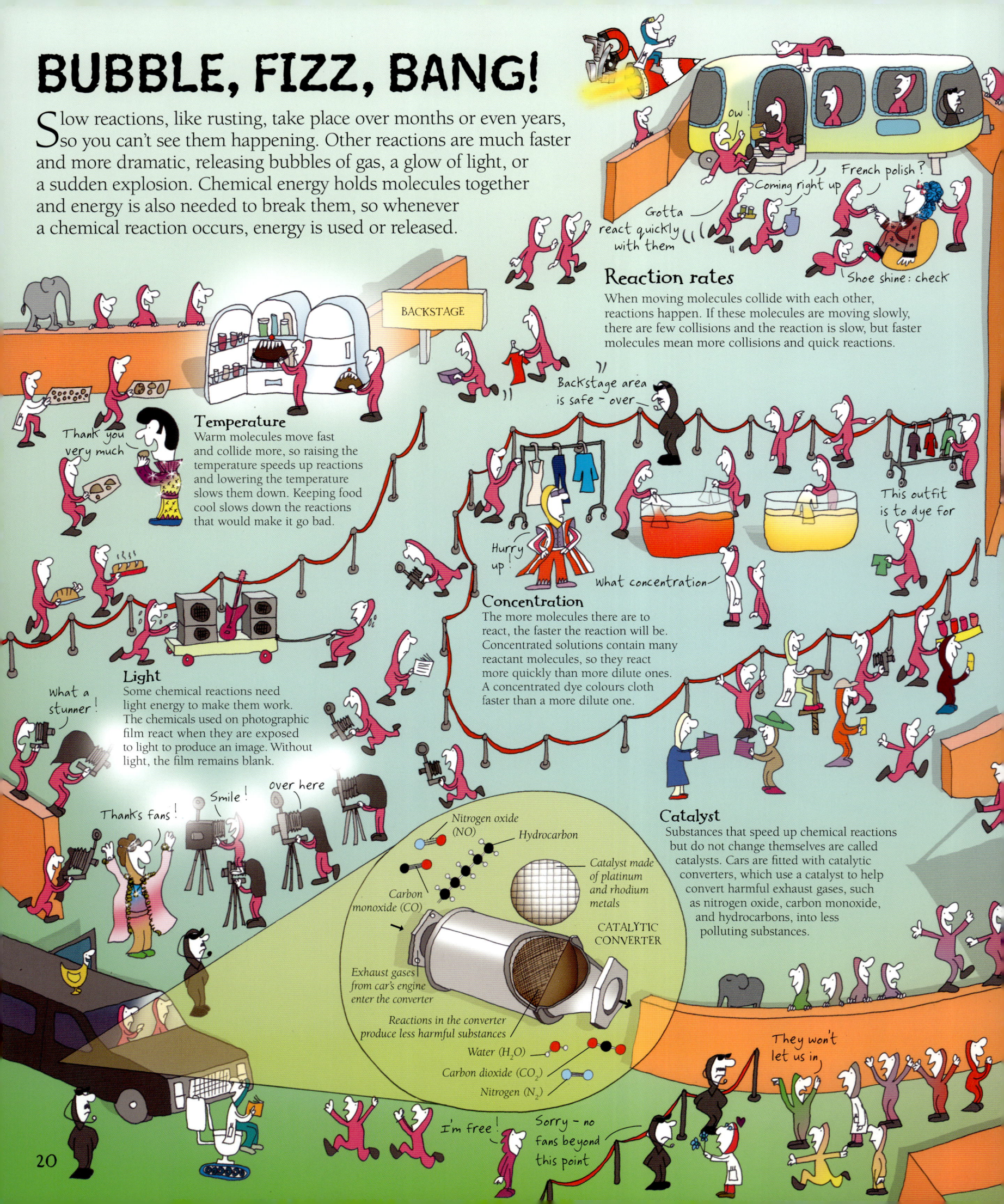

Slow reactions, like rusting, take place over months or even years, so you can't see them happening. Other reactions are much faster and more dramatic, releasing bubbles of gas, a glow of light, or a sudden explosion. Chemical energy holds molecules together and energy is also needed to break them, so whenever a chemical reaction occurs, energy is used or released.

Reaction rates
When moving molecules collide with each other, reactions happen. If these molecules are moving slowly, there are few collisions and the reaction is slow, but faster molecules mean more collisions and quick reactions.

Temperature
Warm molecules move fast and collide more, so raising the temperature speeds up reactions and lowering the temperature slows them down. Keeping food cool slows down the reactions that would make it go bad.

Concentration
The more molecules there are to react, the faster the reaction will be. Concentrated solutions contain many reactant molecules, so they react more quickly than more dilute ones. A concentrated dye colours cloth faster than a more dilute one.

Light
Some chemical reactions need light energy to make them work. The chemicals used on photographic film react when they are exposed to light to produce an image. Without light, the film remains blank.

Catalyst
Substances that speed up chemical reactions but do not change themselves are called catalysts. Cars are fitted with catalytic converters, which use a catalyst to help convert harmful exhaust gases, such as nitrogen oxide, carbon monoxide, and hydrocarbons, into less polluting substances.

Nitrogen oxide (NO)
Hydrocarbon
Catalyst made of platinum and rhodium metals
Carbon monoxide (CO)
CATALYTIC CONVERTER
Exhaust gases from car's engine enter the converter
Reactions in the converter produce less harmful substances
Water (H_2O)
Carbon dioxide (CO_2)
Nitrogen (N_2)

Splitting

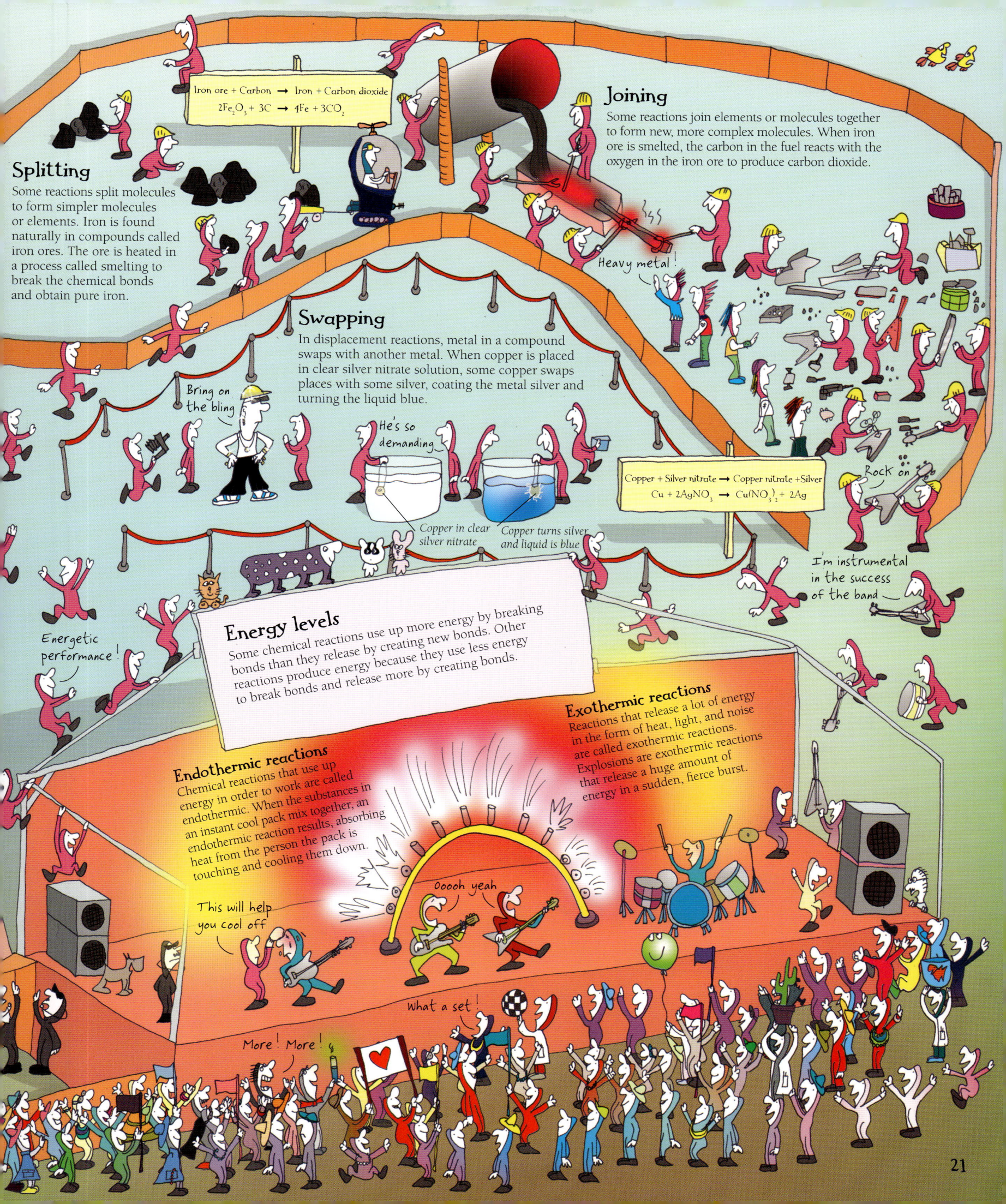

Some reactions split molecules to form simpler molecules or elements. Iron is found naturally in compounds called iron ores. The ore is heated in a process called smelting to break the chemical bonds and obtain pure iron.

Iron ore + Carbon → Iron + Carbon dioxide
$2Fe_2O_3 + 3C \rightarrow 4Fe + 3CO_2$

Joining

Some reactions join elements or molecules together to form new, more complex molecules. When iron ore is smelted, the carbon in the fuel reacts with the oxygen in the iron ore to produce carbon dioxide.

Heavy metal!

Swapping

In displacement reactions, metal in a compound swaps with another metal. When copper is placed in clear silver nitrate solution, some copper swaps places with some silver, coating the metal silver and turning the liquid blue.

Bring on the bling

He's so demanding

Copper in clear silver nitrate

Copper turns silver and liquid is blue

Copper + Silver nitrate → Copper nitrate + Silver
$Cu + 2AgNO_3 \rightarrow Cu(NO_3)_2 + 2Ag$

Rock on

I'm instrumental in the success of the band

Energetic performance!

Energy levels

Some chemical reactions use up more energy by breaking bonds than they release by creating new bonds. Other reactions produce energy because they use less energy to break bonds and release more by creating bonds.

Endothermic reactions

Chemical reactions that use up energy in order to work are called endothermic. When the substances in an instant cool pack mix together, an endothermic reaction results, absorbing heat from the person the pack is touching and cooling them down.

Exothermic reactions

Reactions that release a lot of energy in the form of heat, light, and noise are called exothermic reactions. Explosions are exothermic reactions that release a huge amount of energy in a sudden, fierce burst.

This will help you cool off

Ooooh yeah

What a set!

More! More!

ACIDS AND BASES

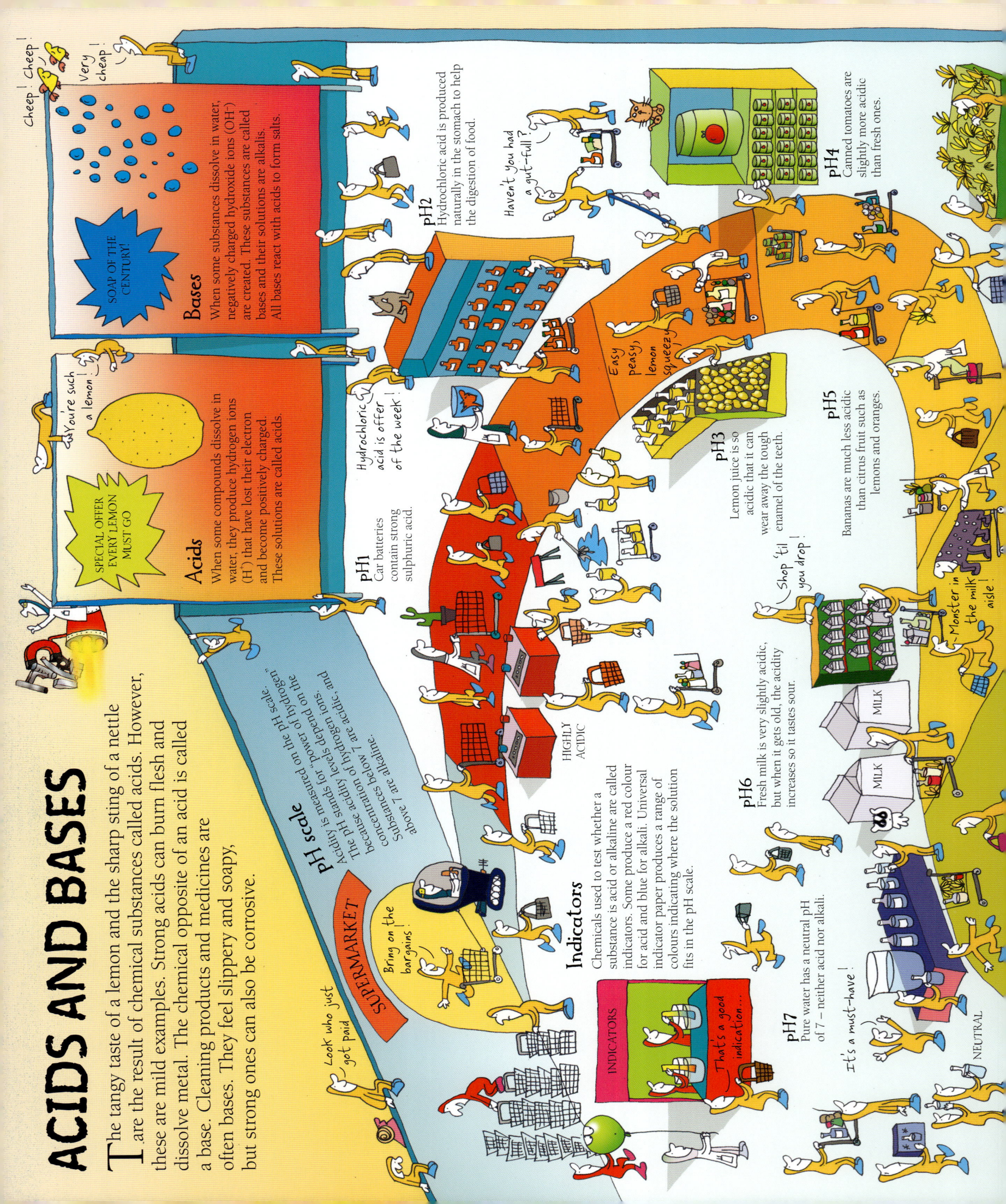

The tangy taste of a lemon and the sharp sting of a nettle are the result of chemical substances called acids. However, these are mild examples. Strong acids can burn flesh and dissolve metal. The chemical opposite of an acid is called a base. Cleaning products and medicines are often bases. They feel slippery and soapy, but strong ones can also be corrosive.

Bases
When some substances dissolve in water, negatively charged hydroxide ions (OH⁻) are created. These substances are called bases and their solutions are alkalis. All bases react with acids to form salts.

Acids
When some compounds dissolve in water, they produce hydrogen ions (H⁺) that have lost their electron and become positively charged. These solutions are called acids.

pH scale
Acidity is measured on the pH scale. pH stands for "power of the hydrogen" because acidity levels depend on the pH acidity of hydrogen ions. The pH scale runs from acidic, and concentration below 7 are acidic, and above 7 are alkaline.

Indicators
Chemicals used to test whether a substance is acid or alkaline are called indicators. Some produce a red colour for acid and blue for alkali. Universal indicator paper produces a range of colours indicating where the solution fits in the pH scale.

pH1 Car batteries contain strong sulphuric acid. HIGHLY ACIDIC

pH2 Hydrochloric acid is produced naturally in the stomach to help the digestion of food.

pH3 Lemon juice is so acidic that it can wear away the tough enamel of the teeth.

pH4 Canned tomatoes are slightly more acidic than fresh ones.

pH5 Bananas are much less acidic than citrus fruit such as lemons and oranges.

pH6 Fresh milk is very slightly acidic, but when it gets old, the acidity increases so it tastes sour.

pH7 Pure water has a neutral pH of 7 – neither acid nor alkali. NEUTRAL

Neutralizing acids

When acids and alkalis mix, the acid's hydrogen ions combine with the alkali's hydroxide ions to form water. If all the ions are used up, the solution will be neither acid nor alkaline, but neutral.

pH8
The pH of blood is regulated by the body's kidneys and lungs working together.

pH9
Alkaline toothpaste neutralizes plaque acids, which cause tooth decay.

pH10
Milk of magnesia or magnesium hydroxide is used as an antacid – a medicine that soothes excessive acid levels in the stomach.

pH11
Household ammonia, a solution of ammonia in water, is used in cleaning products.

pH12
Soap is made by combining fatty acids with very strong alkalis.

pH13
Bleach is used for cleaning and for whitening fabrics.

pH14
Caustic soda or sodium hydroxide is used to clean ovens.

HIGHLY ALKALINE (OR BASIC)

Acid rain

When it rains, carbon dioxide in the air dissolves to form carbonic acid, so all rainwater is slightly acidic. Polluting compounds of nitrogen and sulphur in the air can also form acids, lowering rain's pH to 1.5. This acid rain kills vegetation and wears away rocks and stone buildings.

23

BLUE PLANET

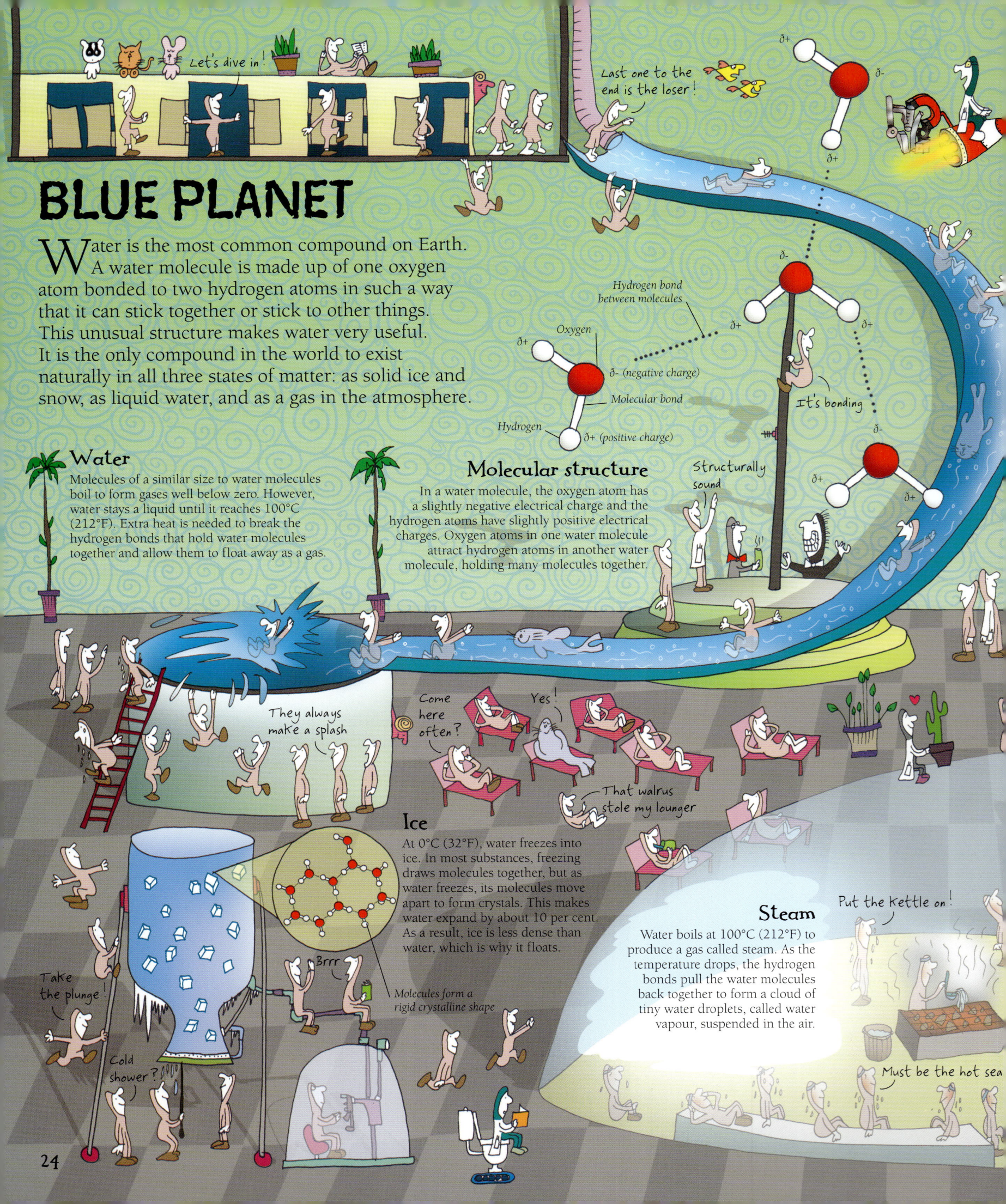

Water is the most common compound on Earth. A water molecule is made up of one oxygen atom bonded to two hydrogen atoms in such a way that it can stick together or stick to other things. This unusual structure makes water very useful. It is the only compound in the world to exist naturally in all three states of matter: as solid ice and snow, as liquid water, and as a gas in the atmosphere.

Water

Molecules of a similar size to water molecules boil to form gases well below zero. However, water stays a liquid until it reaches 100°C (212°F). Extra heat is needed to break the hydrogen bonds that hold water molecules together and allow them to float away as a gas.

Molecular structure

In a water molecule, the oxygen atom has a slightly negative electrical charge and the hydrogen atoms have slightly positive electrical charges. Oxygen atoms in one water molecule attract hydrogen atoms in another water molecule, holding many molecules together.

Ice

At 0°C (32°F), water freezes into ice. In most substances, freezing draws molecules together, but as water freezes, its molecules move apart to form crystals. This makes water expand by about 10 per cent. As a result, ice is less dense than water, which is why it floats.

Steam

Water boils at 100°C (212°F) to produce a gas called steam. As the temperature drops, the hydrogen bonds pull the water molecules back together to form a cloud of tiny water droplets, called water vapour, suspended in the air.

THE BLUE PLANET SPA

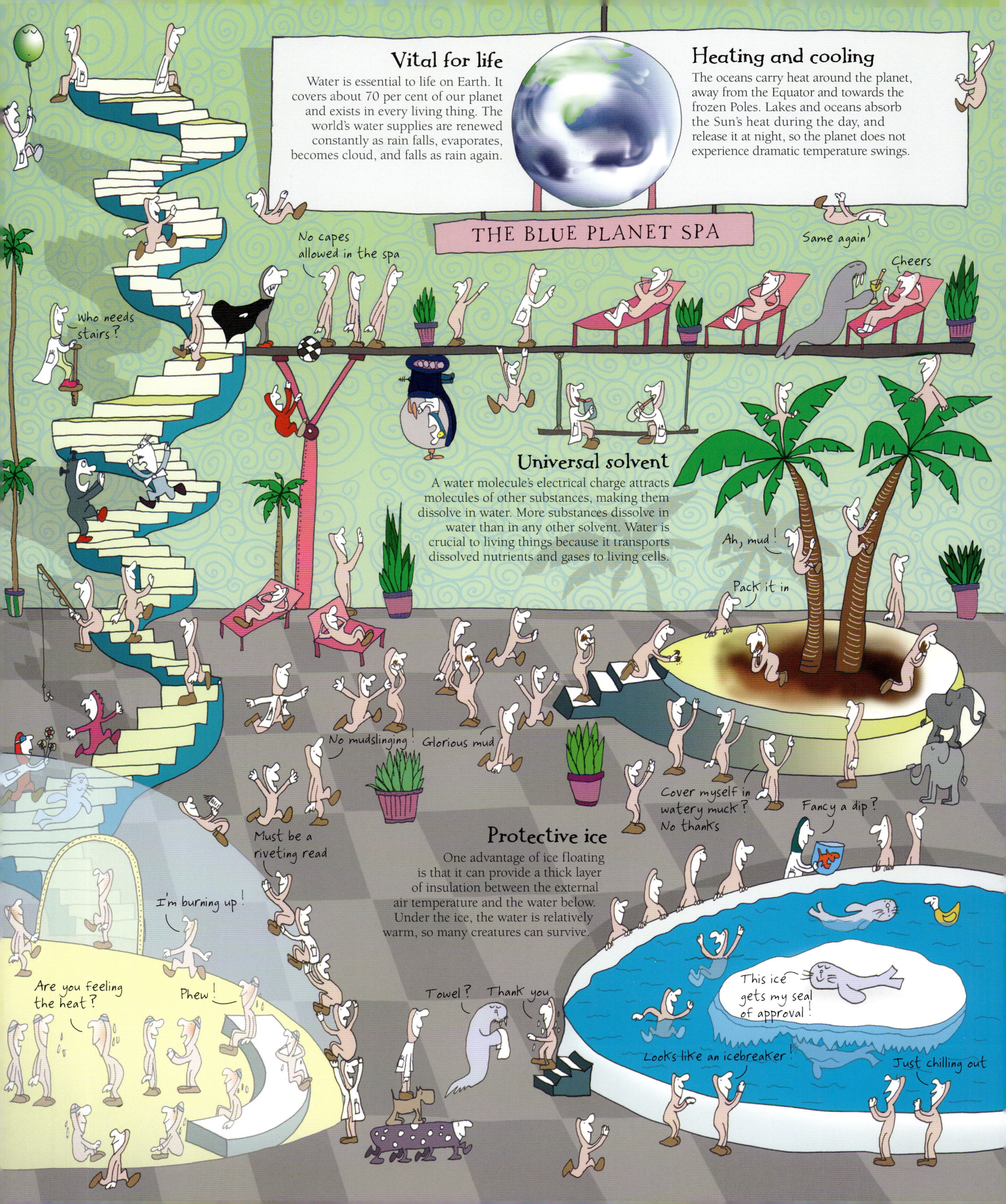

Vital for life
Water is essential to life on Earth. It covers about 70 per cent of our planet and exists in every living thing. The world's water supplies are renewed constantly as rain falls, evaporates, becomes cloud, and falls as rain again.

Heating and cooling
The oceans carry heat around the planet, away from the Equator and towards the frozen Poles. Lakes and oceans absorb the Sun's heat during the day, and release it at night, so the planet does not experience dramatic temperature swings.

Universal solvent
A water molecule's electrical charge attracts molecules of other substances, making them dissolve in water. More substances dissolve in water than in any other solvent. Water is crucial to living things because it transports dissolved nutrients and gases to living cells.

Protective ice
One advantage of ice floating is that it can provide a thick layer of insulation between the external air temperature and the water below. Under the ice, the water is relatively warm, so many creatures can survive.

MIXING IT UP

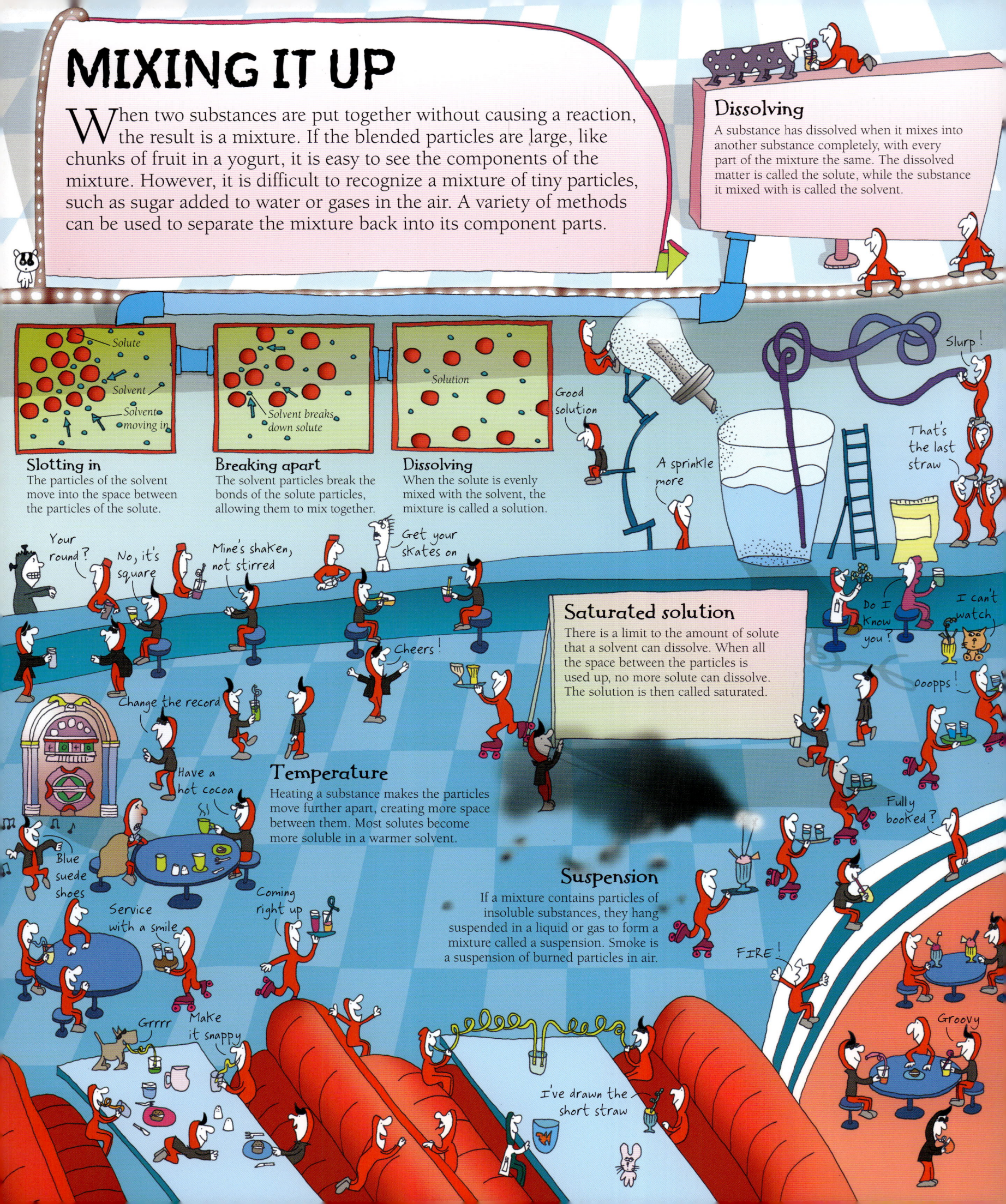

When two substances are put together without causing a reaction, the result is a mixture. If the blended particles are large, like chunks of fruit in a yogurt, it is easy to see the components of the mixture. However, it is difficult to recognize a mixture of tiny particles, such as sugar added to water or gases in the air. A variety of methods can be used to separate the mixture back into its component parts.

Dissolving

A substance has dissolved when it mixes into another substance completely, with every part of the mixture the same. The dissolved matter is called the solute, while the substance it mixed with is called the solvent.

Slotting in
The particles of the solvent move into the space between the particles of the solute.

Breaking apart
The solvent particles break the bonds of the solute particles, allowing them to mix together.

Dissolving
When the solute is evenly mixed with the solvent, the mixture is called a solution.

Saturated solution

There is a limit to the amount of solute that a solvent can dissolve. When all the space between the particles is used up, no more solute can dissolve. The solution is then called saturated.

Temperature

Heating a substance makes the particles move further apart, creating more space between them. Most solutes become more soluble in a warmer solvent.

Suspension

If a mixture contains particles of insoluble substances, they hang suspended in a liquid or gas to form a mixture called a suspension. Smoke is a suspension of burned particles in air.

Separating mixtures

The components of mixtures are not chemically bonded, so it does not take a chemical reaction to separate them. Mixtures are separated using methods that make use of the different physical properties of the components.

Emulsion

Liquids that do not form a solution when mixed together are called immiscible. It is possible to force immiscible liquids to form a suspension, called an emulsion, by shaking them, but they separate into layers eventually.

Colloid

In most suspensions, the suspended particles settle eventually at the bottom, but in a suspension called a colloid, the particles are too small and light to settle. Whipped cream is a colloid of air suspended in liquid.

Distillation

Substances with different boiling points can be separated by distillation. The mixture is heated and as it reaches the boiling point of each component, that component evaporates. As the gas cools, the component turns back into a liquid, ready to be collected.

DISTILLING CRUDE OIL
- 20°C (68°F) Gas for fuel
- 40°C (104°F) Petrol for cars
- 111°C (232°F) Naphtha for chemical production
- 180°C (356°F) Kerosene for jet fuel
- 260°C (500°F) Diesel oil for diesel engines
- 340°C (644°F) Fuel for ships, road surfaces, and paraffin wax

Filtration

When a mixture is made of substances with different-sized particles, it can be separated by filtration. The simplest form of filtration is to use a sieve, which allows small particles to fit through the holes, while catching the large ones.

Chromatography

Chemists sometimes analyze substances in a solution by placing them on absorbent paper with one end dipped in a solvent. The components of the solution travel different distances up the material. Food scientists can use chromatography to discover what colourings have been added to food.

Centrifuging

Substances with varying densities can be separated by centrifuging. The mixture is spun at great speed in a machine, so the denser particles are forced to the bottom of the container, and the lighter particles rise to the top. Blood can be separated in this way.

27

WARNING! CHEMISTS AT WORK

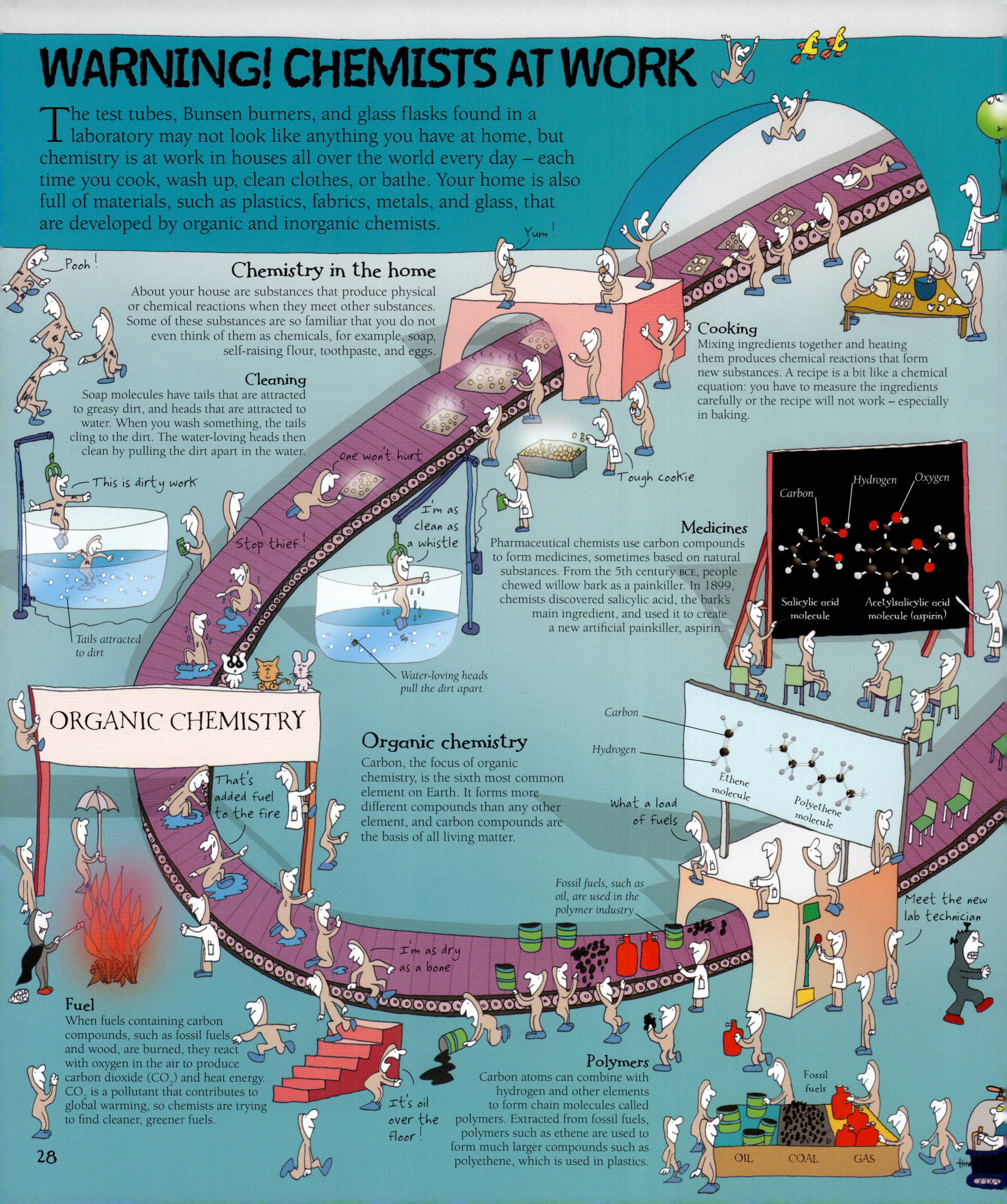

The test tubes, Bunsen burners, and glass flasks found in a laboratory may not look like anything you have at home, but chemistry is at work in houses all over the world every day – each time you cook, wash up, clean clothes, or bathe. Your home is also full of materials, such as plastics, fabrics, metals, and glass, that are developed by organic and inorganic chemists.

Chemistry in the home
About your house are substances that produce physical or chemical reactions when they meet other substances. Some of these substances are so familiar that you do not even think of them as chemicals, for example, soap, self-raising flour, toothpaste, and eggs.

Cleaning
Soap molecules have tails that are attracted to greasy dirt, and heads that are attracted to water. When you wash something, the tails cling to the dirt. The water-loving heads then clean by pulling the dirt apart in the water.

Cooking
Mixing ingredients together and heating them produces chemical reactions that form new substances. A recipe is a bit like a chemical equation: you have to measure the ingredients carefully or the recipe will not work – especially in baking.

Medicines
Pharmaceutical chemists use carbon compounds to form medicines, sometimes based on natural substances. From the 5th century BCE, people chewed willow bark as a painkiller. In 1899, chemists discovered salicylic acid, the bark's main ingredient, and used it to create a new artificial painkiller, aspirin.

ORGANIC CHEMISTRY

Organic chemistry
Carbon, the focus of organic chemistry, is the sixth most common element on Earth. It forms more different compounds than any other element, and carbon compounds are the basis of all living matter.

Fuel
When fuels containing carbon compounds, such as fossil fuels and wood, are burned, they react with oxygen in the air to produce carbon dioxide (CO_2) and heat energy. CO_2 is a pollutant that contributes to global warming, so chemists are trying to find cleaner, greener fuels.

Polymers
Carbon atoms can combine with hydrogen and other elements to form chain molecules called polymers. Extracted from fossil fuels, polymers such as ethene are used to form much larger compounds such as polyethene, which is used in plastics.

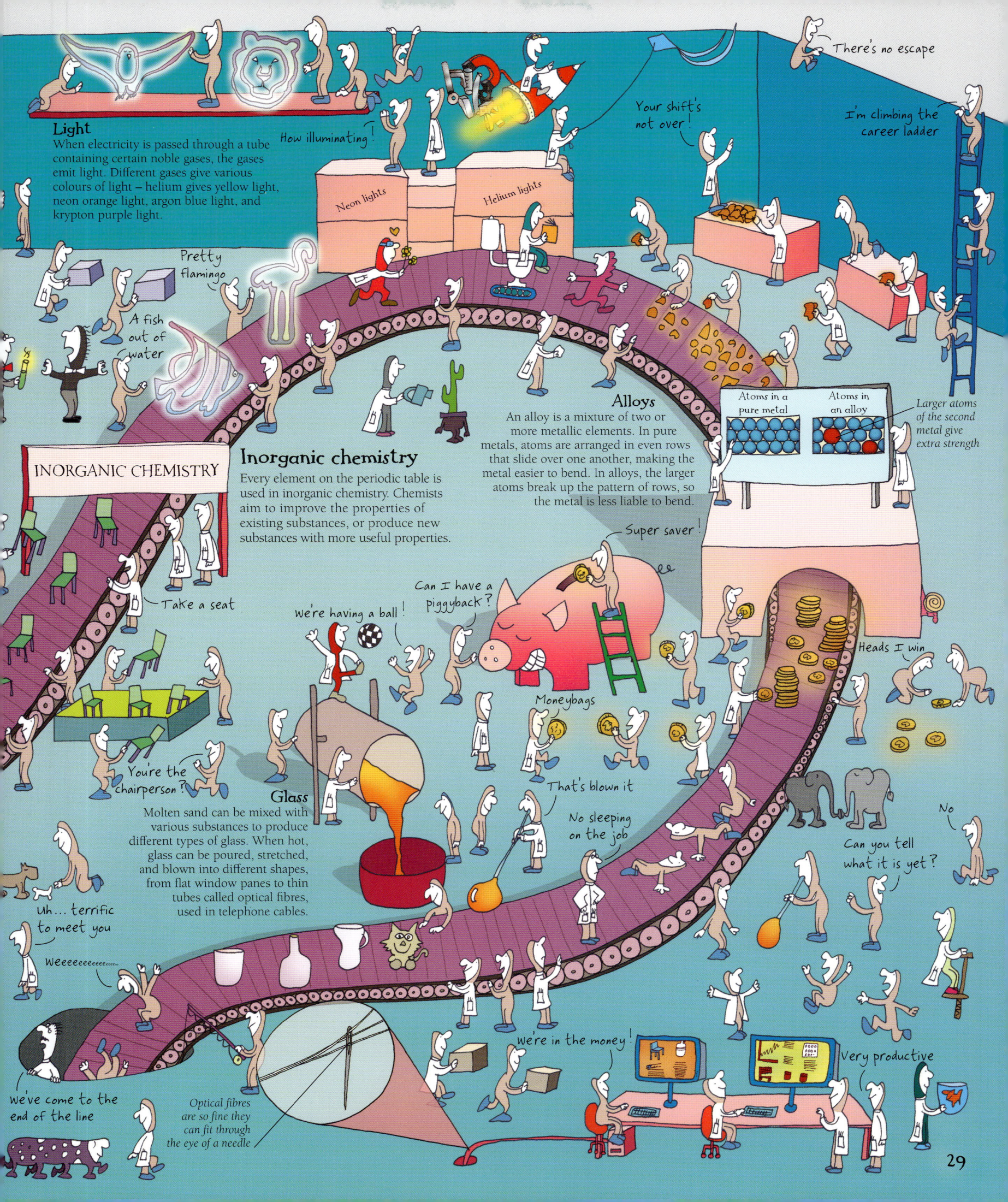

Light
When electricity is passed through a tube containing certain noble gases, the gases emit light. Different gases give various colours of light – helium gives yellow light, neon orange light, argon blue light, and krypton purple light.

Inorganic chemistry
Every element on the periodic table is used in inorganic chemistry. Chemists aim to improve the properties of existing substances, or produce new substances with more useful properties.

Alloys
An alloy is a mixture of two or more metallic elements. In pure metals, atoms are arranged in even rows that slide over one another, making the metal easier to bend. In alloys, the larger atoms break up the pattern of rows, so the metal is less liable to bend.

Glass
Molten sand can be mixed with various substances to produce different types of glass. When hot, glass can be poured, stretched, and blown into different shapes, from flat window panes to thin tubes called optical fibres, used in telephone cables.

Optical fibres are so fine they can fit through the eye of a needle.

ENDLESS ENERGY

Everything from turning on an electric fan to playing a game uses energy. But for scientists, energy goes beyond making machines work and bodies move. They recognize the energy involved in every process, every chemical reaction, and every living thing. Energy cannot be created or destroyed. Instead, it is just stored and transferred in different ways.

GREEN'S GYM

Forms of energy
Energy comes in many different forms, such as light, heat, sound, electrical, and mechanical energy. All forms of energy can be converted from one form to another.

Potential energy
Stored energy that can be converted into another form of energy in the future is called potential energy. Bouncing down on a trampoline stretches the fabric, giving it potential energy. When the fabric springs back, the trampolinist is flung into the air and the potential energy is released as kinetic energy.

Chemical energy
Molecules are bonded together by a form of potential energy called chemical energy. When these bonds are made and broken by chemical reactions, energy may be released. In the digestive process, chemical energy is released from food for our bodies to use.

Kinetic energy
A moving object, such as a ball, has a form of energy called kinetic energy. The more kinetic energy the object has, the faster it moves. When the object stops moving, it no longer has kinetic energy.

Work

The energy needed to perform a task is called "work". The amount of work done equals the amount of energy used, and both are measured in joules. One joule is the amount of work done to move one newton (the unit used to measure forces) across 1 m (3 ft).

Efficiency

An efficient machine, such as a bicycle, turns most of the energy put into it into useful work. An inefficient machine, such as a lightbulb, wastes some of the energy by turning it into heat instead of light.

Power

This is the amount of work carried out in a certain time, and is measured in watts. Powerful machines can do a specific amount of work more quickly than others, or do more work in a set time.

Conservation of energy

Physical and chemical processes convert energy into other forms. When a fan is turned on, electrical energy is converted to mechanical energy moving the blades. As they move, the blades have kinetic energy, which is transferred to the surrounding air.

Nuclear reactions

Matter is destroyed and energy is produced in nuclear reactions. The energy produced is calculated using scientist Albert Einstein's formula $E=mc^2$. Energy (E) is equal to matter destroyed (m), multiplied by the speed of light squared (c^2), which is a huge number.

Renewable energy

Solar energy and wind power are sources of energy that will never run out. These resources directly harness the energy of the Sun and wind, converting it into useable forms of power, such as heat, light, and electricity.

Energy sources

Fossil fuels started life as plants, but are now used to provide power. Early on, these plants used light energy from the Sun to grow. Over time, they fossilized, so the energy was stored as chemical energy. When the fuels are burned, this energy is released as heat and light.

GOOD VIBRATIONS

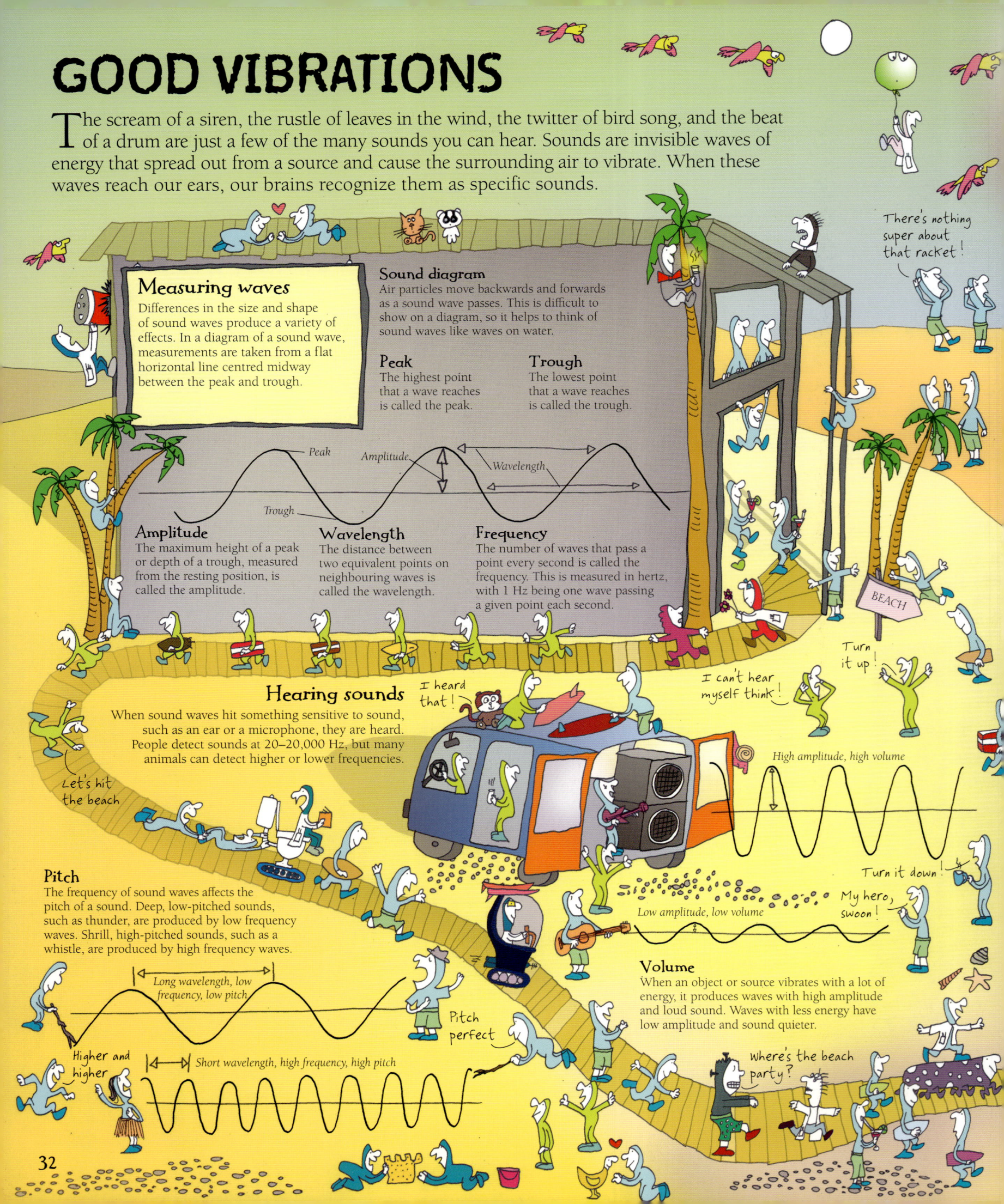

The scream of a siren, the rustle of leaves in the wind, the twitter of bird song, and the beat of a drum are just a few of the many sounds you can hear. Sounds are invisible waves of energy that spread out from a source and cause the surrounding air to vibrate. When these waves reach our ears, our brains recognize them as specific sounds.

Measuring waves
Differences in the size and shape of sound waves produce a variety of effects. In a diagram of a sound wave, measurements are taken from a flat horizontal line centred midway between the peak and trough.

Sound diagram
Air particles move backwards and forwards as a sound wave passes. This is difficult to show on a diagram, so it helps to think of sound waves like waves on water.

Peak
The highest point that a wave reaches is called the peak.

Trough
The lowest point that a wave reaches is called the trough.

Amplitude
The maximum height of a peak or depth of a trough, measured from the resting position, is called the amplitude.

Wavelength
The distance between two equivalent points on neighbouring waves is called the wavelength.

Frequency
The number of waves that pass a point every second is called the frequency. This is measured in hertz, with 1 Hz being one wave passing a given point each second.

Hearing sounds
When sound waves hit something sensitive to sound, such as an ear or a microphone, they are heard. People detect sounds at 20–20,000 Hz, but many animals can detect higher or lower frequencies.

Pitch
The frequency of sound waves affects the pitch of a sound. Deep, low-pitched sounds, such as thunder, are produced by low frequency waves. Shrill, high-pitched sounds, such as a whistle, are produced by high frequency waves.

Long wavelength, low frequency, low pitch

Short wavelength, high frequency, high pitch

Volume
When an object or source vibrates with a lot of energy, it produces waves with high amplitude and loud sound. Waves with less energy have low amplitude and sound quieter.

High amplitude, high volume

Low amplitude, low volume

Supersonic flight
When a supersonic aircraft reaches the speed of sound, it catches up with its own sound waves. This produces a big bang called a sonic boom, and sometimes a halo of water vapour.

Wind instrument
Blowing into a wind instrument makes the column of air inside vibrate. Where you put your fingers changes the length of the air column and makes different sounds.

Percussion instrument
Banging a percussion instrument, such as a drum, creates a sharp sound wave and a crashing sound.

Stringed instrument
When the strings on a stringed instrument, such as a harp, are plucked, they vibrate to produce a bright, harmonic sound.

Recording sounds
Sounds are stored by turning sound energy into electrical signals and then recording them. To listen to the sounds, the electrical signals are converted back into sound waves.

Music
Playing a musical instrument produces a pattern of sound waves. Every note has a fundamental pitch, or frequency, but can include many other harmonics – waves at different frequencies that vibrate in harmony with the fundamental pitch.

Doppler effect
Sound waves from an approaching ambulance are high-pitched because they are compressed by the movement. As the ambulance moves off, the waves stretch out and the sound is lower-pitched.

Echoes
When sound waves hit hard surfaces, part of the wave bounces off. The reflected sound travels back and is heard at the source as an echo.

Sound in water
When sound travels through substances denser than air, the closely packed molecules allow the waves to travel faster. Sound travels four times faster in water than air.

Travelling sound
Sound waves can travel through air, water, or any other type of matter, but they cannot travel where there is no matter – in a vacuum or out in space. The speed of sound in dry air at 0°C (32°F) is 1,190 kph (740 mph).

33

HEAT WAVE

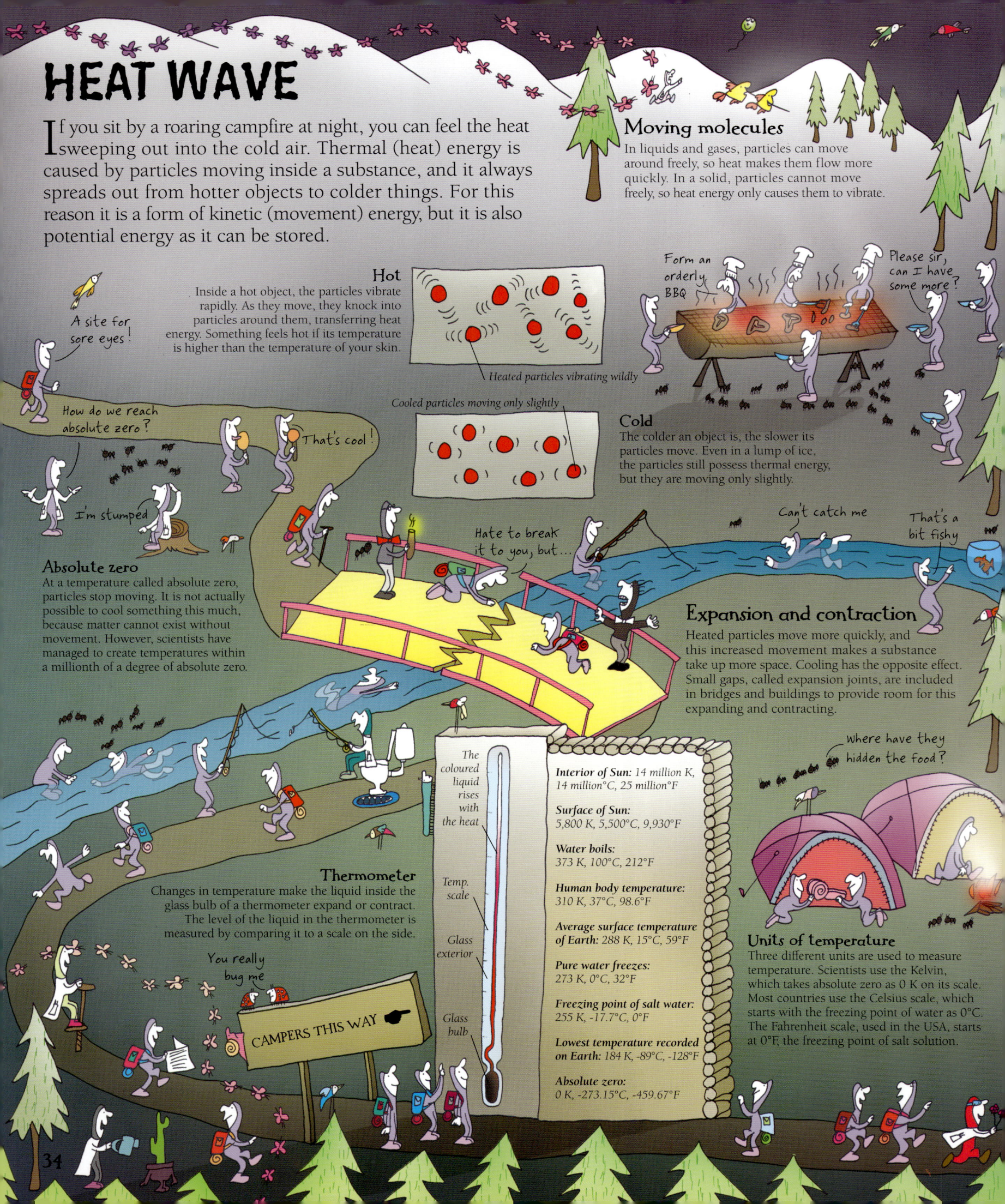

If you sit by a roaring campfire at night, you can feel the heat sweeping out into the cold air. Thermal (heat) energy is caused by particles moving inside a substance, and it always spreads out from hotter objects to colder things. For this reason it is a form of kinetic (movement) energy, but it is also potential energy as it can be stored.

Moving molecules
In liquids and gases, particles can move around freely, so heat makes them flow more quickly. In a solid, particles cannot move freely, so heat energy only causes them to vibrate.

Hot
Inside a hot object, the particles vibrate rapidly. As they move, they knock into particles around them, transferring heat energy. Something feels hot if its temperature is higher than the temperature of your skin.

Heated particles vibrating wildly

Cooled particles moving only slightly

Cold
The colder an object is, the slower its particles move. Even in a lump of ice, the particles still possess thermal energy, but they are moving only slightly.

Absolute zero
At a temperature called absolute zero, particles stop moving. It is not actually possible to cool something this much, because matter cannot exist without movement. However, scientists have managed to create temperatures within a millionth of a degree of absolute zero.

Expansion and contraction
Heated particles move more quickly, and this increased movement makes a substance take up more space. Cooling has the opposite effect. Small gaps, called expansion joints, are included in bridges and buildings to provide room for this expanding and contracting.

Thermometer
Changes in temperature make the liquid inside the glass bulb of a thermometer expand or contract. The level of the liquid in the thermometer is measured by comparing it to a scale on the side.

The coloured liquid rises with the heat
Temp. scale
Glass exterior
Glass bulb

Interior of Sun: 14 million K, 14 million°C, 25 million°F

Surface of Sun: 5,800 K, 5,500°C, 9,930°F

Water boils: 373 K, 100°C, 212°F

Human body temperature: 310 K, 37°C, 98.6°F

Average surface temperature of Earth: 288 K, 15°C, 59°F

Pure water freezes: 273 K, 0°C, 32°F

Freezing point of salt water: 255 K, -17.7°C, 0°F

Lowest temperature recorded on Earth: 184 K, -89°C, -128°F

Absolute zero: 0 K, -273.15°C, -459.67°F

Units of temperature
Three different units are used to measure temperature. Scientists use the Kelvin, which takes absolute zero as 0 K on its scale. Most countries use the Celsius scale, which starts with the freezing point of water as 0°C. The Fahrenheit scale, used in the USA, starts at 0°F; the freezing point of salt solution.

Insulation

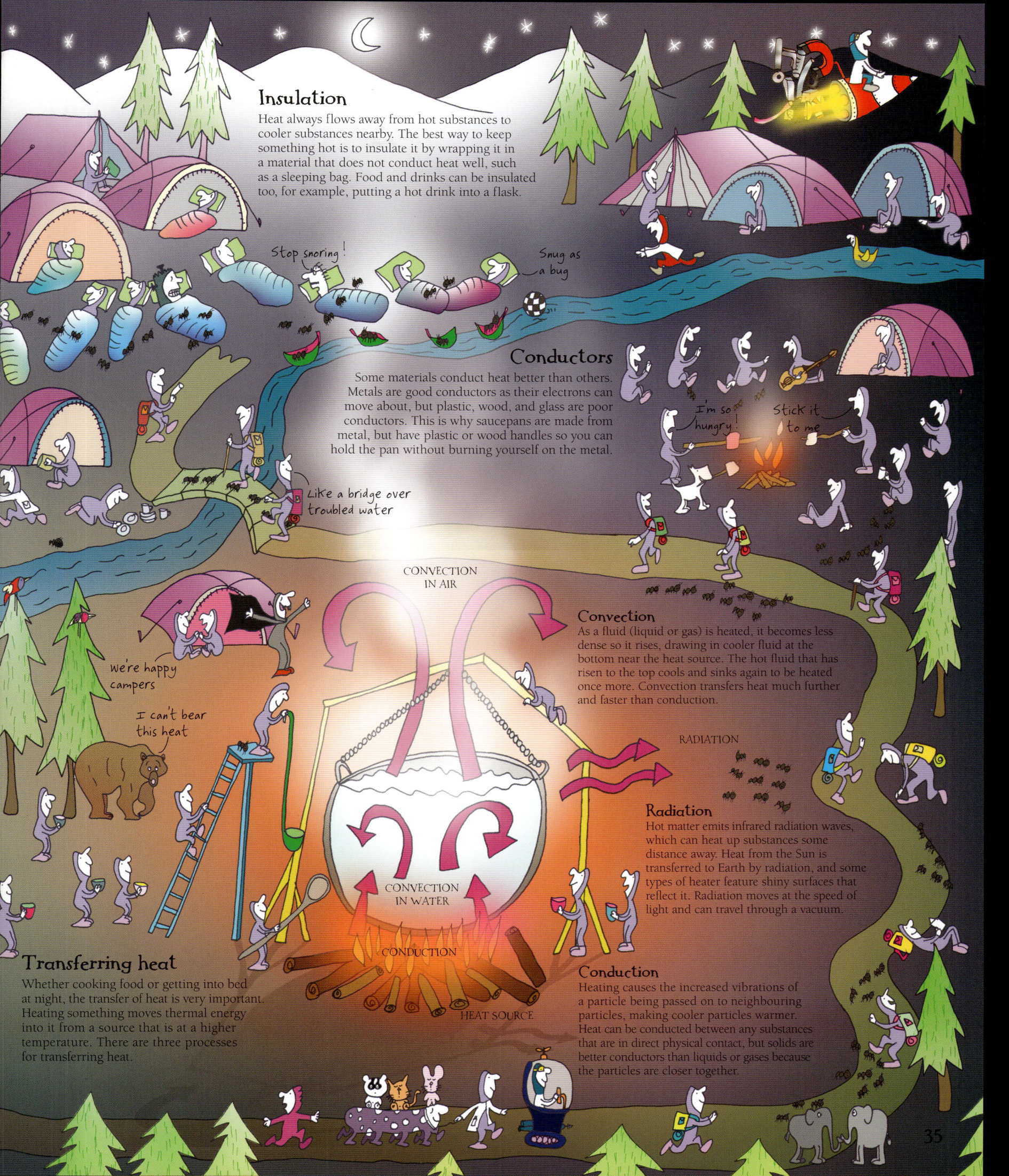

Heat always flows away from hot substances to cooler substances nearby. The best way to keep something hot is to insulate it by wrapping it in a material that does not conduct heat well, such as a sleeping bag. Food and drinks can be insulated too, for example, putting a hot drink into a flask.

Conductors

Some materials conduct heat better than others. Metals are good conductors as their electrons can move about, but plastic, wood, and glass are poor conductors. This is why saucepans are made from metal, but have plastic or wood handles so you can hold the pan without burning yourself on the metal.

Convection

As a fluid (liquid or gas) is heated, it becomes less dense so it rises, drawing in cooler fluid at the bottom near the heat source. The hot fluid that has risen to the top cools and sinks again to be heated once more. Convection transfers heat much further and faster than conduction.

Radiation

Hot matter emits infrared radiation waves, which can heat up substances some distance away. Heat from the Sun is transferred to Earth by radiation, and some types of heater feature shiny surfaces that reflect it. Radiation moves at the speed of light and can travel through a vacuum.

Transferring heat

Whether cooking food or getting into bed at night, the transfer of heat is very important. Heating something moves thermal energy into it from a source that is at a higher temperature. There are three processes for transferring heat.

Conduction

Heating causes the increased vibrations of a particle being passed on to neighbouring particles, making cooler particles warmer. Heat can be conducted between any substances that are in direct physical contact, but solids are better conductors than liquids or gases because the particles are closer together.

35

Telescope

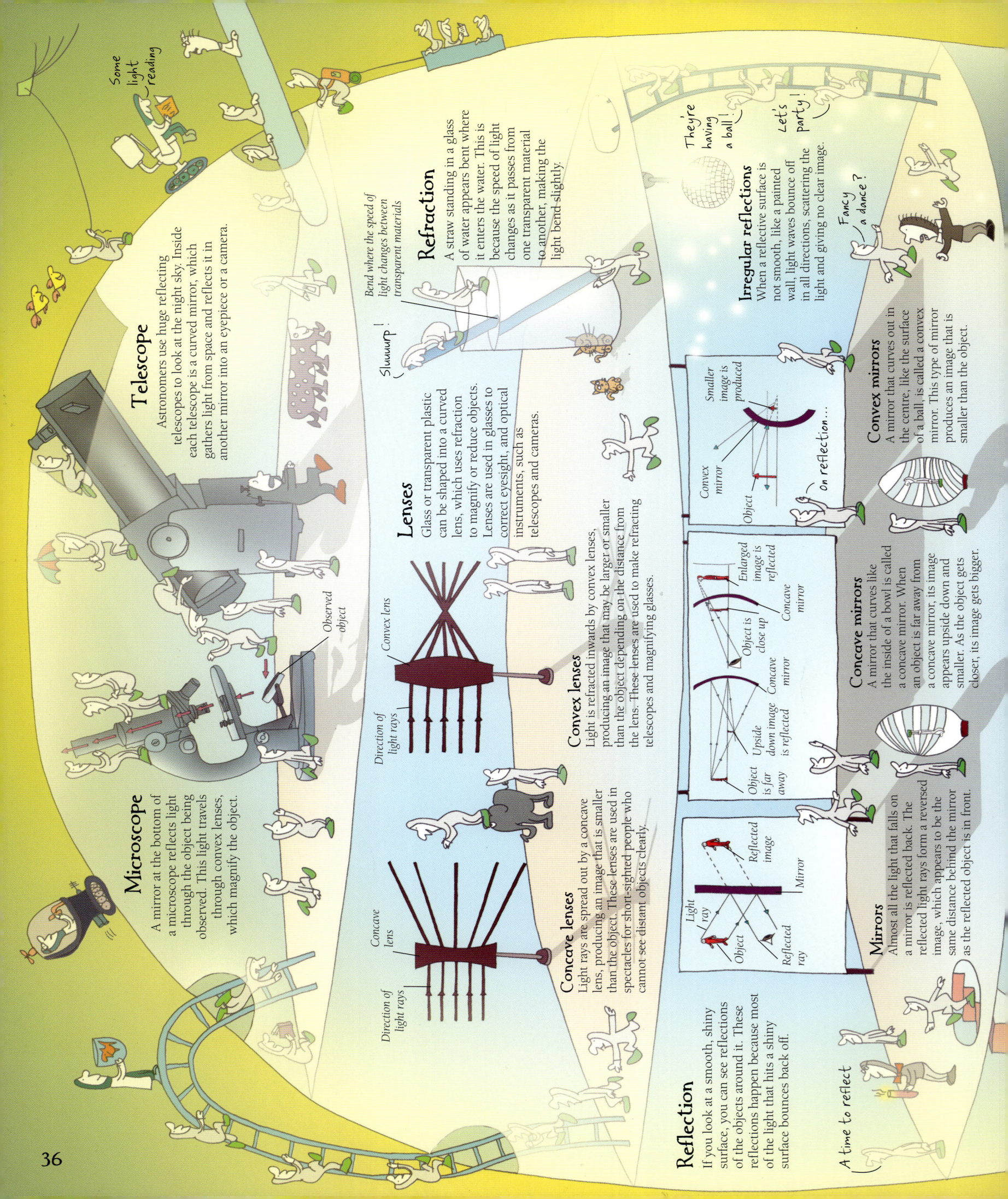

Astronomers use huge reflecting telescopes to look at the night sky. Inside each telescope is a curved mirror, which gathers light from space and reflects it in another mirror into an eyepiece or a camera.

Microscope

A mirror at the bottom of a microscope reflects light through the object being observed. This light travels through convex lenses, which magnify the object.

Observed object

Refraction

A straw standing in a glass of water appears bent where it enters the water. This is because the speed of light changes as it passes from one transparent material to another, making the light bend slightly.

Bend where the speed of light changes between transparent materials

Shuuurp!

Lenses

Glass or transparent plastic can be shaped into a curved lens, which uses refraction to magnify or reduce objects. Lenses are used in glasses to correct eyesight, and optical instruments, such as telescopes and cameras.

Convex lenses

Light is refracted inwards by convex lenses, producing an image that may be larger or smaller than the object depending on the distance from the lens. These lenses are used to make refracting telescopes and magnifying glasses.

Convex lens

Direction of light rays

Concave lenses

Light rays are spread out by a concave lens, producing an image that is smaller than the object. These lenses are used in spectacles for short-sighted people who cannot see distant objects clearly.

Concave lens

Direction of light rays

Irregular reflections

When a reflective surface is not smooth, like a painted wall, light waves bounce off in all directions, scattering the light and giving no clear image.

They're having a ball!

Let's party!

Fancy a dance?

Convex mirrors

A mirror that curves out in the centre, like the surface of a ball, is called a convex mirror. This type of mirror produces an image that is smaller than the object.

Smaller image is produced

Convex mirror

Object

on reflection...

Concave mirrors

A mirror that curves like the inside of a bowl is called a concave mirror. When an object is far away from a concave mirror, its image appears upside down and smaller. As the object gets closer, its image gets bigger.

Enlarged image is reflected

Concave mirror

Object is close up

Upside down image is reflected

Object is far away

Mirrors

Almost all the light that falls on a mirror is reflected back. The reflected light rays form a reversed image, which appears to be the same distance behind the mirror as the reflected object is in front.

Light ray

Reflected image

Mirror

Object

Reflected ray

Reflection

If you look at a smooth, shiny surface, you can see reflections of the objects around it. These reflections happen because most of the light that hits a shiny surface bounces back off.

A time to reflect

Some light reading

LET THERE BE LIGHT!

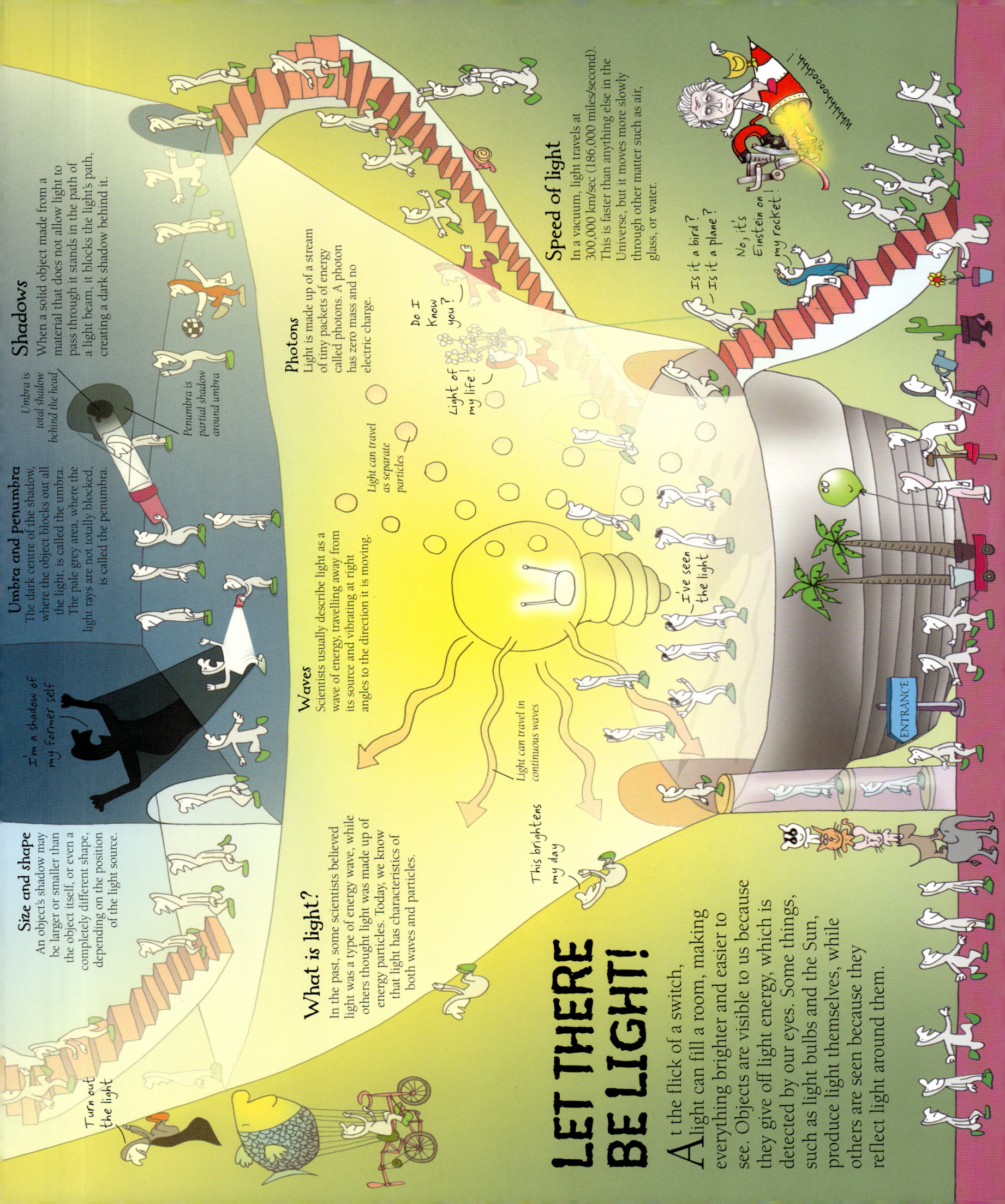

At the flick of a switch, a light can fill a room, making everything brighter and easier to see. Objects are visible to us because they give off light energy, which is detected by our eyes. Some things, such as light bulbs and the Sun, produce light themselves, while others are seen because they reflect light around them.

What is light?
In the past, some scientists believed light was a type of energy wave, while others thought light was made up of energy particles. Today, we know that light has characteristics of both waves and particles.

Waves
Scientists usually describe light as a wave of energy, travelling away from its source and vibrating at right angles to the direction it is moving.

Light can travel in continuous waves

Photons
Light is made up of a stream of tiny packets of energy called photons. A photon has zero mass and no electric charge.

Light can travel as separate particles

Speed of light
In a vacuum, light travels at 300,000 km/sec (186,000 miles/second). This is faster than anything else in the Universe, but it moves more slowly through other matter such as air, glass, or water.

Shadows
When a solid object made from a material that does not allow light to pass through it stands in the path of a light beam, it blocks the light's path, creating a dark shadow behind it.

Umbra and penumbra
The dark centre of the shadow, where the object blocks out all the light, is called the umbra. The pale grey area, where the light rays are not totally blocked, is called the penumbra.

Umbra is total shadow behind the head

Penumbra is partial shadow around umbra

Size and shape
An object's shadow may be larger or smaller than the object itself, or even a completely different shape, depending on the position of the light source.

Turn out the light

I'm a shadow of my former self

This brightens my day

Do I know you?

Light of my life!

I've seen the light

Is it a bird? Is it a plane?

No, it's Einstein on my rocket!

whhhooooshhh

BEYOND THE RAINBOW

The waves of energy you see as light are only a small part of a larger range of energy waves called electromagnetic radiation. Just as our ears can only hear certain wavelengths of sound, our eyes can detect the wavelengths of visible light, but cannot detect longer electromagnetic wavelengths such as radio waves or shorter wavelengths such as X-rays.

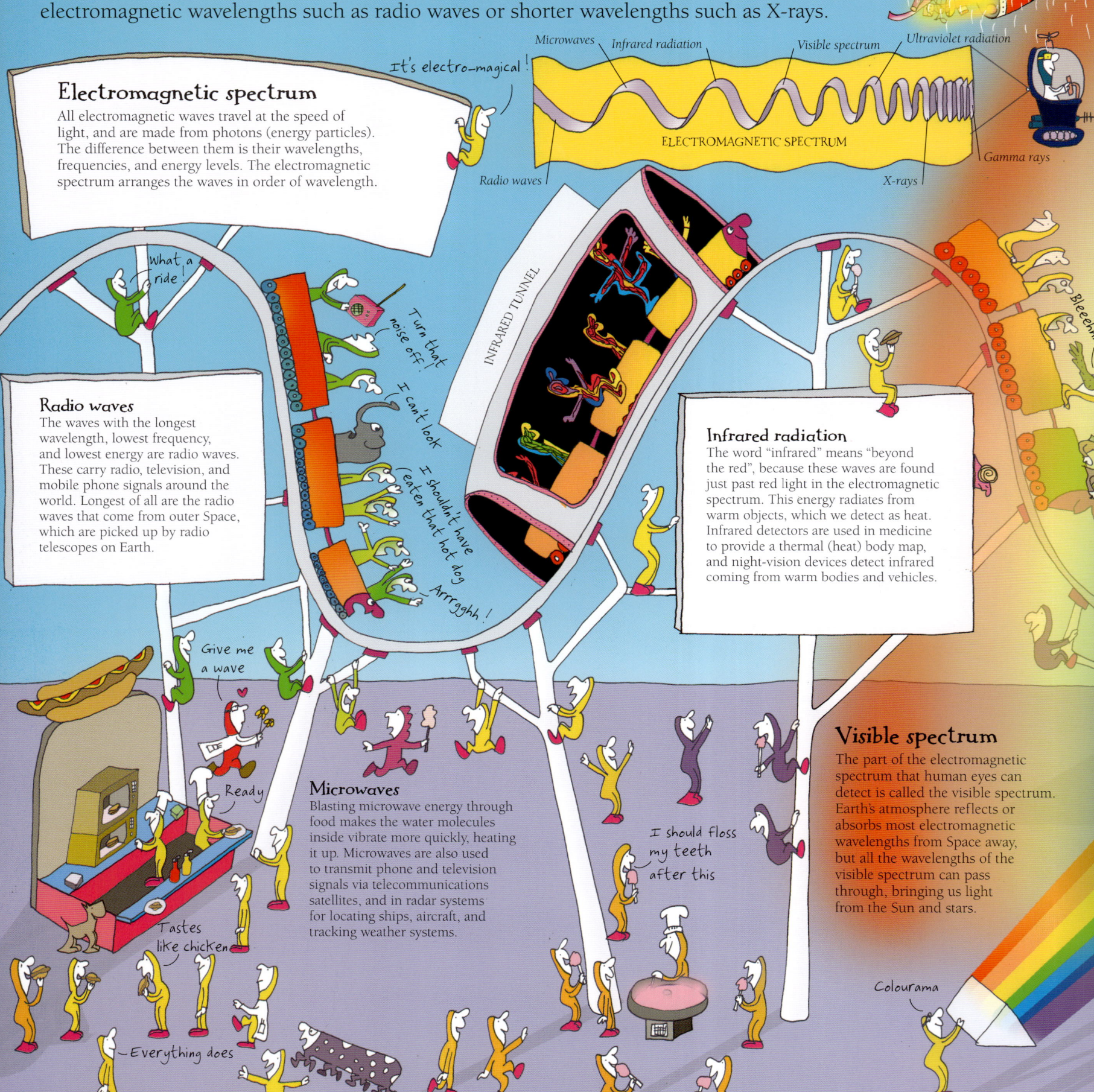

Electromagnetic spectrum

All electromagnetic waves travel at the speed of light, and are made from photons (energy particles). The difference between them is their wavelengths, frequencies, and energy levels. The electromagnetic spectrum arranges the waves in order of wavelength.

ELECTROMAGNETIC SPECTRUM

Radio waves — Microwaves — Infrared radiation — Visible spectrum — Ultraviolet radiation — X-rays — Gamma rays

Radio waves

The waves with the longest wavelength, lowest frequency, and lowest energy are radio waves. These carry radio, television, and mobile phone signals around the world. Longest of all are the radio waves that come from outer Space, which are picked up by radio telescopes on Earth.

Infrared radiation

The word "infrared" means "beyond the red", because these waves are found just past red light in the electromagnetic spectrum. This energy radiates from warm objects, which we detect as heat. Infrared detectors are used in medicine to provide a thermal (heat) body map, and night-vision devices detect infrared coming from warm bodies and vehicles.

Microwaves

Blasting microwave energy through food makes the water molecules inside vibrate more quickly, heating it up. Microwaves are also used to transmit phone and television signals via telecommunications satellites, and in radar systems for locating ships, aircraft, and tracking weather systems.

Visible spectrum

The part of the electromagnetic spectrum that human eyes can detect is called the visible spectrum. Earth's atmosphere reflects or absorbs most electromagnetic wavelengths from Space away, but all the wavelengths of the visible spectrum can pass through, bringing us light from the Sun and stars.

Colours

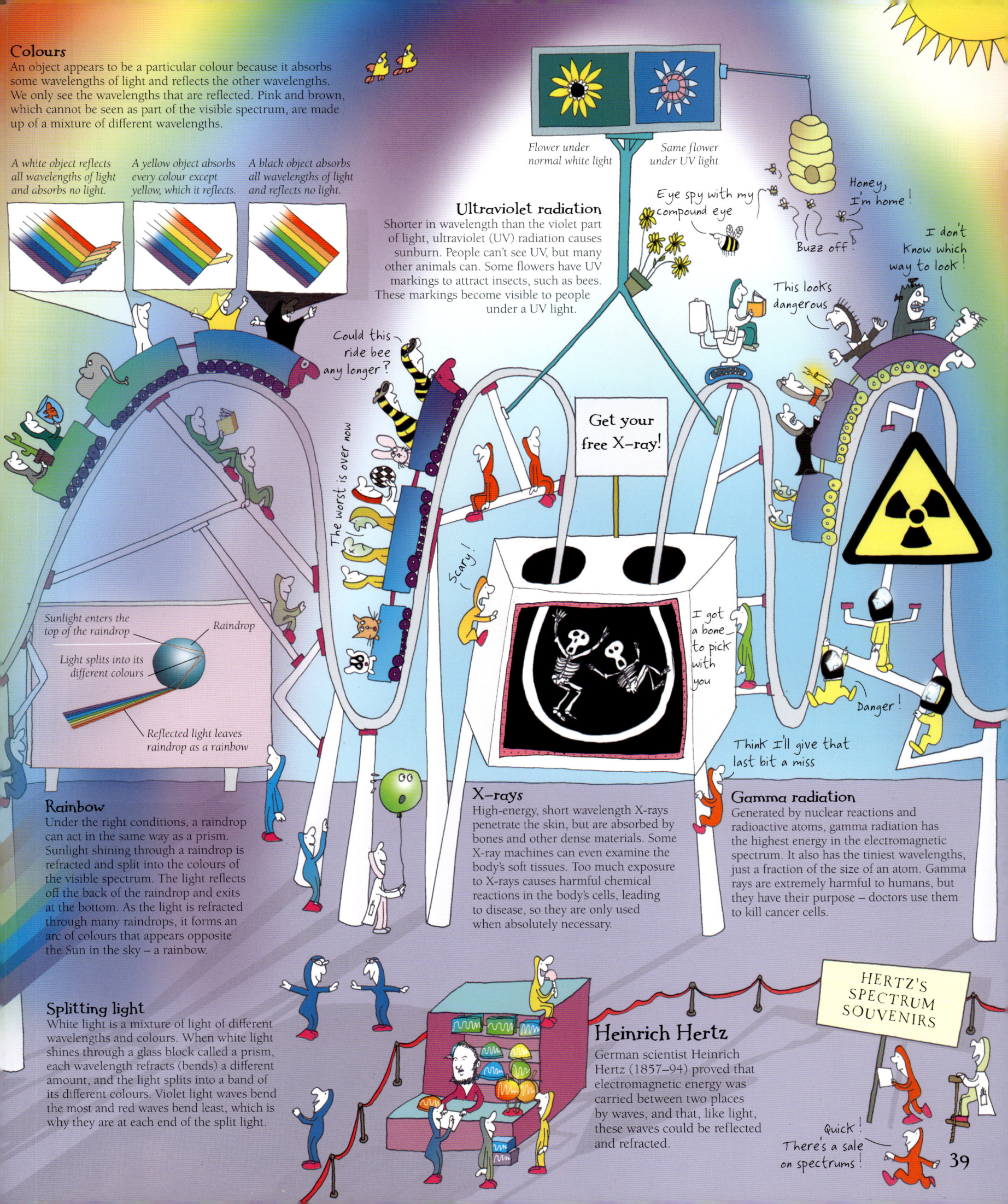

An object appears to be a particular colour because it absorbs some wavelengths of light and reflects the other wavelengths. We only see the wavelengths that are reflected. Pink and brown, which cannot be seen as part of the visible spectrum, are made up of a mixture of different wavelengths.

A white object reflects all wavelengths of light and absorbs no light.

A yellow object absorbs every colour except yellow, which it reflects.

A black object absorbs all wavelengths of light and reflects no light.

Flower under normal white light

Same flower under UV light

Ultraviolet radiation

Shorter in wavelength than the violet part of light, ultraviolet (UV) radiation causes sunburn. People can't see UV, but many other animals can. Some flowers have UV markings to attract insects, such as bees. These markings become visible to people under a UV light.

Sunlight enters the top of the raindrop

Raindrop

Light splits into its different colours

Reflected light leaves raindrop as a rainbow

Rainbow

Under the right conditions, a raindrop can act in the same way as a prism. Sunlight shining through a raindrop is refracted and split into the colours of the visible spectrum. The light reflects off the back of the raindrop and exits at the bottom. As the light is refracted through many raindrops, it forms an arc of colours that appears opposite the Sun in the sky – a rainbow.

X-rays

High-energy, short wavelength X-rays penetrate the skin, but are absorbed by bones and other dense materials. Some X-ray machines can even examine the body's soft tissues. Too much exposure to X-rays causes harmful chemical reactions in the body's cells, leading to disease, so they are only used when absolutely necessary.

Gamma radiation

Generated by nuclear reactions and radioactive atoms, gamma radiation has the highest energy in the electromagnetic spectrum. It also has the tiniest wavelengths, just a fraction of the size of an atom. Gamma rays are extremely harmful to humans, but they have their purpose – doctors use them to kill cancer cells.

Splitting light

White light is a mixture of light of different wavelengths and colours. When white light shines through a glass block called a prism, each wavelength refracts (bends) a different amount, and the light splits into a band of its different colours. Violet light waves bend the most and red waves bend least, which is why they are at each end of the split light.

Heinrich Hertz

German scientist Heinrich Hertz (1857–94) proved that electromagnetic energy was carried between two places by waves, and that, like light, these waves could be reflected and refracted.

39

BRUTE FORCE

Whether throwing a snowball or skating on ice, every action requires a force to create the movement. A force is a push or pull that causes an object to change its speed, direction, or shape. Forces control every movement in the Universe, from huge planets right down to tiny atoms. Some forces act directly on an object, such as pulling a sled, while others act at a distance, such as the force of gravity keeping the stars in motion.

Movement
If you start pushing a ball of snow along, it will begin to roll. Your push creates a force that acts on the snowball, causing it to move.

Direction
A force can change the direction of a movement. If an object moving in a straight line hits an obstacle, the force created by the impact sends the object bouncing off in a different direction.

Balanced forces
When an object is still, all the forces acting on it are balanced. If you stand on a flat surface, the force of gravity pulling you down is equal to the force of the ground pushing you up, so you stay still. Balanced forces on a moving object means it will not change its speed or direction.

Full force
A group of people all pulling together can move a much heavier sled than one person can. This is because the bigger the force that acts on something is, the more movement it will create.

Three laws of motion
Isaac Newton's laws explain how forces affect the direction or speed of objects. Scientists call any change of direction or speed an "acceleration", even when the object gets slower.

Isaac Newton
The unit used for measuring forces is the newton (N), named after English scientist Isaac Newton (1642–1727), who came up with the three laws of motion.

First law
Newton's first law states that a still object will remain still until a force acts upon it, and an object moving along at a steady speed in a straight line will continue moving at the same speed and in the same direction until a force acts upon it.

Inertia
The tendency of objects to resist changes in motion is called inertia. The heavier an object, the more inertia it has, so it is harder to move heavy objects than light ones.

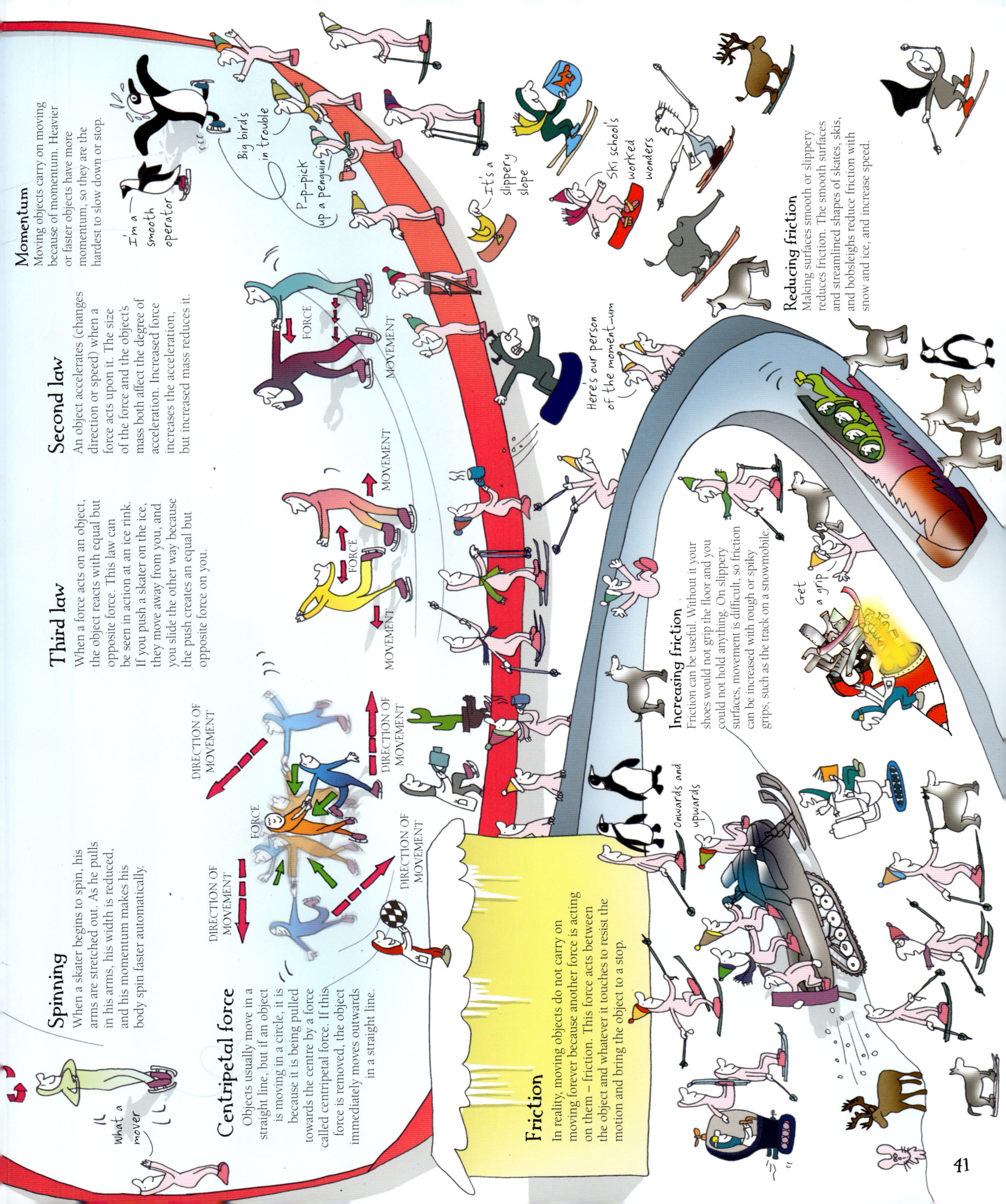

Momentum
Moving objects carry on moving because of momentum. Heavier or faster objects have more momentum, so they are the hardest to slow down or stop.

Second law
An object accelerates (changes direction or speed) when a force acts upon it. The size of the force and the object's mass both affect the degree of acceleration. Increased force increases the acceleration, but increased mass reduces it.

Third law
When a force acts on an object, the object reacts with equal but opposite force. This law can be seen in action at an ice rink. If you push a skater on the ice, they move away from you, and you slide the other way because the push creates an equal but opposite force on you.

Spinning
When a skater begins to spin, his arms are stretched out. As he pulls in his arms, his width is reduced, and his momentum makes his body spin faster automatically.

Centripetal force
Objects usually move in a straight line, but if an object is moving in a circle, it is because it is being pulled towards the centre by a force called centripetal force. If this force is removed, the object immediately moves outwards in a straight line.

Friction
In reality, moving objects do not carry on moving forever because another force is acting on them – friction. This force acts between the object and whatever it touches to resist the motion and bring the object to a stop.

Increasing friction
Friction can be useful. Without it your shoes would not grip the floor and you could not hold anything. On slippery surfaces, movement is difficult, so friction can be increased with rough or spiky grips, such as the track on a snowmobile.

Reducing friction
Making surfaces smooth or slippery reduces friction. The smooth surfaces and streamlined shapes of skates, skis, and bobsleighs reduce friction with snow and ice, and increase speed.

HARD AT WORK

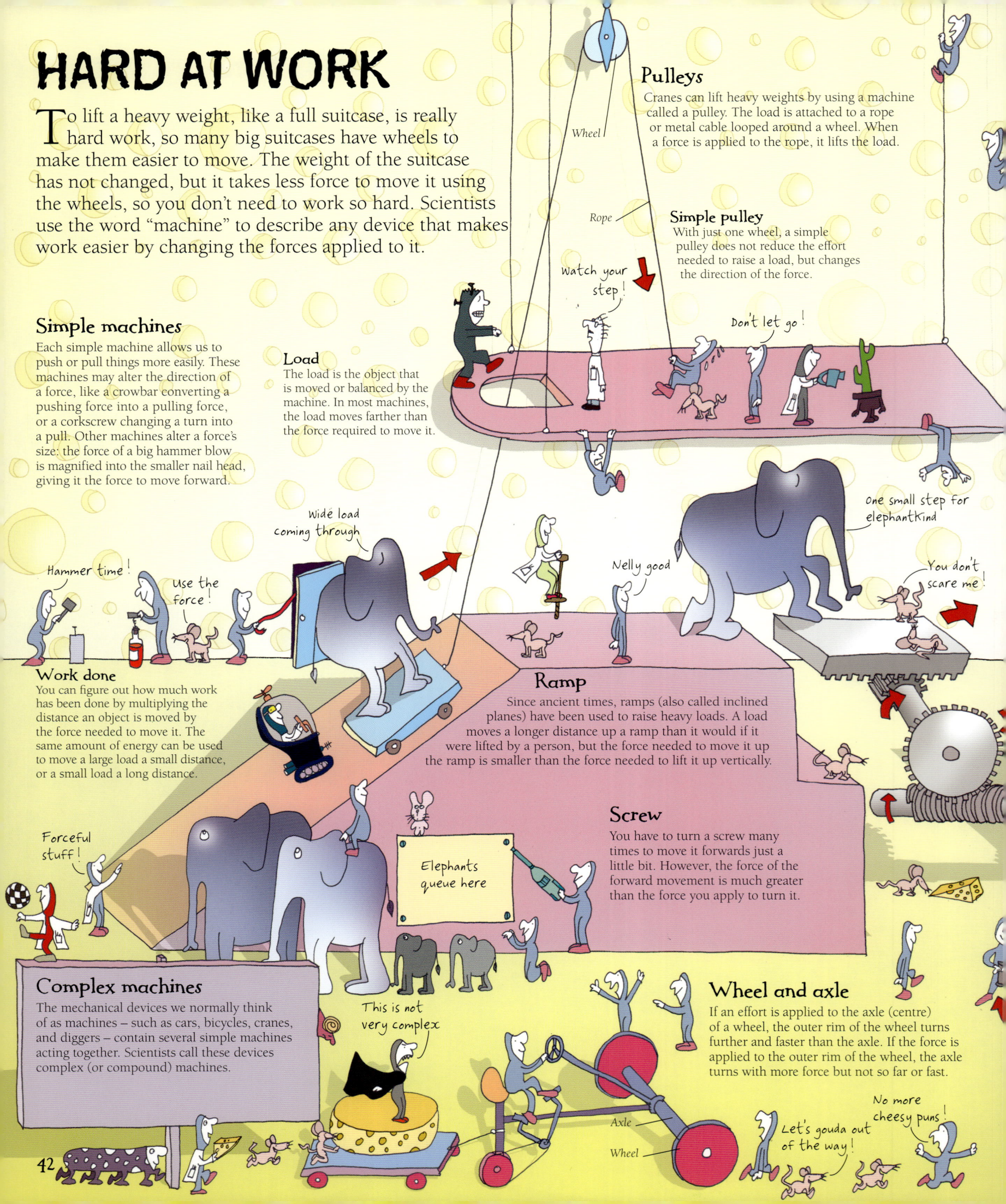

To lift a heavy weight, like a full suitcase, is really hard work, so many big suitcases have wheels to make them easier to move. The weight of the suitcase has not changed, but it takes less force to move it using the wheels, so you don't need to work so hard. Scientists use the word "machine" to describe any device that makes work easier by changing the forces applied to it.

Simple machines
Each simple machine allows us to push or pull things more easily. These machines may alter the direction of a force, like a crowbar converting a pushing force into a pulling force, or a corkscrew changing a turn into a pull. Other machines alter a force's size: the force of a big hammer blow is magnified into the smaller nail head, giving it the force to move forward.

Work done
You can figure out how much work has been done by multiplying the distance an object is moved by the force needed to move it. The same amount of energy can be used to move a large load a small distance, or a small load a long distance.

Complex machines
The mechanical devices we normally think of as machines – such as cars, bicycles, cranes, and diggers – contain several simple machines acting together. Scientists call these devices complex (or compound) machines.

Pulleys
Cranes can lift heavy weights by using a machine called a pulley. The load is attached to a rope or metal cable looped around a wheel. When a force is applied to the rope, it lifts the load.

Simple pulley
With just one wheel, a simple pulley does not reduce the effort needed to raise a load, but changes the direction of the force.

Load
The load is the object that is moved or balanced by the machine. In most machines, the load moves farther than the force required to move it.

Ramp
Since ancient times, ramps (also called inclined planes) have been used to raise heavy loads. A load moves a longer distance up a ramp than it would if it were lifted by a person, but the force needed to move it up the ramp is smaller than the force needed to lift it up vertically.

Screw
You have to turn a screw many times to move it forwards just a little bit. However, the force of the forward movement is much greater than the force you apply to turn it.

Wheel and axle
If an effort is applied to the axle (centre) of a wheel, the outer rim of the wheel turns further and faster than the axle. If the force is applied to the outer rim of the wheel, the axle turns with more force but not so far or fast.

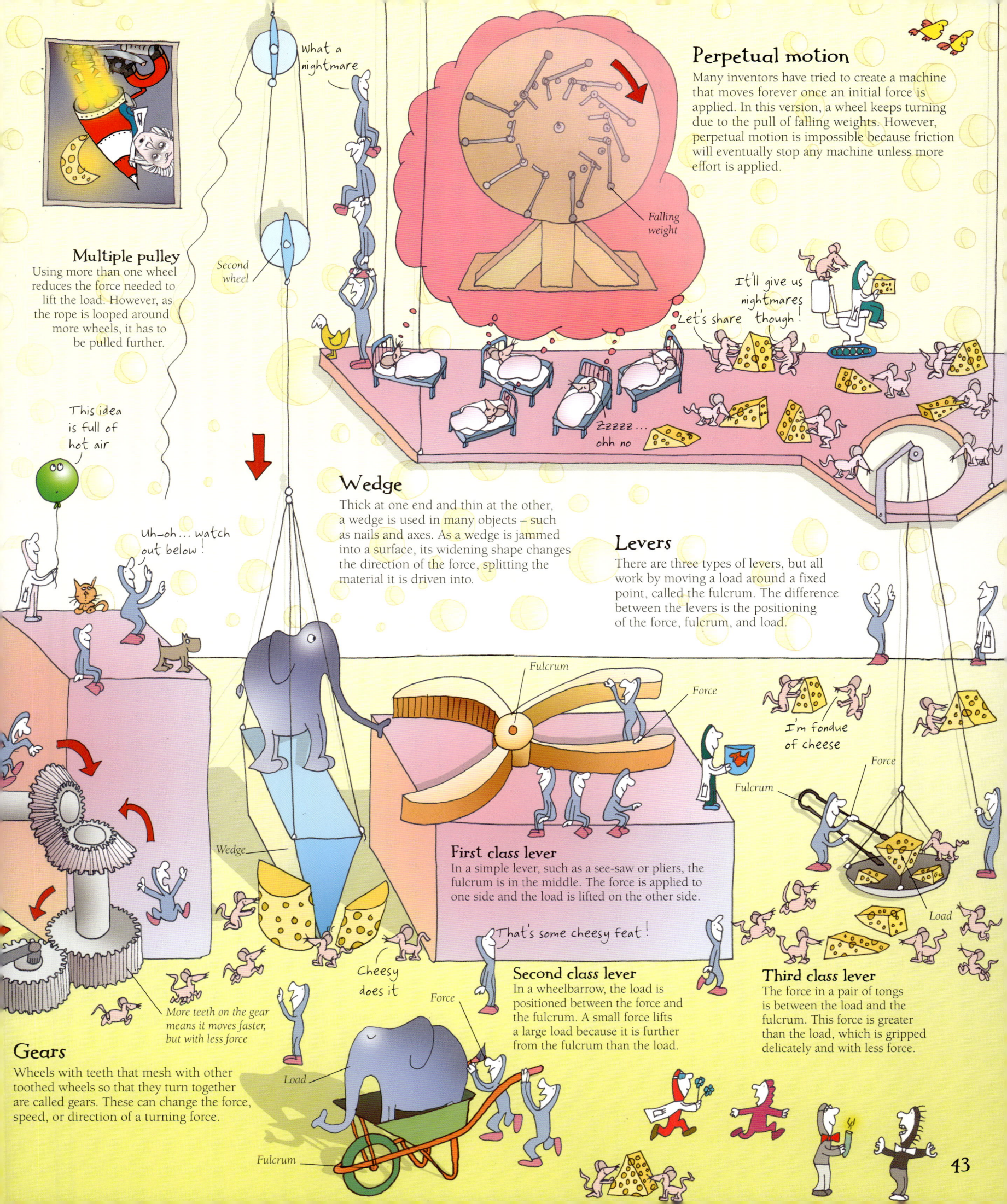

Multiple pulley
Using more than one wheel reduces the force needed to lift the load. However, as the rope is looped around more wheels, it has to be pulled further.

Perpetual motion
Many inventors have tried to create a machine that moves forever once an initial force is applied. In this version, a wheel keeps turning due to the pull of falling weights. However, perpetual motion is impossible because friction will eventually stop any machine unless more effort is applied.

Wedge
Thick at one end and thin at the other, a wedge is used in many objects – such as nails and axes. As a wedge is jammed into a surface, its widening shape changes the direction of the force, splitting the material it is driven into.

Levers
There are three types of levers, but all work by moving a load around a fixed point, called the fulcrum. The difference between the levers is the positioning of the force, fulcrum, and load.

First class lever
In a simple lever, such as a see-saw or pliers, the fulcrum is in the middle. The force is applied to one side and the load is lifted on the other side.

Second class lever
In a wheelbarrow, the load is positioned between the force and the fulcrum. A small force lifts a large load because it is further from the fulcrum than the load.

Third class lever
The force in a pair of tongs is between the load and the fulcrum. This force is greater than the load, which is gripped delicately and with less force.

Gears
Wheels with teeth that mesh with other toothed wheels so that they turn together are called gears. These can change the force, speed, or direction of a turning force.

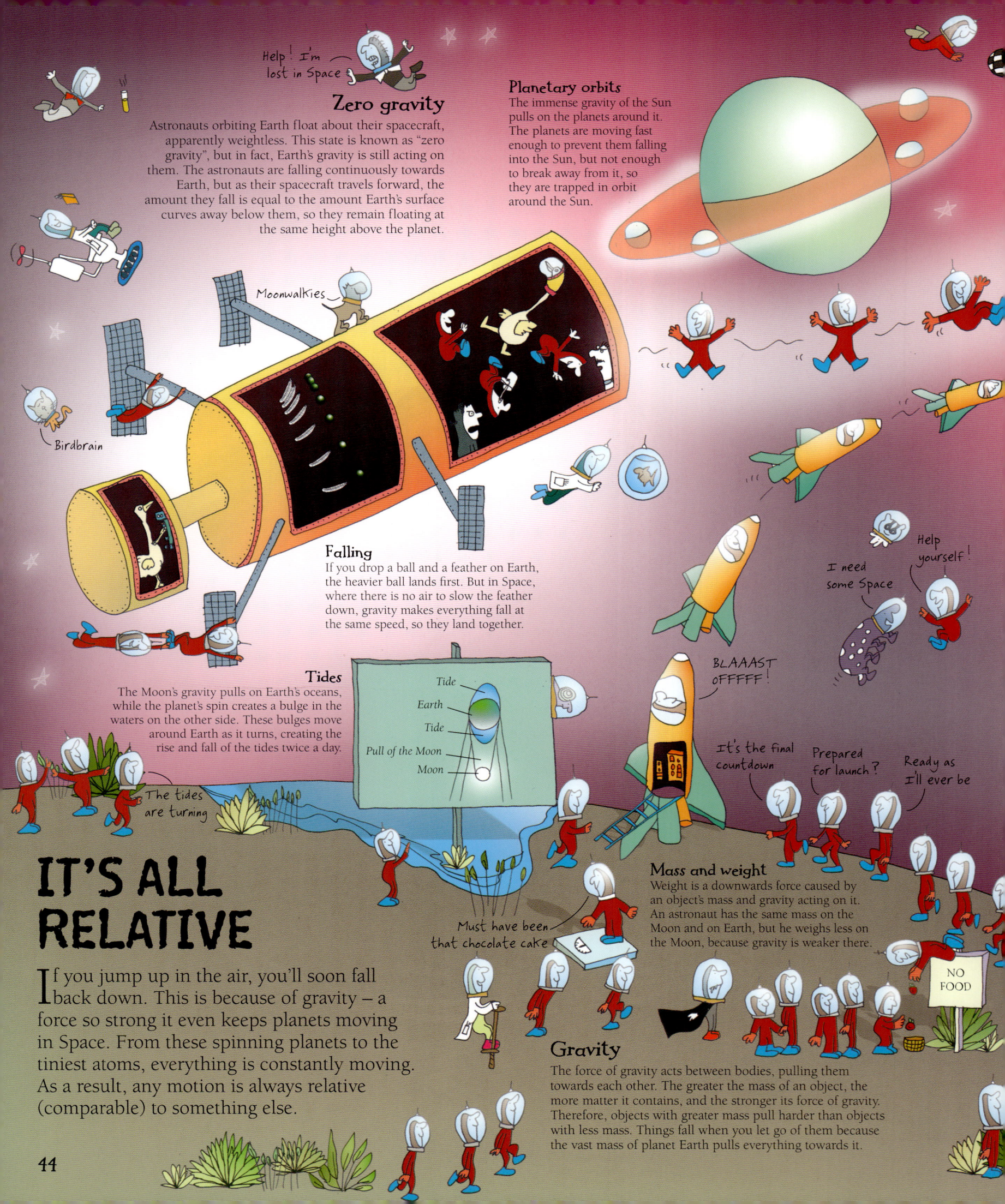

Zero gravity
Astronauts orbiting Earth float about their spacecraft, apparently weightless. This state is known as "zero gravity", but in fact, Earth's gravity is still acting on them. The astronauts are falling continuously towards Earth, but as their spacecraft travels forward, the amount they fall is equal to the amount Earth's surface curves away below them, so they remain floating at the same height above the planet.

Planetary orbits
The immense gravity of the Sun pulls on the planets around it. The planets are moving fast enough to prevent them falling into the Sun, but not enough to break away from it, so they are trapped in orbit around the Sun.

Falling
If you drop a ball and a feather on Earth, the heavier ball lands first. But in Space, where there is no air to slow the feather down, gravity makes everything fall at the same speed, so they land together.

Tides
The Moon's gravity pulls on Earth's oceans, while the planet's spin creates a bulge in the waters on the other side. These bulges move around Earth as it turns, creating the rise and fall of the tides twice a day.

IT'S ALL RELATIVE

If you jump up in the air, you'll soon fall back down. This is because of gravity – a force so strong it even keeps planets moving in Space. From these spinning planets to the tiniest atoms, everything is constantly moving. As a result, any motion is always relative (comparable) to something else.

Mass and weight
Weight is a downwards force caused by an object's mass and gravity acting on it. An astronaut has the same mass on the Moon and on Earth, but he weighs less on the Moon, because gravity is weaker there.

Gravity
The force of gravity acts between bodies, pulling them towards each other. The greater the mass of an object, the more matter it contains, and the stronger its force of gravity. Therefore, objects with greater mass pull harder than objects with less mass. Things fall when you let go of them because the vast mass of planet Earth pulls everything towards it.

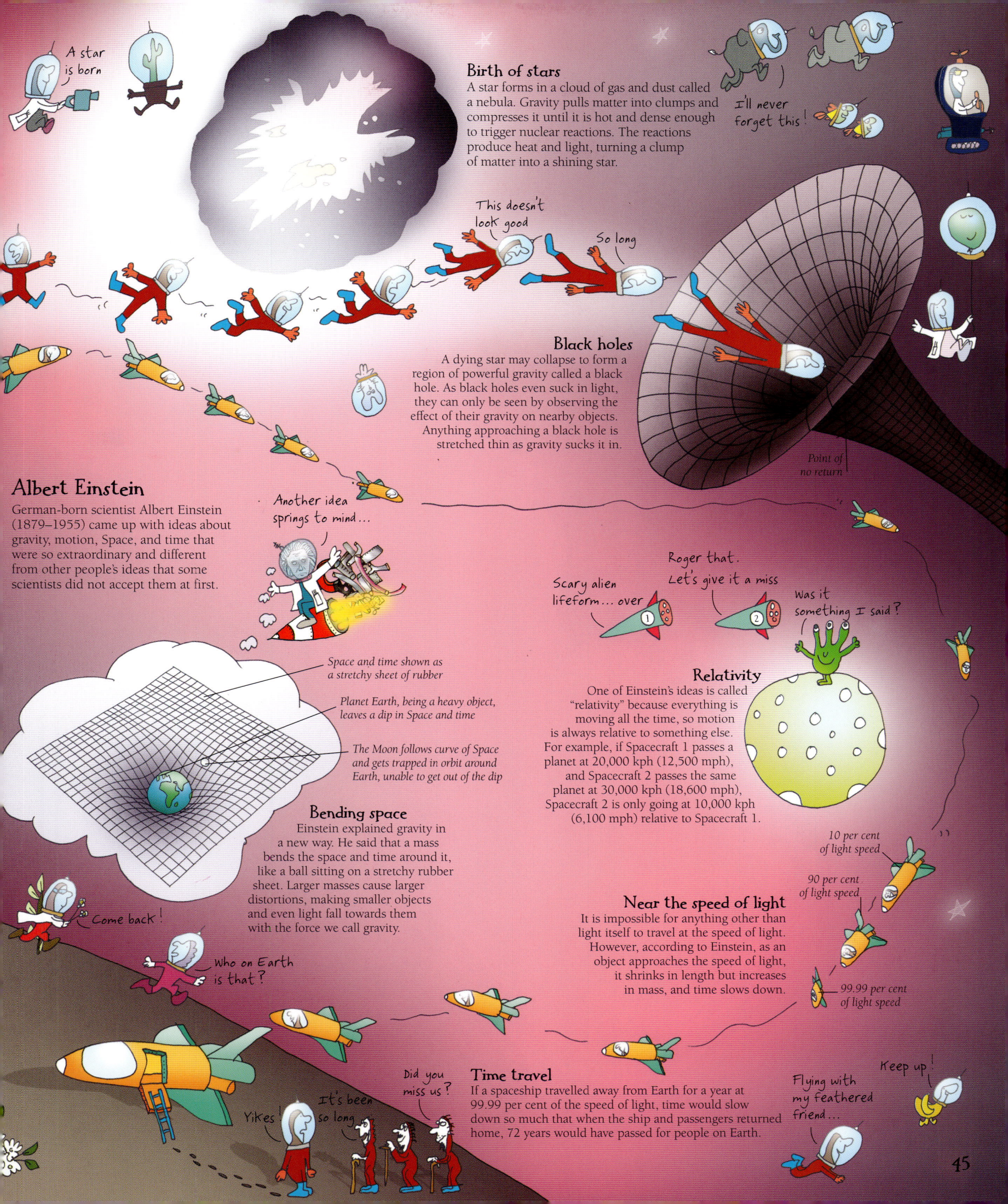

Birth of stars
A star forms in a cloud of gas and dust called a nebula. Gravity pulls matter into clumps and compresses it until it is hot and dense enough to trigger nuclear reactions. The reactions produce heat and light, turning a clump of matter into a shining star.

Black holes
A dying star may collapse to form a region of powerful gravity called a black hole. As black holes even suck in light, they can only be seen by observing the effect of their gravity on nearby objects. Anything approaching a black hole is stretched thin as gravity sucks it in.

Albert Einstein
German-born scientist Albert Einstein (1879–1955) came up with ideas about gravity, motion, Space, and time that were so extraordinary and different from other people's ideas that some scientists did not accept them at first.

Space and time shown as a stretchy sheet of rubber

Planet Earth, being a heavy object, leaves a dip in Space and time

The Moon follows curve of Space and gets trapped in orbit around Earth, unable to get out of the dip

Bending space
Einstein explained gravity in a new way. He said that a mass bends the space and time around it, like a ball sitting on a stretchy rubber sheet. Larger masses cause larger distortions, making smaller objects and even light fall towards them with the force we call gravity.

Relativity
One of Einstein's ideas is called "relativity" because everything is moving all the time, so motion is always relative to something else. For example, if Spacecraft 1 passes a planet at 20,000 kph (12,500 mph), and Spacecraft 2 passes the same planet at 30,000 kph (18,600 mph), Spacecraft 2 is only going at 10,000 kph (6,100 mph) relative to Spacecraft 1.

Near the speed of light
It is impossible for anything other than light itself to travel at the speed of light. However, according to Einstein, as an object approaches the speed of light, it shrinks in length but increases in mass, and time slows down.

Time travel
If a spaceship travelled away from Earth for a year at 99.99 per cent of the speed of light, time would slow down so much that when the ship and passengers returned home, 72 years would have passed for people on Earth.

POWERFUL ATTRACTION

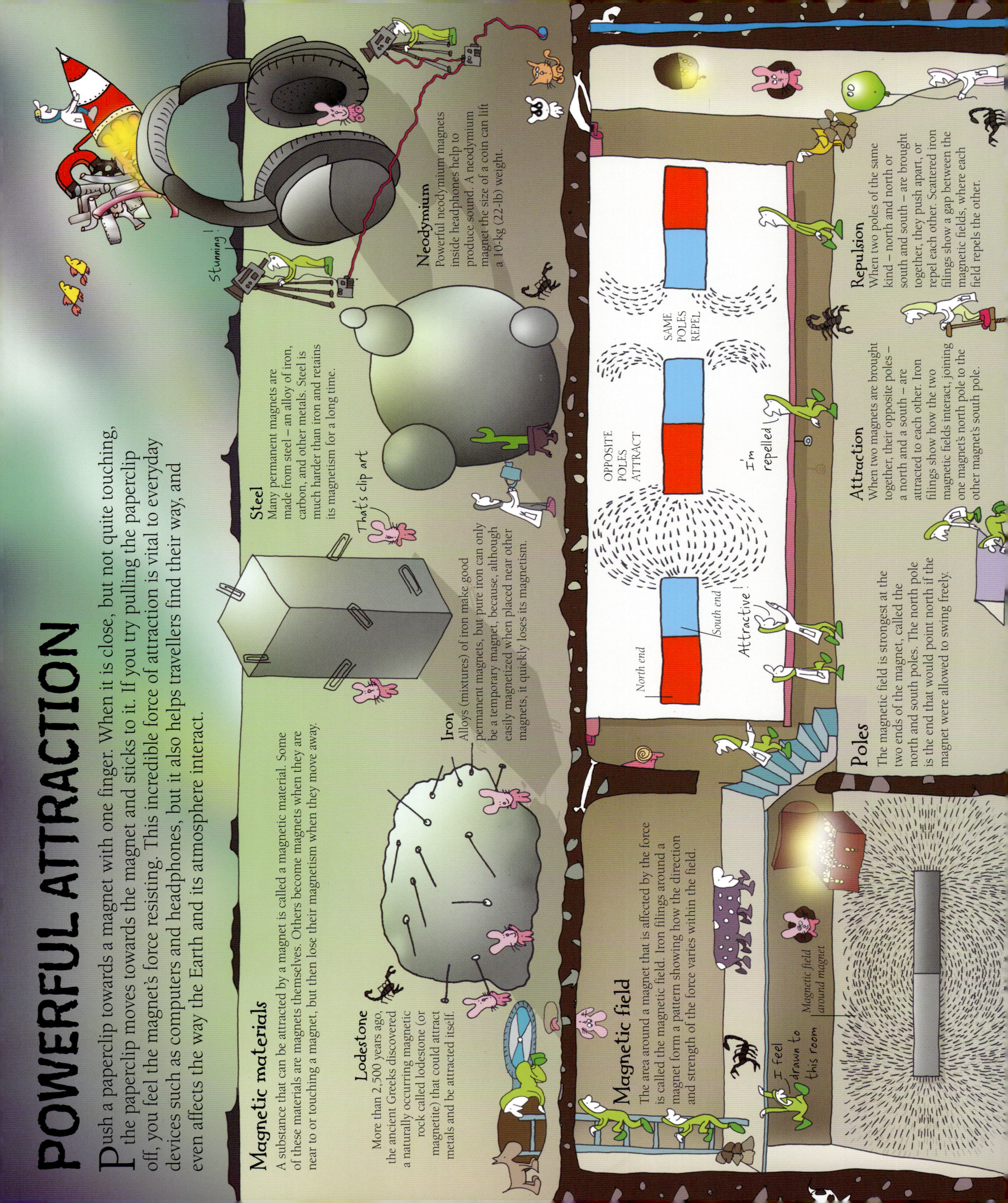

Push a paperclip towards a magnet with one finger. When it is close, but not quite touching, the paperclip moves towards the magnet and sticks to it. If you try pulling the paperclip off, you feel the magnet's force resisting. This incredible force of attraction is vital to everyday devices such as computers and headphones, but it also helps travellers find their way, and even affects the way the Earth and its atmosphere interact.

Magnetic materials
A substance that can be attracted by a magnet is called a magnetic material. Some of these materials are magnets themselves. Others become magnets when they are near to or touching a magnet, but then lose their magnetism when they move away.

Lodestone
More than 2,500 years ago, the ancient Greeks discovered a naturally occurring magnetic rock called lodestone (or magnetite) that could attract metals and be attracted itself.

Iron
Alloys (mixtures) of iron make good permanent magnets, but pure iron can only be a temporary magnet, because, although easily magnetized when placed near other magnets, it quickly loses its magnetism.

Steel
Many permanent magnets are made from steel – an alloy of iron, carbon, and other metals. Steel is much harder than iron and retains its magnetism for a long time.

Neodymium
Powerful neodymium magnets inside headphones help to produce sound. A neodymium magnet the size of a coin can lift a 10-kg (22-lb) weight.

Magnetic field
The area around a magnet that is affected by the force is called the magnetic field. Iron filings around a magnet form a pattern showing how the direction and strength of the force varies within the field.

Poles
The magnetic field is strongest at the two ends of the magnet, called the north and south poles. The north pole is the end that would point north if the magnet were allowed to swing freely.

Attraction
When two magnets are brought together, their opposite poles – a north and a south – are attracted to each other. Iron filings show how the two magnetic fields interact, joining one magnet's north pole to the other magnet's south pole.

Repulsion
When two poles of the same kind – north and north or south and south – are brought together, they push apart, or repel each other. Scattered iron filings show a gap between the magnetic fields, where each field repels the other.

Earth's magnetic field

Planet Earth behaves like a huge magnet, surrounded by a magnetic field called the magnetosphere, which extends out into space. The field is probably created by charged material circulating deep inside the planet.

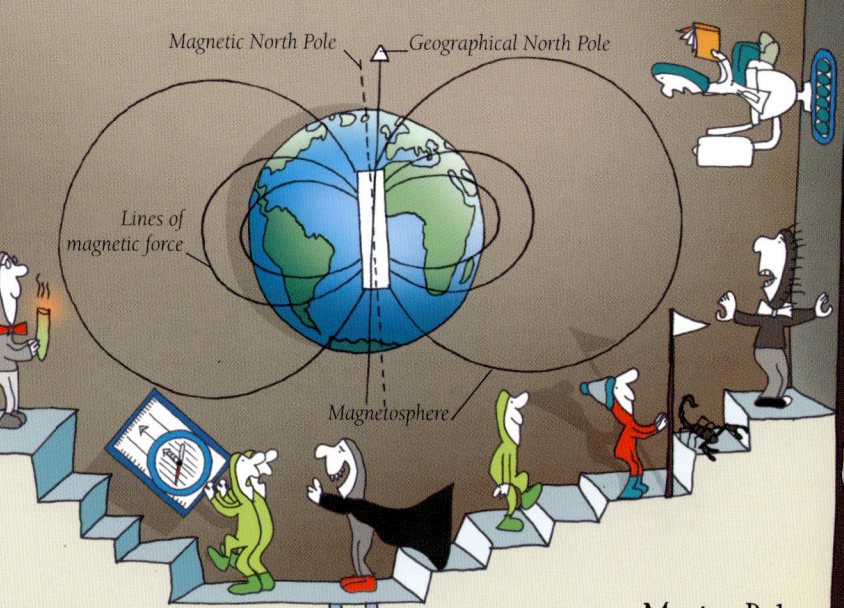

Magnetic North Pole
Geographical North Pole
Magnetosphere
Lines of magnetic force

Moving Pole

The Magnetic North Pole is not in the same place as the geographical North Pole, but in northern Canada. The precise location changes, because Earth's magnetic field moves over time and is now travelling at up to 40 km (25 miles) per year.

Compasses

The fine magnetic needle inside a compass spins on a pivot and always points towards Earth's Magnetic North Pole. Chinese and European sailors first used compasses made from lodestone in the 12th century.

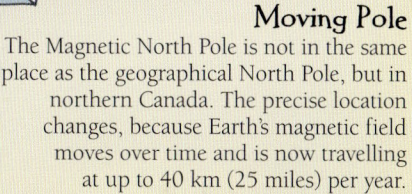

Auroras

Patterns of swirling lights sometimes fill the sky near the magnetic poles. These effects, called the Aurora Borealis (Northern Lights) and Aurora Australis (Southern Lights), happen when high-energy charged particles from the Sun are attracted to the poles, making atoms in the atmosphere glow.

Ooooh! *Aaahh!*

Magnetic domains

Inside magnetic materials are regions called magnetic domains. These resemble tiny magnets each with a north and south pole. When the material is unmagnetized, the poles of the domains point randomly in any direction, so the material has no overall north and south pole.

Magnetic domains
UNMAGNETIZED
MAGNETIZED

Magnetizing

When a magnetic material is placed in a magnetic field, the magnetic domains line up so that all the north poles point in one direction and all the south poles in the opposite direction, turning it into a magnet.

Domains aligned by stroking with another magnet

Lining up domains

A magnetic material can become a magnet by repeatedly stroking it in one direction with one pole of a magnet. This lines up the magnetic domains within the material.

Demagnetizing

Striking a magnet hard jumbles up the magnetic domains, demagnetizing the magnet. When heated, magnets also become demagnetized because moving molecules in the hot material destroy the alignment of the domains.

Jumbled domains

Keeper

A horseshoe magnet is bent so that its north and south poles face the same direction. Putting an iron plate called a keeper across the poles forms a magnetic circuit, which keeps the domains aligned and prevents the magnet from gradually losing its magnetism.

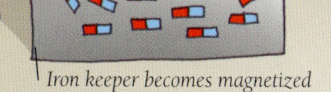

Horseshoe magnet
Iron keeper becomes magnetized

Keep out!

47

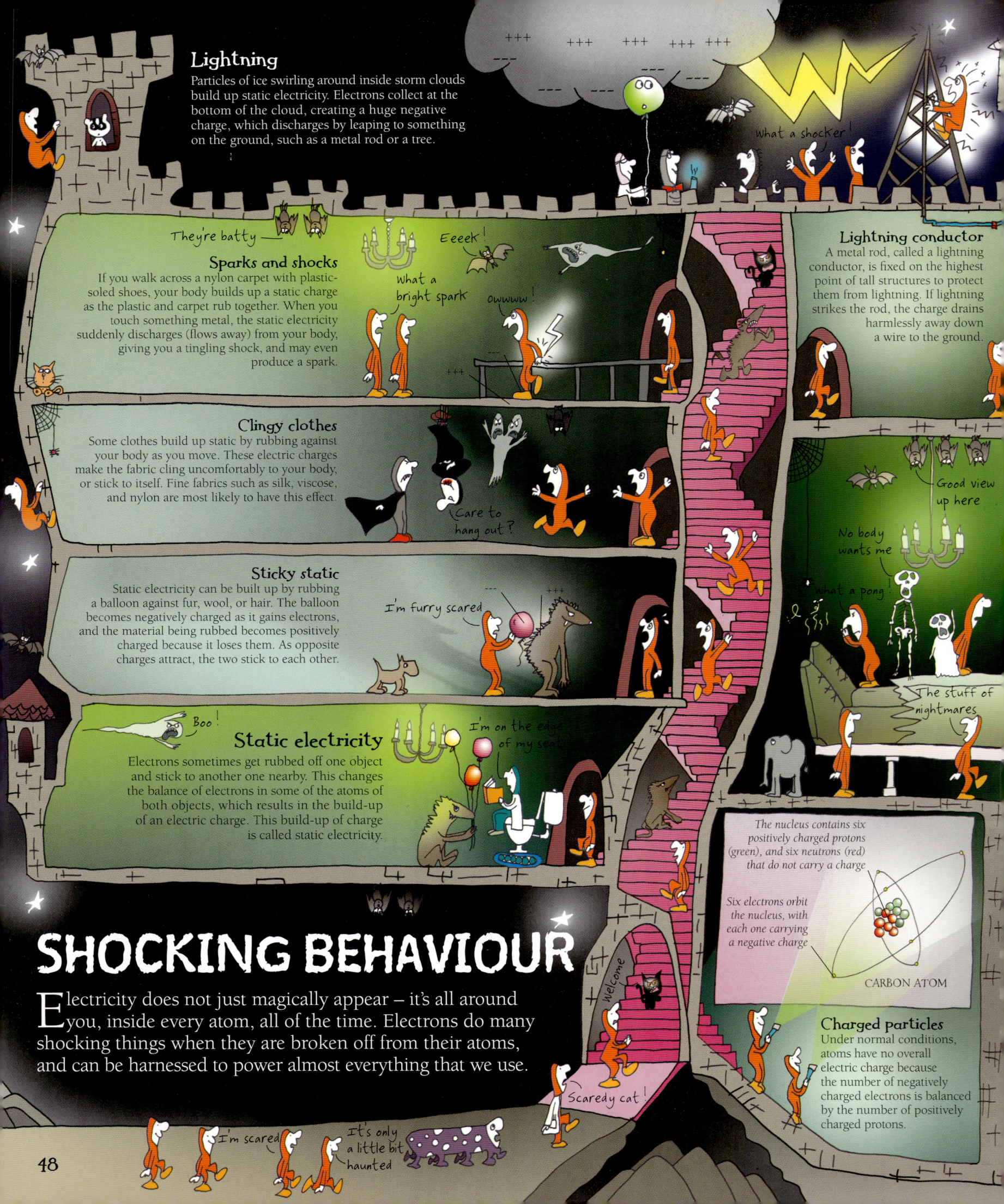

Lightning
Particles of ice swirling around inside storm clouds build up static electricity. Electrons collect at the bottom of the cloud, creating a huge negative charge, which discharges by leaping to something on the ground, such as a metal rod or a tree.

Sparks and shocks
If you walk across a nylon carpet with plastic-soled shoes, your body builds up a static charge as the plastic and carpet rub together. When you touch something metal, the static electricity suddenly discharges (flows away) from your body, giving you a tingling shock, and may even produce a spark.

Clingy clothes
Some clothes build up static by rubbing against your body as you move. These electric charges make the fabric cling uncomfortably to your body, or stick to itself. Fine fabrics such as silk, viscose, and nylon are most likely to have this effect.

Sticky static
Static electricity can be built up by rubbing a balloon against fur, wool, or hair. The balloon becomes negatively charged as it gains electrons, and the material being rubbed becomes positively charged because it loses them. As opposite charges attract, the two stick to each other.

Static electricity
Electrons sometimes get rubbed off one object and stick to another one nearby. This changes the balance of electrons in some of the atoms of both objects, which results in the build-up of an electric charge. This build-up of charge is called static electricity.

Lightning conductor
A metal rod, called a lightning conductor, is fixed on the highest point of tall structures to protect them from lightning. If lightning strikes the rod, the charge drains harmlessly away down a wire to the ground.

The nucleus contains six positively charged protons (green), and six neutrons (red) that do not carry a charge

Six electrons orbit the nucleus, with each one carrying a negative charge

CARBON ATOM

Charged particles
Under normal conditions, atoms have no overall electric charge because the number of negatively charged electrons is balanced by the number of positively charged protons.

SHOCKING BEHAVIOUR
Electricity does not just magically appear – it's all around you, inside every atom, all of the time. Electrons do many shocking things when they are broken off from their atoms, and can be harnessed to power almost everything that we use.

48

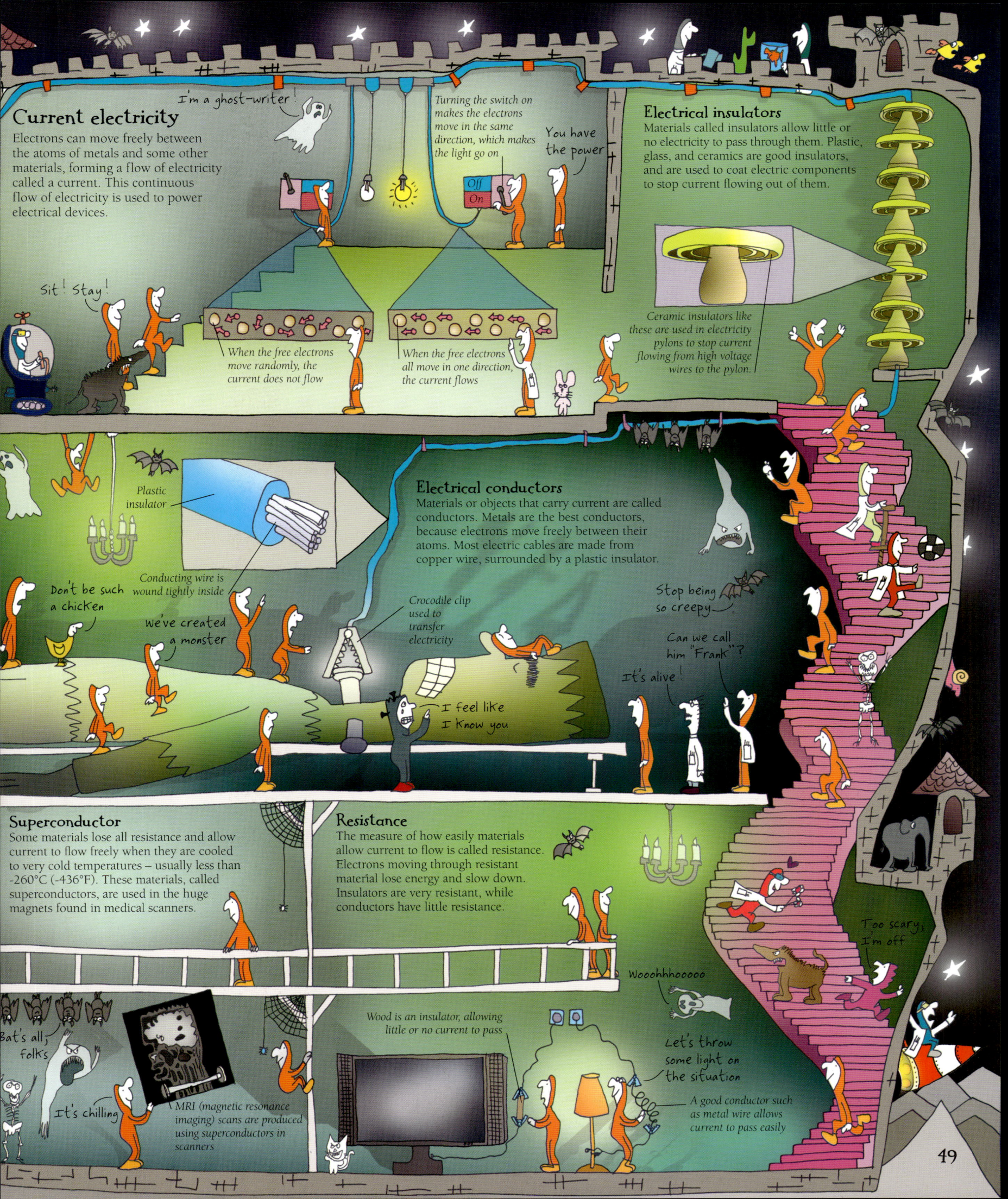

Current electricity

Electrons can move freely between the atoms of metals and some other materials, forming a flow of electricity called a current. This continuous flow of electricity is used to power electrical devices.

Turning the switch on makes the electrons move in the same direction, which makes the light go on

When the free electrons move randomly, the current does not flow

When the free electrons all move in one direction, the current flows

Electrical insulators

Materials called insulators allow little or no electricity to pass through them. Plastic, glass, and ceramics are good insulators, and are used to coat electric components to stop current flowing out of them.

Ceramic insulators like these are used in electricity pylons to stop current flowing from high voltage wires to the pylon.

Electrical conductors

Materials or objects that carry current are called conductors. Metals are the best conductors, because electrons move freely between their atoms. Most electric cables are made from copper wire, surrounded by a plastic insulator.

Plastic insulator

Conducting wire is wound tightly inside

Crocodile clip used to transfer electricity

Superconductor

Some materials lose all resistance and allow current to flow freely when they are cooled to very cold temperatures – usually less than -260°C (-436°F). These materials, called superconductors, are used in the huge magnets found in medical scanners.

MRI (magnetic resonance imaging) scans are produced using superconductors in scanners

Resistance

The measure of how easily materials allow current to flow is called resistance. Electrons moving through resistant material lose energy and slow down. Insulators are very resistant, while conductors have little resistance.

Wood is an insulator, allowing little or no current to pass

A good conductor such as metal wire allows current to pass easily

49

BRIGHT SPARKS

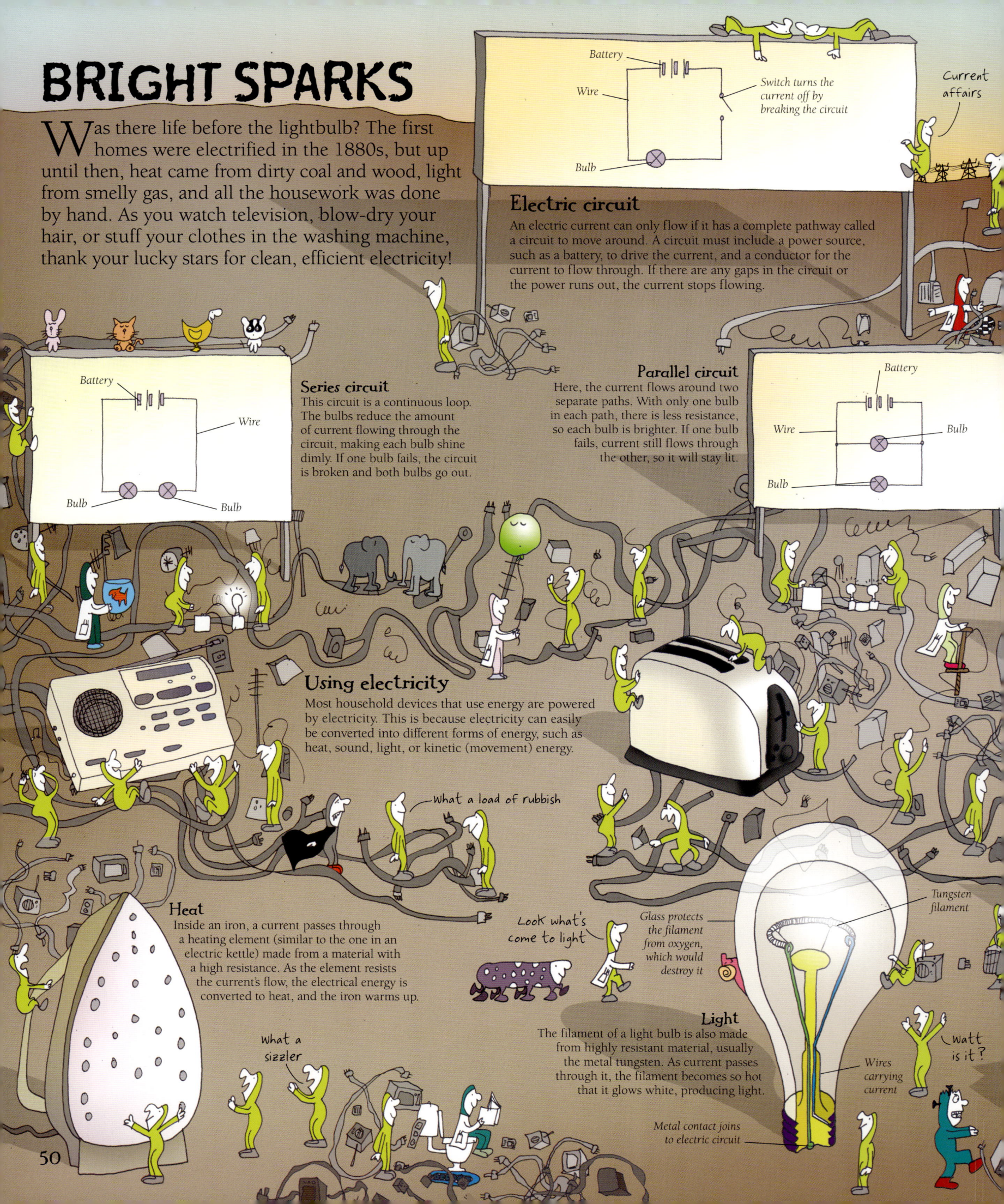

Was there life before the lightbulb? The first homes were electrified in the 1880s, but up until then, heat came from dirty coal and wood, light from smelly gas, and all the housework was done by hand. As you watch television, blow-dry your hair, or stuff your clothes in the washing machine, thank your lucky stars for clean, efficient electricity!

Electric circuit
An electric current can only flow if it has a complete pathway called a circuit to move around. A circuit must include a power source, such as a battery, to drive the current, and a conductor for the current to flow through. If there are any gaps in the circuit or the power runs out, the current stops flowing.

Series circuit
This circuit is a continuous loop. The bulbs reduce the amount of current flowing through the circuit, making each bulb shine dimly. If one bulb fails, the circuit is broken and both bulbs go out.

Parallel circuit
Here, the current flows around two separate paths. With only one bulb in each path, there is less resistance, so each bulb is brighter. If one bulb fails, current still flows through the other, so it will stay lit.

Using electricity
Most household devices that use energy are powered by electricity. This is because electricity can easily be converted into different forms of energy, such as heat, sound, light, or kinetic (movement) energy.

Heat
Inside an iron, a current passes through a heating element (similar to the one in an electric kettle) made from a material with a high resistance. As the element resists the current's flow, the electrical energy is converted to heat, and the iron warms up.

Light
The filament of a light bulb is also made from highly resistant material, usually the metal tungsten. As current passes through it, the filament becomes so hot that it glows white, producing light.

Electromagnetism

An electric current flowing through a wire produces a magnetic field around the wire. When the current is switched off, the magnetic field disappears. The bigger the current and the more wire there is, the stronger the electromagnet's magnetic force.

Diagram labels: South pole, Magnetic field, North pole, Flow of current, Battery

Electromagnets at work
Loads of scrap metal can be moved easily using giant electromagnets. The current is turned on to pick up and transport the load, then turned off to shut off the magnetic field, releasing the metal in a new location.

Diagram labels: Magnetic field, Commutator reverses the flow of current each half turn, reversing the coil's poles, Coil, Direction of current, Battery

Motor
In a motor, a current passes through a wire coil in one direction and then the other, creating a changing magnetic field. Magnets on either side of the wire alternately attract and repel the coil, forcing it to turn. This energy can be harnessed to power machines.

Generator
When a coil of wire is turned inside a magnetic field or a magnet is moved past a stationery wire, an electric current passes through the wire. A generator uses this effect to create current from movement, the opposite principle to how a motor works.

Diagram labels: Coil, Magnetic field, Commutator, Magnet, Bulb lights up when handle is turned, Handle turns coil, Direction of current flow

Michael Faraday
English scientist Michael Faraday (1791–1867) proved that magnetism could produce electricity by pushing a magnet in and out of a coil of wire to create a current. He invented the electric motor and a basic generator.

Hans Christian Ørsted
Danish scientist Hans Christian Ørsted (1777–1851) discovered the link between magnetism and electricity when he noticed that turning a current on and off made the needle of a nearby compass jump.

Clap hands for Hans!

Electricity supply
The electrical energy we use is supplied by power stations, and is brought to us via a system of metal cables carried by pylons. When the cables reach city streets, they are usually run underground to deliver electricity to buildings.

Power station
Most of our electricity comes from fossil fuels, such as coal, oil, and gas. These are burned to heat water, which in turn drives spinning blades called turbines inside massive generators to produce electricity. Nuclear energy – the harnessing of the energy inside an atom's nucleus – can also be used to make electricity.

Power rangers

I get a real buzz off you

MAINS TRANSFORMER diagram labels: Wire coils wound around inside of the transformer, Outer plastic covering, High voltage in, Iron core, Lower voltage out

Transformer
The electrical pressure that drives current is called voltage. Cables carrying current from power stations have a dangerously high voltage. Before electricity arrives in homes and workplaces, a device called a transformer lowers the voltage to make it safer.

51

ELECTRIC CHEMISTRY

Just as some chemical reactions need light or heat to make them work, other reactions require electrical energy. Some chemical reactions even create an electric current. Electrochemical reactions are used to extract metals from ores, separate hydrogen from sea water, and produce the portable power source we use every day – the battery.

Electrolysis
The process of passing an electric current through a compound to split it into simpler parts is called electrolysis. When salt water undergoes electrolysis, it breaks apart to form chlorine gas, hydrogen gas, and sodium hydroxide.

ELECTROLYSIS OF SALT WATER
- Power supply
- Flow of electrons
- Anode (+)
- Cathode (−)
- Negative chlorine (Cl-) ions move to anode
- Electrolyte of salt water (H_2O + NaCl)
- Positive hydrogen (H^+) ions move to cathode
- Liquid becomes sodium hydroxide (NaOH) solution

Electrolyte of salt water (H_2O + NaCl)
Positive electrode
Negative electrode
Chlorine (Cl_2)
Hydrogen (H_2)

Electrode
A battery is connected to two electrical conductor rods, called electrodes. Each electrode becomes electrically charged when the circuit is complete. The negatively charged electrode is called the cathode and the positively charged electrode is called the anode.

Electrolyte
The electrodes are placed in a mixture called an electrolyte, which may be solid or liquid. The electrolyte is a conductor, so the current now has a complete circuit to move around, from the battery to the cathode, across the electrolyte to the anode, and back to the battery.

Hydrogen cars
The gas used to fuel hydrogen cars is often produced by electrolysis of salt water. Unlike diesel-fuelled or petrol-fuelled cars, hydrogen cars produce no harmful emissions. The engine is driven by the reaction of hydrogen with oxygen, producing one simple, clean waste product – water.

Humphrey Davy
In 1807, British scientist Sir Humphrey Davy (1778–1829) built a battery more powerful than any that had existed previously. He used the power to split compounds apart using electrolysis, and discovered many new elements, including potassium, sodium, calcium, magnesium, boron, and barium.

Electroplating

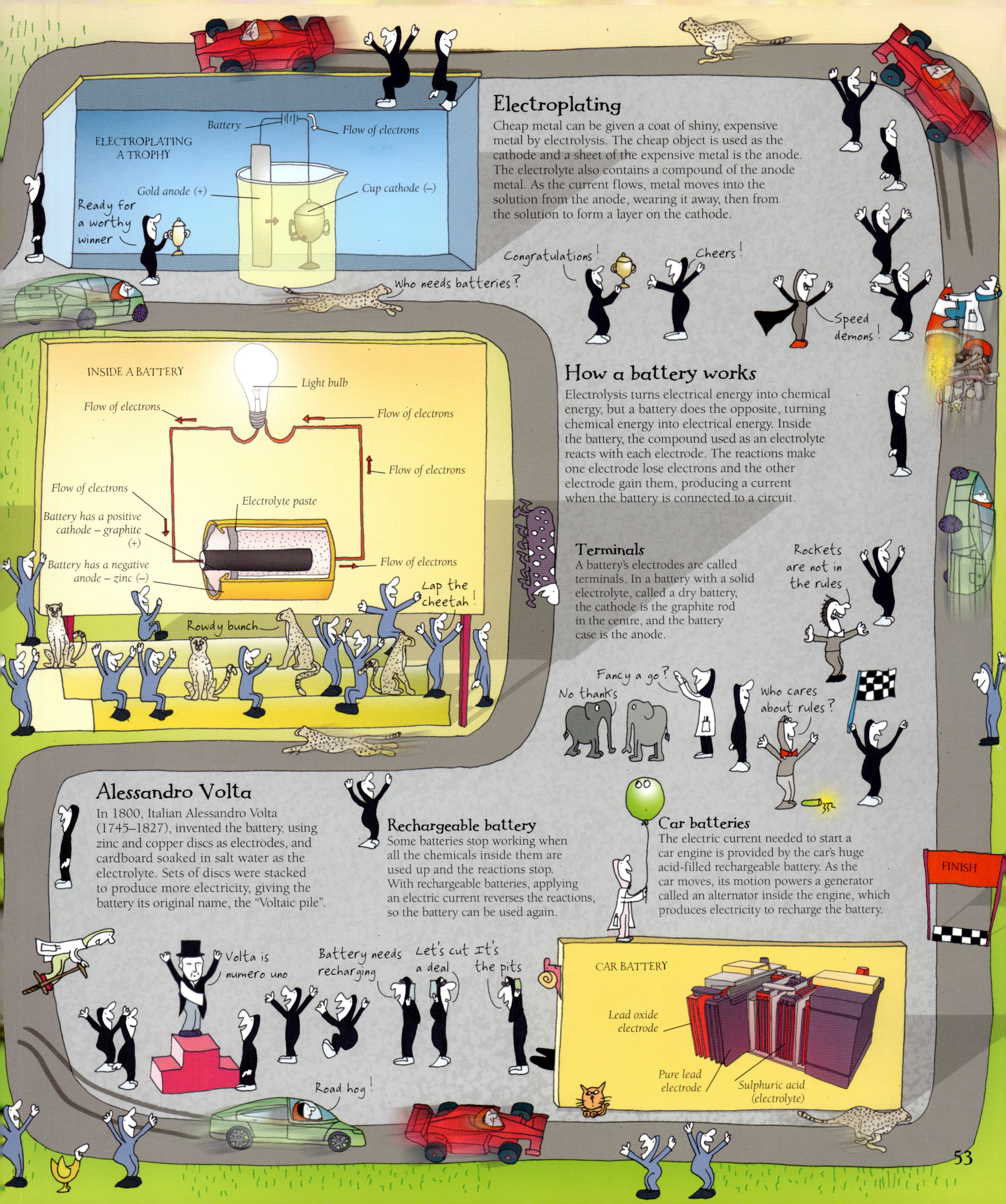

Cheap metal can be given a coat of shiny, expensive metal by electrolysis. The cheap object is used as the cathode and a sheet of the expensive metal is the anode. The electrolyte also contains a compound of the anode metal. As the current flows, metal moves into the solution from the anode, wearing it away, then from the solution to form a layer on the cathode.

ELECTROPLATING A TROPHY — Battery, Flow of electrons, Gold anode (+), Cup cathode (−)

How a battery works

Electrolysis turns electrical energy into chemical energy, but a battery does the opposite, turning chemical energy into electrical energy. Inside the battery, the compound used as an electrolyte reacts with each electrode. The reactions make one electrode lose electrons and the other electrode gain them, producing a current when the battery is connected to a circuit.

INSIDE A BATTERY — Light bulb, Flow of electrons, Electrolyte paste, Battery has a positive cathode – graphite (+), Battery has a negative anode – zinc (−)

Terminals
A battery's electrodes are called terminals. In a battery with a solid electrolyte, called a dry battery, the cathode is the graphite rod in the centre, and the battery case is the anode.

Alessandro Volta

In 1800, Italian Alessandro Volta (1745–1827), invented the battery, using zinc and copper discs as electrodes, and cardboard soaked in salt water as the electrolyte. Sets of discs were stacked to produce more electricity, giving the battery its original name, the "Voltaic pile".

Rechargeable battery

Some batteries stop working when all the chemicals inside them are used up and the reactions stop. With rechargeable batteries, applying an electric current reverses the reactions, so the battery can be used again.

Car batteries

The electric current needed to start a car engine is provided by the car's huge acid-filled rechargeable battery. As the car moves, its motion powers a generator called an alternator inside the engine, which produces electricity to recharge the battery.

CAR BATTERY — Lead oxide electrode, Pure lead electrode, Sulphuric acid (electrolyte)

53

RECIPE FOR LIFE

We all start life as a single cell – a fertilized egg. This basic unit of life divides repeatedly to produce a human body made of thirty trillion cells. These cells are not identical – there are more than 200 different types, each with its own job, including fat, nerve, and bone cells. Each cell contains the genes (instructions) to construct and run not just a cell, but also an entire body.

Cell ingredients

Nucleus (containing a nucleolus, where ribosomes are made)

Cytoplasm containing:
  Mitochondria
  Rough endoplasmic reticulum
  Golgi body
  Ribosomes

Cell membrane (the outer coating)

Chromosomes and DNA

Inside each nucleus are 46 gene-carrying chromosomes made of DNA – a long molecule of two strands that spiral round each other like a twisted ladder. The rungs of this ladder, called bases, form coded instructions for making proteins, which construct and run the cell.

Ribosome makes proteins
Rough endoplasmic reticulum (ER) transports the proteins made by the ribosome
Golgi body packages the proteins made by the ribosome
Mitochondrion provides the cell with energy
Cytoplasm
Nucleus
Cell membrane

Cell structure

Whatever their shape and size, all cells share the same basic structure. Each has an outer cell membrane, a nucleus (the control centre), and a jelly-like cytoplasm containing tiny organelles that bring the cell to life, including ribosomes, rough ER, the Golgi body, and mitochondria.

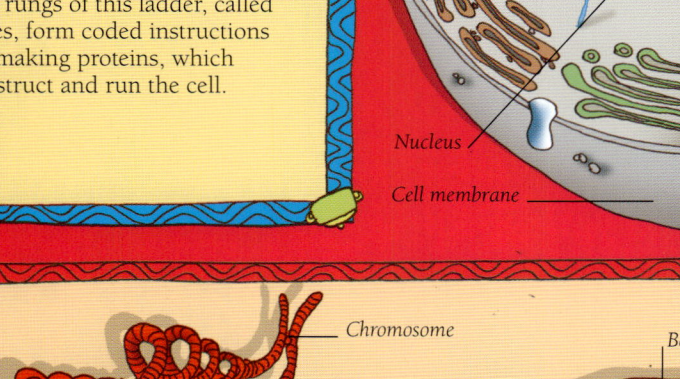

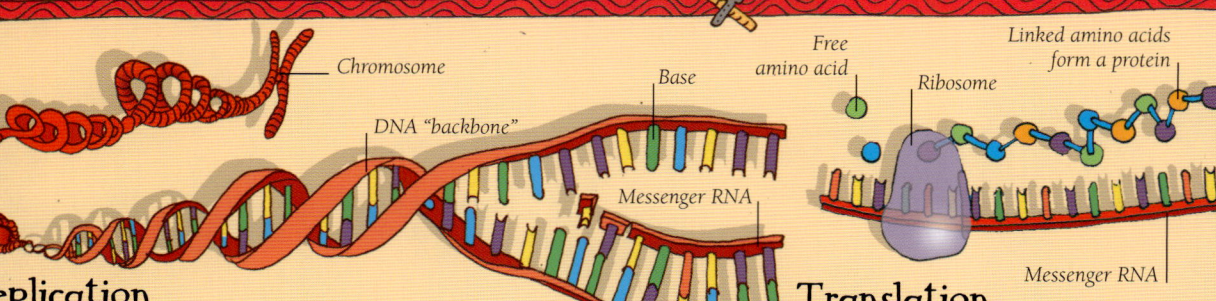

Replication

In the nucleus, a short section of DNA, representing a single gene (instruction), "unzips" to expose its coded message. This is copied onto a single-stranded substance, similar to the DNA "backbone", called messenger RNA. The messenger RNA then passes out of the nucleus into the cell's cytoplasm.

Chromosome · *DNA "backbone"* · *Base* · *Messenger RNA*

Translation

Passing through a ribosome in the cytoplasm, the RNA "message" is translated into a specific sequence for free amino acids in the cytoplasm to link up correctly and form a protein.

Free amino acid · *Ribosome* · *Linked amino acids form a protein* · *Messenger RNA*

Folding up

The new protein now detaches itself from the ribosome and folds up into its specific shape, determined by the order of amino acids.

Fat cells

The space inside these cells is mainly occupied by a globule of fat. Fat cells make adipose tissue, which provides an energy store and insulates the body.

Nerve cells

Nerve cells provide the wiring for the nervous system. Connected together in a massive network, they transmit electrical signals at high speed.

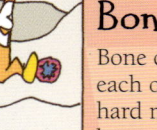

Bone cells

Bone cells live in isolation of each other, surrounded by the hard material that makes up bones, but still communicate to maintain bone tissue.

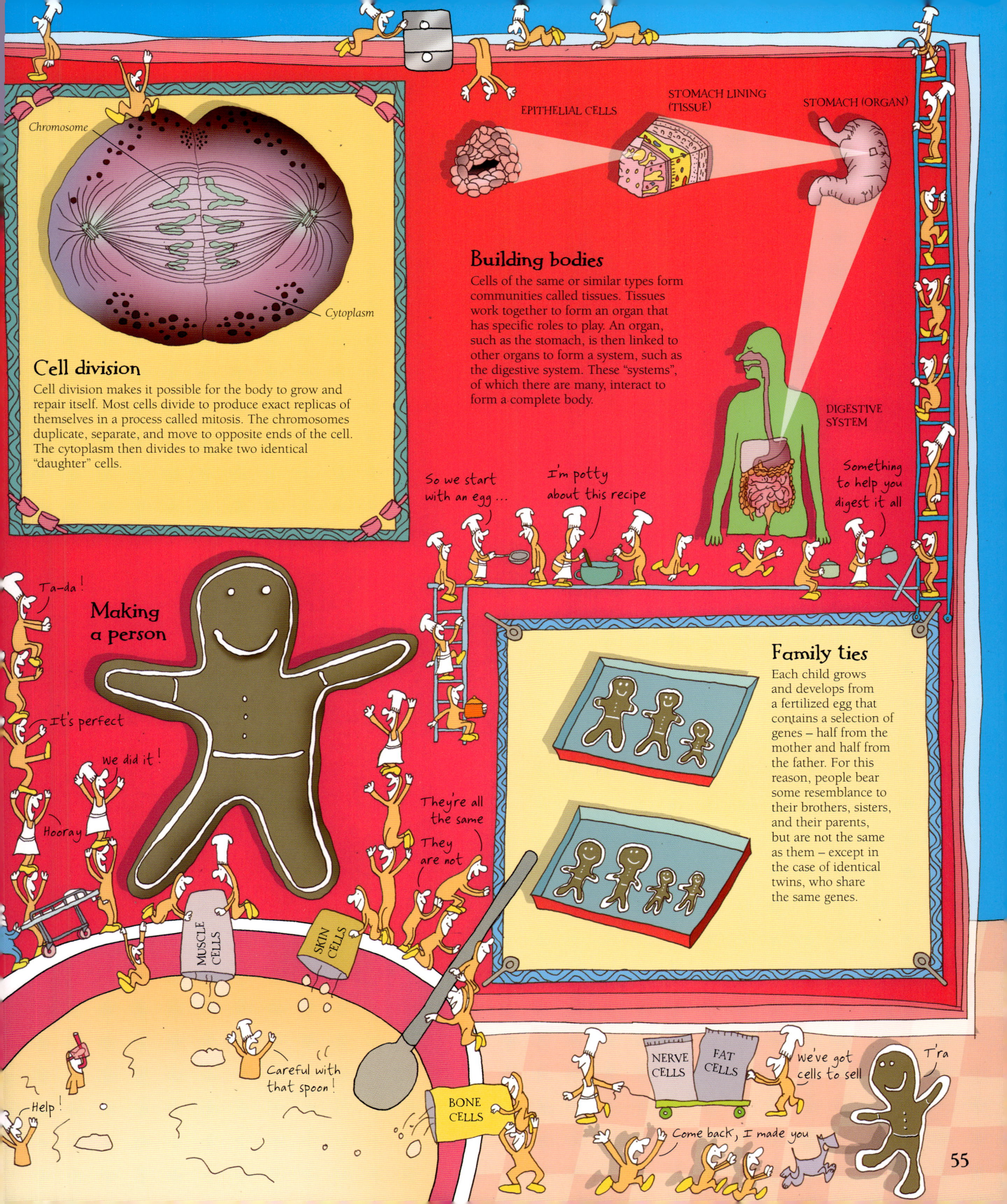

EPITHELIAL CELLS   STOMACH LINING (TISSUE)   STOMACH (ORGAN)

Cell division

Cell division makes it possible for the body to grow and repair itself. Most cells divide to produce exact replicas of themselves in a process called mitosis. The chromosomes duplicate, separate, and move to opposite ends of the cell. The cytoplasm then divides to make two identical "daughter" cells.

Chromosome
Cytoplasm

Building bodies

Cells of the same or similar types form communities called tissues. Tissues work together to form an organ that has specific roles to play. An organ, such as the stomach, is then linked to other organs to form a system, such as the digestive system. These "systems", of which there are many, interact to form a complete body.

DIGESTIVE SYSTEM

So we start with an egg...
I'm potty about this recipe
Something to help you digest it all

Making a person

Ta-da!
It's perfect
We did it!
Hooray
They're all the same
They are not
Careful with that spoon!
Help!
MUSCLE CELLS
SKIN CELLS
BONE CELLS
NERVE CELLS
FAT CELLS
We've got cells to sell
Come back, I made you
T'ra

Family ties

Each child grows and develops from a fertilized egg that contains a selection of genes – half from the mother and half from the father. For this reason, people bear some resemblance to their brothers, sisters, and their parents, but are not the same as them – except in the case of identical twins, who share the same genes.

55

Simultaneous discoveries
Often in the history of science, several scientists have worked on the same problem at the same time, in a race to be the first to make a breakthrough. This has sometimes led to two scientists coming up with a new idea at once, making it impossible to decide who should get the credit for the discovery.

Calculus
In 1675, English physicist Sir Isaac Newton and German physicist Gottfried Leibniz both came up with a mathematical theory called calculus. Newton insisted that Leibniz had stolen his ideas.

This was a calculated act of robbery

I don't know what you mean

Chance discoveries
Most scientific discoveries are the result of years of study and hard work. But from time to time, something unexpected is revealed, which leads to an entirely new discovery. For this reason, scientists always observe every aspect of whatever they are studying, even tiny factors that may seem irrelevant.

Microwave oven
While working with microwave radar signals in 1945, American engineer Percy Lebaron Spencer noticed his chocolate bar had melted. He double-checked the effect by popping some corn in the path of the beam. He had discovered the principle of the microwave oven!

1939
American scientist Linus Pauling explains the nsature of chemical bonds.

1930s
Scientists investigate subatomic particles and this leads to the splitting of the atom. The process is explained and called nuclear fission in 1939.

Modern chemistry
Chemists now know how atoms are made and how they bond to create molecules, so they can alter substances by manipulating the atoms and molecules. The alchemists' dream of changing one element into another may yet become a reality.

1911
New Zealand physicist Ernest Rutherford discovers the structure of the atom.

1905
German physicist Albert Einstein publishes his theory of special relativity. A decade later, he establishes his theory of general relativity.

Alchemy
The study of alchemy spread from ancient China, reaching Europe in the 13th century. Alchemists were searching for the secret to eternal life, and a way to create gold from other metals. These aims seemed impossible, but their experiments led to developments in chemistry and medicine.

Going for gold!

Medieval methods
In the Middle Ages, scientific principles were applied to practical purposes, creating great leaps in technology. The crank (a type of gear), along with previously invented waterwheels and wheelbarrows, made it possible to construct huge buildings.

1220–25
English philosopher Robert Grosseteste develops the first scientific method. He works with mirrors and lenses on actual experiments, concluding that light is the basic substance in the Universe.

12th–16th centuries
Gothic cathedrals built in Europe, using scientific principles.

13th century CE
Qutb al-Din al-Shirazi and Kamal al-Din al-Farisi explain why rainbows occur.

9th century CE
Ja'far Muhammad ibn Musa ibn Shakir proposes the idea of gravitational pull between planets and stars.

8th century CE
Ja'far al-Sadiq suggests that tiny particles (atoms) have positive and negative charge.

I'm in charge

Islamic ideas
The Arabian empire spread through western Asia and around the Mediterranean from the 7th century CE. The Arabs' religion, Islam, encouraged the study of medicine, astronomy, and mathematics. Islamic philosophers translated the scientific works of ancient Greece, then began to analyze and improve on their ideas.

BURSTS OF IDEAS

Throughout history, there have been periods when science was considered all-important and great discoveries came thick and fast, as well as times when science was virtually forgotten, with scholars merely accepting the ideas of the past. While science has often been at the forefront of new technology, many inventions were developed long before scientists worked out the principles behind them.

LIBRARY (please be quiet)

Your returns are overdue!

The spread of knowledge
Today, new scientific ideas spread around the world very quickly. However, in the past, there were long periods when one region was much more scientifically advanced than another. This timeline shows the history of science, including revolutionary ideas and discoveries.

The numbers in brackets indicate the pages to look at to learn more about these ground-breaking ideas.

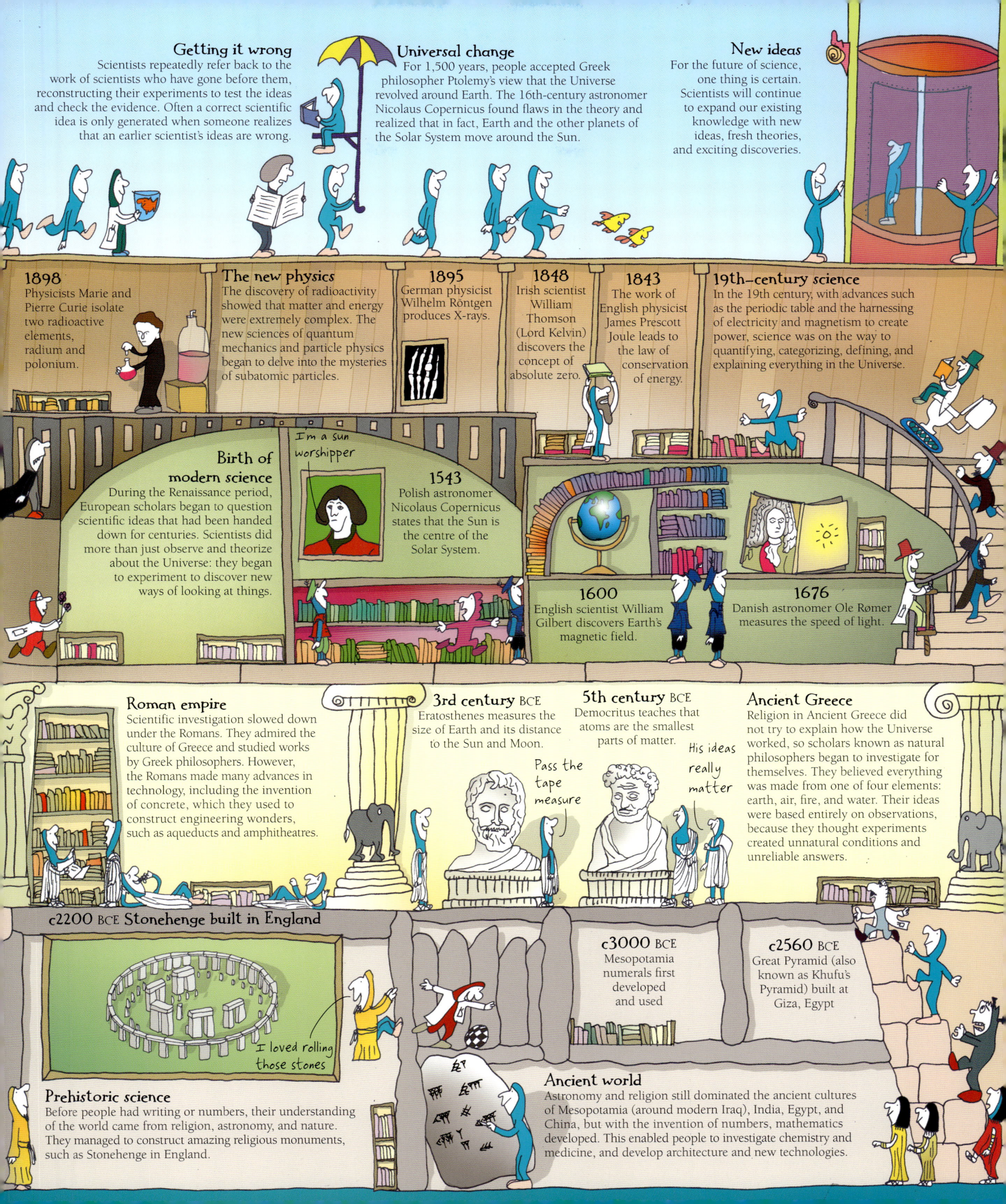

Getting it wrong
Scientists repeatedly refer back to the work of scientists who have gone before them, reconstructing their experiments to test the ideas and check the evidence. Often a correct scientific idea is only generated when someone realizes that an earlier scientist's ideas are wrong.

Universal change
For 1,500 years, people accepted Greek philosopher Ptolemy's view that the Universe revolved around Earth. The 16th-century astronomer Nicolaus Copernicus found flaws in the theory and realized that in fact, Earth and the other planets of the Solar System move around the Sun.

New ideas
For the future of science, one thing is certain. Scientists will continue to expand our existing knowledge with new ideas, fresh theories, and exciting discoveries.

1898
Physicists Marie and Pierre Curie isolate two radioactive elements, radium and polonium.

The new physics
The discovery of radioactivity showed that matter and energy were extremely complex. The new sciences of quantum mechanics and particle physics began to delve into the mysteries of subatomic particles.

1895
German physicist Wilhelm Röntgen produces X-rays.

1848
Irish scientist William Thomson (Lord Kelvin) discovers the concept of absolute zero.

1843
The work of English physicist James Prescott Joule leads to the law of conservation of energy.

19th-century science
In the 19th century, with advances such as the periodic table and the harnessing of electricity and magnetism to create power, science was on the way to quantifying, categorizing, defining, and explaining everything in the Universe.

Birth of modern science
During the Renaissance period, European scholars began to question scientific ideas that had been handed down for centuries. Scientists did more than just observe and theorize about the Universe: they began to experiment to discover new ways of looking at things.

I'm a sun worshipper

1543
Polish astronomer Nicolaus Copernicus states that the Sun is the centre of the Solar System.

1600
English scientist William Gilbert discovers Earth's magnetic field.

1676
Danish astronomer Ole Rømer measures the speed of light.

Roman empire
Scientific investigation slowed down under the Romans. They admired the culture of Greece and studied works by Greek philosophers. However, the Romans made many advances in technology, including the invention of concrete, which they used to construct engineering wonders, such as aqueducts and amphitheatres.

3rd century BCE
Eratosthenes measures the size of Earth and its distance to the Sun and Moon.

Pass the tape measure

5th century BCE
Democritus teaches that atoms are the smallest parts of matter.

His ideas really matter

Ancient Greece
Religion in Ancient Greece did not try to explain how the Universe worked, so scholars known as natural philosophers began to investigate for themselves. They believed everything was made from one of four elements: earth, air, fire, and water. Their ideas were based entirely on observations, because they thought experiments created unnatural conditions and unreliable answers.

c2200 BCE Stonehenge built in England

I loved rolling those stones

c3000 BCE
Mesopotamia numerals first developed and used

c2560 BCE
Great Pyramid (also known as Khufu's Pyramid) built at Giza, Egypt

Prehistoric science
Before people had writing or numbers, their understanding of the world came from religion, astronomy, and nature. They managed to construct amazing religious monuments, such as Stonehenge in England.

Ancient world
Astronomy and religion still dominated the ancient cultures of Mesopotamia (around modern Iraq), India, Egypt, and China, but with the invention of numbers, mathematics developed. This enabled people to investigate chemistry and medicine, and develop architecture and new technologies.

Theoretical science

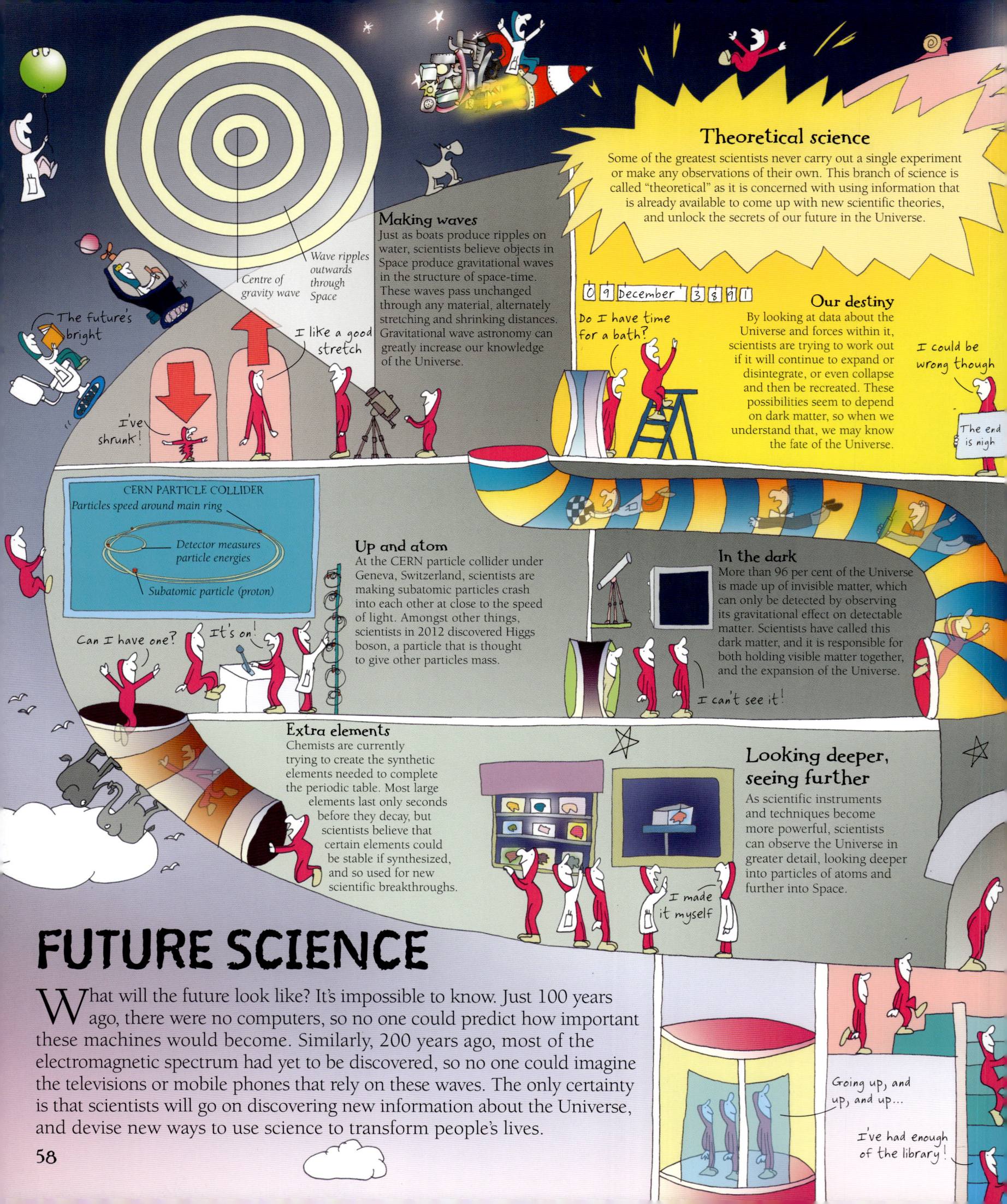

Some of the greatest scientists never carry out a single experiment or make any observations of their own. This branch of science is called "theoretical" as it is concerned with using information that is already available to come up with new scientific theories, and unlock the secrets of our future in the Universe.

Making waves

Just as boats produce ripples on water, scientists believe objects in Space produce gravitational waves in the structure of space-time. These waves pass unchanged through any material, alternately stretching and shrinking distances. Gravitational wave astronomy can greatly increase our knowledge of the Universe.

Our destiny

By looking at data about the Universe and forces within it, scientists are trying to work out if it will continue to expand or disintegrate, or even collapse and then be recreated. These possibilities seem to depend on dark matter, so when we understand that, we may know the fate of the Universe.

Up and atom

At the CERN particle collider under Geneva, Switzerland, scientists are making subatomic particles crash into each other at close to the speed of light. Amongst other things, scientists in 2012 discovered Higgs boson, a particle that is thought to give other particles mass.

In the dark

More than 96 per cent of the Universe is made up of invisible matter, which can only be detected by observing its gravitational effect on detectable matter. Scientists have called this dark matter, and it is responsible for both holding visible matter together, and the expansion of the Universe.

Extra elements

Chemists are currently trying to create the synthetic elements needed to complete the periodic table. Most large elements last only seconds before they decay, but scientists believe that certain elements could be stable if synthesized, and so used for new scientific breakthroughs.

Looking deeper, seeing further

As scientific instruments and techniques become more powerful, scientists can observe the Universe in greater detail, looking deeper into particles of atoms and further into Space.

FUTURE SCIENCE

What will the future look like? It's impossible to know. Just 100 years ago, there were no computers, so no one could predict how important these machines would become. Similarly, 200 years ago, most of the electromagnetic spectrum had yet to be discovered, so no one could imagine the televisions or mobile phones that rely on these waves. The only certainty is that scientists will go on discovering new information about the Universe, and devise new ways to use science to transform people's lives.

Incredible innovations

Inventors and manufacturers can use the latest scientific ideas to invent new technology, providing practical innovations that will make people's lives easier or more entertaining, such as artificially intelligent robots.

Theory of everything

There are four fundamental forces at work in the Universe: gravity, electromagnetism, and the strong and weak nuclear forces that hold atoms together. Quantum theory explains how the last three fit together, but gravity does not seem to fit. Scientists are searching for one theory that will explain how all these forces are connected.

Small world

Scientists can now manipulate individual molecules to create new materials and build microscopic machine parts. At present, nanotechnology is mainly used to make specialist fabrics and pharmaceuticals, but eventually it could be used to create tiny engines or robots powered by nanobatteries.

Union fusion

The solution to the world's energy problems could be nuclear fusion, if scientists discover an economical way to achieve it on a large scale. Today's nuclear power stations use nuclear fission, splitting atoms and producing deadly radioactive waste. Nuclear fusion joins atoms together and produces no dangerous waste.

Cleaner cars

Hydrogen-fuelled cars emit less pollution than most other vehicles, but producing hydrogen uses vast quantities of fossil fuels, which contribute to global warming. Future technology will aim to discover a clean, cheap, and efficient method of producing hydrogen, using renewable sources such as wind or solar power.

Time travellers

According to Albert Einstein, it might be possible to time travel back into the past, but it would be impossible to travel into the future. But you never know – scientists have declared lots of things impossible, and then turned out to be wrong.

Revolutionary robots

Although electronic computers have been around since the mid-20th century, there are still no machines that can compete with the flexibility of the human mind. In the future, the artificial intelligence of computers and robots will develop, enabling them to reason and learn from past experiences, solve problems, understand environments, and use language.

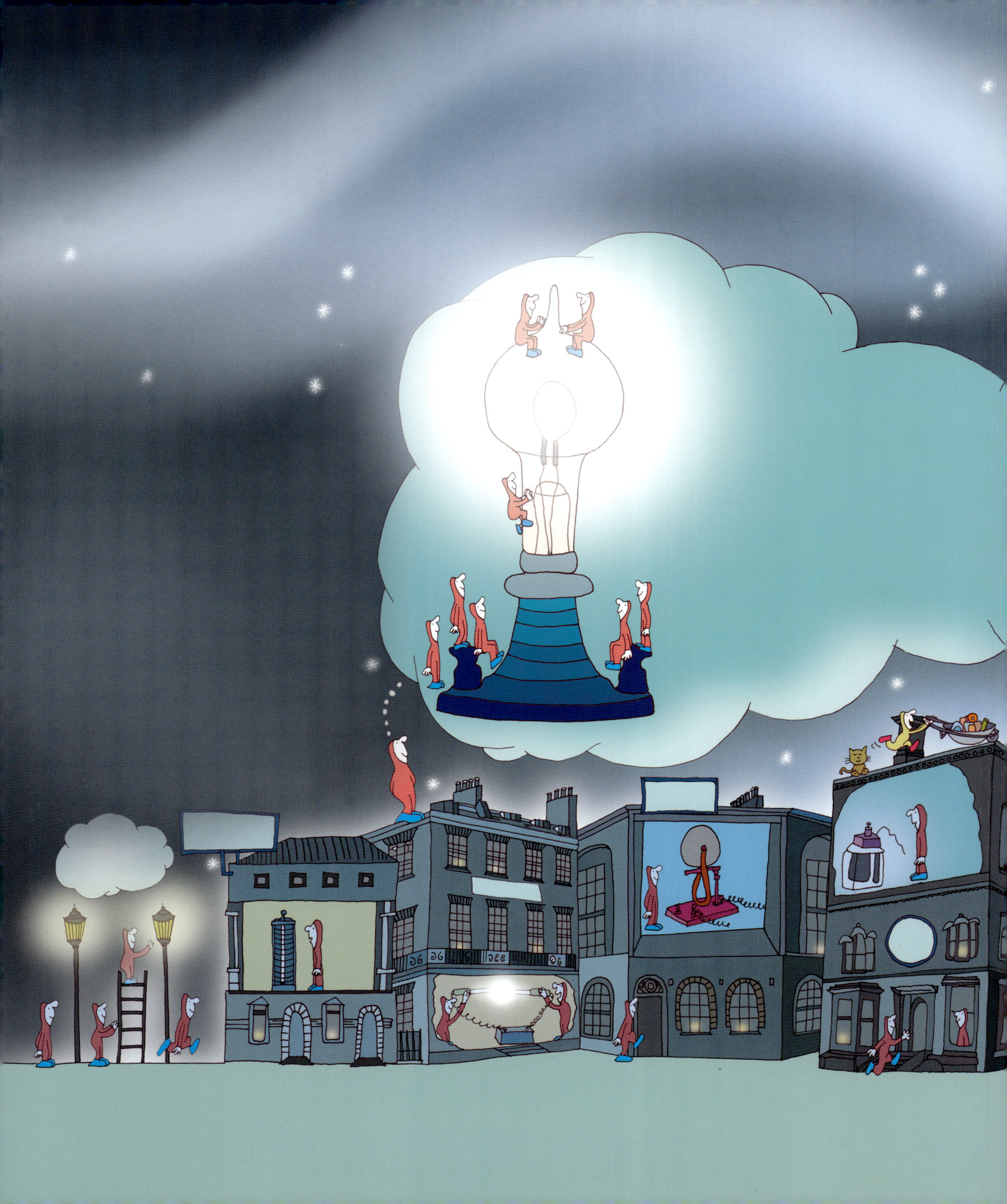

How NEARLY EVERYTHING WAS INVENTED

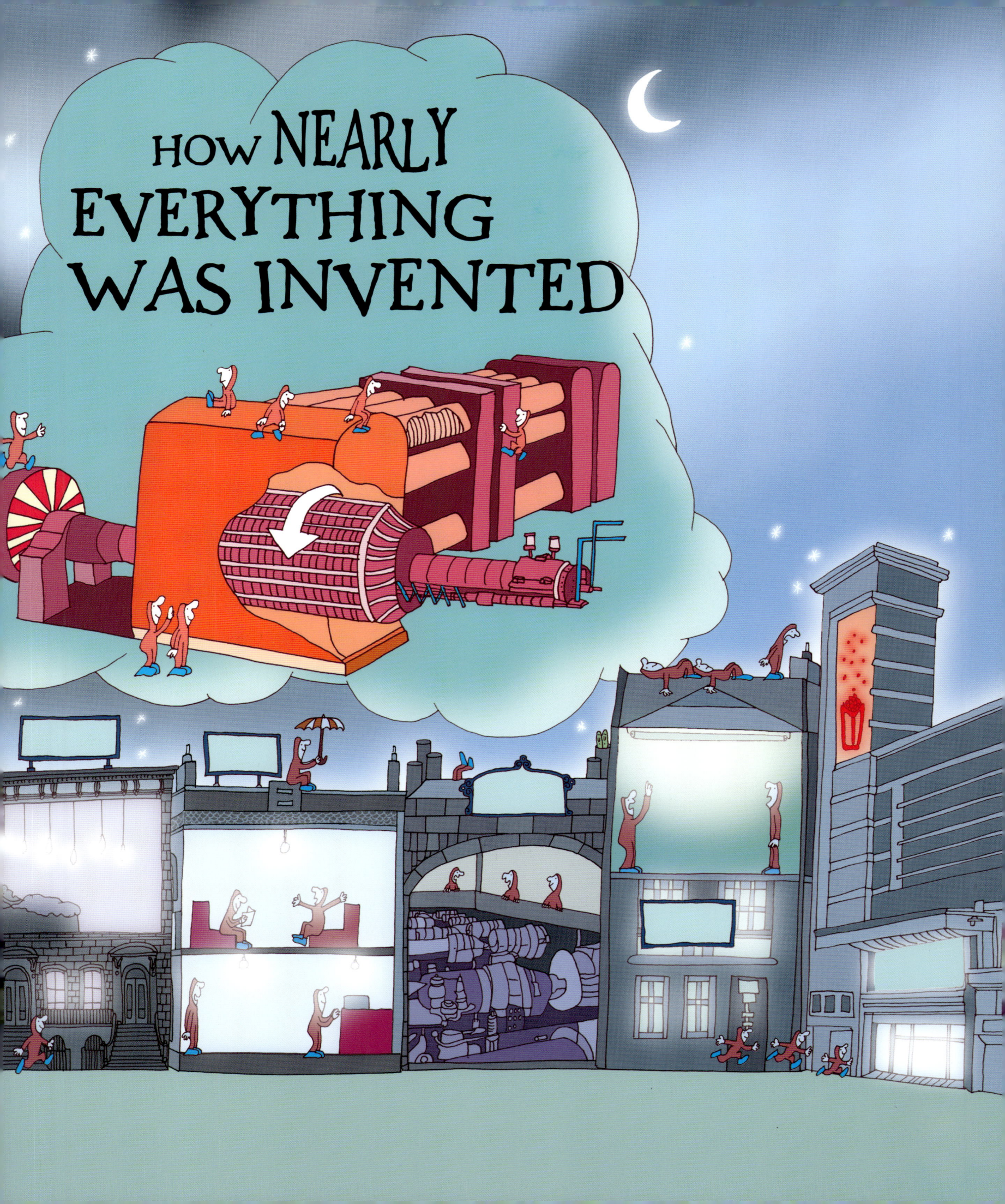

FINDING A BETTER WAY

Since people first roamed the planet more than a million years ago, the conviction that "there must be a better way than this" has inspired them to invent things. Some inventions are the brainchild of an individual working alone, while others are the result of teamwork. Many evolved over long periods of time, with numerous people taking a hand in their development; others were conceived within days. However they came about, one thing's for certain – without inventions we would all still be living in caves!

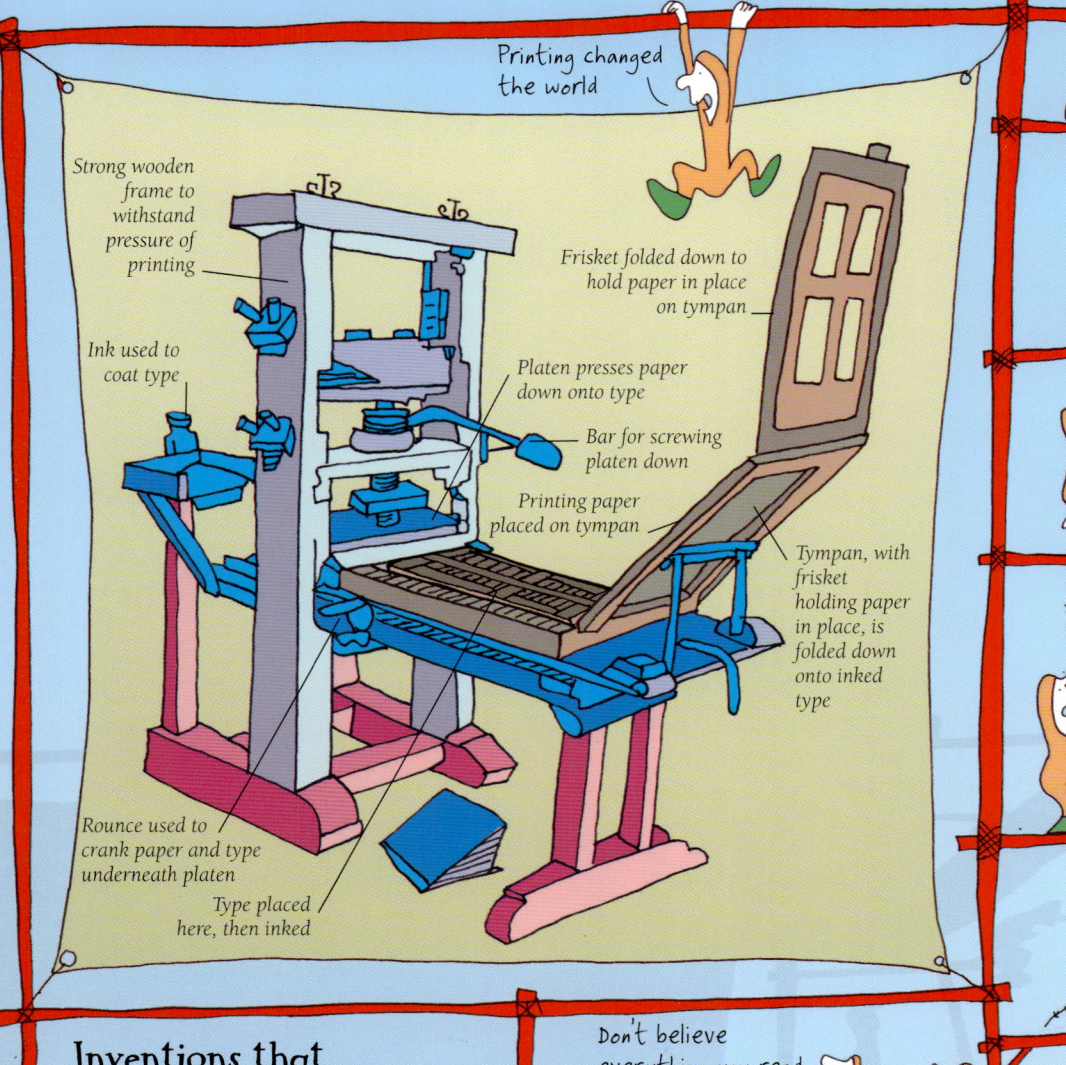

Printing changed the world

- Strong wooden frame to withstand pressure of printing
- Ink used to coat type
- Frisket folded down to hold paper in place on tympan
- Platen presses paper down onto type
- Bar for screwing platen down
- Printing paper placed on tympan
- Tympan, with frisket holding paper in place, is folded down onto inked type
- Rounce used to crank paper and type underneath platen
- Type placed here, then inked

Early inventions

The world's earliest inventions were simple tools made by chipping away at lumps of stone to create a sharp cutting edge. These "handaxes" were used to butcher meat, prepare hides, and cut branches. They served their purpose for more than a million years until someone had the bright idea of adding a handle to improve the swing, and the axe was born!

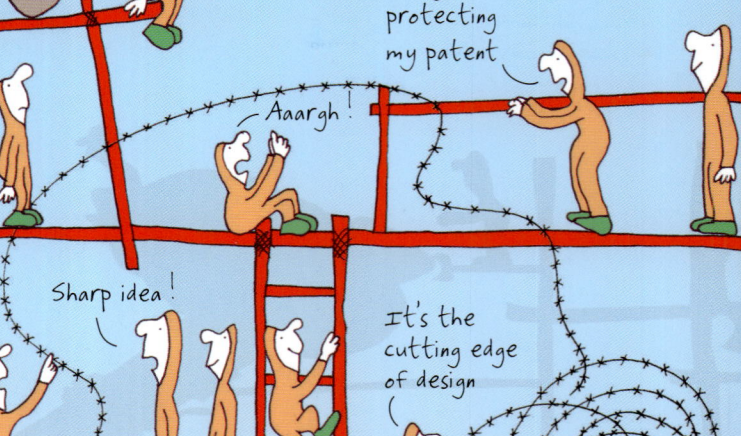

I'm just protecting my patent

Aaargh!

Sharp idea!

It's the cutting edge of design

Inventions that changed the world

Some inventions have such a big impact on society that they change the world. One such invention was the method of printing developed in Germany by Johannes Gutenberg in about 1439. Before this in Europe, books were laboriously copied out by hand and were the sole preserve of churchmen, scholars, and kings. Afterwards, books could be mass-produced and new ideas shared by anyone who could read. Things would never be the same again!

Don't believe everything you read

Patent protection

Patents were developed in the 15th century to give inventors legal protection against people stealing their ideas and making money from them. To get a patent, an invention has to differ significantly from similar ideas. In the 19th century, for example, hundreds of patents were granted for barbed wire, each one for a different design.

Alpha foxtrot Iggy iggy tango Dot dot dash

It's either gibberish, martian, or some sort of secret code

Codes and languages

Some people are famous for inventing codes and languages rather than devices. Samuel Morse is best known for his Morse code, a dot-and-dash code that was once widely used to send telegraph messages. Computer pioneer Grace Hopper, on the other hand, invented a new language called COBOL that transformed the way computers were programmed.

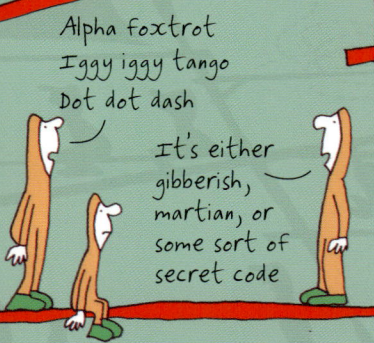

Who gets the credit?

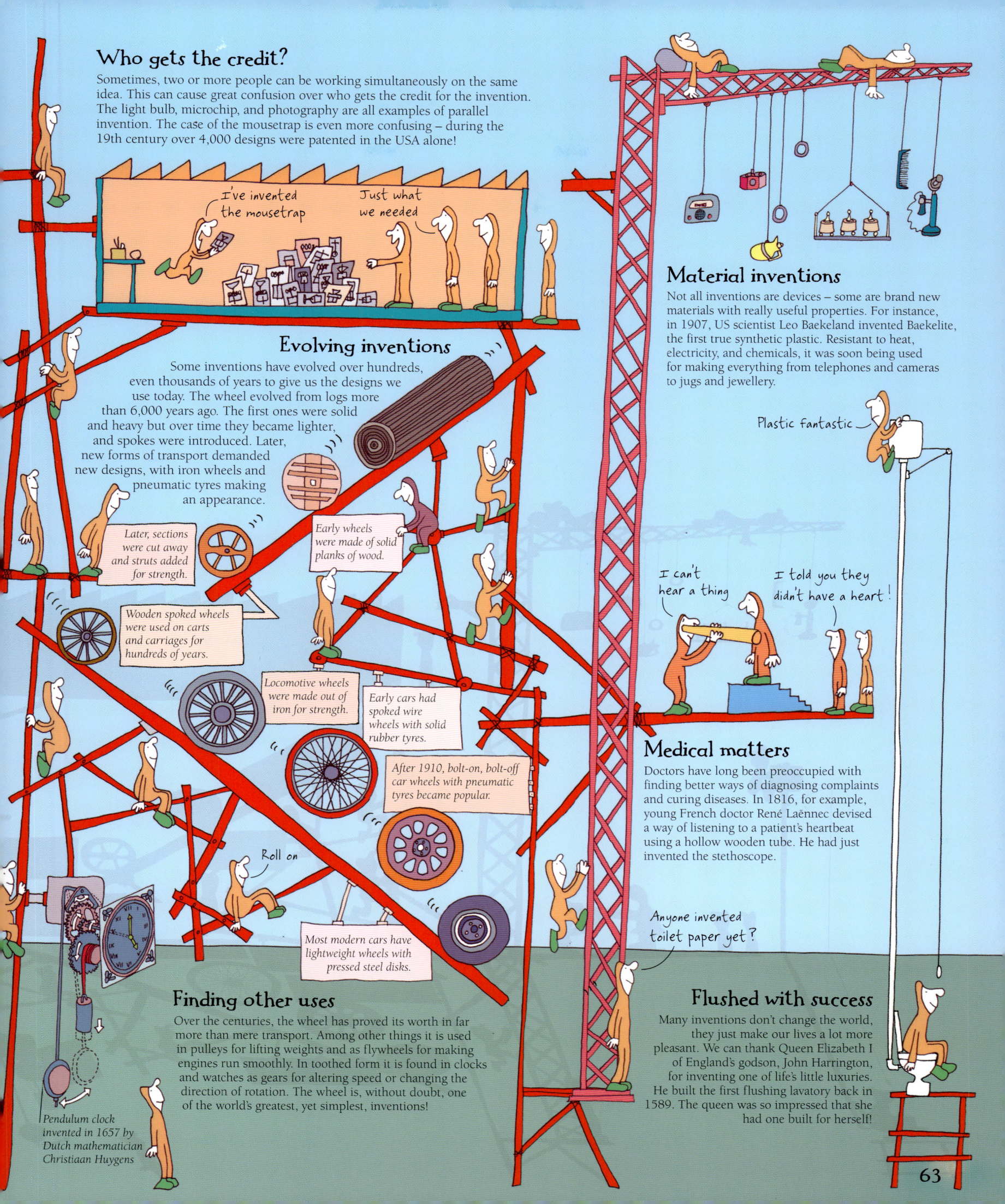

Sometimes, two or more people can be working simultaneously on the same idea. This can cause great confusion over who gets the credit for the invention. The light bulb, microchip, and photography are all examples of parallel invention. The case of the mousetrap is even more confusing – during the 19th century over 4,000 designs were patented in the USA alone!

I've invented the mousetrap

Just what we needed

Evolving inventions

Some inventions have evolved over hundreds, even thousands of years to give us the designs we use today. The wheel evolved from logs more than 6,000 years ago. The first ones were solid and heavy but over time they became lighter, and spokes were introduced. Later, new forms of transport demanded new designs, with iron wheels and pneumatic tyres making an appearance.

Later, sections were cut away and struts added for strength.

Early wheels were made of solid planks of wood.

Wooden spoked wheels were used on carts and carriages for hundreds of years.

Locomotive wheels were made out of iron for strength.

Early cars had spoked wire wheels with solid rubber tyres.

After 1910, bolt-on, bolt-off car wheels with pneumatic tyres became popular.

Roll on

Most modern cars have lightweight wheels with pressed steel disks.

Material inventions

Not all inventions are devices – some are brand new materials with really useful properties. For instance, in 1907, US scientist Leo Baekeland invented Baekelite, the first true synthetic plastic. Resistant to heat, electricity, and chemicals, it was soon being used for making everything from telephones and cameras to jugs and jewellery.

Plastic fantastic

I can't hear a thing

I told you they didn't have a heart!

Medical matters

Doctors have long been preoccupied with finding better ways of diagnosing complaints and curing diseases. In 1816, for example, young French doctor René Laënnec devised a way of listening to a patient's heartbeat using a hollow wooden tube. He had just invented the stethoscope.

Anyone invented toilet paper yet?

Finding other uses

Over the centuries, the wheel has proved its worth in far more than mere transport. Among other things it is used in pulleys for lifting weights and as flywheels for making engines run smoothly. In toothed form it is found in clocks and watches as gears for altering speed or changing the direction of rotation. The wheel is, without doubt, one of the world's greatest, yet simplest, inventions!

Pendulum clock invented in 1657 by Dutch mathematician Christiaan Huygens

Flushed with success

Many inventions don't change the world, they just make our lives a lot more pleasant. We can thank Queen Elizabeth I of England's godson, John Harrington, for inventing one of life's little luxuries. He built the first flushing lavatory back in 1589. The queen was so impressed that she had one built for herself!

63

SEEING IS BELIEVING

Lenses were invented in the Roman empire around 2,000 years ago. It took until 1200 to invent the magnifying glass, and then another 90 years for spectacles to be created. By the 17th century, they were being incorporated into powerful new instruments designed to view objects that were either too far away or too small to see with the naked eye. Telescopes and microscopes heralded a new age in scientific research and transformed the way we see our world and the cosmos beyond.

Beyond belief
In 1609, Italian astronomer Galileo Galilei became the first person to view the heavens through a telescope. But he soon got into trouble when he claimed his observations showed that the Earth revolved around the Sun, contradicting the Church's belief that the Earth was at the centre of the Universe. He was thrown into jail, under threat of death, until he took it all back!

The lens
Lenses are curved pieces of glass that work by bending, or refracting, light rays passing through them. There are two types of lens: convex and concave, each of which works according to the way it bends light (see opposite). Convex lenses are used to make small objects look bigger; concave lenses make distant objects look closer (but smaller).

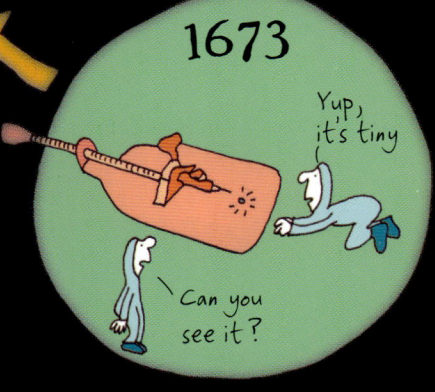

Electron microscope
Powerful light microscopes can only magnify up to 2,000 times, and, as the magnification goes up, the sharpness of the image goes down. So in 1933 German physicist Ernst Ruska invented a new kind of microscope that used an electron beam instead of light, which gave much better definition. Modern electron microscopes magnify more than a million times to show molecules.

Leeuwenhoek's microscope
Dutch draper Antoni van Leeuwenhoek built at least 247 single-lens microscopes. They were so powerful that, in 1673, Leeuwenhoek became the first person to see bacteria, taken from inside his own mouth.

Compound microscope
The compound microscope – that is, a microscope with two or more lenses – was probably invented by Dutch spectacle-maker Hans Janssen in about 1600.

Microscopic enquiry

English scientist Robert Hooke built one of the first successful microscopes. Called a compound microscope, it had a second lens, or eyepiece, to enlarge the magnified image. Hooke used it to study tiny animals and plants, publishing his findings in 1665 in a famous book called *Micrographia*, which featured a huge drawing of a flea 60 cm (2 ft) long.

Observer views image of specimen through eyepiece

Specially designed lighting system focuses light on specimen

Large "eyepiece" lens magnifies the image

Screw fitting raises or lowers microscope to focus it

Small but powerful "objective" lens magnifies the specimen

Specimen

1999 — Chandra space telescope
A new kind of telescope was launched into space in 1999. Forming part of NASA's Chandra observatory, it is designed to collect X-rays and is used for studying supernovae, black holes, and dark matter.

Hubble space telescope
In 1990, the Hubble space telescope was launched into orbit to study emissions such as ultra-violet light that don't penetrate the Earth's atmosphere. It can view objects up to 10 billion light years away, seeing much further into space than Earth-based telescopes.

So many stars!

1990

Great reception

Radio telescope
US radio engineer Grote Reber built a new kind of telescope in his back garden in 1937. Designed to collect radio waves instead of light waves, and therefore show aspects of the Universe not visible to the eye, his radio telescope was the only one of its kind for almost 10 years.

1937

Herschel's telescope
In 1789, British astronomer William Herschel built the largest reflecting telescope of his day. Almost 12 m (40 ft) long with a 1.2 m (4 ft) mirror, it was so big it had to be supported on scaffolding and moved around on circular tracks to view different parts of the night sky.

I'm on top of the world!

1789

Up close and personal

1608

Such a starry night!

1663

Refracting telescope
In 1608, Dutch spectacle-maker Hans Lippershey built what is often regarded as the first telescope, based on his discovery that a pair of lenses could make distant objects look closer. He called his invention a "looker" and thought it might be useful in warfare. Galileo built his own telescope (shown here) the following year.

Reflecting telescope
Early refracting or lens-based telescopes gave images with coloured edges. In 1663, Scottish mathematician James Gregory proposed a solution – to swap the objective lens for a concave mirror. He'd just designed the reflecting telescope! Five years later, the famous British scientist Isaac Newton designed his own model (shown here) to view the stars.

How lenses work

Convex lens
A convex, outward curved lens bends light inwards, making an object look bigger and further away than it actually is.

Image Object

Concave lens
A concave, inward curved lens bends light outwards, making a distant object look smaller and closer than it actually is.

Object Image

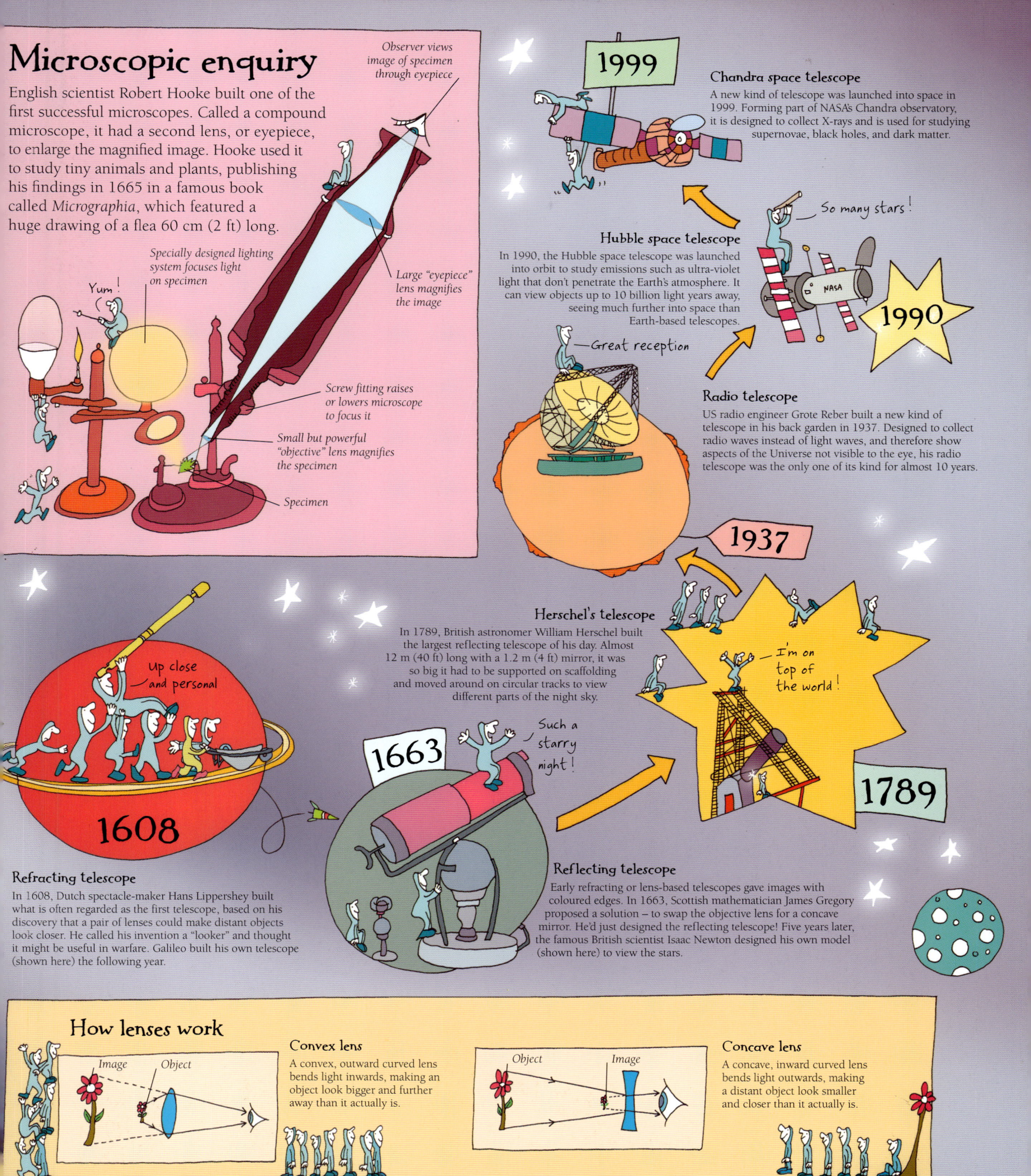

65

Ancient lighthouses

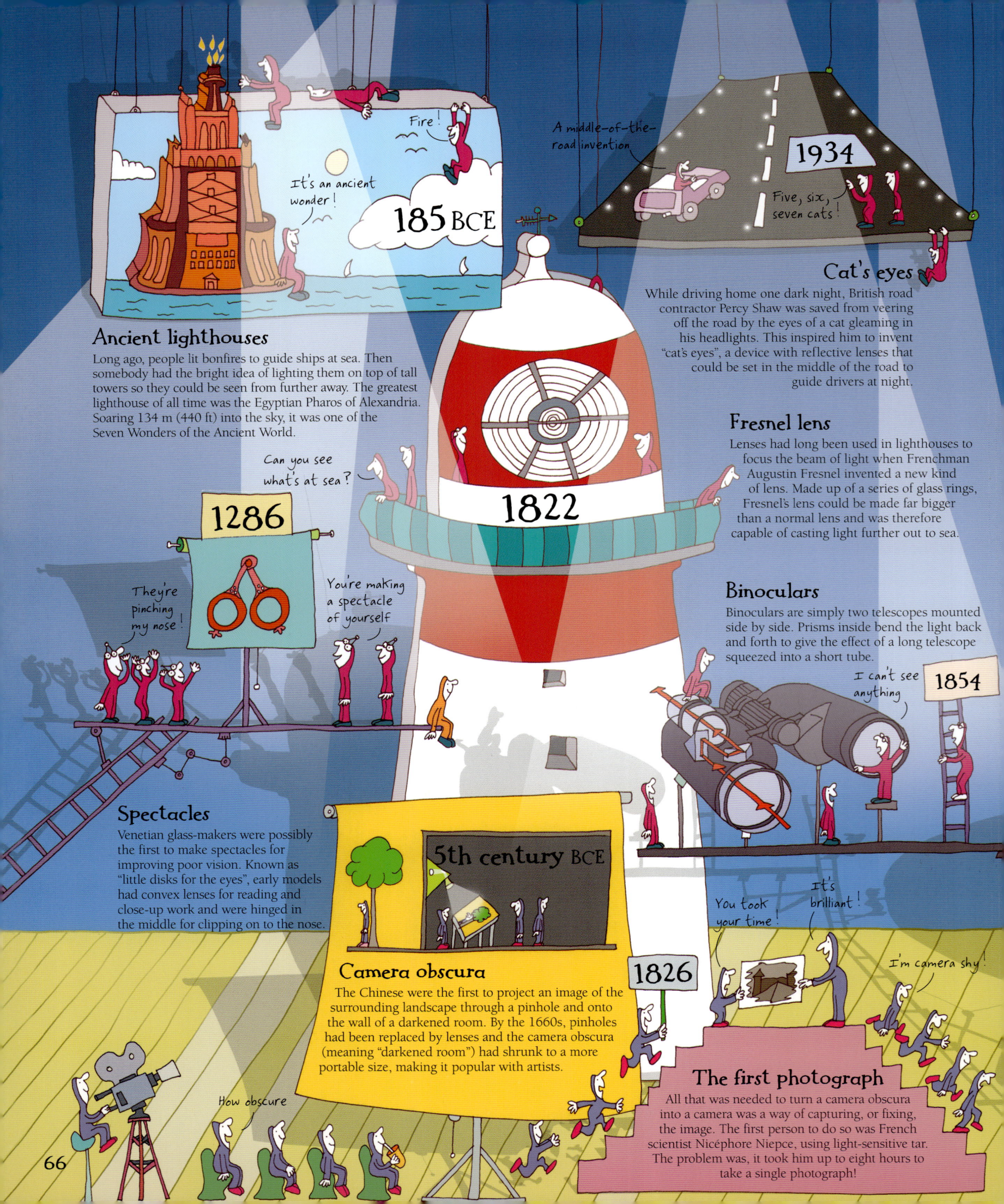

Long ago, people lit bonfires to guide ships at sea. Then somebody had the bright idea of lighting them on top of tall towers so they could be seen from further away. The greatest lighthouse of all time was the Egyptian Pharos of Alexandria. Soaring 134 m (440 ft) into the sky, it was one of the Seven Wonders of the Ancient World.

Cat's eyes

While driving home one dark night, British road contractor Percy Shaw was saved from veering off the road by the eyes of a cat gleaming in his headlights. This inspired him to invent "cat's eyes", a device with reflective lenses that could be set in the middle of the road to guide drivers at night.

Fresnel lens

Lenses had long been used in lighthouses to focus the beam of light when Frenchman Augustin Fresnel invented a new kind of lens. Made up of a series of glass rings, Fresnel's lens could be made far bigger than a normal lens and was therefore capable of casting light further out to sea.

Binoculars

Binoculars are simply two telescopes mounted side by side. Prisms inside bend the light back and forth to give the effect of a long telescope squeezed into a short tube.

Spectacles

Venetian glass-makers were possibly the first to make spectacles for improving poor vision. Known as "little disks for the eyes", early models had convex lenses for reading and close-up work and were hinged in the middle for clipping on to the nose.

Camera obscura

The Chinese were the first to project an image of the surrounding landscape through a pinhole and onto the wall of a darkened room. By the 1660s, pinholes had been replaced by lenses and the camera obscura (meaning "darkened room") had shrunk to a more portable size, making it popular with artists.

The first photograph

All that was needed to turn a camera obscura into a camera was a way of capturing, or fixing, the image. The first person to do so was French scientist Nicéphore Niepce, using light-sensitive tar. The problem was, it took him up to eight hours to take a single photograph!

Endoscope

Microscopes had long been used in medicine. In the early 19th century, lenses were put to new medical use in a device called an endoscope. Comprising a long tube with a lens at each end, endoscopes were inserted into an orifice and used to study internal organs such as the stomach and bladder.

Goodness, this old lady's swallowed a spider

1806

Laser scalpel

Using a lens to focus a laser beam, the laser scalpel is designed to slice through flesh, sealing the ends of tiny blood vessels even as it cuts through them. It causes less pain than a normal scalpel and can even cut around corners!

I've forgotten my lines!
Does it hurt?

1964

Just look at those blinding inventions!

This is a truly moving experience

It's all spin

LIGHTS, CAMERA, ACTION!

Lenses had long been used for scientific research and improving vision when, in the 19th century, they found a new role in the art of photography. Photography captured the Victorian imagination like no other invention, and developed into one of our age's most popular and thrilling forms of entertainment – the cinema.

What's on?

c1833

Zoetrope

Toys that made pictures appear to move were popular in the 19th century. One such toy was the zoetrope, comprising a sequence of images pasted inside a slotted, spinning drum. The images merged when viewed through the slots, giving the illusion of movement.

Leaping lizards!
Flying billiard balls

1888

The birth of photography

The first practical photographic process was invented by Niepce's partner Louis Daguerre. He used silvered copper plates to capture the image, producing one-off "positive" photographs that couldn't be copied. But it was Englishman William Fox Talbot who invented the negative-positive process we still use today. This involves taking "negative" images – such that dark areas are light and light areas dark – from which multiple "positive" copies can be made.

Say cheese!
Give me a copy

1839

Film camera

Early photography was strictly for the experts. American manufacturer George Eastman changed all that by inventing the Kodak roll film camera. Hot on his heels with an alternative roll film – celluloid photographic film – was Reverend Hannibal Goodwin. Budding photographers simply had to snap their shots then send the camera off to have the film developed. Soon, everyone wanted a camera!

I want a camera
This is our best seller

continued...

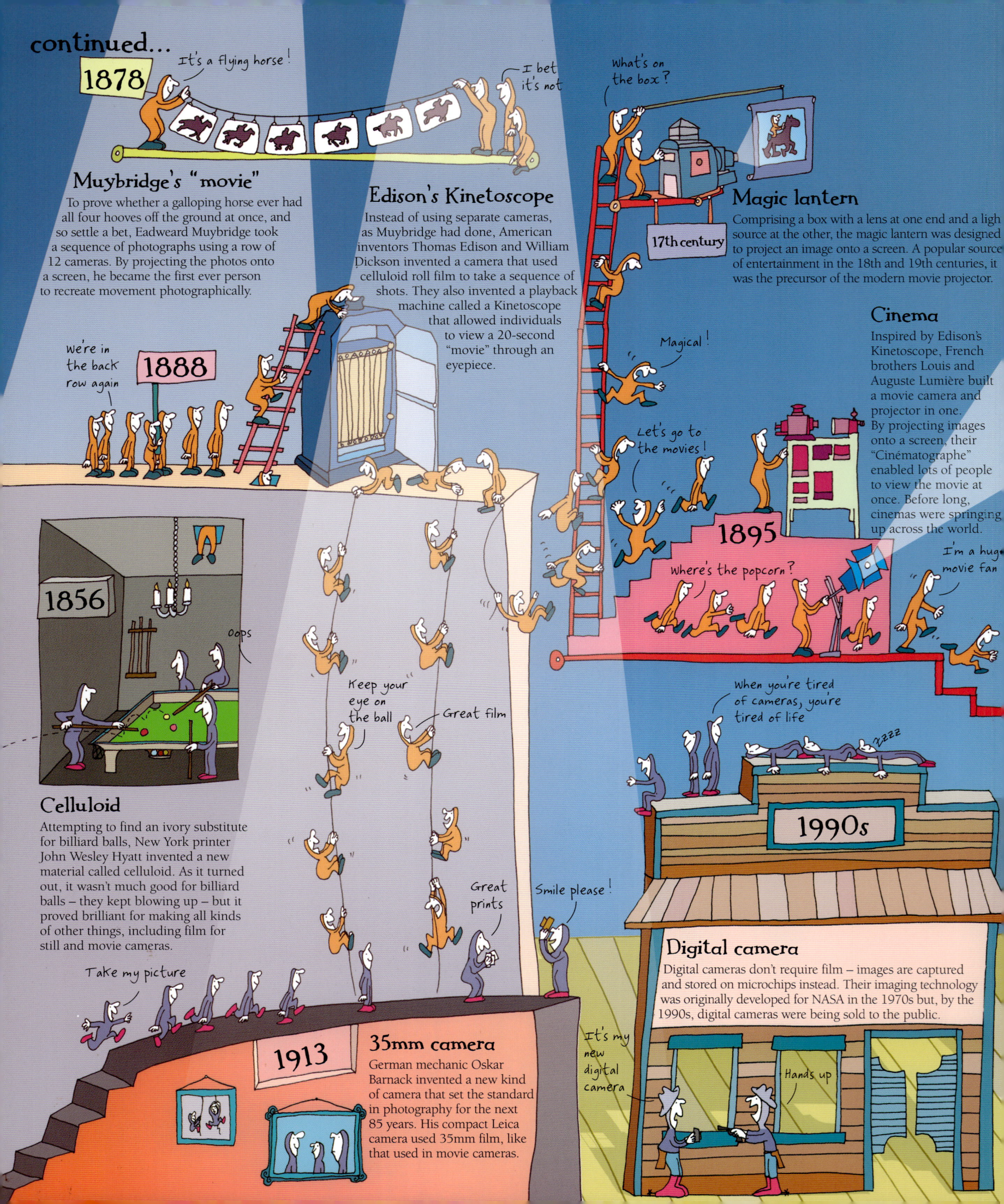

1878

Muybridge's "movie"
To prove whether a galloping horse ever had all four hooves off the ground at once, and so settle a bet, Eadweard Muybridge took a sequence of photographs using a row of 12 cameras. By projecting the photos onto a screen, he became the first ever person to recreate movement photographically.

Edison's Kinetoscope
Instead of using separate cameras, as Muybridge had done, American inventors Thomas Edison and William Dickson invented a camera that used celluloid roll film to take a sequence of shots. They also invented a playback machine called a Kinetoscope that allowed individuals to view a 20-second "movie" through an eyepiece.

Magic lantern
17th century

Comprising a box with a lens at one end and a light source at the other, the magic lantern was designed to project an image onto a screen. A popular source of entertainment in the 18th and 19th centuries, it was the precursor of the modern movie projector.

1888

Cinema
Inspired by Edison's Kinetoscope, French brothers Louis and Auguste Lumière built a movie camera and projector in one. By projecting images onto a screen, their "Cinématographe" enabled lots of people to view the movie at once. Before long, cinemas were springing up across the world.

1895

1856

Celluloid
Attempting to find an ivory substitute for billiard balls, New York printer John Wesley Hyatt invented a new material called celluloid. As it turned out, it wasn't much good for billiard balls – they kept blowing up – but it proved brilliant for making all kinds of other things, including film for still and movie cameras.

1990s

Digital camera
Digital cameras don't require film – images are captured and stored on microchips instead. Their imaging technology was originally developed for NASA in the 1970s but, by the 1990s, digital cameras were being sold to the public.

1913

35mm camera
German mechanic Oskar Barnack invented a new kind of camera that set the standard in photography for the next 85 years. His compact Leica camera used 35mm film, like that used in movie cameras.

Talkies

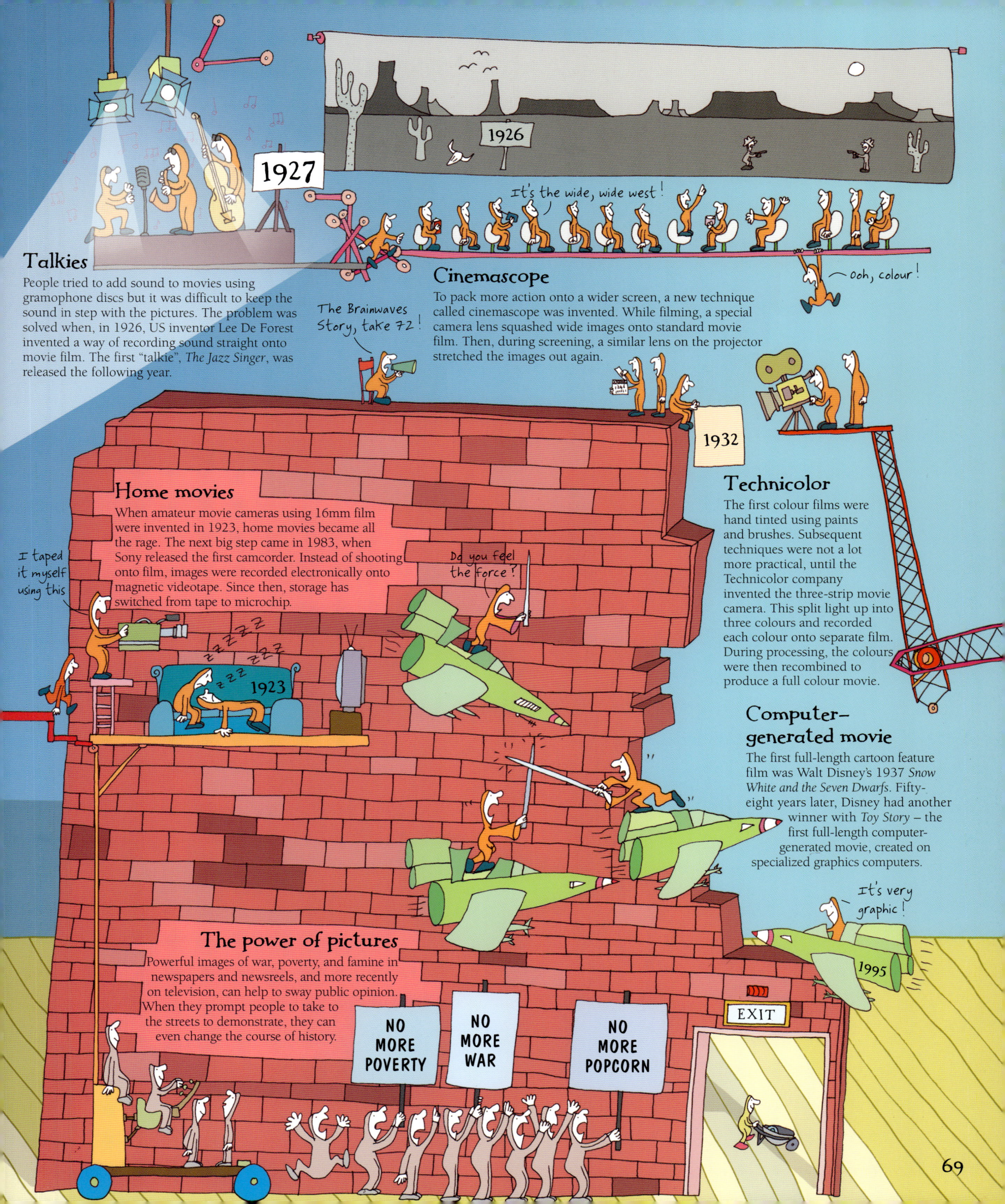

People tried to add sound to movies using gramophone discs but it was difficult to keep the sound in step with the pictures. The problem was solved when, in 1926, US inventor Lee De Forest invented a way of recording sound straight onto movie film. The first "talkie", *The Jazz Singer*, was released the following year.

Cinemascope

To pack more action onto a wider screen, a new technique called cinemascope was invented. While filming, a special camera lens squashed wide images onto standard movie film. Then, during screening, a similar lens on the projector stretched the images out again.

Home movies

When amateur movie cameras using 16mm film were invented in 1923, home movies became all the rage. The next big step came in 1983, when Sony released the first camcorder. Instead of shooting onto film, images were recorded electronically onto magnetic videotape. Since then, storage has switched from tape to microchip.

Technicolor

The first colour films were hand tinted using paints and brushes. Subsequent techniques were not a lot more practical, until the Technicolor company invented the three-strip movie camera. This split light up into three colours and recorded each colour onto separate film. During processing, the colours were then recombined to produce a full colour movie.

Computer-generated movie

The first full-length cartoon feature film was Walt Disney's 1937 *Snow White and the Seven Dwarfs*. Fifty-eight years later, Disney had another winner with *Toy Story* – the first full-length computer-generated movie, created on specialized graphics computers.

The power of pictures

Powerful images of war, poverty, and famine in newspapers and newsreels, and more recently on television, can help to sway public opinion. When they prompt people to take to the streets to demonstrate, they can even change the course of history.

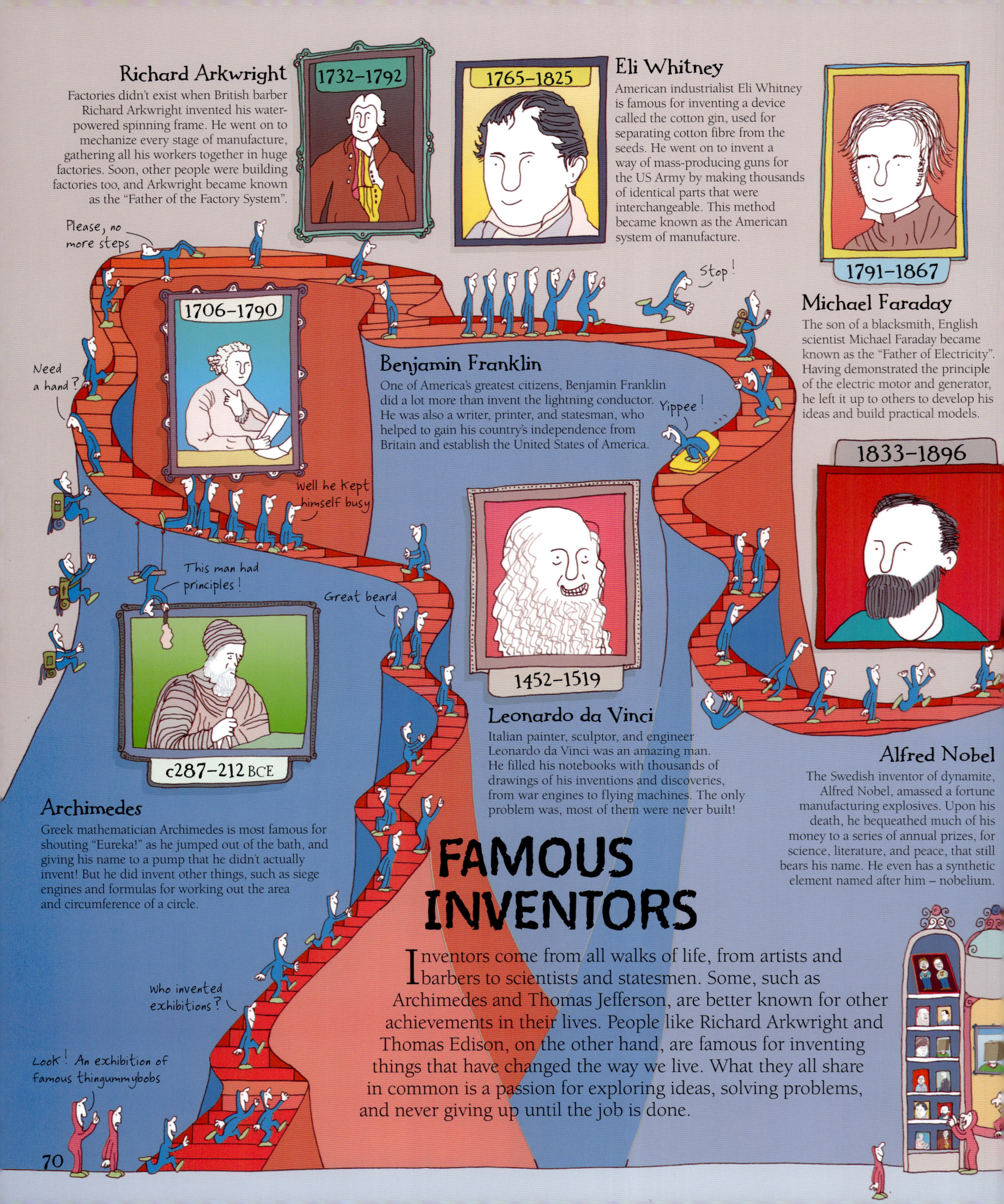

Richard Arkwright
1732–1792
Factories didn't exist when British barber Richard Arkwright invented his water-powered spinning frame. He went on to mechanize every stage of manufacture, gathering all his workers together in huge factories. Soon, other people were building factories too, and Arkwright became known as the "Father of the Factory System".

Eli Whitney
1765–1825
American industrialist Eli Whitney is famous for inventing a device called the cotton gin, used for separating cotton fibre from the seeds. He went on to invent a way of mass-producing guns for the US Army by making thousands of identical parts that were interchangeable. This method became known as the American system of manufacture.

Michael Faraday
1791–1867
The son of a blacksmith, English scientist Michael Faraday became known as the "Father of Electricity". Having demonstrated the principle of the electric motor and generator, he left it up to others to develop his ideas and build practical models.

Benjamin Franklin
1706–1790
One of America's greatest citizens, Benjamin Franklin did a lot more than invent the lightning conductor. He was also a writer, printer, and statesman, who helped to gain his country's independence from Britain and establish the United States of America.

Leonardo da Vinci
1452–1519
Italian painter, sculptor, and engineer Leonardo da Vinci was an amazing man. He filled his notebooks with thousands of drawings of his inventions and discoveries, from war engines to flying machines. The only problem was, most of them were never built!

Alfred Nobel
1833–1896
The Swedish inventor of dynamite, Alfred Nobel, amassed a fortune manufacturing explosives. Upon his death, he bequeathed much of his money to a series of annual prizes, for science, literature, and peace, that still bears his name. He even has a synthetic element named after him – nobelium.

Archimedes
c287–212 BCE
Greek mathematician Archimedes is most famous for shouting "Eureka!" as he jumped out of the bath, and giving his name to a pump that he didn't actually invent! But he did invent other things, such as siege engines and formulas for working out the area and circumference of a circle.

FAMOUS INVENTORS

Inventors come from all walks of life, from artists and barbers to scientists and statesmen. Some, such as Archimedes and Thomas Jefferson, are better known for other achievements in their lives. People like Richard Arkwright and Thomas Edison, on the other hand, are famous for inventing things that have changed the way we live. What they all share in common is a passion for exploring ideas, solving problems, and never giving up until the job is done.

Mattie Knight

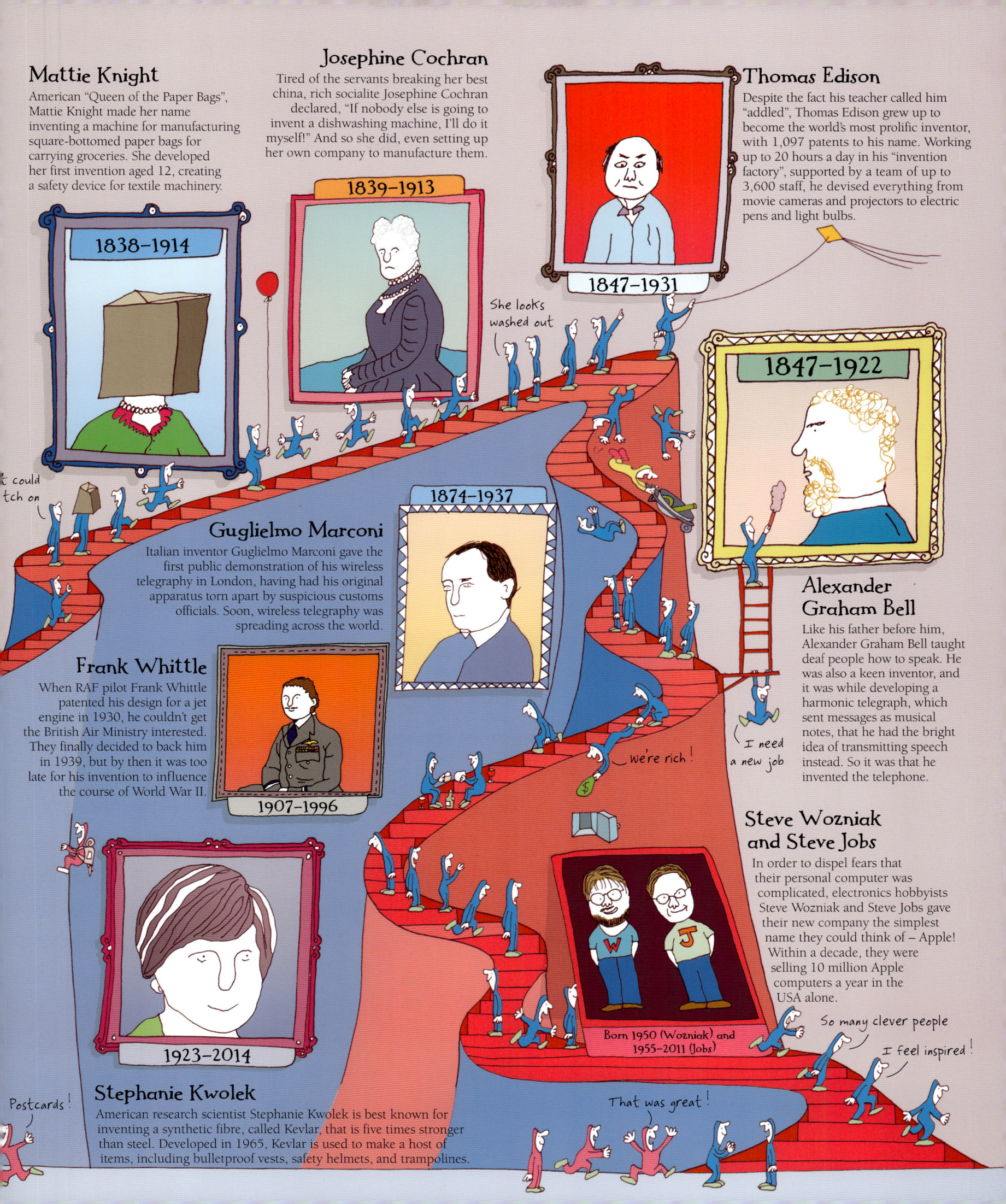

American "Queen of the Paper Bags", Mattie Knight made her name inventing a machine for manufacturing square-bottomed paper bags for carrying groceries. She developed her first invention aged 12, creating a safety device for textile machinery.

1838–1914

Josephine Cochran

Tired of the servants breaking her best china, rich socialite Josephine Cochran declared, "If nobody else is going to invent a dishwashing machine, I'll do it myself!" And so she did, even setting up her own company to manufacture them.

1839–1913

She looks washed out

Thomas Edison

Despite the fact his teacher called him "addled", Thomas Edison grew up to become the world's most prolific inventor, with 1,097 patents to his name. Working up to 20 hours a day in his "invention factory", supported by a team of up to 3,600 staff, he devised everything from movie cameras and projectors to electric pens and light bulbs.

1847–1931

1847–1922

Alexander Graham Bell

Like his father before him, Alexander Graham Bell taught deaf people how to speak. He was also a keen inventor, and it was while developing a harmonic telegraph, which sent messages as musical notes, that he had the bright idea of transmitting speech instead. So it was that he invented the telephone.

I need a new job

Guglielmo Marconi

Italian inventor Guglielmo Marconi gave the first public demonstration of his wireless telegraphy in London, having had his original apparatus torn apart by suspicious customs officials. Soon, wireless telegraphy was spreading across the world.

1874–1937

Frank Whittle

When RAF pilot Frank Whittle patented his design for a jet engine in 1930, he couldn't get the British Air Ministry interested. They finally decided to back him in 1939, but by then it was too late for his invention to influence the course of World War II.

1907–1996

We're rich!

Steve Wozniak and Steve Jobs

In order to dispel fears that their personal computer was complicated, electronics hobbyists Steve Wozniak and Steve Jobs gave their new company the simplest name they could think of – Apple! Within a decade, they were selling 10 million Apple computers a year in the USA alone.

Born 1950 (Wozniak) and 1955–2011 (Jobs)

So many clever people

I feel inspired!

1923–2014

Stephanie Kwolek

American research scientist Stephanie Kwolek is best known for inventing a synthetic fibre, called Kevlar, that is five times stronger than steel. Developed in 1965, Kevlar is used to make a host of items, including bulletproof vests, safety helmets, and trampolines.

Postcards!

That was great!

STEAM MACHINE

Until the 18th century, the main sources of power were water, wind, and horses. The development of the steam engine changed all that, and life was never the same again. The first steam engines were used to pump water out of mines, but in 1782 Scottish engineer James Watt built a new engine that was soon put to work driving machinery. Then Richard Trevithick had the brilliant idea of using steam power to pull carriages along rails and the rest, as they say, is history!

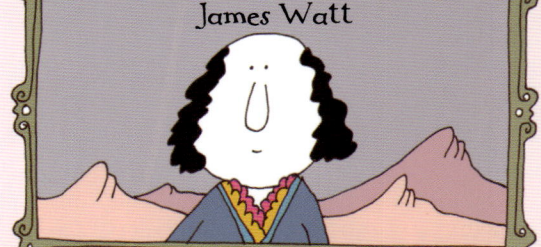

Watt a guy

King of steam
When Scottish engineer James Watt was asked to mend an old steam engine, he realized he could do far better and by 1769 had designed a much more efficient model. With his partner Matthew Boulton, he went on to manufacture steam engines that sold across the world.

The rotary steam engine

In common with other early steam engines, Watt's first model could only create an up-down motion, ideal for pumping water. Then, in 1782, he designed a new engine that converted the up-down action into a circular, or rotary, motion using special gears called sun and planet gears. This meant his engines could be used instead of water wheels to drive textile mills and other machinery.

1. Boiler turns water into steam
2. Steam fed into the cylinder, forcing the piston inside the cylinder up and down
3. Beam is rocked up and down by the moving piston
4. Governor regulates the engine's speed
5. Sun and planet gears, turned by the rocking beam, translate the up-down motion into a rotary motion
6. Flywheel helps to keep the engine running smoothly

Stephenson's Rocket
1829
In 1829, a contest was held to find the best locomotive ever. Stephenson's *Rocket* won with flying colours and was soon put to work on the Manchester and Liverpool line, the first regular passenger service.

Death on the tracks
Stephenson's *Rocket* was the fastest locomotive of its day, with a top speed of 56 kph (35 mph). Many people feared that they'd suffocate or go mad travelling at such high speeds. But it wasn't suffocation that killed poor William Huskisson MP – he was run over by the *Rocket* on its first day in service!

Aaargh, I've met my death!

Steam locomotive
1803
In 1803, English engineer Richard Trevithick built the world's first steam locomotive, for hauling coal. He took his idea to London in 1808, where he built a circular track for his new engine – called *Catch Me Who Can* – offering delighted passengers a ride for a shilling a go.

Crossing continents
1869
The first railway to straddle an entire continent was built across the USA during the 1860s. Starting out from both east and west, and crossing over 3,000 km (1,860 miles) of wilderness, the two lines finally came together at Promontory Point, Utah, in May 1869. A nation was united and a journey that used to last six months now took seven days!

Where's it gone?
Mind the gap!
All aboard

Public railway
1825
The first public railway was only 20 km (13 miles) long. Set up in 1825, it carried goods and passengers between Stockton and Darlington in the north of England, powered by engineer Robert Stephenson's *Locomotion No. 1*.

Going underground
1863
In 1863 the world's first underground service, powered by steam train, was launched in London. On the opening day, even future Prime Minister William Gladstone came along for the ride!

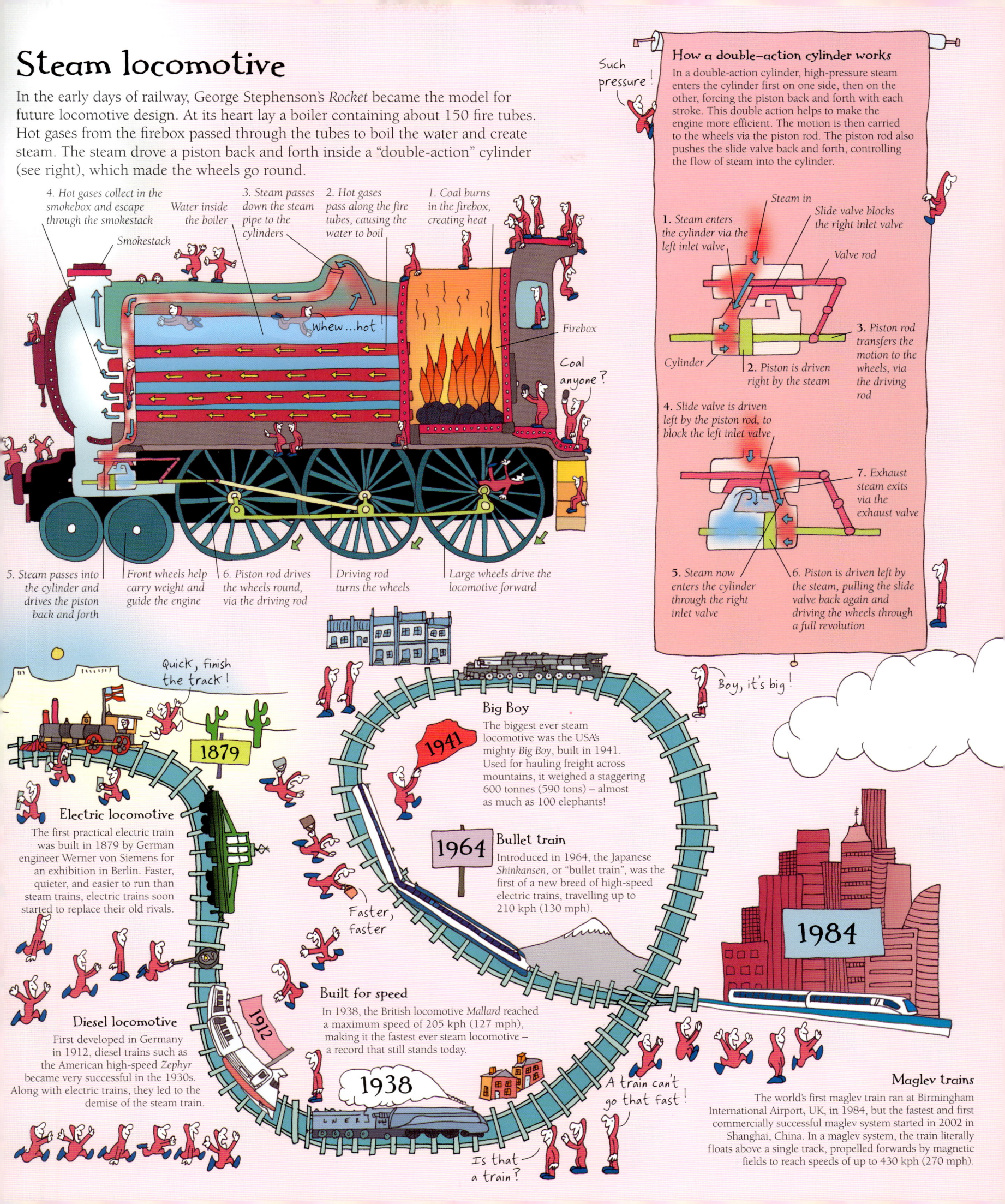

Steam locomotive

In the early days of railway, George Stephenson's *Rocket* became the model for future locomotive design. At its heart lay a boiler containing about 150 fire tubes. Hot gases from the firebox passed through the tubes to boil the water and create steam. The steam drove a piston back and forth inside a "double-action" cylinder (see right), which made the wheels go round.

4. Hot gases collect in the smokebox and escape through the smokestack

Smokestack

Water inside the boiler

3. Steam passes down the steam pipe to the cylinders

2. Hot gases pass along the fire tubes, causing the water to boil

1. Coal burns in the firebox, creating heat

Firebox

Whew...hot!

Coal anyone?

5. Steam passes into the cylinder and drives the piston back and forth

Front wheels help carry weight and guide the engine

6. Piston rod drives the wheels round, via the driving rod

Driving rod turns the wheels

Large wheels drive the locomotive forward

How a double-action cylinder works

In a double-action cylinder, high-pressure steam enters the cylinder first on one side, then on the other, forcing the piston back and forth with each stroke. This double action helps to make the engine more efficient. The motion is then carried to the wheels via the piston rod. The piston rod also pushes the slide valve back and forth, controlling the flow of steam into the cylinder.

Such pressure!

1. Steam enters the cylinder via the left inlet valve

Steam in

Slide valve blocks the right inlet valve

Valve rod

Cylinder

2. Piston is driven right by the steam

3. Piston rod transfers the motion to the wheels, via the driving rod

4. Slide valve is driven left by the piston rod, to block the left inlet valve

7. Exhaust steam exits via the exhaust valve

5. Steam now enters the cylinder through the right inlet valve

6. Piston is driven left by the steam, pulling the slide valve back again and driving the wheels through a full revolution

Quick, finish the track!

1879

Electric locomotive

The first practical electric train was built in 1879 by German engineer Werner von Siemens for an exhibition in Berlin. Faster, quieter, and easier to run than steam trains, electric trains soon started to replace their old rivals.

1941

Big Boy

The biggest ever steam locomotive was the USA's mighty *Big Boy*, built in 1941. Used for hauling freight across mountains, it weighed a staggering 600 tonnes (590 tons) – almost as much as 100 elephants!

Boy, it's big!

1964

Bullet train

Introduced in 1964, the Japanese *Shinkansen*, or "bullet train", was the first of a new breed of high-speed electric trains, travelling up to 210 kph (130 mph).

Faster, faster

1984

Diesel locomotive

First developed in Germany in 1912, diesel trains such as the American high-speed *Zephyr* became very successful in the 1930s. Along with electric trains, they led to the demise of the steam train.

1912

Built for speed

In 1938, the British locomotive *Mallard* reached a maximum speed of 205 kph (127 mph), making it the fastest ever steam locomotive – a record that still stands today.

1938

A train can't go that fast!

Is that a train?

Maglev trains

The world's first maglev train ran at Birmingham International Airport, UK, in 1984, but the fastest and first commercially successful maglev system started in 2002 in Shanghai, China. In a maglev system, the train literally floats above a single track, propelled forwards by magnetic fields to reach speeds of up to 430 kph (270 mph).

Iron smelting

People had worked with iron since 4000 BCE, hammering it into shape to make tools and weapons. In 1800 BCE, people in Anatolia (in what is now Turkey) found a way of "smelting" iron ore – heating it so they could extract the iron and work it more easily. It was the dawn of a new age, known as the Iron Age.

I thought I smelt marshmallows

Getting kind of hot up here!

1800 BCE

Smelting with coke

Englishman Abraham Darby invented a quicker way of smelting iron using coke (made from coal) instead of wood, providing a good source of iron for building steam engines and other machinery.

Smelt away

1709

Water wheel

Before the steam engine, water was a major source of power. The water wheel was invented by the Greeks for irrigation and grinding grain into flour and olives into oil. Water wheels were later used to drive the first power looms.

Show offs!

250 BCE

Spinning wheel

For thousands of years, thread for making cloth was spun on hand-held spindles. Then, about 1,000 years ago, textile workers in India developed a better way of turning the spindle, using a wheel. By the early 14th century, spinning wheels had reached Europe.

c1000

I'm flying!

1733

Mechanized weaving

Englishman John Kay revolutionized weaving when he invented an automatic device called a "flying shuttle", which enabled cloth to be woven faster and wider than ever before. In 1787, clergyman Edmond Cartwright speeded up the process even more by developing the first steam-powered loom.

Back-and-forth path of the flying shuttle

Handloom

The first handlooms for weaving cloth were invented about 9,000 years ago. They consisted of a frame holding a set of parallel "warp" threads. A cross thread, called the "weft", was woven through the warp using a wooden "shuttle" containing a spool of thread.

c7000 BCE

Hero's engine

Greek scientist Hero of Alexandria became the first person to make a steam-powered machine. The problem was, no-one knew what to do with it!

c50 CE

What's that for? *Who knows!*

Savery pump

English engineer Thomas Savery designed the world's first steam engine for pumping water out of flooded mines. Placed half way down a mineshaft, it worked by condensing steam alternately inside a pair of tanks (A and B) to create a vacuum that sucked up the floodwater. Using more steam power, the water was then pumped up and out of the shaft.

Fumes from the boiler escape through the chimney

Water is pumped up and out of the spout by steam in the tank

Steam condenses in the tank to create a vacuum that sucks water out of the mine

Boiler feeds steam into each tank alternately

1698

Water is sucked up

Flooded mine

Archimedes screw

Greek engineer Archimedes gave his name to a special screw device for pumping water from one level to another in irrigation systems. The Archimedes screw was the forerunner of early steam pumps.

c236 BCE

I'm a genius

My bottom feels wet!

Industrial Revolution

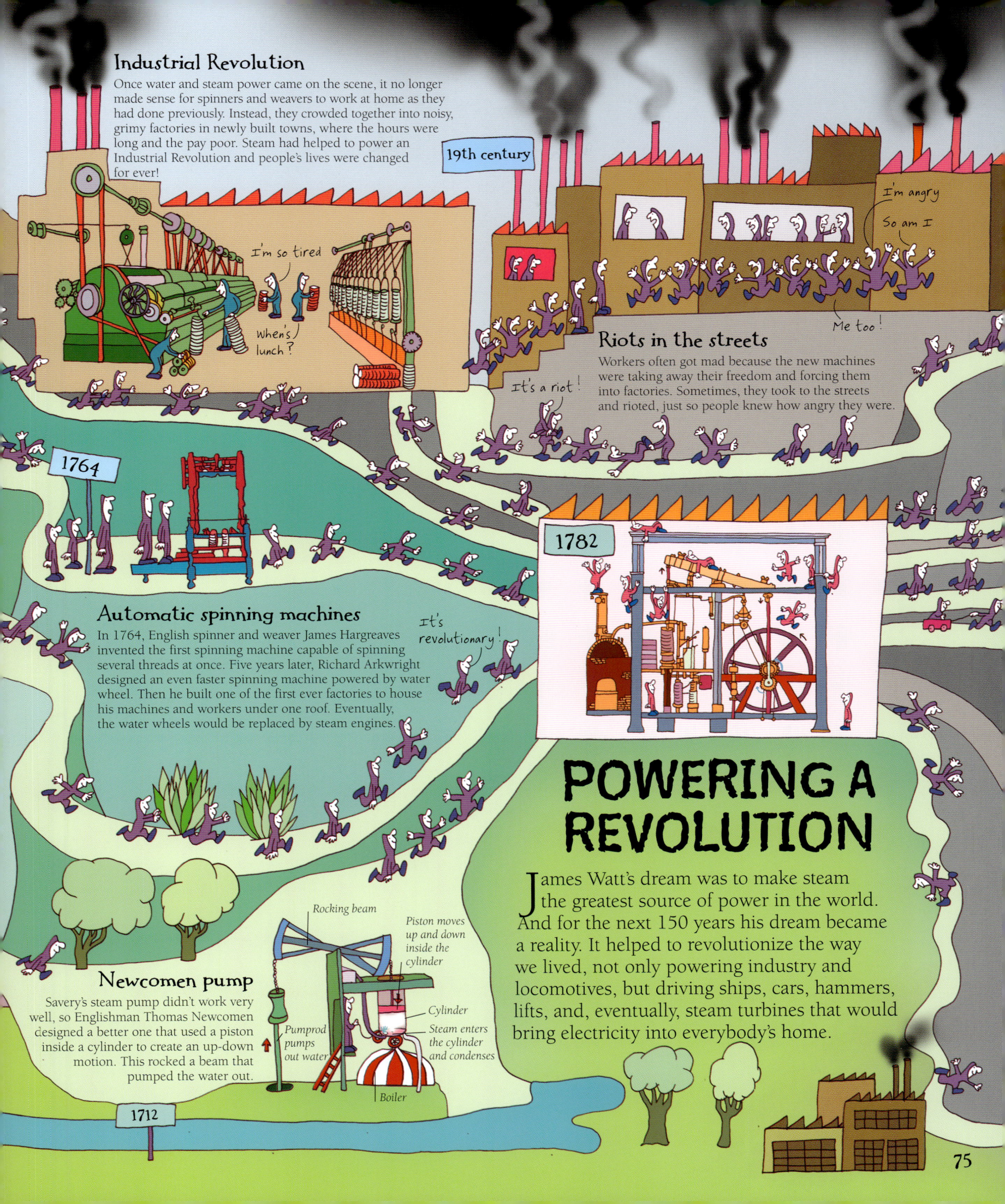

Once water and steam power came on the scene, it no longer made sense for spinners and weavers to work at home as they had done previously. Instead, they crowded together into noisy, grimy factories in newly built towns, where the hours were long and the pay poor. Steam had helped to power an Industrial Revolution and people's lives were changed for ever!

19th century

Riots in the streets

Workers often got mad because the new machines were taking away their freedom and forcing them into factories. Sometimes, they took to the streets and rioted, just so people knew how angry they were.

1764

Automatic spinning machines

In 1764, English spinner and weaver James Hargreaves invented the first spinning machine capable of spinning several threads at once. Five years later, Richard Arkwright designed an even faster spinning machine powered by water wheel. Then he built one of the first ever factories to house his machines and workers under one roof. Eventually, the water wheels would be replaced by steam engines.

1782

POWERING A REVOLUTION

James Watt's dream was to make steam the greatest source of power in the world. And for the next 150 years his dream became a reality. It helped to revolutionize the way we lived, not only powering industry and locomotives, but driving ships, cars, hammers, lifts, and, eventually, steam turbines that would bring electricity into everybody's home.

Newcomen pump

Savery's steam pump didn't work very well, so Englishman Thomas Newcomen designed a better one that used a piston inside a cylinder to create an up-down motion. This rocked a beam that pumped the water out.

Rocking beam
Piston moves up and down inside the cylinder
Pumprod pumps out water
Cylinder
Steam enters the cylinder and condenses
Boiler

1712

continued... **1860s**

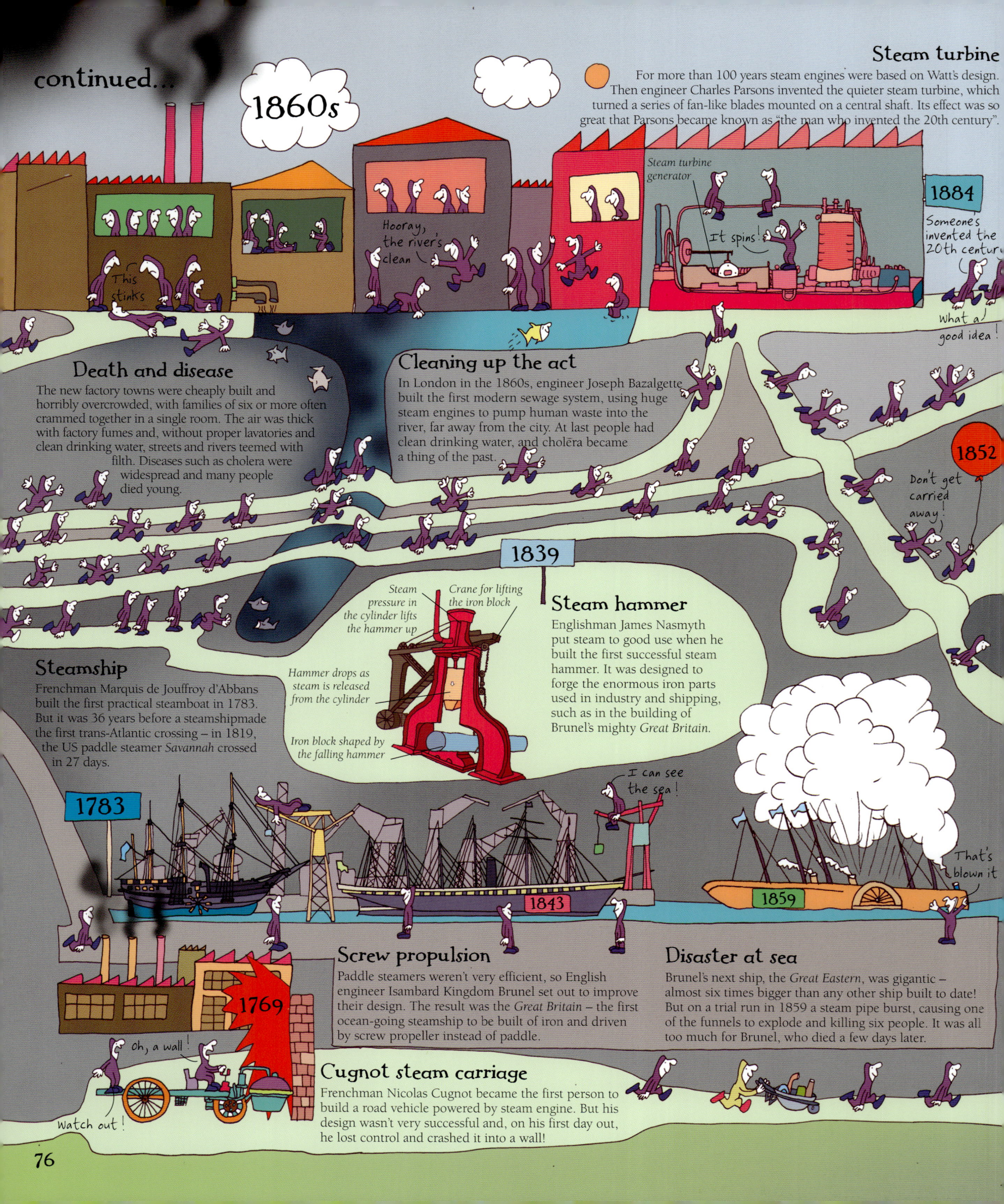

Steam turbine
For more than 100 years steam engines were based on Watt's design. Then engineer Charles Parsons invented the quieter steam turbine, which turned a series of fan-like blades mounted on a central shaft. Its effect was so great that Parsons became known as "the man who invented the 20th century".

1884

Death and disease
The new factory towns were cheaply built and horribly overcrowded, with families of six or more often crammed together in a single room. The air was thick with factory fumes and, without proper lavatories and clean drinking water, streets and rivers teemed with filth. Diseases such as cholera were widespread and many people died young.

Cleaning up the act
In London in the 1860s, engineer Joseph Bazalgette built the first modern sewage system, using huge steam engines to pump human waste into the river, far away from the city. At last people had clean drinking water, and cholera became a thing of the past.

1852

1839

Steam hammer
Englishman James Nasmyth put steam to good use when he built the first successful steam hammer. It was designed to forge the enormous iron parts used in industry and shipping, such as in the building of Brunel's mighty *Great Britain*.

Steamship
Frenchman Marquis de Jouffroy d'Abbans built the first practical steamboat in 1783. But it was 36 years before a steamship made the first trans-Atlantic crossing – in 1819, the US paddle steamer *Savannah* crossed in 27 days.

1783

1843

1859

1769

Screw propulsion
Paddle steamers weren't very efficient, so English engineer Isambard Kingdom Brunel set out to improve their design. The result was the *Great Britain* – the first ocean-going steamship to be built of iron and driven by screw propeller instead of paddle.

Disaster at sea
Brunel's next ship, the *Great Eastern*, was gigantic – almost six times bigger than any other ship built to date! But on a trial run in 1859 a steam pipe burst, causing one of the funnels to explode and killing six people. It was all too much for Brunel, who died a few days later.

Cugnot steam carriage
Frenchman Nicolas Cugnot became the first person to build a road vehicle powered by steam engine. But his design wasn't very successful and, on his first day out, he lost control and crashed it into a wall!

Power to the people

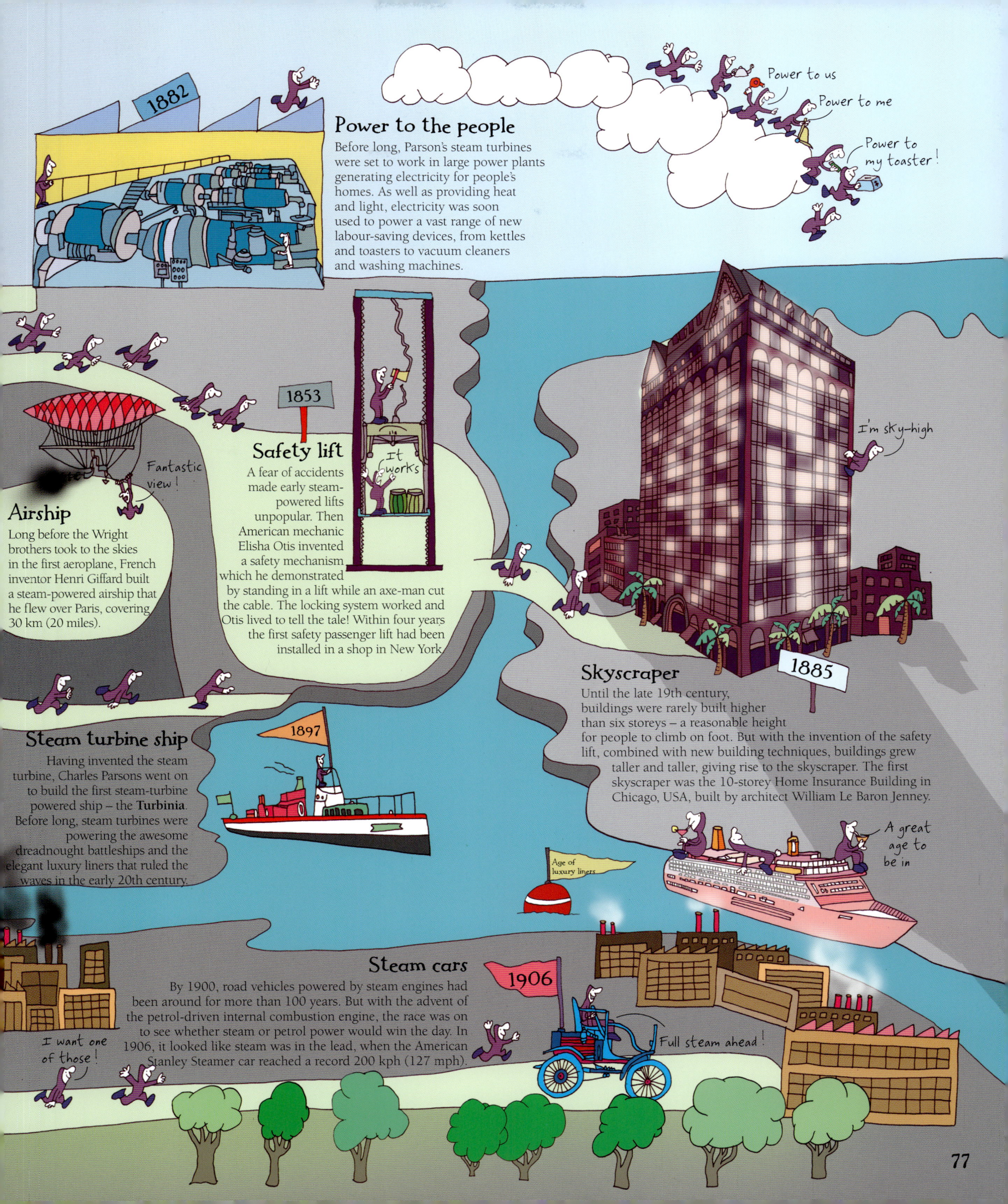

Before long, Parson's steam turbines were set to work in large power plants generating electricity for people's homes. As well as providing heat and light, electricity was soon used to power a vast range of new labour-saving devices, from kettles and toasters to vacuum cleaners and washing machines.

1882

Power to us
Power to me
Power to my toaster!

Safety lift

1853

A fear of accidents made early steam-powered lifts unpopular. Then American mechanic Elisha Otis invented a safety mechanism which he demonstrated by standing in a lift while an axe-man cut the cable. The locking system worked and Otis lived to tell the tale! Within four years the first safety passenger lift had been installed in a shop in New York.

It works

Airship

Long before the Wright brothers took to the skies in the first aeroplane, French inventor Henri Giffard built a steam-powered airship that he flew over Paris, covering 30 km (20 miles).

Fantastic view!

Skyscraper

1885

Until the late 19th century, buildings were rarely built higher than six storeys – a reasonable height for people to climb on foot. But with the invention of the safety lift, combined with new building techniques, buildings grew taller and taller, giving rise to the skyscraper. The first skyscraper was the 10-storey Home Insurance Building in Chicago, USA, built by architect William Le Baron Jenney.

I'm sky-high

Steam turbine ship

1897

Having invented the steam turbine, Charles Parsons went on to build the first steam-turbine powered ship – the **Turbinia**. Before long, steam turbines were powering the awesome dreadnought battleships and the elegant luxury liners that ruled the waves in the early 20th century.

Age of luxury liners

A great age to be in

Steam cars

1906

By 1900, road vehicles powered by steam engines had been around for more than 100 years. But with the advent of the petrol-driven internal combustion engine, the race was on to see whether steam or petrol power would win the day. In 1906, it looked like steam was in the lead, when the American Stanley Steamer car reached a record 200 kph (127 mph).

I want one of those!

Full steam ahead!

77

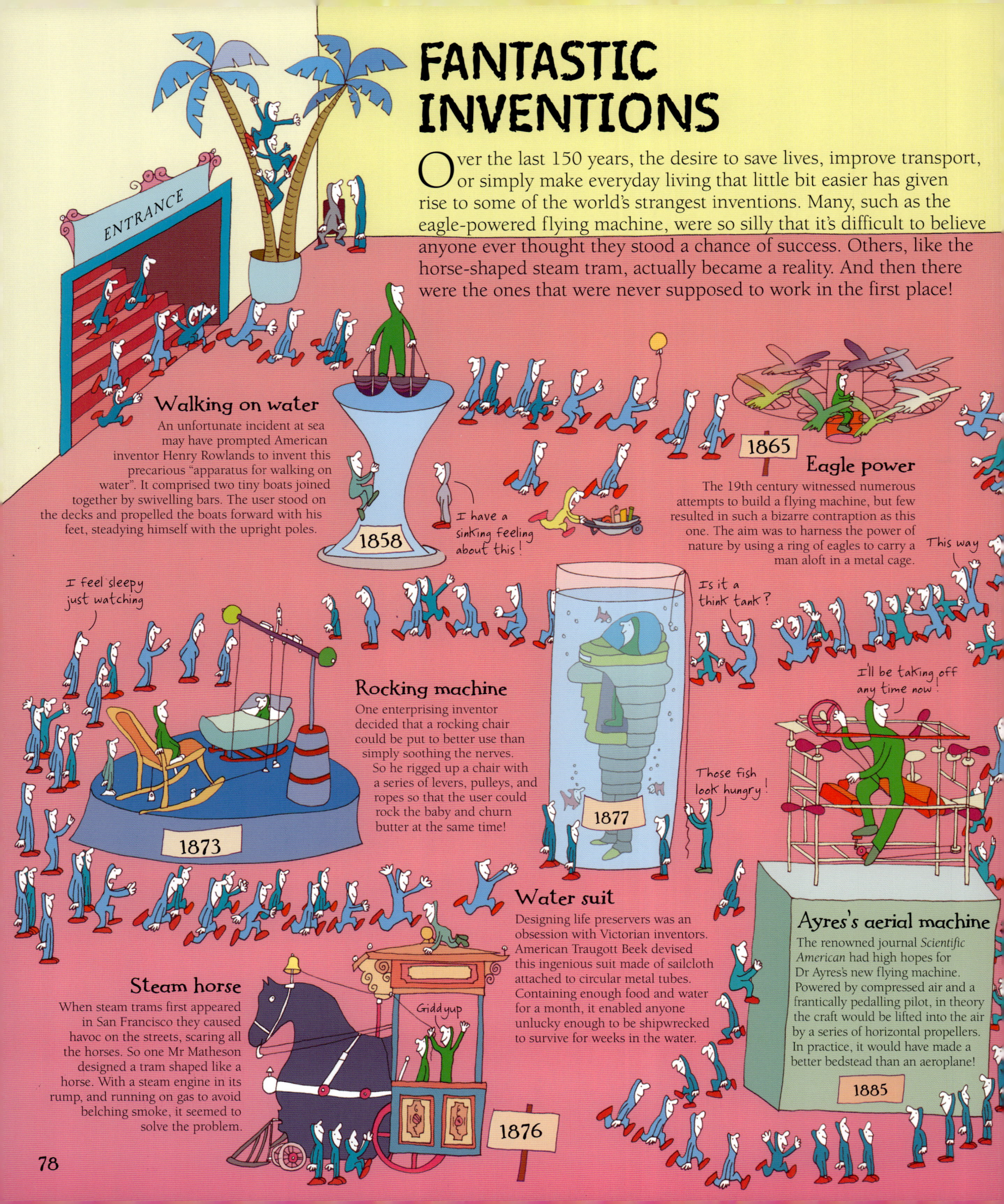

FANTASTIC INVENTIONS

Over the last 150 years, the desire to save lives, improve transport, or simply make everyday living that little bit easier has given rise to some of the world's strangest inventions. Many, such as the eagle-powered flying machine, were so silly that it's difficult to believe anyone ever thought they stood a chance of success. Others, like the horse-shaped steam tram, actually became a reality. And then there were the ones that were never supposed to work in the first place!

Walking on water
An unfortunate incident at sea may have prompted American inventor Henry Rowlands to invent this precarious "apparatus for walking on water". It comprised two tiny boats joined together by swivelling bars. The user stood on the decks and propelled the boats forward with his feet, steadying himself with the upright poles.

I have a sinking feeling about this!

1858

Eagle power
The 19th century witnessed numerous attempts to build a flying machine, but few resulted in such a bizarre contraption as this one. The aim was to harness the power of nature by using a ring of eagles to carry a man aloft in a metal cage.

1865

I feel sleepy just watching

Rocking machine
One enterprising inventor decided that a rocking chair could be put to better use than simply soothing the nerves. So he rigged up a chair with a series of levers, pulleys, and ropes so that the user could rock the baby and churn butter at the same time!

1873

Is it a think tank?

Those fish look hungry!

Water suit
Designing life preservers was an obsession with Victorian inventors. American Traugott Beek devised this ingenious suit made of sailcloth attached to circular metal tubes. Containing enough food and water for a month, it enabled anyone unlucky enough to be shipwrecked to survive for weeks in the water.

1877

This way

I'll be taking off any time now!

Ayres's aerial machine
The renowned journal *Scientific American* had high hopes for Dr Ayres's new flying machine. Powered by compressed air and a frantically pedalling pilot, in theory the craft would be lifted into the air by a series of horizontal propellers. In practice, it would have made a better bedstead than an aeroplane!

1885

Steam horse
When steam trams first appeared in San Francisco they caused havoc on the streets, scaring all the horses. So one Mr Matheson designed a tram shaped like a horse. With a steam engine in its rump, and running on gas to avoid belching smoke, it seemed to solve the problem.

Giddyup

1876

78

Suitcase lifejacket
What better way to ensure safety at sea than to have a suitcase that doubles as a lifejacket? A German named Krankel did just that by inventing a case with two removable panels. The user simply took these out, sealed the hole with a rubber ring and slipped the case over his body.

Uniwheel
Even after the invention of the bicycle, some people still thought the future lay with single-wheeled cycles, or uniwheels. Designs such as this one were almost impossible to steer and, with spokes on either side, seemingly impossible to get into!

Self-raising hat
What was a Victorian gentleman to do upon encountering a lady if he had his hands full? The answer lay in James Boyle's self-tipping hat. By simply nodding, the wearer activated a clockwork mechanism that automatically tipped his hat for him!

Bicycle shower
One enterprising cyclist had the bright idea of combining the morning shower with a bit of exercise. His "Vélodouche" used pedal power to pump water into the shower. The harder you pedalled, the more powerful the shower!

Patting the baby
American inventor Thomas Zelenka, possibly tired of patting the baby to sleep, invented an electrically powered mechanical arm to do it for him. Attached to the side of the cot, the arm pats a baby's bottom to send the tiny tot off to sleep.

Rolling ball
Designed by Alessandro Dandini, this curious marine craft comprises a large motorized ball with two cabins attached on either side. In theory, if something goes wrong, the cabins can be released by firing explosive bolts. The problem is, having released one cabin, the whole contraption would become unbalanced and keel over on its side!

Chindogu
Japanese comedian Kenji Kawakami created a craze for nonsensical devices when he started inventing Chindogu – meaning "weird tool". Designed to create more problems than they solve, they include a solar-powered torch, a portable zebra crossing, and a motorized noodle fork.

LEADING LIGHTS

City streets were dark and dangerous places at night until gas lamps were introduced in the early 19th century. Lighting homes was not so simple. Wax candles were expensive, oil lamps were smelly, and gas lighting gave off fumes, stained furniture, and killed the pot plants! In the 1870s, two men independently set out to invent an alternative that was cheap, clean, and could be controlled by the flick of a switch – the result was the electric light bulb.

Bright sparks
Although Swan beat Edison to invent the light bulb by a few months, the two men were soon caught up in a legal battle over patent rights. But by 1883 they had seen the light and combined forces to produce the "Ediswan" light bulb!

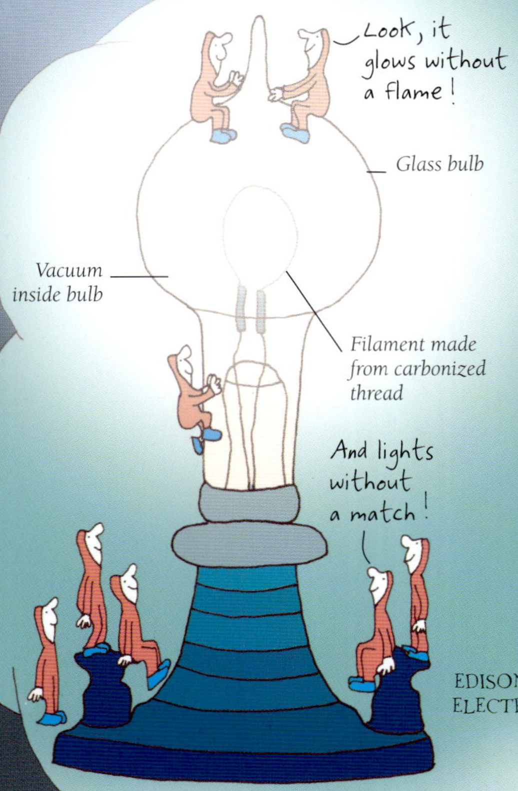

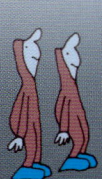

How light bulbs work
Edison and Swan's light bulbs worked on the principle of "incandescence" – meaning, a filament will glow with heat when an electric current is passed through it. Modern incandescent bulbs work in a similar way, only now they have a tungsten filament instead of carbon, which lasts longer and gives a brighter light.

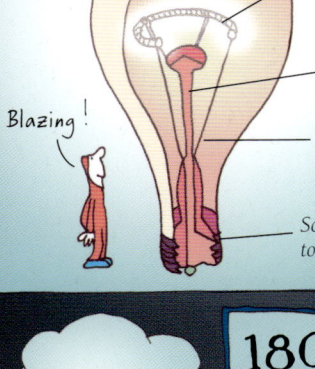

- Glass bulb contains inert gas that prevents the filament burning
- Tungsten filament glows when the current passes through it
- Glass mount supports the filament
- Support wires carry the electric current to the tungsten filament
- Screw thread contact to mains electricity

The light bulb
In 1879, British chemist Joseph Swan and US inventor Thomas Edison both demonstrated a practical light bulb, comprising a glowing filament inside a vacuum. The problem had been finding a filament that wouldn't burn away within minutes. After 1,200 experiments using different materials, including fishing line and coconut hair, Edison discovered that carbonized sewing thread worked best!

EDISON'S FIRST ELECTRIC LAMP

Gas lighting
William Murdock became the first person to install gas lighting in his house, in Cornwall, England, in 1792. By the early 19th century, city streets across Europe and the USA were being lit by gas.

Volta's pile
The first electric battery was invented by Italian scientist Alessandro Volta. Comprising a stack of metal and brine-soaked cardboard disks, Volta's "pile" produced the first reliable current, making experiments into electricity easier to perform.

Arc lights
English chemist Sir Humphrey Davy used a battery to power his invention – the arc light. But arc lights weren't used for street lighting until the 1870s, once a practical power source had been developed. Even then, they were too bright for use in the home.

Dynamo
History was made in 1831 when Michael Faraday discovered that by moving a magnet inside a coil of wire he could create, or "induce," an electric current. He had just invented the dynamo, the forerunner of electric generators.

Leclanché battery
Using a glass jar containing zinc and carbon rods in chemical solutions, French engineer Georges Leclanché invented a new kind of battery in 1866. It was the forerunner of modern dry cell batteries, which are used to power countless items from toys to torches.

The generator

What good was an electric light bulb without the means of supplying electricity to people's homes? It was Edison who made it feasible, designing an entire electricity supply system, from high-voltage generators and insulated cables to screw sockets and light switches. In 1882, he opened the first public power station in Pearl Street, New York, using generators driven by steam engines to light 13,000 lamps in homes and offices across several city blocks.

EDISON'S PEARL STREET GENERATORS

Flywheel, driven by a steam engine, turns the armature

1. Electromagnet creates a magnetic field
2. Rotating "armature" (wire coil) induces an alternating current (which fluctuates back and forth)
3. "Commutator" turns the alternating current into a direct current
4. Carbon brushes pick up the direct current
5. Electric current flows to homes and offices

Generators at work

Generators work on the principle of "electromagnetic induction" – that is, an electric current can be induced to flow by moving a wire coil inside a magnetic field. In this diagram, the movement is created by turning a handle; Edison used steam engines to do the same job. As generators produce an alternating current (one that fluctuates backwards and forwards), Edison used a device called a commutator to turn it into a direct current (one that flows in one direction only) for sending to homes and offices.

Diagram labels: Magnetic field created between the magnet's poles; South pole; North pole; Commutator; Wire coil (armature) rotates; Bulb glows when the current flows through the circuit; Current flows through the circuit

---

1880 — Bulbs for sale
Within a year of inventing his incandescent bulb, Thomas Edison was selling light bulbs commercially. His new, improved design used carbonized bamboo as a filament and worked for more than 1,100 hours!

1882 — Power to Pearl Street
Edison's Pearl Street power station of 1882 kicked off the age of electricity, and soon other power stations using rival systems were opening up across the western world. Edison's biggest rival was George Westinghouse, who supplied alternating current.

1888 — Steam turbine power
Irishman Charles Parsons invented a new kind of steam engine – the steam turbine. By 1888 it had been put to work driving electricity generators, and is still used today in modern power stations and large ships such as ocean cruisers.

1901 — Fluorescent lighting
In 1901, US electrical engineer Peter Cooper-Hewitt designed a light bulb that worked without a filament. Called a mercury vapour lamp, it had to be tilted to get it going! It wasn't very successful but the idea re-emerged in 1935 as the tubular fluorescent lamp.

1910 — Neon signs
French physicist Georges Claude discovered that passing a current through a glass tube filled with neon gas produced a bright red glow. By 1910, he had put his find to practical use and invented the neon sign.

18th century

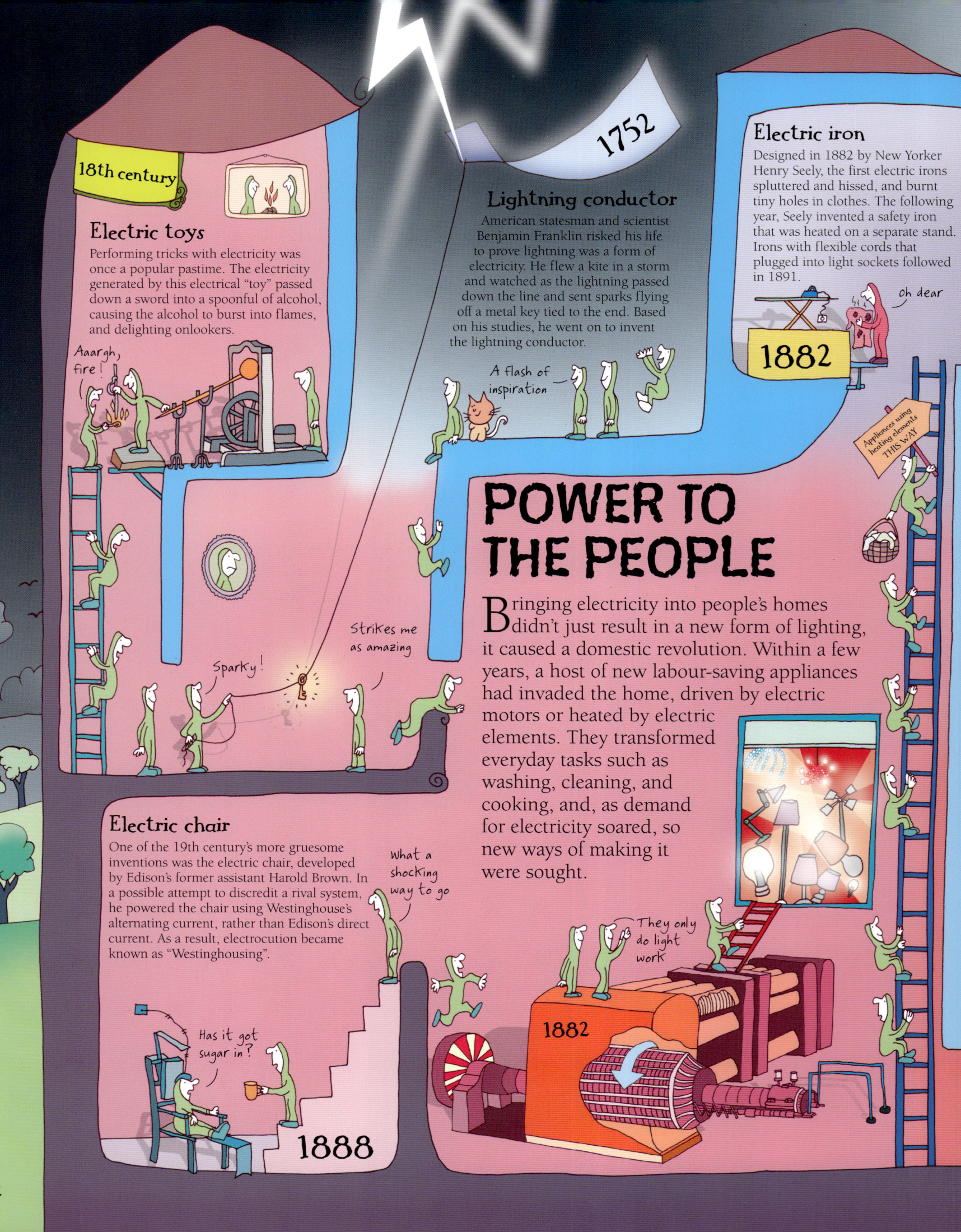

Electric toys
Performing tricks with electricity was once a popular pastime. The electricity generated by this electrical "toy" passed down a sword into a spoonful of alcohol, causing the alcohol to burst into flames, and delighting onlookers.

1752

Lightning conductor
American statesman and scientist Benjamin Franklin risked his life to prove lightning was a form of electricity. He flew a kite in a storm and watched as the lightning passed down the line and sent sparks flying off a metal key tied to the end. Based on his studies, he went on to invent the lightning conductor.

Electric iron
Designed in 1882 by New Yorker Henry Seely, the first electric irons spluttered and hissed, and burnt tiny holes in clothes. The following year, Seely invented a safety iron that was heated on a separate stand. Irons with flexible cords that plugged into light sockets followed in 1891.

1882

POWER TO THE PEOPLE

Bringing electricity into people's homes didn't just result in a new form of lighting, it caused a domestic revolution. Within a few years, a host of new labour-saving appliances had invaded the home, driven by electric motors or heated by electric elements. They transformed everyday tasks such as washing, cleaning, and cooking, and, as demand for electricity soared, so new ways of making it were sought.

Electric chair
One of the 19th century's more gruesome inventions was the electric chair, developed by Edison's former assistant Harold Brown. In a possible attempt to discredit a rival system, he powered the chair using Westinghouse's alternating current, rather than Edison's direct current. As a result, electrocution became known as "Westinghousing".

1888

1882

82

Electric kettle
1891

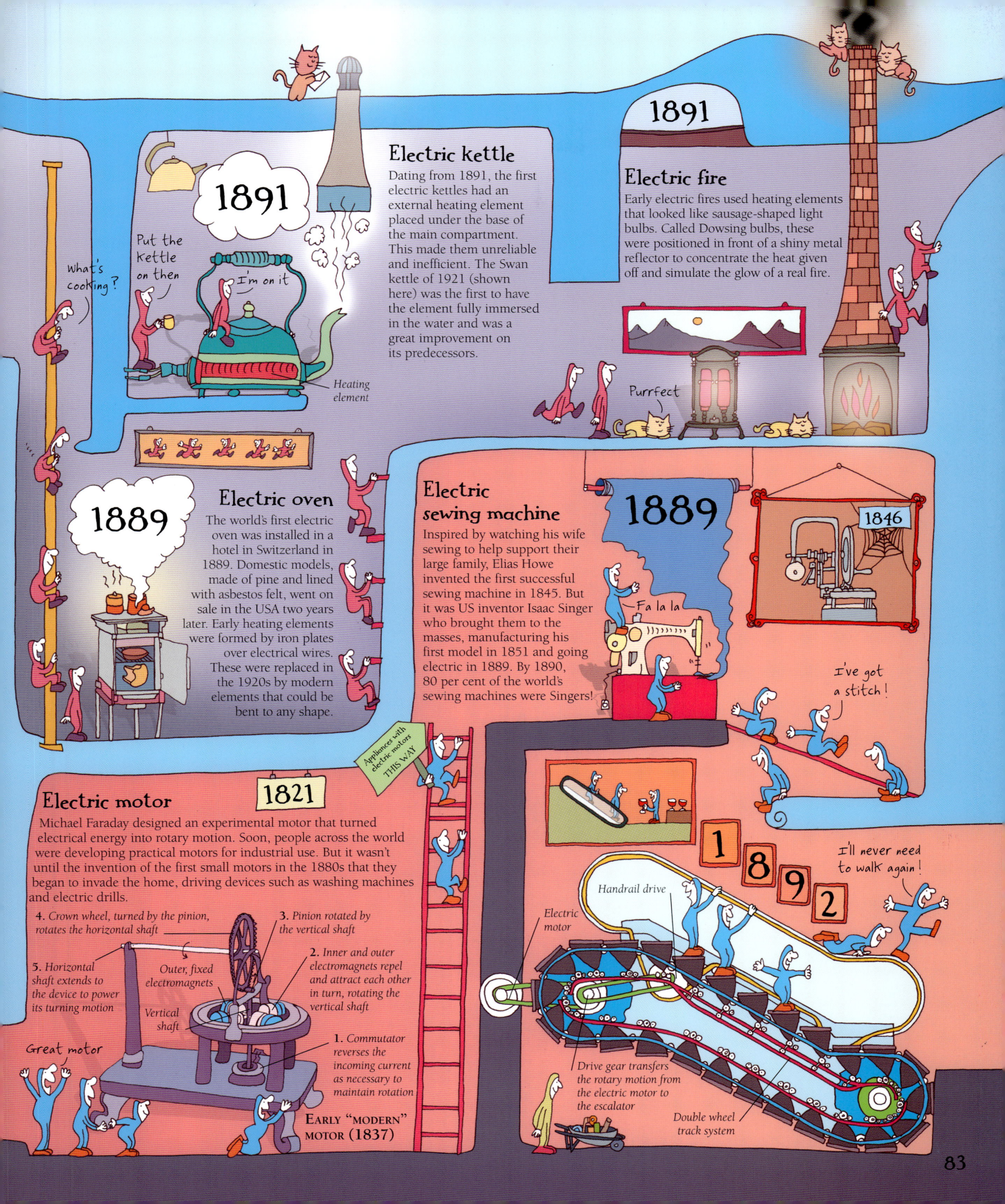

Dating from 1891, the first electric kettles had an external heating element placed under the base of the main compartment. This made them unreliable and inefficient. The Swan kettle of 1921 (shown here) was the first to have the element fully immersed in the water and was a great improvement on its predecessors.

Heating element

1891
Electric fire

Early electric fires used heating elements that looked like sausage-shaped light bulbs. Called Dowsing bulbs, these were positioned in front of a shiny metal reflector to concentrate the heat given off and simulate the glow of a real fire.

Electric oven
1889

The world's first electric oven was installed in a hotel in Switzerland in 1889. Domestic models, made of pine and lined with asbestos felt, went on sale in the USA two years later. Early heating elements were formed by iron plates over electrical wires. These were replaced in the 1920s by modern elements that could be bent to any shape.

Electric sewing machine
1889

Inspired by watching his wife sewing to help support their large family, Elias Howe invented the first successful sewing machine in 1845. But it was US inventor Isaac Singer who brought them to the masses, manufacturing his first model in 1851 and going electric in 1889. By 1890, 80 per cent of the world's sewing machines were Singers!

1846

Electric motor
1821

Michael Faraday designed an experimental motor that turned electrical energy into rotary motion. Soon, people across the world were developing practical motors for industrial use. But it wasn't until the invention of the first small motors in the 1880s that they began to invade the home, driving devices such as washing machines and electric drills.

4. Crown wheel, turned by the pinion, rotates the horizontal shaft
5. Horizontal shaft extends to the device to power its turning motion
3. Pinion rotated by the vertical shaft
2. Inner and outer electromagnets repel and attract each other in turn, rotating the vertical shaft
1. Commutator reverses the incoming current as necessary to maintain rotation

Outer, fixed electromagnets
Vertical shaft

EARLY "MODERN" MOTOR (1837)

1892

Handrail drive
Electric motor
Drive gear transfers the rotary motion from the electric motor to the escalator
Double wheel track system

Appliances with electric motors THIS WAY

83

continued...

You're toast!

Washing machine
US engineer Alva Fisher mechanized the weekly wash by inventing an electric washing machine he called Thor. It was little more than a wooden tub with an electric motor bolted underneath. Not surprisingly, washing machines weren't popular until the 1960s, when the first "twin tubs" appeared.

1907

Is there a wool wash?

Electric dishwasher
During the late 19th century, more than 30 women took out patents for dishwashers in the USA. The first machine to be manufactured was invented by Josephine Cochran, who had had enough of washing her own dishes. Initially powered by handle or steam engine, dishwashers didn't go electric until 1912. Even then, they didn't catch on in the home until the 1950s.

1912

Pop-up toaster
Burnt toast became commonplace once electric toasters had appeared on the breakfast table in 1893. In 1921, all that changed when American inventor Charles Strite patented the pop-up toaster. Originally designed for caterers, by 1925 it had reached the home in the form of the Toastmaster.

1921

I'll just pop up stairs

Electric drill
1895 Having improved the design of the telephone, and invented the first electric fire alarm, German electrical engineer Wilhelm Fein went on to create the world's first electric hand drill.

Very handy

Electric refrigerator
In 1851, US doctor John Gorrie patented a refrigerator that relied on the expansion of a compressed gas (refrigerant) for its cooling effect. But refrigerators didn't go domestic until after 1913 when the first electric model was introduced, with a motorized compressor mounted on top that forced the refrigerant through metal coils.

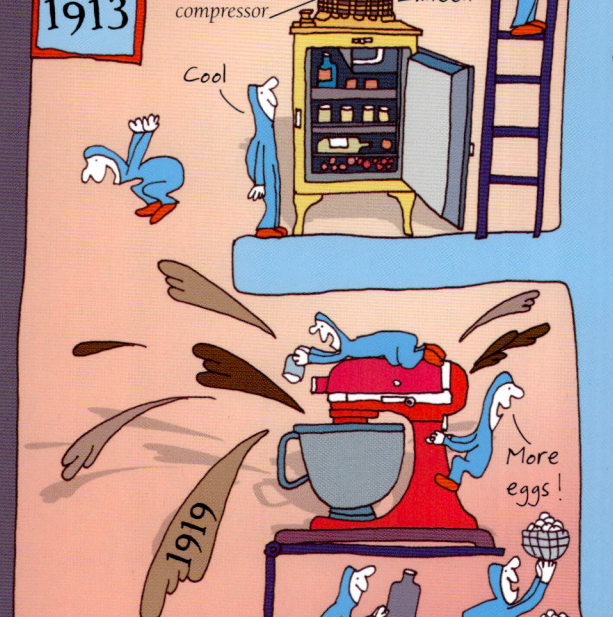

1913

Motorized compressor *Indeed!* *Cool*

Electric hover-mower
Lawnmowers date back to 1830 when Englishm[an] Edwin Budding invented a machine with blade[s] arranged around a cylinder. Nearly 100 yea[rs] later, the first electric models appeared. But the basic concept didn't change until the hover-mower was introduced in the 1960s, with rotary cutting blades replacing the cylinder.

1830

1964

Escalator
The escalator was invented by American engineer Jesse Reno. Called an inclined elevator, it was driven by an electric motor and had a continuous sloping belt instead of steps. It was so novel that, when one was fitted in London's famous Harrods department store in 1896, a man was on hand to dispense brandy to passengers overcome by the experience! Modern-style escalators with steps used a clever double wheel track system (see left), but they didn't appear until 1921.

KitchenAid
Early food mixers were little more than motorized egg whisks. Then American engineer Herbert Johnson invented a new kind of multi-purpose mixer in which the beaters and bowl turned in opposite directions. Originally designed for the US Navy, within three years it was being sold to the public as the KitchenAid.

1919

More eggs!

Hairdryer
Hand-held hairdryers were made possible thanks to the small, high-speed motors developed by American inventor Chester Beach in the early years of the 20th century. Containing a motorized fan that blew air over a heated element, early hairdryers were big, heavy, and noisy, with metal casing and a wooden handle.

Me next! *Purrr....*

1920

Microwave oven — 1946

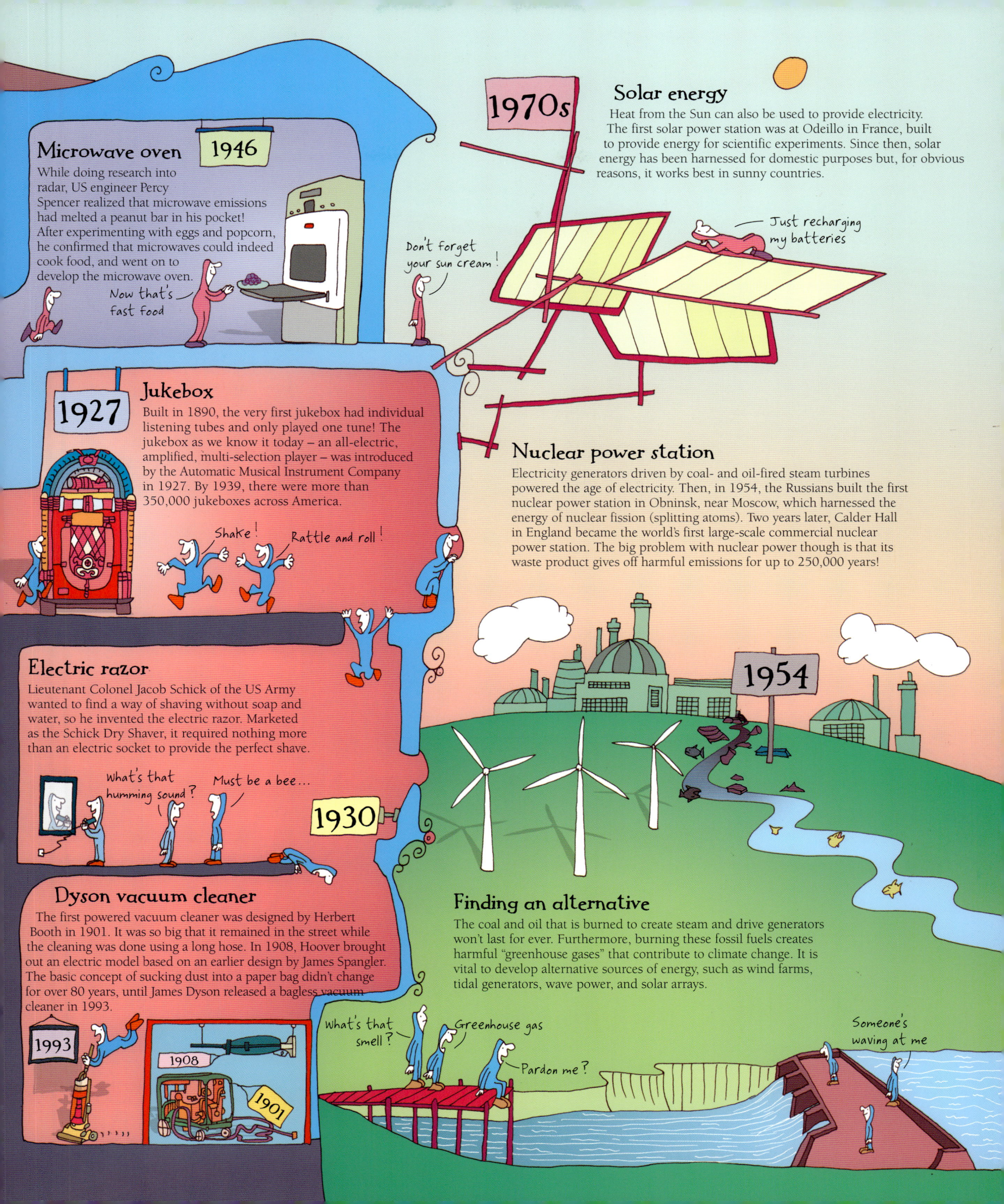

While doing research into radar, US engineer Percy Spencer realized that microwave emissions had melted a peanut bar in his pocket! After experimenting with eggs and popcorn, he confirmed that microwaves could indeed cook food, and went on to develop the microwave oven.

Jukebox — 1927

Built in 1890, the very first jukebox had individual listening tubes and only played one tune! The jukebox as we know it today – an all-electric, amplified, multi-selection player – was introduced by the Automatic Musical Instrument Company in 1927. By 1939, there were more than 350,000 jukeboxes across America.

Electric razor

Lieutenant Colonel Jacob Schick of the US Army wanted to find a way of shaving without soap and water, so he invented the electric razor. Marketed as the Schick Dry Shaver, it required nothing more than an electric socket to provide the perfect shave.

1930

Dyson vacuum cleaner

The first powered vacuum cleaner was designed by Herbert Booth in 1901. It was so big that it remained in the street while the cleaning was done using a long hose. In 1908, Hoover brought out an electric model based on an earlier design by James Spangler. The basic concept of sucking dust into a paper bag didn't change for over 80 years, until James Dyson released a bagless vacuum cleaner in 1993.

Solar energy — 1970s

Heat from the Sun can also be used to provide electricity. The first solar power station was at Odeillo in France, built to provide energy for scientific experiments. Since then, solar energy has been harnessed for domestic purposes but, for obvious reasons, it works best in sunny countries.

Nuclear power station

Electricity generators driven by coal- and oil-fired steam turbines powered the age of electricity. Then, in 1954, the Russians built the first nuclear power station in Obninsk, near Moscow, which harnessed the energy of nuclear fission (splitting atoms). Two years later, Calder Hall in England became the world's first large-scale commercial nuclear power station. The big problem with nuclear power though is that its waste product gives off harmful emissions for up to 250,000 years!

1954

Finding an alternative

The coal and oil that is burned to create steam and drive generators won't last for ever. Furthermore, burning these fossil fuels creates harmful "greenhouse gases" that contribute to climate change. It is vital to develop alternative sources of energy, such as wind farms, tidal generators, wave power, and solar arrays.

FASCINATING FIRSTS

Have you ever wondered who invented sliced bread, when roller skates were first made, or how blue jeans came into existence? Even the most basic things we use every day, such as safety pins and tinned food, were invented by someone, sometime. Inventions such as false teeth may date back to Roman times, whereas others, like the artificial heart and the ejector seat, are very much a product of our modern age.

False teeth

The Etruscans, who ruled central Italy before the Romans, were the first to wear false teeth. They made them out of animal teeth held together by gold bridgework. Poor people couldn't afford false teeth, and had to cure the toothache with a mouthwash made by boiling dogs' teeth in wine!

Roller skates

The first roller skates on record were worn by theatre performers in London, UK, when actors attached wheels to the bottom of their footwear. They were designed to copy the movement of ice-skating on stage.

Tinned food

The first patent for preserving food using "vessels of tin or other metals" was taken out by Englishman Peter Durand in 1810. Two years later, Bryan Donkin and John Hall set up the first canning factory to supply the army and navy with provisions. But the can-opener wasn't invented for another 43 years!

Elastic band

Six years after the invention of vulcanized rubber, English rubber manufacturer Stephen Perry invented the elastic band as a means of holding bundles of papers together. It wasn't long before kids had found another use for the elastic band – firing projectiles at hapless friends and foes!

Safety pin

Where would we be without the safety pin? Clasp-type pins possibly date back to Roman times, but it was American inventor Walter Hunt who patented the design we still use today. As someone joked upon Hunt's death, "Without him we would be undone!"

Jeans

When Californian tailor Jacob Davis was asked if he could design some work trousers with pockets that wouldn't keep tearing, he had the bright idea of using metal rivets on the pocket corners to take the strain. Before long he'd teamed up with denim supplier Levi Strauss, and Levi jeans were born!

Zip
1893

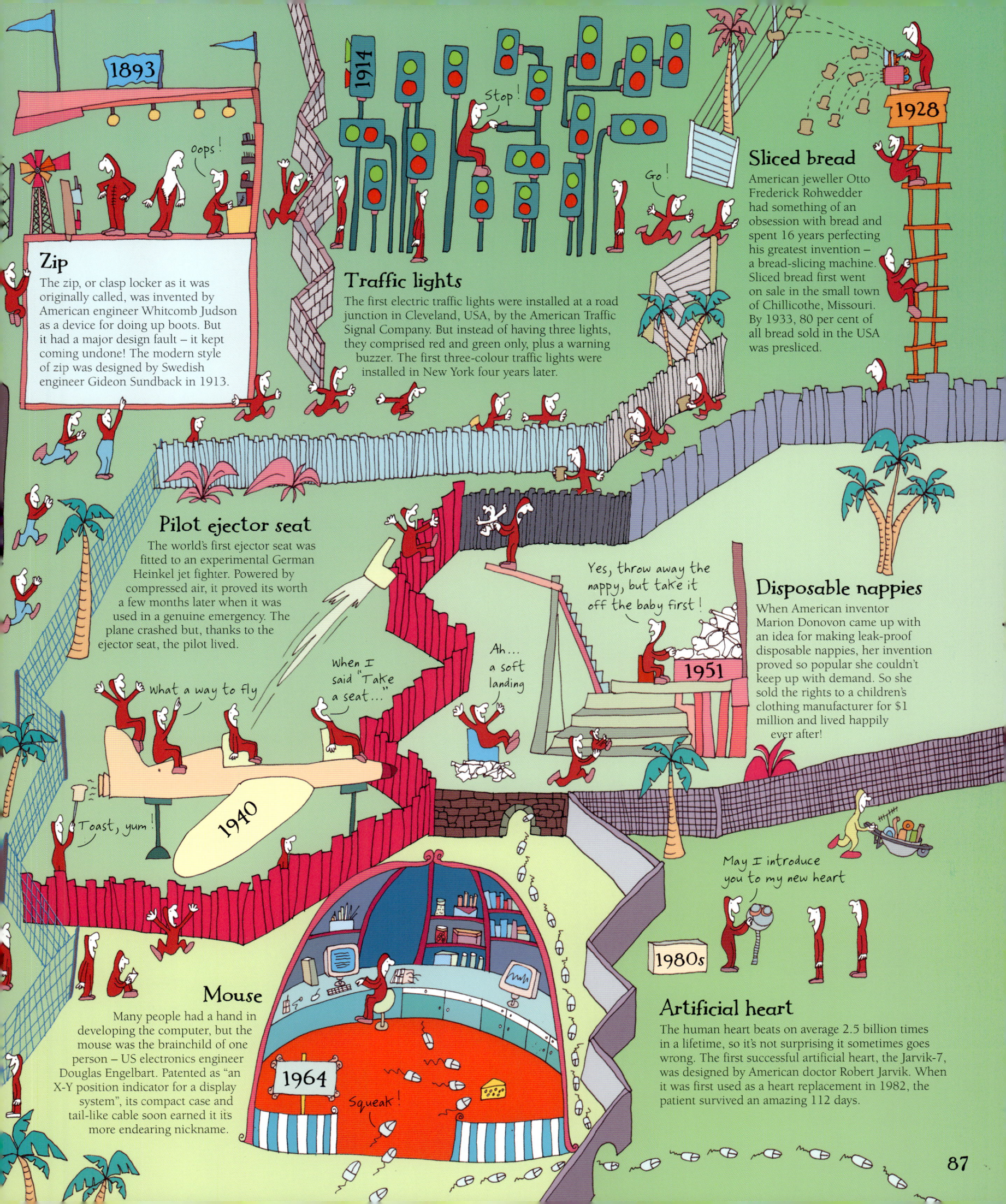

The zip, or clasp locker as it was originally called, was invented by American engineer Whitcomb Judson as a device for doing up boots. But it had a major design fault – it kept coming undone! The modern style of zip was designed by Swedish engineer Gideon Sundback in 1913.

Traffic lights
1914

The first electric traffic lights were installed at a road junction in Cleveland, USA, by the American Traffic Signal Company. But instead of having three lights, they comprised red and green only, plus a warning buzzer. The first three-colour traffic lights were installed in New York four years later.

Sliced bread
1928

American jeweller Otto Frederick Rohwedder had something of an obsession with bread and spent 16 years perfecting his greatest invention – a bread-slicing machine. Sliced bread first went on sale in the small town of Chillicothe, Missouri. By 1933, 80 per cent of all bread sold in the USA was presliced.

Pilot ejector seat
1940

The world's first ejector seat was fitted to an experimental German Heinkel jet fighter. Powered by compressed air, it proved its worth a few months later when it was used in a genuine emergency. The plane crashed but, thanks to the ejector seat, the pilot lived.

Disposable nappies
1951

When American inventor Marion Donovon came up with an idea for making leak-proof disposable nappies, her invention proved so popular she couldn't keep up with demand. So she sold the rights to a children's clothing manufacturer for $1 million and lived happily ever after!

Mouse
1964

Many people had a hand in developing the computer, but the mouse was the brainchild of one person – US electronics engineer Douglas Engelbart. Patented as "an X-Y position indicator for a display system", its compact case and tail-like cable soon earned it its more endearing nickname.

Artificial heart
1980s

The human heart beats on average 2.5 billion times in a lifetime, so it's not surprising it sometimes goes wrong. The first successful artificial heart, the Jarvik-7, was designed by American doctor Robert Jarvik. When it was first used as a heart replacement in 1982, the patient survived an amazing 112 days.

87

ON THE ROAD

The steam engine had powered a revolution in industry and transport. But, although it rivalled the petrol engine for more than 20 years, it was too impractical, and took too long to get started, ever to become master of the roads. Beginning life as a stationary engine for driving industrial machinery, it was the internal combustion engine that caused the transport revolution of the 20th century, evolving into a light and highly efficient machine that made the motor car the "must-have" mode of transport for the masses.

First car — 1885
Karl Benz built the first successful motor car in 1885. It was powered by petrol engine and steered by a tiller, but only had three wheels!

Driven men
Karl Benz and Gottlieb Daimler competed against each other in the development of the motor car.

The internal combustion engine

The first internal combustion engines ran on coal gas. Then, in 1885, German engineers Gottlieb Daimler and Wilhelm Maybach developed a successful petrol engine. With a single cylinder that operated on a four-stroke cycle (see right), the engine soon evolved into the four-cylinder type that is still used in cars today. The power comes from burning fuel inside the cylinders, which drives the pistons down and turns the crankshaft.

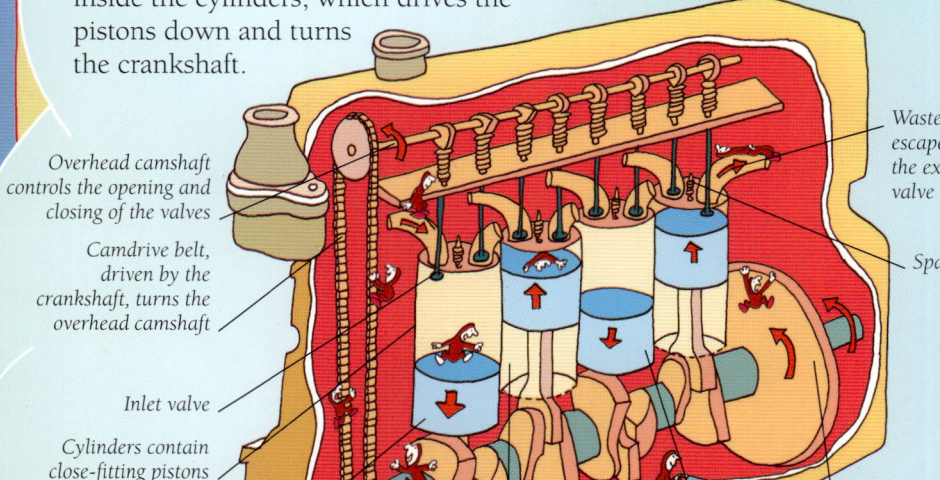

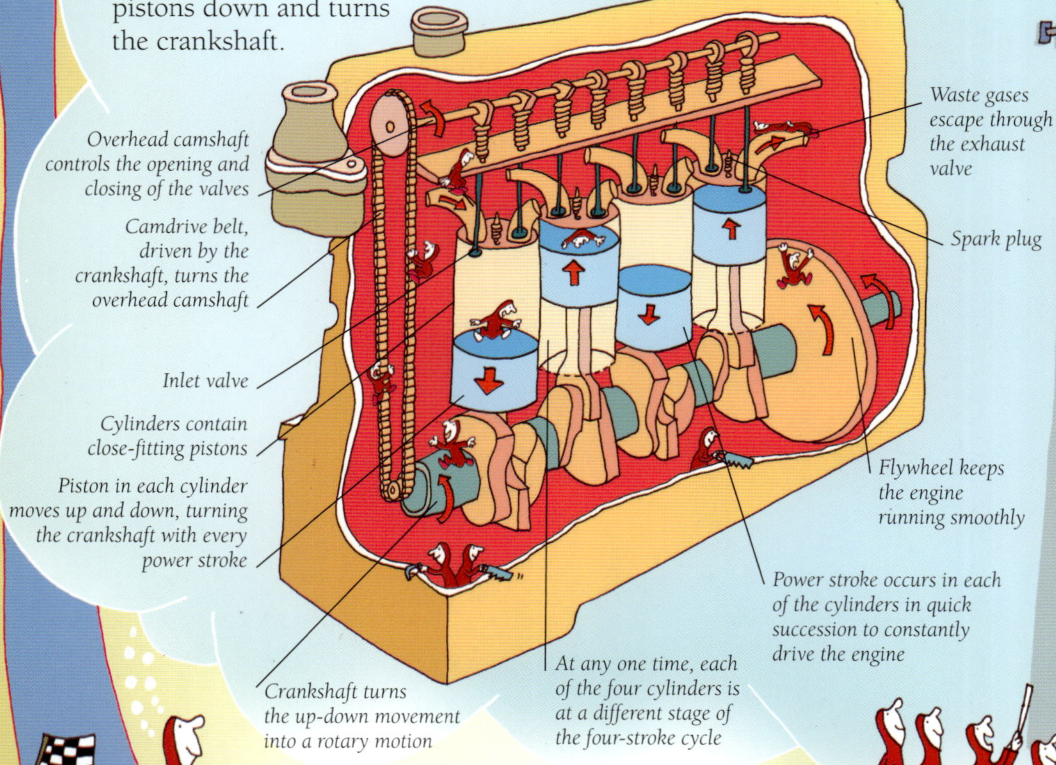

- *Overhead camshaft controls the opening and closing of the valves*
- *Camdrive belt, driven by the crankshaft, turns the overhead camshaft*
- *Inlet valve*
- *Cylinders contain close-fitting pistons*
- *Piston in each cylinder moves up and down, turning the crankshaft with every power stroke*
- *Crankshaft turns the up-down movement into a rotary motion*
- *At any one time, each of the four cylinders is at a different stage of the four-stroke cycle*
- *Waste gases escape through the exhaust valve*
- *Spark plug*
- *Flywheel keeps the engine running smoothly*
- *Power stroke occurs in each of the cylinders in quick succession to constantly drive the engine*

Four-stroke cycle

When the engine is running, each cylinder continuously performs a cycle of four events, called the four-stroke cycle. The events occur in sequence across the four cylinders, so that as one cylinder is carrying out the intake stroke, the next is completing the compression stroke, and so on.

1. Intake stroke
Piston moves down, drawing a fuel-air mix into the cylinder via the inlet valve.

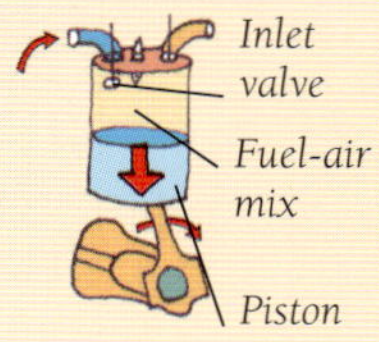

2. Compression stroke
Piston moves up again, compressing the fuel-air mix.

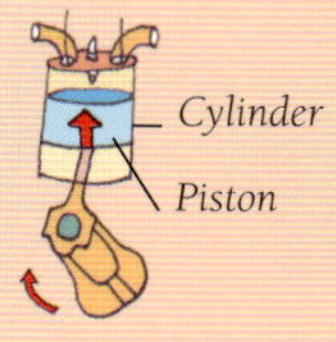

3. Power stroke
Spark from the spark plug ignites the fuel, and expanding gases drive the piston down.

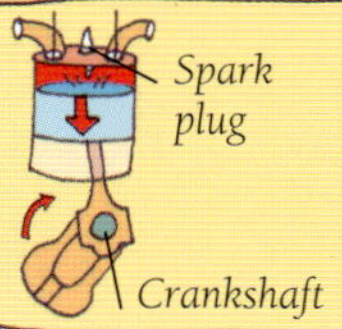

4. Exhaust stroke
Piston moves up again, forcing burnt gases out through the exhaust valve.

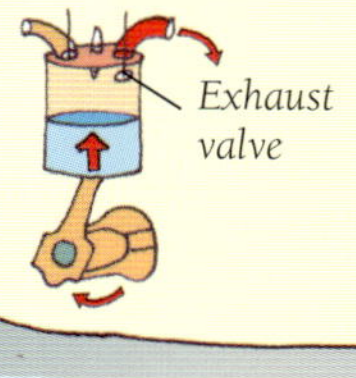

Fast car — 2005
One of the fastest and most expensive production cars is the awesome Bugatti Veyron. With a 16-cylinder engine, it reaches a staggering 400 kph (250 mph).

Cleaning up the act — 1997
Launched in 1997, Toyota Prius was one of the first hybrid cars. It runs on petrol at higher speeds but uses an electric motor at lower ones, reducing pollution. In the 2010s, all-electric cars became more popular, powered by a lithium-ion battery that was invented in the 1980s

The first "modern" motor car

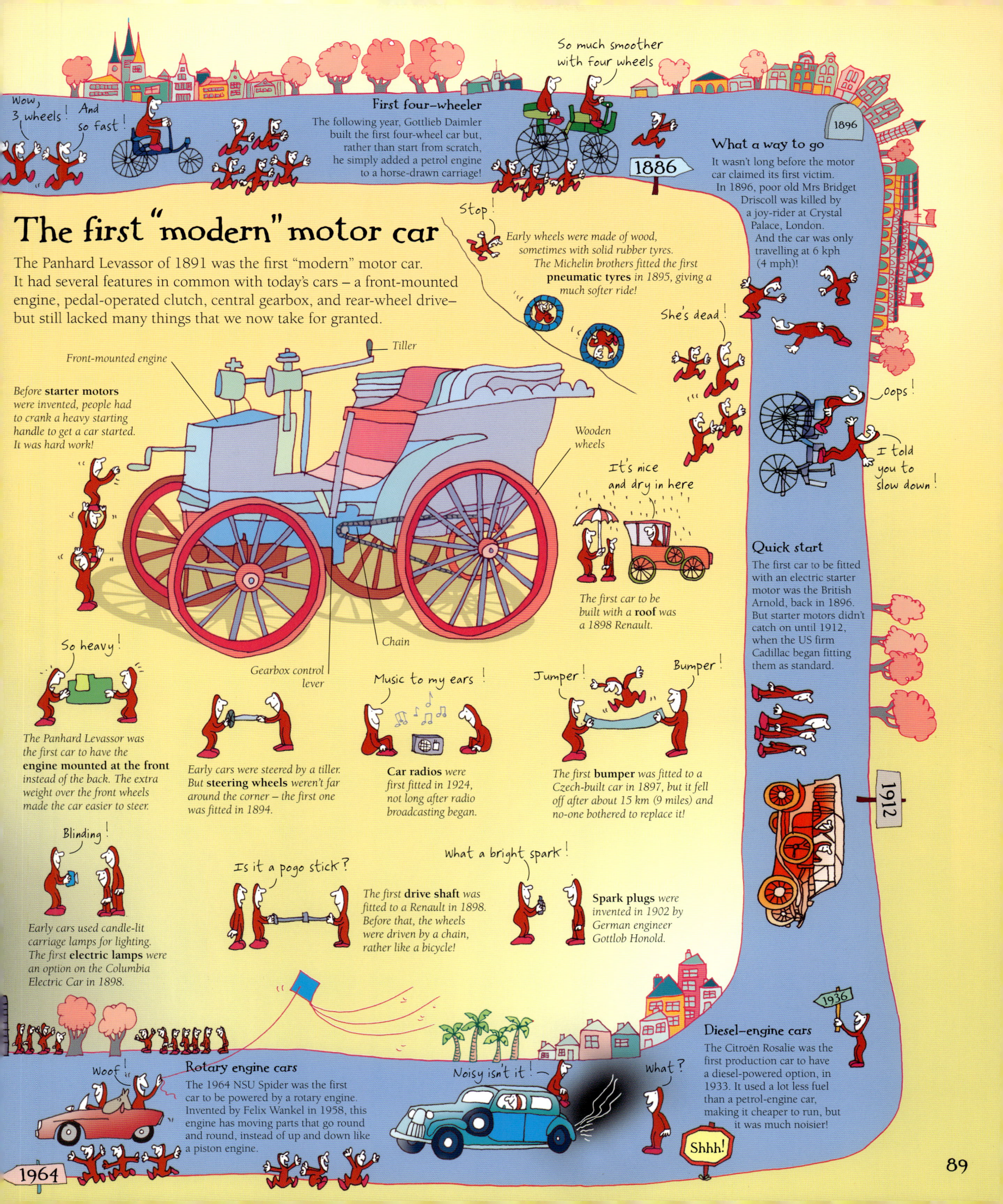

The Panhard Levassor of 1891 was the first "modern" motor car. It had several features in common with today's cars – a front-mounted engine, pedal-operated clutch, central gearbox, and rear-wheel drive – but still lacked many things that we now take for granted.

Front-mounted engine

Before **starter motors** were invented, people had to crank a heavy starting handle to get a car started. It was hard work!

Tiller

Wooden wheels

Chain

Gearbox control lever

The Panhard Levassor was the first car to have the **engine mounted at the front** instead of the back. The extra weight over the front wheels made the car easier to steer.

Early cars were steered by a tiller. But **steering wheels** weren't far around the corner – the first one was fitted in 1894.

Car radios were first fitted in 1924, not long after radio broadcasting began.

The first **bumper** was fitted to a Czech-built car in 1897, but it fell off after about 15 km (9 miles) and no-one bothered to replace it!

Early cars used candle-lit carriage lamps for lighting. The first **electric lamps** were an option on the Columbia Electric Car in 1898.

The first **drive shaft** was fitted to a Renault in 1898. Before that, the wheels were driven by a chain, rather like a bicycle!

Spark plugs were invented in 1902 by German engineer Gottlob Honold.

Rotary engine cars
The 1964 NSU Spider was the first car to be powered by a rotary engine. Invented by Felix Wankel in 1958, this engine has moving parts that go round and round, instead of up and down like a piston engine.

First four-wheeler
The following year, Gottlieb Daimler built the first four-wheel car but, rather than start from scratch, he simply added a petrol engine to a horse-drawn carriage!

Early wheels were made of wood, sometimes with solid rubber tyres. The Michelin brothers fitted the first **pneumatic tyres** in 1895, giving a much softer ride!

The first car to be built with a **roof** was a 1898 Renault.

What a way to go
It wasn't long before the motor car claimed its first victim. In 1896, poor old Mrs Bridget Driscoll was killed by a joy-rider at Crystal Palace, London. And the car was only travelling at 6 kph (4 mph)!

Quick start
The first car to be fitted with an electric starter motor was the British Arnold, back in 1896. But starter motors didn't catch on until 1912, when the US firm Cadillac began fitting them as standard.

Diesel-engine cars
The Citroën Rosalie was the first production car to have a diesel-powered option, in 1933. It used a lot less fuel than a petrol-engine car, making it cheaper to run, but it was much noisier!

1886 · 1896 · 1912 · 1936 · 1964

89

The wheel

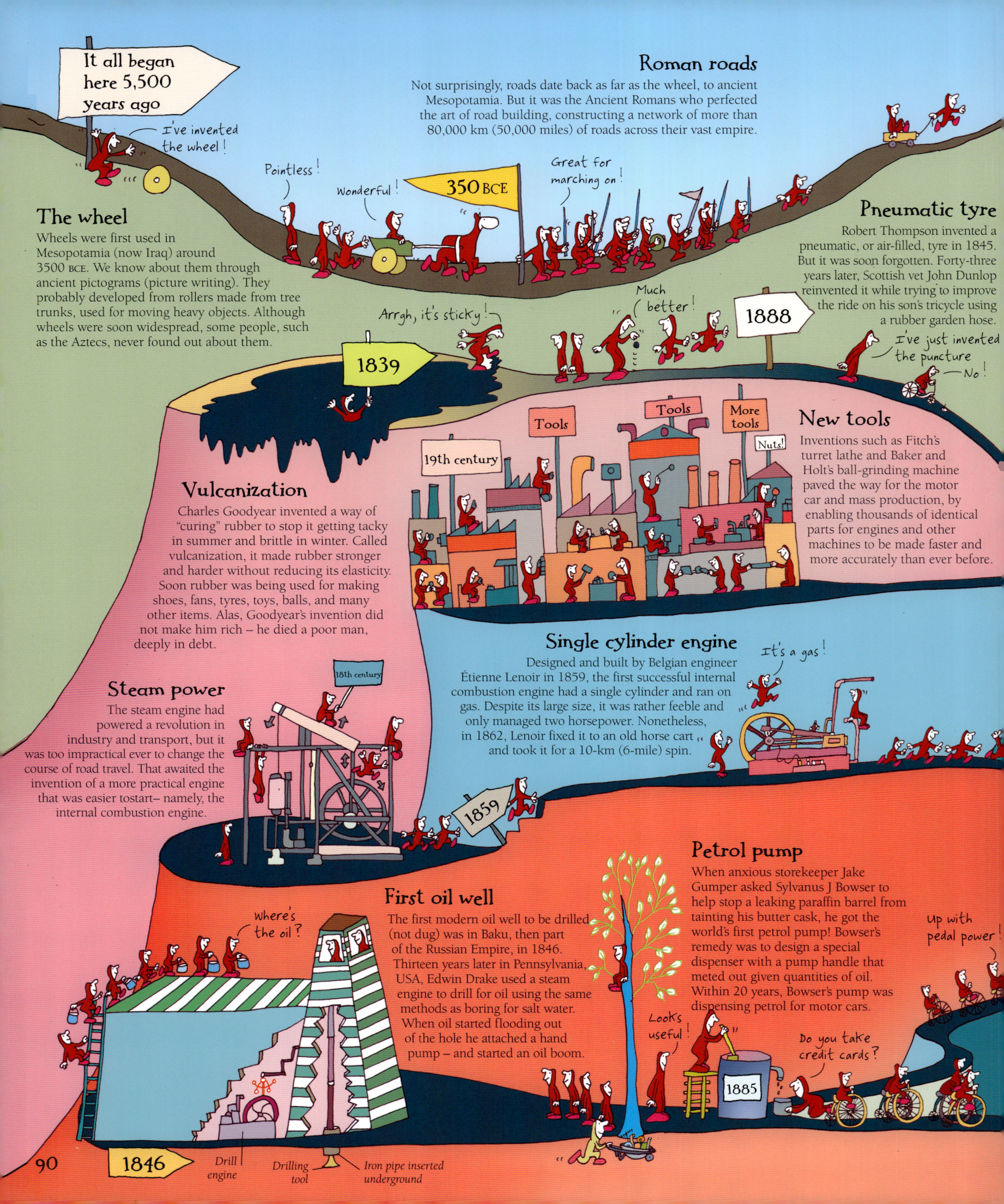

Wheels were first used in Mesopotamia (now Iraq) around 3500 BCE. We know about them through ancient pictograms (picture writing). They probably developed from rollers made from tree trunks, used for moving heavy objects. Although wheels were soon widespread, some people, such as the Aztecs, never found out about them.

Roman roads

Not surprisingly, roads date back as far as the wheel, to ancient Mesopotamia. But it was the Ancient Romans who perfected the art of road building, constructing a network of more than 80,000 km (50,000 miles) of roads across their vast empire.

Pneumatic tyre

Robert Thompson invented a pneumatic, or air-filled, tyre in 1845. But it was soon forgotten. Forty-three years later, Scottish vet John Dunlop reinvented it while trying to improve the ride on his son's tricycle using a rubber garden hose.

Vulcanization

Charles Goodyear invented a way of "curing" rubber to stop it getting tacky in summer and brittle in winter. Called vulcanization, it made rubber stronger and harder without reducing its elasticity. Soon rubber was being used for making shoes, fans, tyres, toys, balls, and many other items. Alas, Goodyear's invention did not make him rich – he died a poor man, deeply in debt.

New tools

Inventions such as Fitch's turret lathe and Baker and Holt's ball-grinding machine paved the way for the motor car and mass production, by enabling thousands of identical parts for engines and other machines to be made faster and more accurately than ever before.

Steam power

The steam engine had powered a revolution in industry and transport, but it was too impractical ever to change the course of road travel. That awaited the invention of a more practical engine that was easier to start – namely, the internal combustion engine.

Single cylinder engine

Designed and built by Belgian engineer Étienne Lenoir in 1859, the first successful internal combustion engine had a single cylinder and ran on gas. Despite its large size, it was rather feeble and only managed two horsepower. Nonetheless, in 1862, Lenoir fixed it to an old horse cart and took it for a 10-km (6-mile) spin.

First oil well

The first modern oil well to be drilled (not dug) was in Baku, then part of the Russian Empire, in 1846. Thirteen years later in Pennsylvania, USA, Edwin Drake used a steam engine to drill for oil using the same methods as boring for salt water. When oil started flooding out of the hole he attached a hand pump – and started an oil boom.

Petrol pump

When anxious storekeeper Jake Gumper asked Sylvanus J Bowser to help stop a leaking paraffin barrel from tainting his butter cask, he got the world's first petrol pump! Bowser's remedy was to design a special dispenser with a pump handle that meted out given quantities of oil. Within 20 years, Bowser's pump was dispensing petrol for motor cars.

McAdam's macadam roads

John McAdam devised a new road-building technique using tightly packed soil covered in stones and smaller pebbles. Passing carriages would crush the pebbles, filling in any gaps and making the surface watertight.

These roads are really hard-wearing!

They're cheap to build too!

First motorway

As more cars were made, bigger and better roads had to be built. The first dual-carriage motorway dates from 1921, when the Germans opened the Avus Autobahn in Berlin. Only 10 km (6 miles) long, it had a loop at either end so it could double as a racetrack.

Consumer age

When companies started adopting Ford's methods of mass production, more and more goods were made cheaper and faster than ever before. "Buy now, pay later" policies brought cars, cookers, fridges, and food mixers within the reach of millions, and by the 1950s the consumer age was in full swing.

If my neighbour's got one, I want one!

It's nonstop!

Modern assembly line

US car manufacturer Henry Ford transformed factory production by inventing the modern assembly line. Workers were each given one task to perform and, instead of walking from car to car, they stood still and waited for the cars to come to them. The time taken to build a car shrank from 12 hours to one and a half!

Otto cycle

In 1876, German engineer Nikolaus Otto invented the engine cycle that still bears his name. Alphonse Beau de Rochas had first described a four-stroke cycle in 1861, but Otto reinvented it, and was soon putting it to the test in his new line of gas engines.

Did I hear someone invented a bike with an engine?

Motorbike

When Gottlieb Daimler developed the petrol engine, instead of putting it straight onto a carriage, he built a wooden bike and tested it on that. He'd just invented the motorbike! But it was nine years before motorbikes went into production.

Hey, the one in front's not pedalling!

BY LAND, SEA, AND AIR

Many inventions contributed to the success of the motor car and the petrol engine, from wheels and roads to turret lathes and petrol pumps. But there was more to come. In 1892, Rudolf Diesel invented a new kind of internal combustion engine, ideal for powering heavy machinery, ships, and locomotives. In 1903, the Wright brothers took to the skies. And by 1937, Frank Whittle had built the world's first jet engine, giving rise to a new age in air transport.

continued...

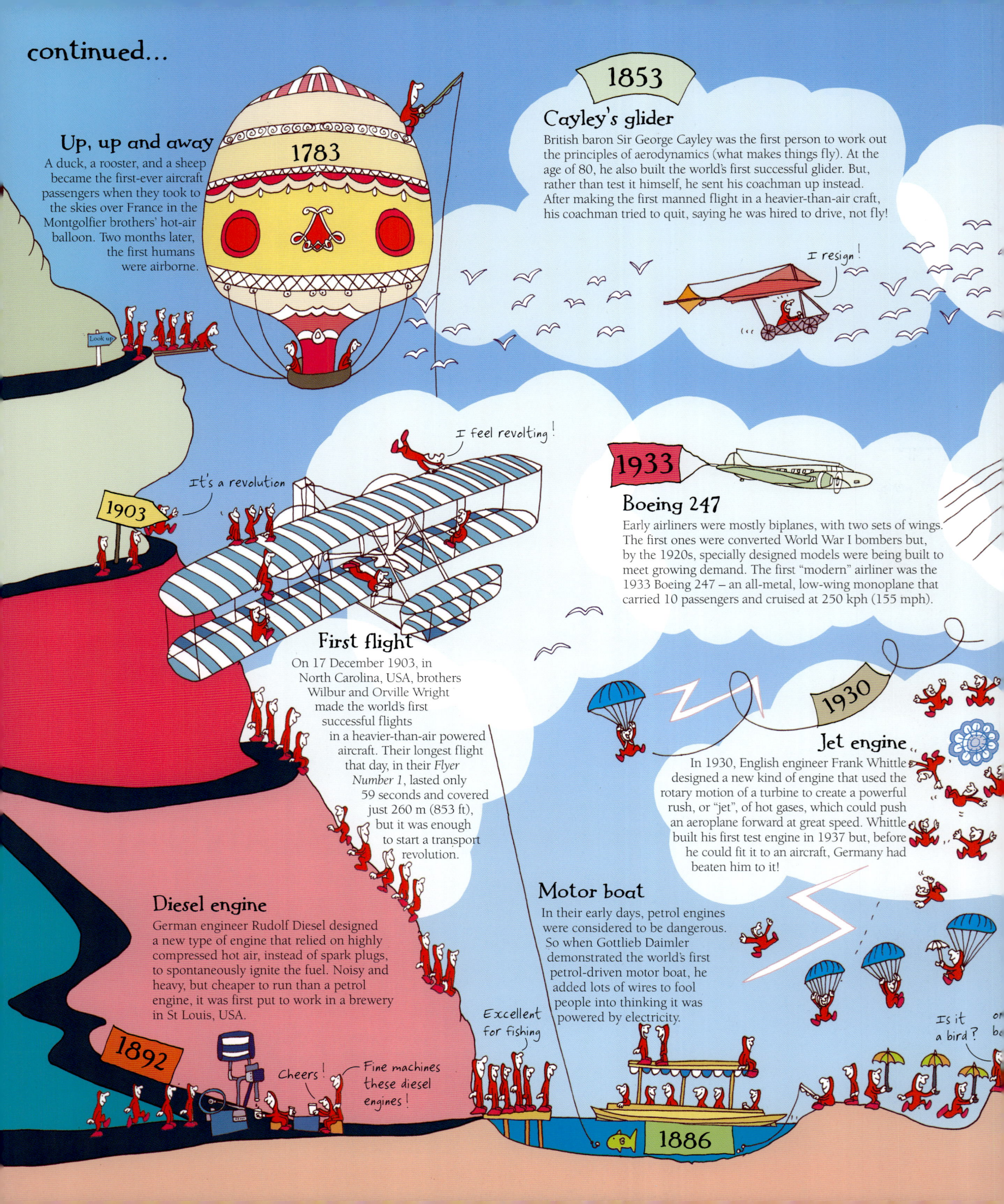

Up, up and away
A duck, a rooster, and a sheep became the first-ever aircraft passengers when they took to the skies over France in the Montgolfier brothers' hot-air balloon. Two months later, the first humans were airborne.

1783

1853
Cayley's glider
British baron Sir George Cayley was the first person to work out the principles of aerodynamics (what makes things fly). At the age of 80, he also built the world's first successful glider. But, rather than test it himself, he sent his coachman up instead. After making the first manned flight in a heavier-than-air craft, his coachman tried to quit, saying he was hired to drive, not fly!

I resign!

I feel revolting!

It's a revolution

1903

1933
Boeing 247
Early airliners were mostly biplanes, with two sets of wings. The first ones were converted World War I bombers but, by the 1920s, specially designed models were being built to meet growing demand. The first "modern" airliner was the 1933 Boeing 247 – an all-metal, low-wing monoplane that carried 10 passengers and cruised at 250 kph (155 mph).

First flight
On 17 December 1903, in North Carolina, USA, brothers Wilbur and Orville Wright made the world's first successful flights in a heavier-than-air powered aircraft. Their longest flight that day, in their *Flyer Number 1*, lasted only 59 seconds and covered just 260 m (853 ft), but it was enough to start a transport revolution.

1930
Jet engine
In 1930, English engineer Frank Whittle designed a new kind of engine that used the rotary motion of a turbine to create a powerful rush, or "jet", of hot gases, which could push an aeroplane forward at great speed. Whittle built his first test engine in 1937 but, before he could fit it to an aircraft, Germany had beaten him to it!

Diesel engine
German engineer Rudolf Diesel designed a new type of engine that relied on highly compressed hot air, instead of spark plugs, to spontaneously ignite the fuel. Noisy and heavy, but cheaper to run than a petrol engine, it was first put to work in a brewery in St Louis, USA.

Motor boat
In their early days, petrol engines were considered to be dangerous. So when Gottlieb Daimler demonstrated the world's first petrol-driven motor boat, he added lots of wires to fool people into thinking it was powered by electricity.

1892

Cheers! *Fine machines these diesel engines!*

Excellent for fishing

1886

Is it a bird?

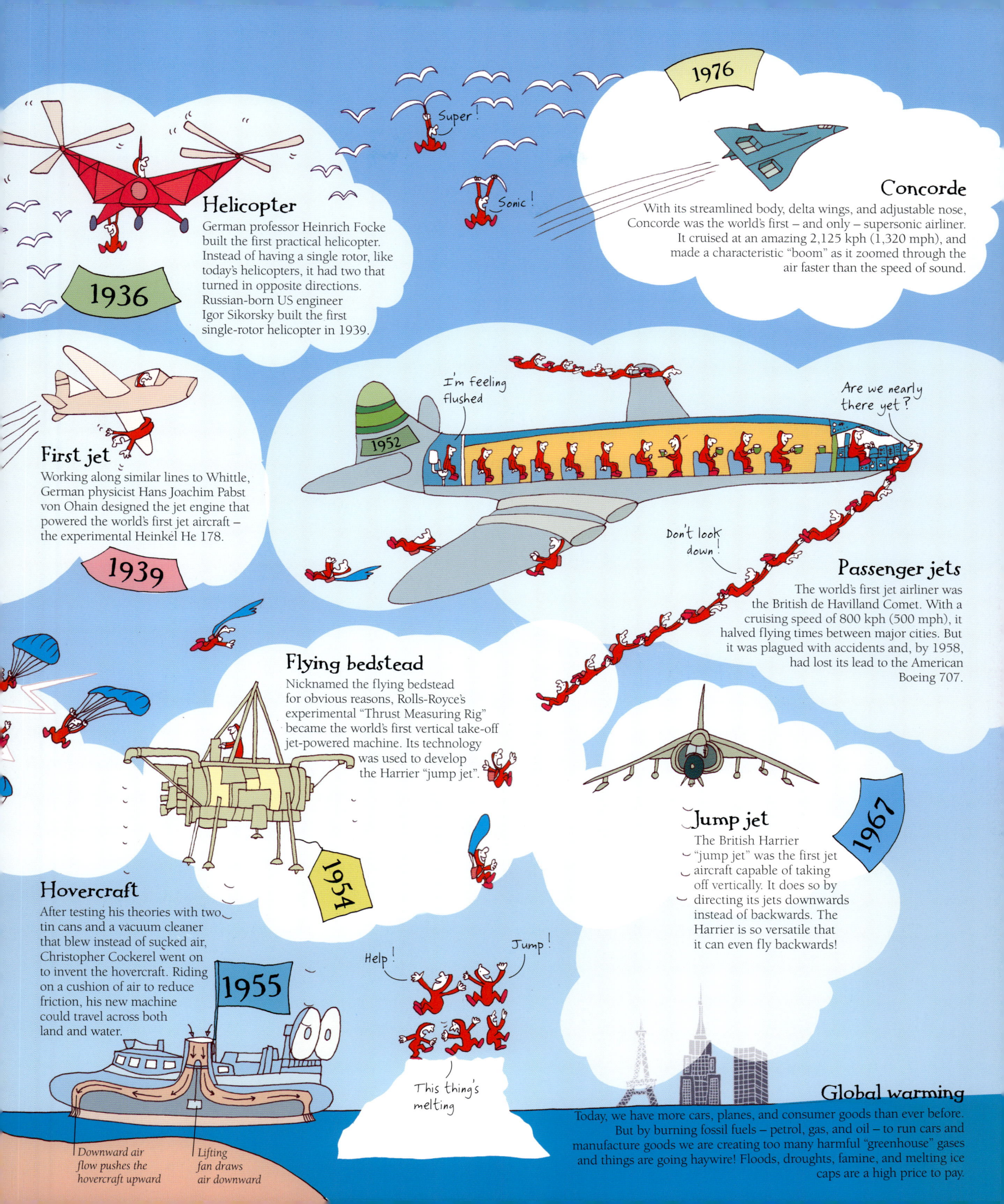

Helicopter
German professor Heinrich Focke built the first practical helicopter. Instead of having a single rotor, like today's helicopters, it had two that turned in opposite directions. Russian-born US engineer Igor Sikorsky built the first single-rotor helicopter in 1939.

1936

1976

Concorde
With its streamlined body, delta wings, and adjustable nose, Concorde was the world's first – and only – supersonic airliner. It cruised at an amazing 2,125 kph (1,320 mph), and made a characteristic "boom" as it zoomed through the air faster than the speed of sound.

Super!
Sonic!

First jet
Working along similar lines to Whittle, German physicist Hans Joachim Pabst von Ohain designed the jet engine that powered the world's first jet aircraft – the experimental Heinkel He 178.

1939

I'm feeling flushed
1952
Are we nearly there yet?
Don't look down!

Passenger jets
The world's first jet airliner was the British de Havilland Comet. With a cruising speed of 800 kph (500 mph), it halved flying times between major cities. But it was plagued with accidents and, by 1958, had lost its lead to the American Boeing 707.

Flying bedstead
Nicknamed the flying bedstead for obvious reasons, Rolls-Royce's experimental "Thrust Measuring Rig" became the world's first vertical take-off jet-powered machine. Its technology was used to develop the Harrier "jump jet".

1954

Jump jet
The British Harrier "jump jet" was the first jet aircraft capable of taking off vertically. It does so by directing its jets downwards instead of backwards. The Harrier is so versatile that it can even fly backwards!

1967

Hovercraft
After testing his theories with two tin cans and a vacuum cleaner that blew instead of sucked air, Christopher Cockerel went on to invent the hovercraft. Riding on a cushion of air to reduce friction, his new machine could travel across both land and water.

1955

Help! *Jump!*
This thing's melting

Downward air flow pushes the hovercraft upward
Lifting fan draws air downward

Global warming
Today, we have more cars, planes, and consumer goods than ever before. But by burning fossil fuels – petrol, gas, and oil – to run cars and manufacture goods we are creating too many harmful "greenhouse" gases and things are going haywire! Floods, droughts, famine, and melting ice caps are a high price to pay.

FABULOUS FLOPS

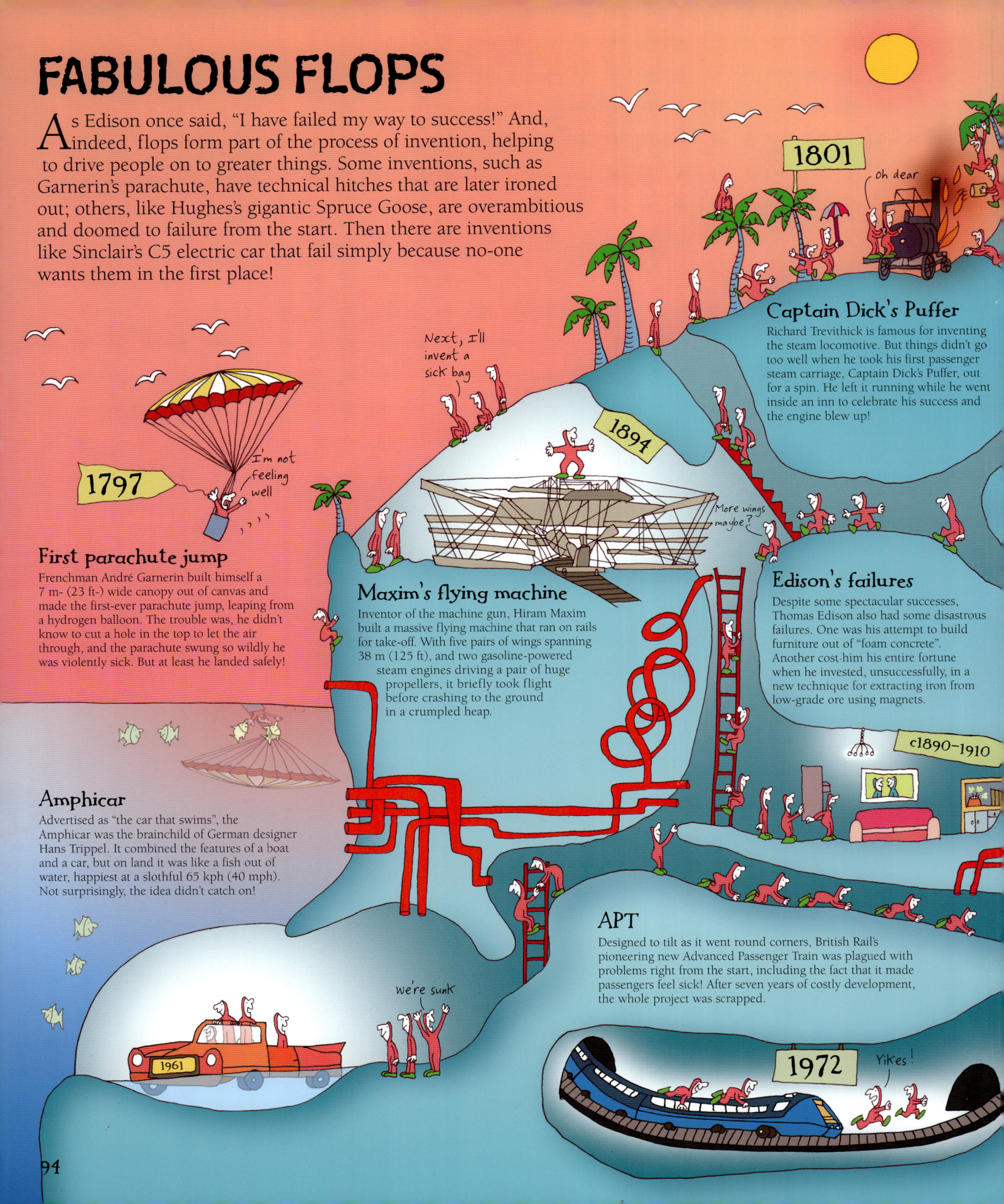

As Edison once said, "I have failed my way to success!" And, indeed, flops form part of the process of invention, helping to drive people on to greater things. Some inventions, such as Garnerin's parachute, have technical hitches that are later ironed out; others, like Hughes's gigantic Spruce Goose, are overambitious and doomed to failure from the start. Then there are inventions like Sinclair's C5 electric car that fail simply because no-one wants them in the first place!

Captain Dick's Puffer
Richard Trevithick is famous for inventing the steam locomotive. But things didn't go too well when he took his first passenger steam carriage, Captain Dick's Puffer, out for a spin. He left it running while he went inside an inn to celebrate his success and the engine blew up!

First parachute jump
Frenchman André Garnerin built himself a 7 m- (23 ft-) wide canopy out of canvas and made the first-ever parachute jump, leaping from a hydrogen balloon. The trouble was, he didn't know to cut a hole in the top to let the air through, and the parachute swung so wildly he was violently sick. But at least he landed safely!

Maxim's flying machine
Inventor of the machine gun, Hiram Maxim built a massive flying machine that ran on rails for take-off. With five pairs of wings spanning 38 m (125 ft), and two gasoline-powered steam engines driving a pair of huge propellers, it briefly took flight before crashing to the ground in a crumpled heap.

Edison's failures
Despite some spectacular successes, Thomas Edison also had some disastrous failures. One was his attempt to build furniture out of "foam concrete". Another cost him his entire fortune when he invested, unsuccessfully, in a new technique for extracting iron from low-grade ore using magnets.

Amphicar
Advertised as "the car that swims", the Amphicar was the brainchild of German designer Hans Trippel. It combined the features of a boat and a car, but on land it was like a fish out of water, happiest at a slothful 65 kph (40 mph). Not surprisingly, the idea didn't catch on!

APT
Designed to tilt as it went round corners, British Rail's pioneering new Advanced Passenger Train was plagued with problems right from the start, including the fact that it made passengers feel sick! After seven years of costly development, the whole project was scrapped.

Aerial steam carriage

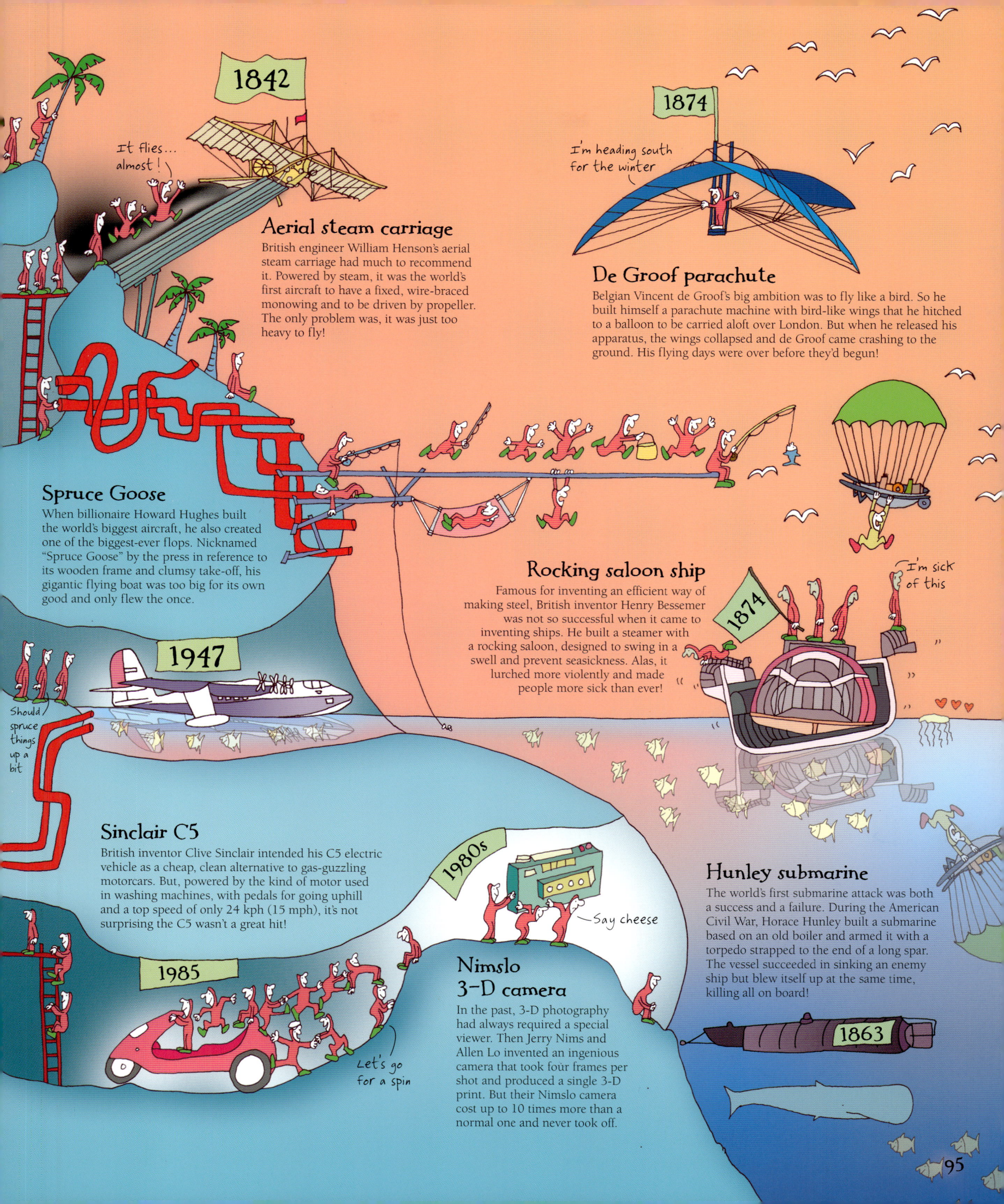

British engineer William Henson's aerial steam carriage had much to recommend it. Powered by steam, it was the world's first aircraft to have a fixed, wire-braced monowing and to be driven by propeller. The only problem was, it was just too heavy to fly!

De Groof parachute

Belgian Vincent de Groof's big ambition was to fly like a bird. So he built himself a parachute machine with bird-like wings that he hitched to a balloon to be carried aloft over London. But when he released his apparatus, the wings collapsed and de Groof came crashing to the ground. His flying days were over before they'd begun!

Spruce Goose

When billionaire Howard Hughes built the world's biggest aircraft, he also created one of the biggest-ever flops. Nicknamed "Spruce Goose" by the press in reference to its wooden frame and clumsy take-off, his gigantic flying boat was too big for its own good and only flew the once.

Rocking saloon ship

Famous for inventing an efficient way of making steel, British inventor Henry Bessemer was not so successful when it came to inventing ships. He built a steamer with a rocking saloon, designed to swing in a swell and prevent seasickness. Alas, it lurched more violently and made people more sick than ever!

Sinclair C5

British inventor Clive Sinclair intended his C5 electric vehicle as a cheap, clean alternative to gas-guzzling motorcars. But, powered by the kind of motor used in washing machines, with pedals for going uphill and a top speed of only 24 kph (15 mph), it's not surprising the C5 wasn't a great hit!

Nimslo 3-D camera

In the past, 3-D photography had always required a special viewer. Then Jerry Nims and Allen Lo invented an ingenious camera that took four frames per shot and produced a single 3-D print. But their Nimslo camera cost up to 10 times more than a normal one and never took off.

Hunley submarine

The world's first submarine attack was both a success and a failure. During the American Civil War, Horace Hunley built a submarine based on an old boiler and armed it with a torpedo strapped to the end of a long spar. The vessel succeeded in sinking an enemy ship but blew itself up at the same time, killing all on board!

95

SUPER-DUPER COMPUTER

Mechanical calculating machines have been around for more than 350 years. But, following the invention of a device called a "triode valve" in the early 20th century, a new type of calculator was born – the electronic computer. Computers differ from calculators in that they are programmable – that is, they have a memory and can store instructions. Early computers had thousands of valves and took up entire rooms. Then, in 1947, three scientists invented something very small that was to have a very big impact on all our lives – the transistor.

Portraits

John Bardeen

William Shockley

Walter Brattain

US physicists John Bardeen, Walter Brattain, and William Shockley invented the transistor in 1947 and were awarded a Nobel Prize for their outstanding work.

The transistor

Set the task of improving the telephone system, a team of scientists at Bell Telephone Laboratories in the USA transformed electronics by inventing the transistor. It did the work of a triode valve, amplifying electrical signals and acting as a "switch" in computers, but was very much smaller and more reliable. As transistors replaced valves, computers got smaller and cheaper, and their numbers exploded.

Pascal's calculator
1642
French physicist and mathematician Blaise Pascal built an elaborate calculator for his father, who was a tax inspector. Comprising a series of dials and gears, it could only do addition, and even then it wasn't very reliable!

Babbage's analytical engine
1837
Mathematician Charles Babbage designed the world's first mechanical computer. Called an analytical engine, it would have been enormous, powered by steam engine and programmed using punched cards. But only a small section was ever built.

Binary computer
1942
US mathematicians John Atanasoff and Clifford Berry tried to build the first electronic computer based on the binary system. Although they never finished their ABC machine, binary became the basis for all future computers.

Electronic computer
1943
During World War II, British engineer Tommy Flowers built the first-ever electronic computer, designed to break enemy codes. Containing 1,800 valves, his Colossus machine was so secret that, for 50 years, hardly anyone knew it existed!

Computers at home

A modern home computer system is made up of many internal and external elements all linked together, each with its own function. Some elements, such as the keyboard, CD-ROM drive, and microphone, are designed to input information, or data, into the computer; others, such as the microprocessor, graphics card, and RAM, are designed to process or store the data. The screen and printer are known as output units, displaying the end results of a computer's task.

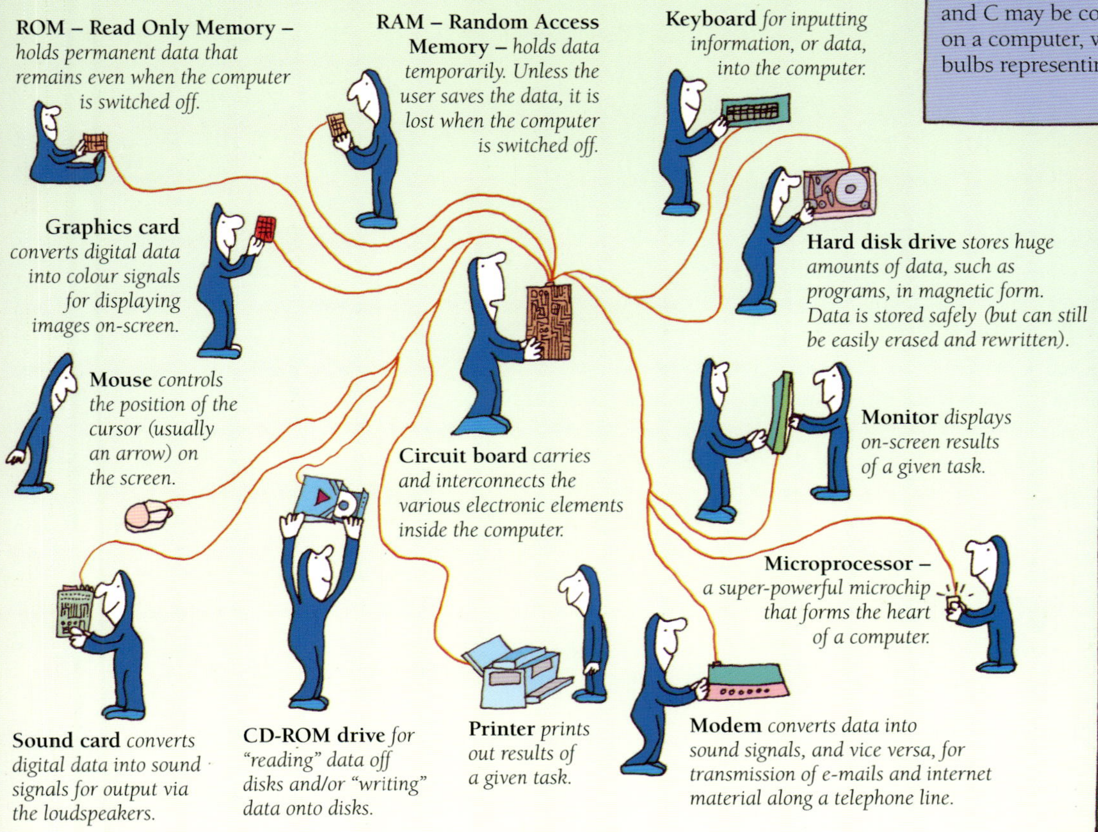

ROM – Read Only Memory – holds permanent data that remains even when the computer is switched off.

RAM – Random Access Memory – holds data temporarily. Unless the user saves the data, it is lost when the computer is switched off.

Keyboard for inputting information, or data, into the computer.

Graphics card converts digital data into colour signals for displaying images on-screen.

Hard disk drive stores huge amounts of data, such as programs, in magnetic form. Data is stored safely (but can still be easily erased and rewritten).

Mouse controls the position of the cursor (usually an arrow) on the screen.

Circuit board carries and interconnects the various electronic elements inside the computer.

Monitor displays on-screen results of a given task.

Microprocessor – a super-powerful microchip that forms the heart of a computer.

Sound card converts digital data into sound signals for output via the loudspeakers.

CD-ROM drive for "reading" data off disks and/or "writing" data onto disks.

Printer prints out results of a given task.

Modem converts data into sound signals, and vice versa, for transmission of e-mails and internet material along a telephone line.

Binary at work

Modern computers operate using a system called binary code. All information is represented as coded sequences of "0"s and "1"s. The transistors act like switches, usually with "off" corresponding to "0" and "on" to "1". This diagram shows how the letters A, B, and C may be coded on a computer, with lit bulbs representing "1".

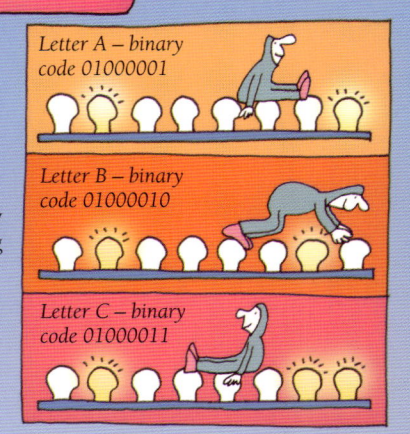

Letter A – binary code 01000001
Letter B – binary code 01000010
Letter C – binary code 01000011

The mighty microchip

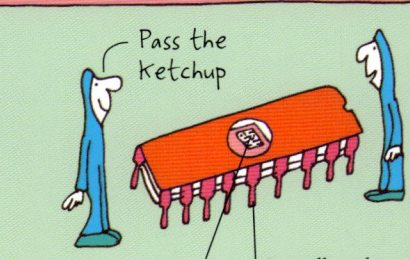

Pass the ketchup

Chip contains thousands of components

Pins allow chip to be plugged into the circuit board

In 1958, electronics experts Jack Kilby and Robert Noyce independently devised ways of integrating miniature transistors and other components into small slices, or chips, of silicon or similar material. Smaller than a penny, yet capable of carrying out a vast number of operations, microchips ultimately brought computers out of the science laboratory and into the home.

Monster machine

1945

This is the compact model!

The first "known" electronic computer was called ENIAC. Built by US scientists to do maths for the military, it had over 18,000 valves, weighed as much as six elephants, and took up a whole room. Even so, in modern terms it wasn't very fast!

Programmable computers

1949

Now do as you're told!

EDSAC   PRO ZAK   UNIVAC

Early machines weren't "real" computers because they could not be programmed (store instructions). The first to do so was called EDSAC, built by a team at Cambridge University, England. The Americans soon followed with BINAC and UNIVAC computers.

Supercomputers

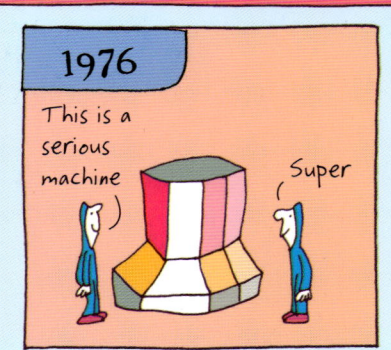

1976

This is a serious machine   *Super*

Really serious mathematics requires really serious computers. The Cray-1 was the first of a new generation of "supercomputers", designed by US engineer Seymour Cray to carry out upwards of 240 million calculations per second.

Personal computing

1977

Fantastic – what is it?   *It'll never catch on!*

Small desktop computers only became possible with the invention of the microprocessor. The first successful one, complete with keyboard and screen, was the Apple II, designed by US techies Steve Jobs and Steve Wozniak.

Semaphore telegraph

Since ancient times people have used smoke signals and drums to send simple messages. The Romans were the first to devise a system of flag waving to spell out words. Then, in 1791, Frenchman Claude Chappé updated the idea by inventing the semaphore telegraph. This comprised a network of wooden posts with hinged "arms" for sending coded messages over long distances.

Edison phonograph

Whilst seeking ways of recording telegraph messages, American inventor Thomas Edison came up with one of his greatest inventions – the phonograph. Sound was recorded using a needle vibrating against a revolving cylinder wrapped in tin foil. For playback, the process was simply repeated, and the vibrations transformed back into sound.

Electric telegraph

Communications were revolutionized when British inventors William Cooke and Charles Wheatstone devised a way of sending messages using electric signals. Their telegraph machine had five needles pointing to 20 letters of the alphabet, so it was hard luck if you wanted to send words with Q, X, or Z!

Microphone

English music professor David Hughes is credited with inventing the first truly effective microphone. Made up of three ordinary nails and some loose wire, his experimental model was so sensitive it could detect a fly's footstep.

Radio broadcasting

It was a big step from wireless telegraphy to broadcasting music and speech over the airwaves. American Reginald Fessenden made the first advertised radio broadcast on Christmas Eve, 1906. By the mid-1920s, public broadcasting was becoming all the rage, with people eagerly tuning in on their new wireless sets.

Wireless telegraphy

The electric telegraph relied on wires to transmit coded messages. Then Italian inventor Guglielmo Marconi invented a way of sending telegraph signals through the air using radio waves instead of electricity. In 1901, he managed to send the first wireless telegraph message across the Atlantic – it was the letter "S"!

Telephone

Electric telegraphy was ideal for sending coded messages over long distances. But Scottish-born inventor Alexander Graham Bell wanted to find a way of transmitting speech. The result was the telephone, in which electrical signals imitate the vibrations of the human voice.

Magnetic recording
1898

In designing the first telephone answering machine, Danish telephone engineer Valdemar Poulsen invented a new way of recording sound, using magnetism. He made recordings by magnetizing piano wire, but the technology didn't really take off until the 1930s, when the first modern tape recorder was invented using plastic tape.

Laser
1960

Just as transistors were designed to amplify electronic signals, so lasers were designed to amplify light. US physicist Theodore Maiman built the first working laser, producing an intense beam of pure light in which the waves were all in step with each other. Within a few years lasers had been put to work in surgery, surveying, metal cutting, and holograms.

Berliner gramophone
1888

It was German engineer Emile Berliner who switched from using cylinders to flat disks for recording sound. The forerunner of the more modern record player, his gramophone produced better sound than Edison's phonograph and soon records were being mass-produced in their thousands.

Triode valve
1906

When US inventor Lee De Forest invented the triode valve, it heralded the dawn of the age of electronics. Looking rather like a light bulb, it was designed to detect radio waves and control electric current. Later, valves came into their own boosting radio and television signals, amplifying sound in record players, and acting as "switches" in computers.

LET'S ALL COMMUNICATE

The transistor not only transformed computer technology, it revolutionized entertainment and communications as well. By packing the power of its predecessor – the triode valve – into a tiny component, it gave rise to a host of smaller, cheaper devices, from transistor radios to portable television sets, and record players. And as it shrunk still further in size, becoming the essential component of microchips, it went on to shape the world we know today.

Radar
1935

Scottish engineer Robert Watson-Watt employed valves in his "radio detection and ranging" system. Better known as radar, it involved bouncing radio waves off enemy aircraft and using the echo to pinpoint the aircraft's distance.

Transistor radio
1954

Early radio sets were large and clumsy, and used a device called a "cat's whisker" or, later, valves to receive radio signals. But with the invention of the transistor, small portable radios became feasible. The first transistor radio was the American Regency TR1 – small enough to fit in a pocket.

continued...

1982
Compact disc player
Electronics giants Sony and Philips pooled resources to invent a new kind of music playback system – the compact disc player. Making full use of laser technology, sound information is stored as a series of pits on the surface of the disk and played back using a laser beam.

1998
MP3 player
The latest way to buy music is to download it from the Internet, using a compression system called MP3. Developed by the Fraunhofer Institut in Germany, MP3 can shrink an audio file down to one-twelfth of its size with little loss of quality.

Microchips and microprocessors
The next big leap forward in electronics was the invention in 1958 of the microchip, followed in 1971 by the more powerful microprocessor. Not only were TVs, radios, and computers transformed yet again, but a host of new devices such as mobile phones, digital cameras, and CD players also came on the scene. Today, everything from washing machines to motorcars contains a microprocessor!

1947

1973
Mobile phone
The first mobile phone was demonstrated by Motorola in 1973. Then, in 1979, Bell Telephone Laboratories developed the "cellular" system for transmitting calls by radio wave. This involved setting up a network of small areas, or cells, each with its own localized transmitter. Early mobile phones were too big and heavy to carry around, but they got smaller after going digital in 1991.

1897
Cathode ray tube
German physicist Ferdinand Braun invented a device for moving a beam of electrons across a screen coated with phosphorescent powder. Where the beam hit the screen the powder glowed, creating patterns of light. Thirty years on, his "cathode ray tube" would form the basis of electronic television.

1926
Baird television
Scottish inventor John Logie Baird was the first to demonstrate television, using a series of spinning disks to transmit an image of a ventriloquist's dummy. His device was mechanical, rather than electronic, and was doomed to be overtaken by developments in America and Britain.

1928
Electronic television
Television was pioneered in America by self-taught whizz kid Philo T Farnsworth. He gave the first demonstration of an all-electronic television system, complete with valves and cathode ray tube.

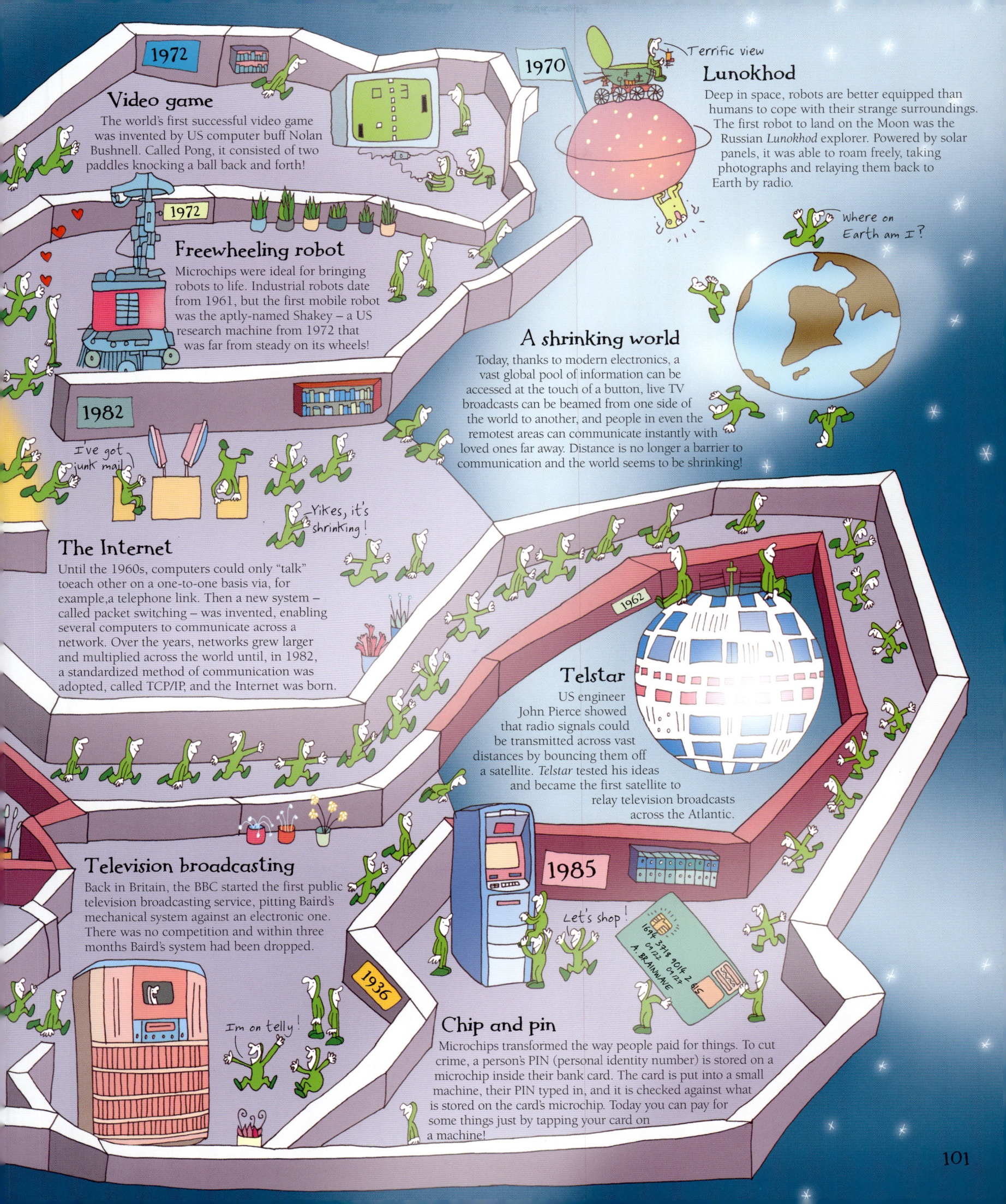

1972
Video game
The world's first successful video game was invented by US computer buff Nolan Bushnell. Called Pong, it consisted of two paddles knocking a ball back and forth!

1972
Freewheeling robot
Microchips were ideal for bringing robots to life. Industrial robots date from 1961, but the first mobile robot was the aptly-named Shakey – a US research machine from 1972 that was far from steady on its wheels!

1982
The Internet
Until the 1960s, computers could only "talk" to each other on a one-to-one basis via, for example, a telephone link. Then a new system – called packet switching – was invented, enabling several computers to communicate across a network. Over the years, networks grew larger and multiplied across the world until, in 1982, a standardized method of communication was adopted, called TCP/IP, and the Internet was born.

Television broadcasting
Back in Britain, the BBC started the first public television broadcasting service, pitting Baird's mechanical system against an electronic one. There was no competition and within three months Baird's system had been dropped.

1936

1970
Lunokhod
Terrific view

Deep in space, robots are better equipped than humans to cope with their strange surroundings. The first robot to land on the Moon was the Russian *Lunokhod* explorer. Powered by solar panels, it was able to roam freely, taking photographs and relaying them back to Earth by radio.

Where on Earth am I?

A shrinking world
Today, thanks to modern electronics, a vast global pool of information can be accessed at the touch of a button, live TV broadcasts can be beamed from one side of the world to another, and people in even the remotest areas can communicate instantly with loved ones far away. Distance is no longer a barrier to communication and the world seems to be shrinking!

I've got junk mail

Yikes, it's shrinking!

1962
Telstar
US engineer John Pierce showed that radio signals could be transmitted across vast distances by bouncing them off a satellite. *Telstar* tested his ideas and became the first satellite to relay television broadcasts across the Atlantic.

1985
Chip and pin
Let's shop!

Microchips transformed the way people paid for things. To cut crime, a person's PIN (personal identity number) is stored on a microchip inside their bank card. The card is put into a small machine, their PIN typed in, and it is checked against what is stored on the card's microchip. Today you can pay for some things just by tapping your card on a machine!

I'm on telly!

101

THE FUTURE

And what of the future? We can get some clue to what it promises by looking at ideas currently being developed, such as growing organs for transplant, harnessing nuclear fusion for pollution-free energy, and building hotels in space. But some concepts, such as travelling through time and making contact with alien life forms, are still so remote that they belong more to works of fiction than to any realistic vision of the future.

Fuel cells

The idea of combining hydrogen with oxygen to make water and release energy dates back to 1838, when Welsh judge William Grove designed the first fuel cell. Since then, fuel cells have been much improved and successfully used to power space flights. But, more importantly, they could help solve our energy crisis by providing pollution-free power for the motorcar.

Solar cars

In 1987, Australia staged the first World Solar Challenge, in which solar cars competed in a 3,000 km (1,864 mile) journey across the continent. In 2005, Nuno 3 was the first to achieve an average speed of more than 100 kph (62 mph). But, if solar cars represent the future of motoring, nobody's going to get very far on a cloudy day!

Nanotechnology

The latest thing in electronics is "nanotechnology" – that is, technology that works on a scale of one billionth (1,000,000,000th) of a metre. It involves creating minuscule machines out of individual molecules that, one day, may be used to fight disease, clean up pollution, and make enough food to feed the world.

Space hotels

Space tourism is already a reality, with some companies aiming to build hotels in space by the year 2027. Shaped like ring doughnuts, such hotels would spin round a central axis to create a sense of gravity in space.

Time travel

According to Einstein, time slows down the faster you travel, and stops altogether when you reach the speed of light. In theory, this means that, by travelling faster than the speed of light, you could go backwards in time. But, as we can only travel at a fraction of light speed, time travel may be a very long way off!

Silent aircraft

In an attempt to make noisy aircraft a thing of the past, Cambridge University and the Massachusetts Institute of Technology have joined forces to design a new generation of aircraft that will be so quiet that no-one will hear them outside an airport.

Implanting ideas

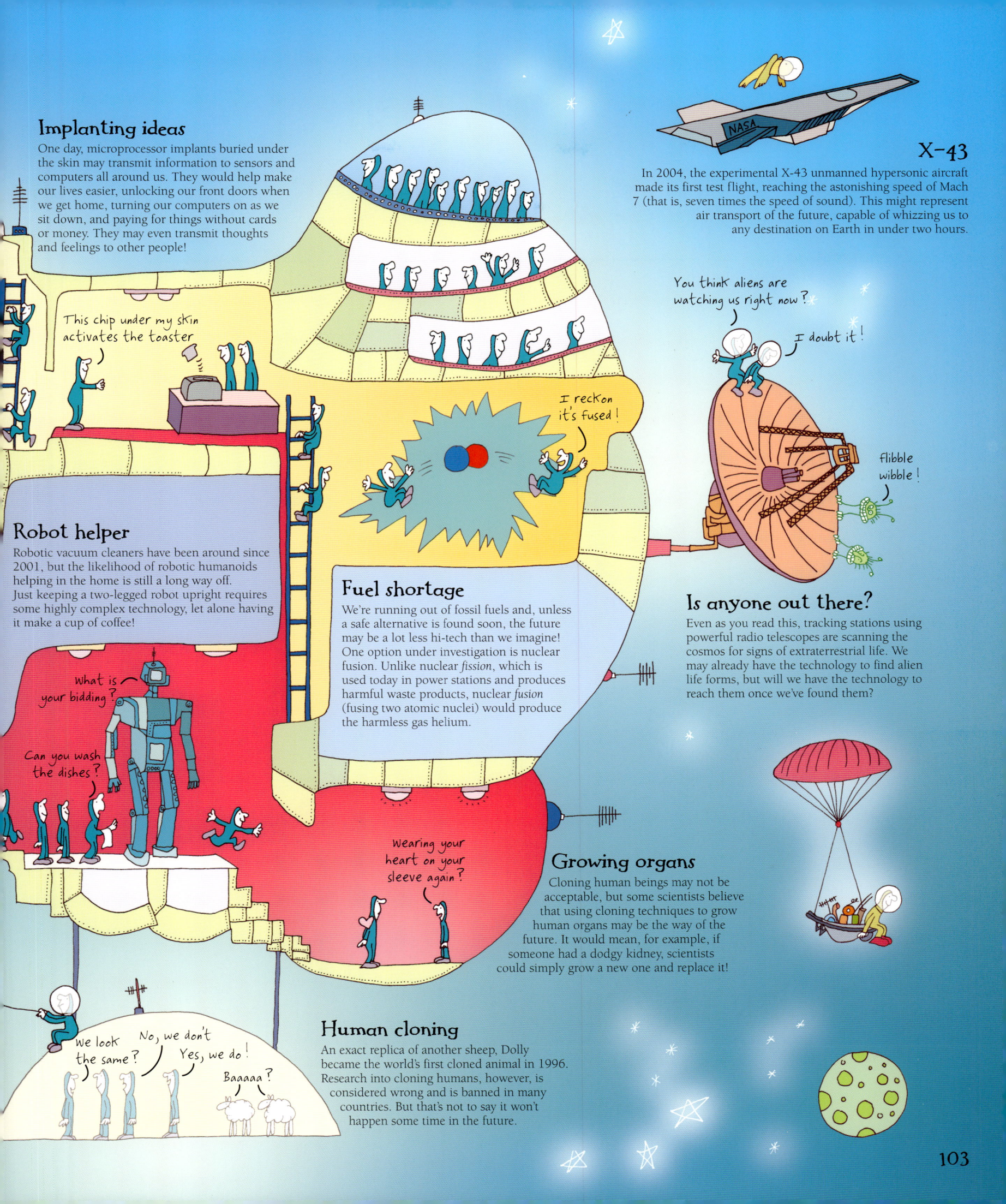

One day, microprocessor implants buried under the skin may transmit information to sensors and computers all around us. They would help make our lives easier, unlocking our front doors when we get home, turning our computers on as we sit down, and paying for things without cards or money. They may even transmit thoughts and feelings to other people!

X-43

In 2004, the experimental X-43 unmanned hypersonic aircraft made its first test flight, reaching the astonishing speed of Mach 7 (that is, seven times the speed of sound). This might represent air transport of the future, capable of whizzing us to any destination on Earth in under two hours.

Robot helper

Robotic vacuum cleaners have been around since 2001, but the likelihood of robotic humanoids helping in the home is still a long way off. Just keeping a two-legged robot upright requires some highly complex technology, let alone having it make a cup of coffee!

Fuel shortage

We're running out of fossil fuels and, unless a safe alternative is found soon, the future may be a lot less hi-tech than we imagine! One option under investigation is nuclear fusion. Unlike nuclear *fission*, which is used today in power stations and produces harmful waste products, nuclear *fusion* (fusing two atomic nuclei) would produce the harmless gas helium.

Is anyone out there?

Even as you read this, tracking stations using powerful radio telescopes are scanning the cosmos for signs of extraterrestrial life. We may already have the technology to find alien life forms, but will we have the technology to reach them once we've found them?

Growing organs

Cloning human beings may not be acceptable, but some scientists believe that using cloning techniques to grow human organs may be the way of the future. It would mean, for example, if someone had a dodgy kidney, scientists could simply grow a new one and replace it!

Human cloning

An exact replica of another sheep, Dolly became the world's first cloned animal in 1996. Research into cloning humans, however, is considered wrong and is banned in many countries. But that's not to say it won't happen some time in the future.

103

Bow and arrow

Cave paintings thousands of years old show people hunting with bows and arrows. Such weapons had a longer range than spears, which made them safer for hunting ferocious beasts. Later, bows and arrows became useful as weapons of war.

Crossbow

The Chinese invented the first mechanical device for pulling back the string of a bow to increase the projectile power of an arrow. Their new weapon was the crossbow. More deadly than a bow and arrow, it had the disadvantage of taking longer to reload, leaving the user vulnerable to attack.

Rocket power

The Chinese invented fireworks around 1000 CE, using gunpowder to make loud bangs and bursts of flame. Within 200 years they had developed the first rocket fireworks, later adapting them for military use by attaching explosive charges.

Catapult

Like bows and arrows, catapults work using the tension of a tightly stretched drawstring or rope. Greek engineers built the first catapults, but soon the Romans were using them to hurl darts or boulders at the enemy in battle or siege warfare. Huge catapults called ballista were capable of hurling rocks weighing 20 kg (44 lb) over 350 m (1,148 ft).

OFF WITH A BANG!

Following the invention of gunpowder, weapons relying on tension were slowly phased out in favour of cannons. As these and their successors – the big guns – became more sophisticated, people found novel ways of using them, building heavily armed warships and land vehicles. Torpedoes, bombs, and high explosives also demanded new forms of delivery, giving rise to submarines, fighting aircraft, and rockets. Then the Americans invented the atomic bomb – the most terrifying weapon of them all.

Cannon

Early cannons were built in a similar way to beer barrels, with iron staves held in place by iron hoops. This made them dangerous weapons in more ways than one, as likely to blow up in the user's face as damage enemy fortifications.

War chariot

Four-wheeled battlewagons were developed in Mesopotamia (now modern Iraq) from oxcarts, but they were very clumsy. Switching from four to two wheels, lightening the construction, and replacing oxen with horses resulted in a more mobile and menacing machine – the war chariot.

Trireme

The Minoans of Crete built the first navy more than 4,000 years ago, but it was the Greeks who built the first truly impressive warships. Called triremes, they had three banks of oars and were capable of reaching speeds of over eight knots.

Nitroglycerine

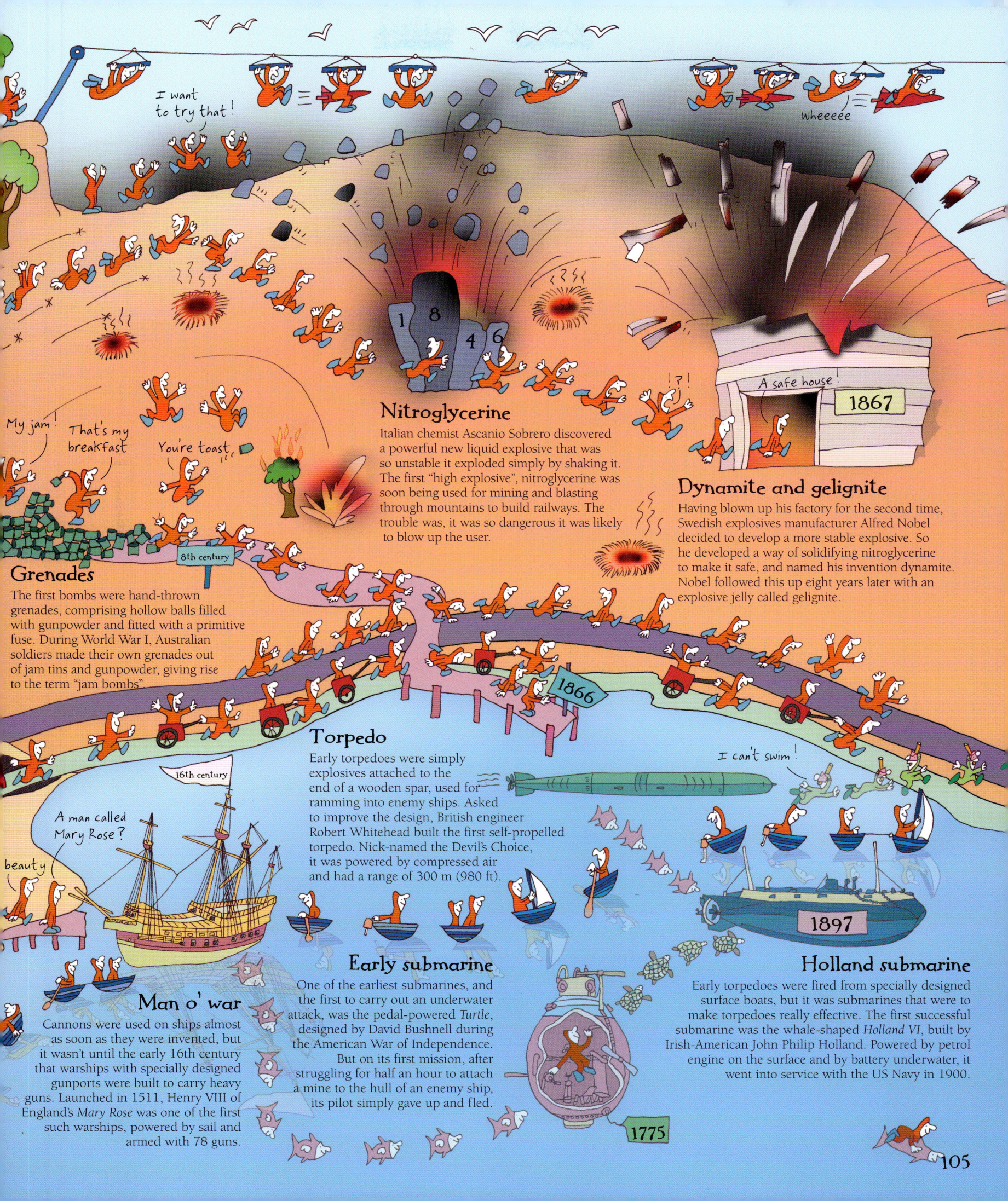

Italian chemist Ascanio Sobrero discovered a powerful new liquid explosive that was so unstable it exploded simply by shaking it. The first "high explosive", nitroglycerine was soon being used for mining and blasting through mountains to build railways. The trouble was, it was so dangerous it was likely to blow up the user.

Dynamite and gelignite

Having blown up his factory for the second time, Swedish explosives manufacturer Alfred Nobel decided to develop a more stable explosive. So he developed a way of solidifying nitroglycerine to make it safe, and named his invention dynamite. Nobel followed this up eight years later with an explosive jelly called gelignite.

Grenades

The first bombs were hand-thrown grenades, comprising hollow balls filled with gunpowder and fitted with a primitive fuse. During World War I, Australian soldiers made their own grenades out of jam tins and gunpowder, giving rise to the term "jam bombs".

Torpedo

Early torpedoes were simply explosives attached to the end of a wooden spar, used for ramming into enemy ships. Asked to improve the design, British engineer Robert Whitehead built the first self-propelled torpedo. Nick-named the Devil's Choice, it was powered by compressed air and had a range of 300 m (980 ft).

Early submarine

One of the earliest submarines, and the first to carry out an underwater attack, was the pedal-powered *Turtle*, designed by David Bushnell during the American War of Independence. But on its first mission, after struggling for half an hour to attach a mine to the hull of an enemy ship, its pilot simply gave up and fled.

Holland submarine

Early torpedoes were fired from specially designed surface boats, but it was submarines that were to make torpedoes really effective. The first successful submarine was the whale-shaped *Holland VI*, built by Irish-American John Philip Holland. Powered by petrol engine on the surface and by battery underwater, it went into service with the US Navy in 1900.

Man o' war

Cannons were used on ships almost as soon as they were invented, but it wasn't until the early 16th century that warships with specially designed gunports were built to carry heavy guns. Launched in 1511, Henry VIII of England's *Mary Rose* was one of the first such warships, powered by sail and armed with 78 guns.

105

continued...

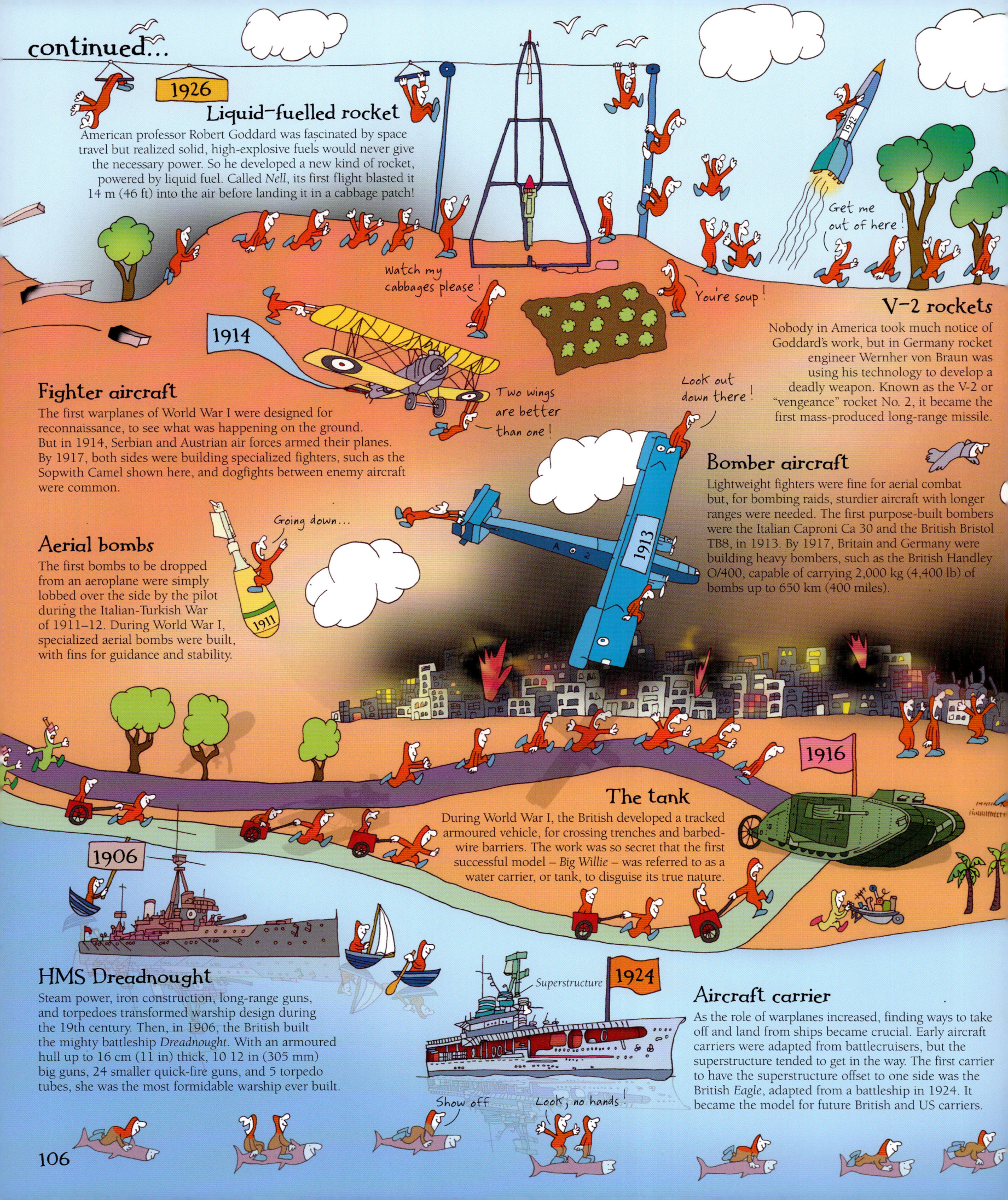

1926 Liquid-fuelled rocket
American professor Robert Goddard was fascinated by space travel but realized solid, high-explosive fuels would never give the necessary power. So he developed a new kind of rocket, powered by liquid fuel. Called *Nell*, its first flight blasted it 14 m (46 ft) into the air before landing it in a cabbage patch!

Fighter aircraft
The first warplanes of World War I were designed for reconnaissance, to see what was happening on the ground. But in 1914, Serbian and Austrian air forces armed their planes. By 1917, both sides were building specialized fighters, such as the Sopwith Camel shown here, and dogfights between enemy aircraft were common.

Aerial bombs
The first bombs to be dropped from an aeroplane were simply lobbed over the side by the pilot during the Italian-Turkish War of 1911–12. During World War I, specialized aerial bombs were built, with fins for guidance and stability.

V-2 rockets
Nobody in America took much notice of Goddard's work, but in Germany rocket engineer Wernher von Braun was using his technology to develop a deadly weapon. Known as the V-2 or "vengeance" rocket No. 2, it became the first mass-produced long-range missile.

Bomber aircraft
Lightweight fighters were fine for aerial combat but, for bombing raids, sturdier aircraft with longer ranges were needed. The first purpose-built bombers were the Italian Caproni Ca 30 and the British Bristol TB8, in 1913. By 1917, Britain and Germany were building heavy bombers, such as the British Handley O/400, capable of carrying 2,000 kg (4,400 lb) of bombs up to 650 km (400 miles).

The tank
During World War I, the British developed a tracked armoured vehicle, for crossing trenches and barbed-wire barriers. The work was so secret that the first successful model – *Big Willie* – was referred to as a water carrier, or tank, to disguise its true nature.

HMS Dreadnought
Steam power, iron construction, long-range guns, and torpedoes transformed warship design during the 19th century. Then, in 1906, the British built the mighty battleship *Dreadnought*. With an armoured hull up to 16 cm (11 in) thick, 10 12 in (305 mm) big guns, 24 smaller quick-fire guns, and 5 torpedo tubes, she was the most formidable warship ever built.

Aircraft carrier
As the role of warplanes increased, finding ways to take off and land from ships became crucial. Early aircraft carriers were adapted from battlecruisers, but the superstructure tended to get in the way. The first carrier to have the superstructure offset to one side was the British *Eagle*, adapted from a battleship in 1924. It became the model for future British and US carriers.

ICBMs

1957

During the 1950s, the USSR and the USA raced to build the first ICBM (Intercontinental Ballistic Missile) – that is, a nuclear-armed rocket capable of reaching a distant continent. After several failed attempts, the Russian team, led by Sergei Korolev, successfully launched its multistage R-7, which covered an astonishing 6,400 km (4,000 miles).

Saturn V

The success of the R-7 heralded the dawn of a new race – the space race – that reached its peak when the USA landed the first man on the Moon. To make this possible, NASA developed the Saturn V rocket to blast its three-manned Apollo craft into space. The height of a 33-storey building, Saturn V was the most powerful rocket to date.

1969

The wages of war

Terrible though war is, the technology developed to wage war has given us many everyday things that we take for granted. Synthetic rubber, tinned food, aviation navigation systems, computers, and the Internet are all the result of military invention. Similarly, bar codes, ready-made meals, and athletic footwear with stay-dry insoles are spin-offs from space technology.

Stealth aircraft

1982

Since the advent of radar, enemy aircraft have been easy to detect. Until, that is, the US Air Force introduced the world's first stealth fighter – the F-117 Nighthawk. A combination of special materials and multiangled surfaces makes this aircraft invisible to radar and therefore almost undetectable.

Atomic bomb

1945

Something as innocuously named as *Little Boy* caused the most devastating explosion ever witnessed in warfare. The first atomic bomb used in action, it obliterated the Japanese city of Hiroshima. Developed in the USA by a team of scientists led by Robert Oppenheimer, it heralded the nuclear age, since when people have lived in fear of it ever being used again.

Humvee

Tanks are designed for their firepower, but armies also need fast and reliable vehicles to transport troops, weapons, and cargo into combat. In 1985, the US Army introduced a revolutionary new vehicle that uniquely fitted the bill – the High Mobility Multipurpose Wheeled Vehicle, or HMMWV (pronounced Humvee)

1985

Nuclear submarine

1954

Battery-powered submarines have to resurface to recharge their batteries. The USS *Nautilus* had no such problem. Its power source was a nuclear reactor, the heat from which created steam to drive a turbine. Without the need to resurface, in 1958 it became the first submarine to sail beneath the polar ice cap and right under the North Pole.

Modular submarine

America's latest range of submarines – the Virginia Class – has a unique modular structure that makes the craft readily upgradable. Individual sections, such as the command centre or weapons module, can be lifted out, modified, and replaced within days, avoiding the need for a lengthy overhaul.

2003

TIMELINE

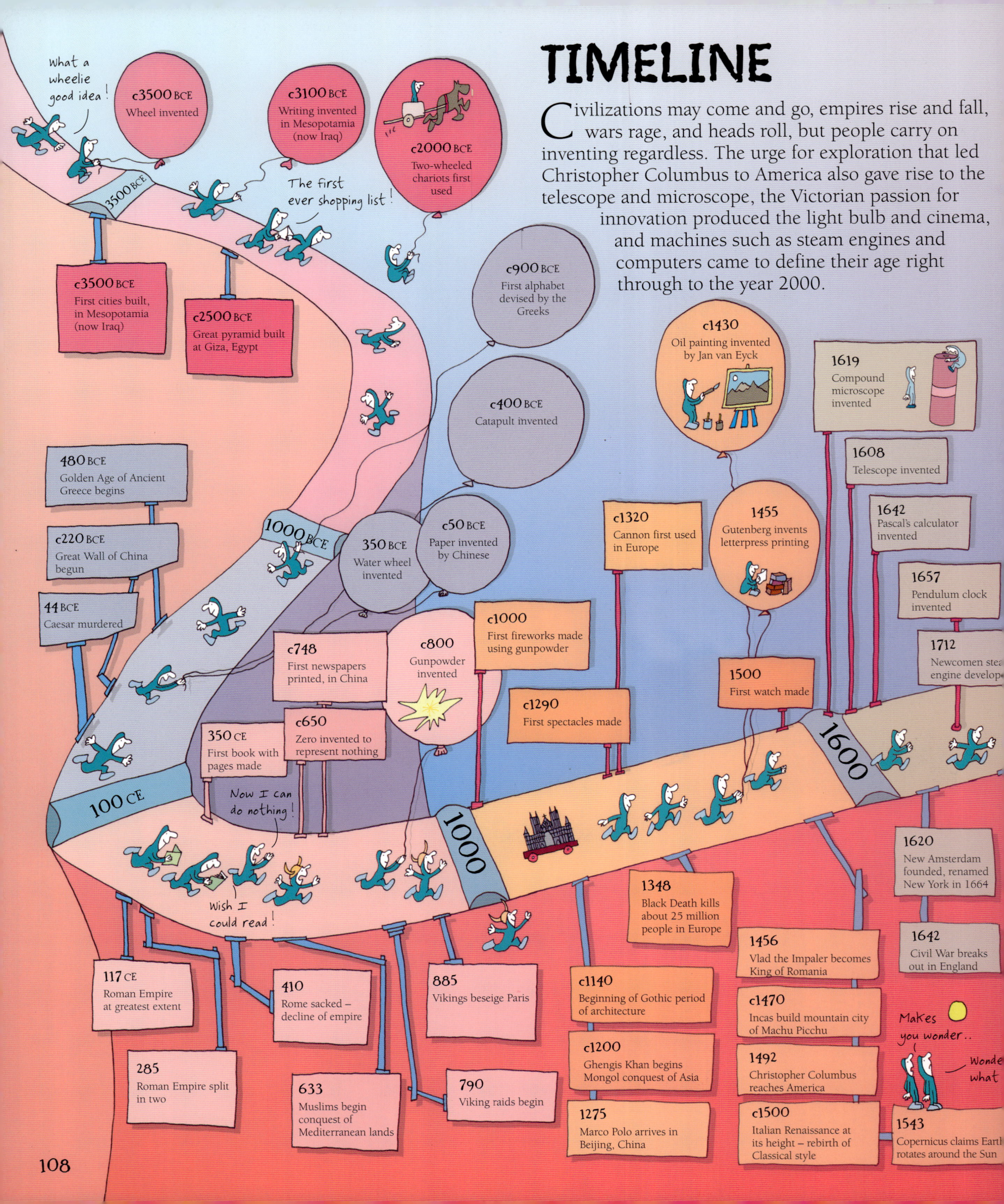

Civilizations may come and go, empires rise and fall, wars rage, and heads roll, but people carry on inventing regardless. The urge for exploration that led Christopher Columbus to America also gave rise to the telescope and microscope, the Victorian passion for innovation produced the light bulb and cinema, and machines such as steam engines and computers came to define their age right through to the year 2000.

What a wheelie good idea!

- **c3500 BCE** Wheel invented
- **c3100 BCE** Writing invented in Mesopotamia (now Iraq) — *The first ever shopping list!*
- **c2000 BCE** Two-wheeled chariots first used
- **c3500 BCE** First cities built, in Mesopotamia (now Iraq)
- **c2500 BCE** Great pyramid built at Giza, Egypt
- **c900 BCE** First alphabet devised by the Greeks
- **c400 BCE** Catapult invented
- **480 BCE** Golden Age of Ancient Greece begins
- **c220 BCE** Great Wall of China begun
- **44 BCE** Caesar murdered
- **350 BCE** Water wheel invented
- **c50 BCE** Paper invented by Chinese
- **350 CE** First book with pages made
- **c650** Zero invented to represent nothing — *Now I can do nothing!*
- **c748** First newspapers printed, in China
- **c800** Gunpowder invented
- **c1000** First fireworks made using gunpowder
- **c1290** First spectacles made
- **c1320** Cannon first used in Europe
- **1455** Gutenberg invents letterpress printing
- **1500** First watch made
- **c1430** Oil painting invented by Jan van Eyck
- **1619** Compound microscope invented
- **1608** Telescope invented
- **1642** Pascal's calculator invented
- **1657** Pendulum clock invented
- **1712** Newcomen steam engine developed
- *Wish I could read!*
- **117 CE** Roman Empire at greatest extent
- **285** Roman Empire split in two
- **410** Rome sacked – decline of empire
- **633** Muslims begin conquest of Mediterranean lands
- **885** Vikings beseige Paris
- **790** Viking raids begin
- **c1140** Beginning of Gothic period of architecture
- **1200** Ghengis Khan begins Mongol conquest of Asia
- **1275** Marco Polo arrives in Beijing, China
- **1348** Black Death kills about 25 million people in Europe
- **1456** Vlad the Impaler becomes King of Romania
- **c1470** Incas build mountain city of Machu Picchu
- **1492** Christopher Columbus reaches America
- **c1500** Italian Renaissance at its height – rebirth of Classical style
- **1620** New Amsterdam founded, renamed New York in 1664
- **1642** Civil War breaks out in England
- **1543** Copernicus claims Earth rotates around the Sun — *Makes you wonder.. Wonder what*

3500 BCE · 1000 BCE · 100 CE · 1000 · 1600

Balloons (top section)

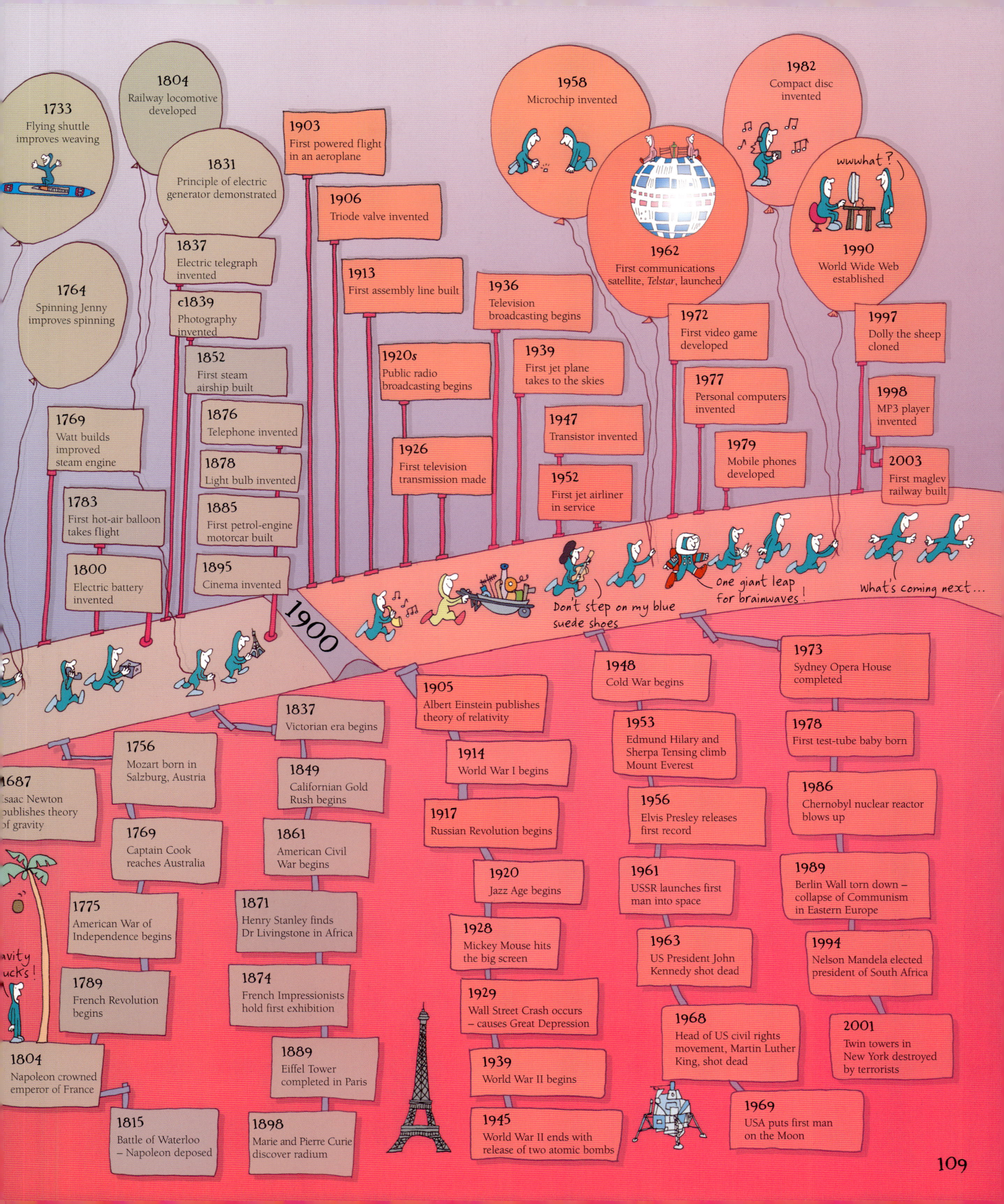

- **1733** Flying shuttle improves weaving
- **1764** Spinning Jenny improves spinning
- **1769** Watt builds improved steam engine
- **1783** First hot-air balloon takes flight
- **1800** Electric battery invented
- **1804** Railway locomotive developed
- **1831** Principle of electric generator demonstrated
- **1837** Electric telegraph invented
- **c1839** Photography invented
- **1852** First steam airship built
- **1876** Telephone invented
- **1878** Light bulb invented
- **1885** First petrol-engine motorcar built
- **1895** Cinema invented
- **1903** First powered flight in an aeroplane
- **1906** Triode valve invented
- **1913** First assembly line built
- **1920s** Public radio broadcasting begins
- **1926** First television transmission made
- **1936** Television broadcasting begins
- **1939** First jet plane takes to the skies
- **1947** Transistor invented
- **1952** First jet airliner in service
- **1958** Microchip invented
- **1962** First communications satellite, *Telstar*, launched
- **1972** First video game developed
- **1977** Personal computers invented
- **1979** Mobile phones developed
- **1982** Compact disc invented
- **1990** World Wide Web established
- **1997** Dolly the sheep cloned
- **1998** MP3 player invented
- **2003** First maglev railway built

Don't step on my blue suede shoes
One giant leap for brainwaves!
What's coming next...
wwwhat?

1900

Lower section

- **1687** Isaac Newton publishes theory of gravity
- *gravity sucks!*
- **1756** Mozart born in Salzburg, Austria
- **1769** Captain Cook reaches Australia
- **1775** American War of Independence begins
- **1789** French Revolution begins
- **1804** Napoleon crowned emperor of France
- **1815** Battle of Waterloo – Napoleon deposed
- **1837** Victorian era begins
- **1849** Californian Gold Rush begins
- **1861** American Civil War begins
- **1871** Henry Stanley finds Dr Livingstone in Africa
- **1874** French Impressionists hold first exhibition
- **1889** Eiffel Tower completed in Paris
- **1898** Marie and Pierre Curie discover radium
- **1905** Albert Einstein publishes theory of relativity
- **1914** World War I begins
- **1917** Russian Revolution begins
- **1920** Jazz Age begins
- **1928** Mickey Mouse hits the big screen
- **1929** Wall Street Crash occurs – causes Great Depression
- **1939** World War II begins
- **1945** World War II ends with release of two atomic bombs
- **1948** Cold War begins
- **1953** Edmund Hilary and Sherpa Tensing climb Mount Everest
- **1956** Elvis Presley releases first record
- **1961** USSR launches first man into space
- **1963** US President John Kennedy shot dead
- **1968** Head of US civil rights movement, Martin Luther King, shot dead
- **1969** USA puts first man on the Moon
- **1973** Sydney Opera House completed
- **1978** First test-tube baby born
- **1986** Chernobyl nuclear reactor blows up
- **1989** Berlin Wall torn down – collapse of Communism in Eastern Europe
- **1994** Nelson Mandela elected president of South Africa
- **2001** Twin towers in New York destroyed by terrorists

109

LUNAR RALLY

INTERGALACTIC GUIDE TO SPACE

COSMIC ZOO

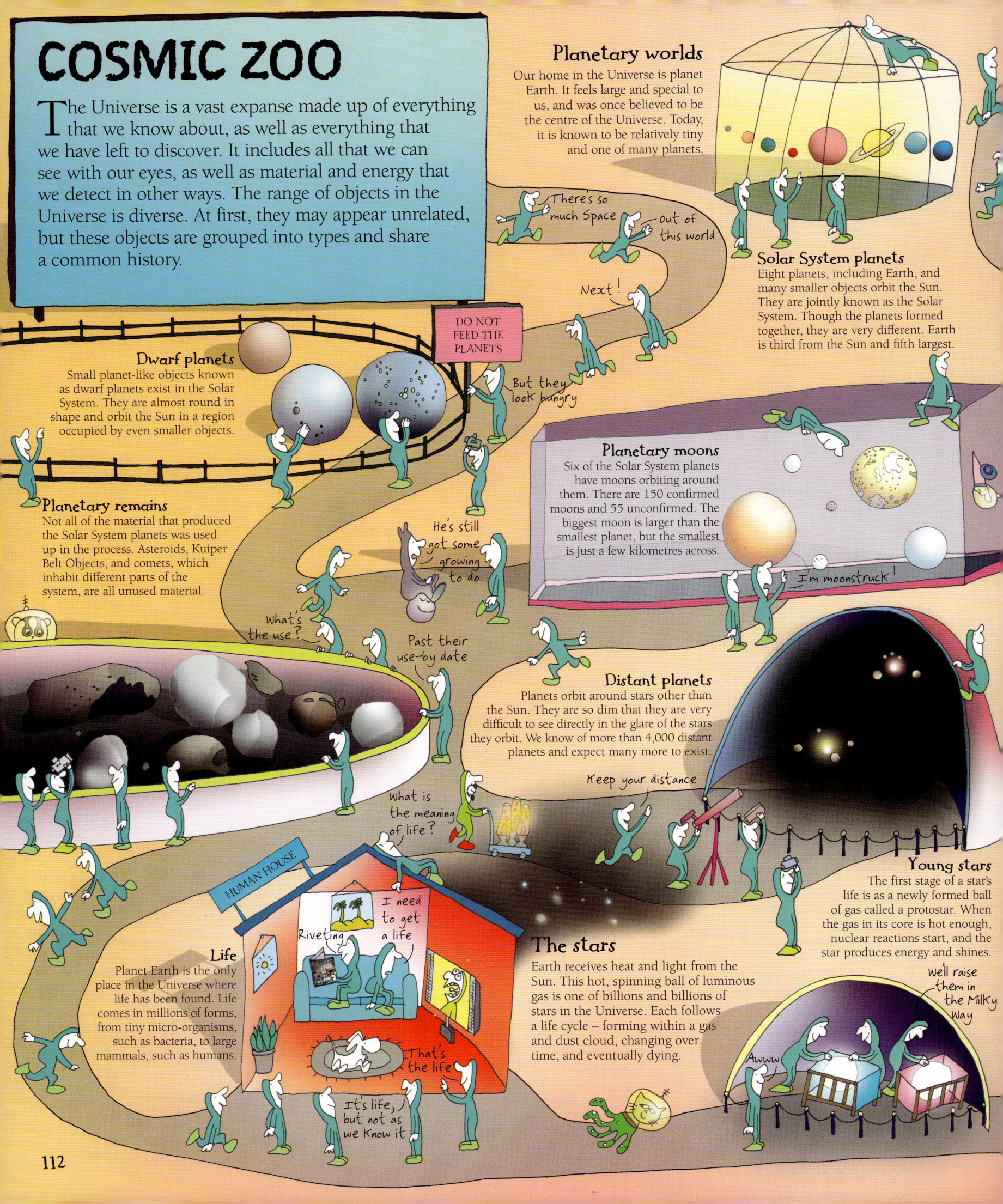

The Universe is a vast expanse made up of everything that we know about, as well as everything that we have left to discover. It includes all that we can see with our eyes, as well as material and energy that we detect in other ways. The range of objects in the Universe is diverse. At first, they may appear unrelated, but these objects are grouped into types and share a common history.

Planetary worlds
Our home in the Universe is planet Earth. It feels large and special to us, and was once believed to be the centre of the Universe. Today, it is known to be relatively tiny and one of many planets.

Solar System planets
Eight planets, including Earth, and many smaller objects orbit the Sun. They are jointly known as the Solar System. Though the planets formed together, they are very different. Earth is third from the Sun and fifth largest.

Dwarf planets
Small planet-like objects known as dwarf planets exist in the Solar System. They are almost round in shape and orbit the Sun in a region occupied by even smaller objects.

Planetary moons
Six of the Solar System planets have moons orbiting around them. There are 150 confirmed moons and 55 unconfirmed. The biggest moon is larger than the smallest planet, but the smallest is just a few kilometres across.

Planetary remains
Not all of the material that produced the Solar System planets was used up in the process. Asteroids, Kuiper Belt Objects, and comets, which inhabit different parts of the system, are all unused material.

Distant planets
Planets orbit around stars other than the Sun. They are so dim that they are very difficult to see directly in the glare of the stars they orbit. We know of more than 4,000 distant planets and expect many more to exist.

Young stars
The first stage of a star's life is as a newly formed ball of gas called a protostar. When the gas in its core is hot enough, nuclear reactions start, and the star produces energy and shines.

Life
Planet Earth is the only place in the Universe where life has been found. Life comes in millions of forms, from tiny micro-organisms, such as bacteria, to large mammals, such as humans.

The stars
Earth receives heat and light from the Sun. This hot, spinning ball of luminous gas is one of billions and billions of stars in the Universe. Each follows a life cycle – forming within a gas and dust cloud, changing over time, and eventually dying.

Universal laws
Scientific rules on Earth apply throughout the Universe. For example, gravity keeps our feet on the ground and stops a star's gas drifting off. Chemical elements change state depending on temperature. Water exists elsewhere, but on Earth the temperature is right for it to be liquid.

Super structures
Superclusters link together in a network of long chains and sheets. These are the largest structures of all, existing throughout the Universe. Voids of virtually empty Space separate them.

Galaxies
There are billions of galaxies all around us in the Universe. Each consists of a vast number of stars, together with gas and dust. The Sun is one star among the billions that make up the Milky Way Galaxy.

Galaxy types
Astronomers classify these huge star systems by their shape. The Milky Way is a spiral galaxy – a disc shape with spiral arms. The Sun lies about two-thirds of the distance from the centre to the edge, in one of the spiral arms.

Galaxy clusters
Clusters consist of tens to thousands of galaxies strung together in superclusters. The Milky Way is part of the Local Group cluster. With other galaxy clusters it makes up the Local Supercluster.

Nebulae
Large clouds of mainly hydrogen gas that produce new stars are called nebulae. These include materials cast off by dying stars and that have no definite shape, such as the Horsehead Nebula.

Star clusters
Stars are born in clusters inside dark clouds of gas and dust. At first, clusters remain intact, but over hundreds of millions of years, the stars tend to drift apart.

Maturing stars
Most stars shine steadily just as the Sun is doing now. The Sun is a single star, but many are in partnerships – two stars orbiting around each other.

Stellar ends
Towards the ends of their lives, most stars swell up to become red giant or supergiant stars. Most die slowly, but the more massive ones blow themselves apart suddenly in huge explosions.

113

BANG!

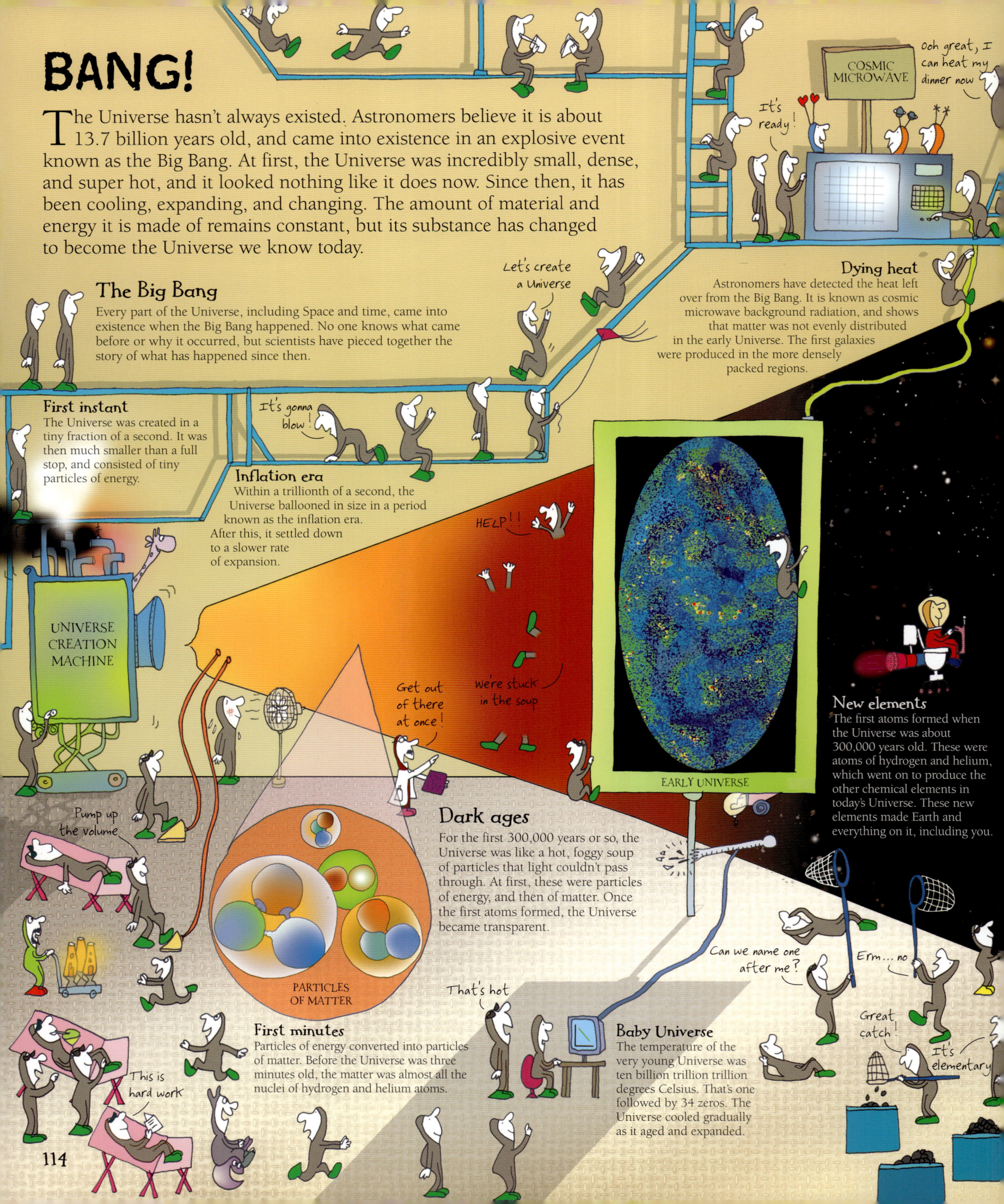

The Universe hasn't always existed. Astronomers believe it is about 13.7 billion years old, and came into existence in an explosive event known as the Big Bang. At first, the Universe was incredibly small, dense, and super hot, and it looked nothing like it does now. Since then, it has been cooling, expanding, and changing. The amount of material and energy it is made of remains constant, but its substance has changed to become the Universe we know today.

The Big Bang
Every part of the Universe, including Space and time, came into existence when the Big Bang happened. No one knows what came before or why it occurred, but scientists have pieced together the story of what has happened since then.

First instant
The Universe was created in a tiny fraction of a second. It was then much smaller than a full stop, and consisted of tiny particles of energy.

Inflation era
Within a trillionth of a second, the Universe ballooned in size in a period known as the inflation era. After this, it settled down to a slower rate of expansion.

Dark ages
For the first 300,000 years or so, the Universe was like a hot, foggy soup of particles that light couldn't pass through. At first, these were particles of energy, and then of matter. Once the first atoms formed, the Universe became transparent.

First minutes
Particles of energy converted into particles of matter. Before the Universe was three minutes old, the matter was almost all the nuclei of hydrogen and helium atoms.

Baby Universe
The temperature of the very young Universe was ten billion trillion trillion degrees Celsius. That's one followed by 34 zeros. The Universe cooled gradually as it aged and expanded.

Dying heat
Astronomers have detected the heat left over from the Big Bang. It is known as cosmic microwave background radiation, and shows that matter was not evenly distributed in the early Universe. The first galaxies were produced in the more densely packed regions.

New elements
The first atoms formed when the Universe was about 300,000 years old. These were atoms of hydrogen and helium, which went on to produce the other chemical elements in today's Universe. These new elements made Earth and everything on it, including you.

First stars and galaxies

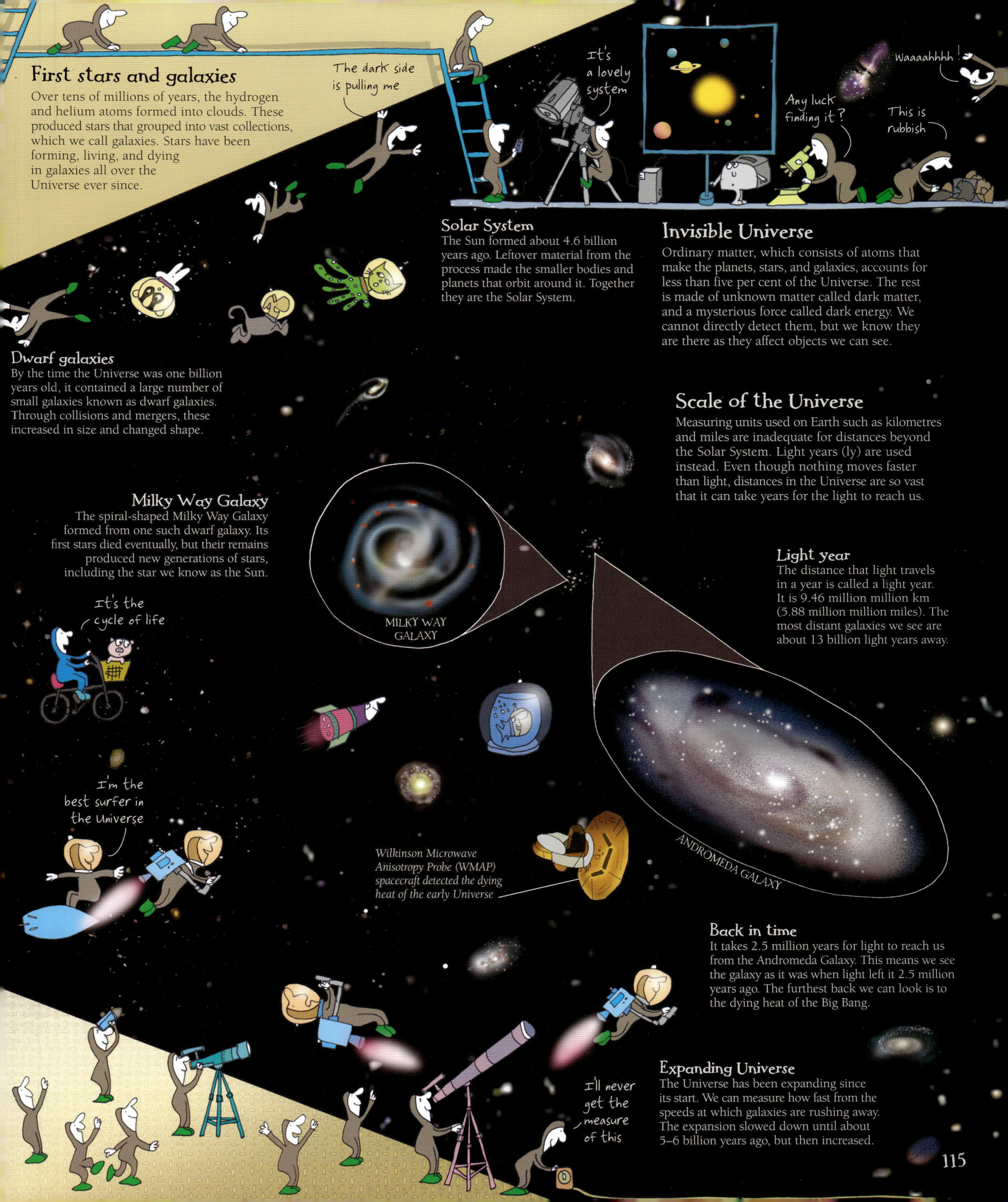

Over tens of millions of years, the hydrogen and helium atoms formed into clouds. These produced stars that grouped into vast collections, which we call galaxies. Stars have been forming, living, and dying in galaxies all over the Universe ever since.

Solar System

The Sun formed about 4.6 billion years ago. Leftover material from the process made the smaller bodies and planets that orbit around it. Together they are the Solar System.

Invisible Universe

Ordinary matter, which consists of atoms that make the planets, stars, and galaxies, accounts for less than five per cent of the Universe. The rest is made of unknown matter called dark matter, and a mysterious force called dark energy. We cannot directly detect them, but we know they are there as they affect objects we can see.

Dwarf galaxies

By the time the Universe was one billion years old, it contained a large number of small galaxies known as dwarf galaxies. Through collisions and mergers, these increased in size and changed shape.

Scale of the Universe

Measuring units used on Earth such as kilometres and miles are inadequate for distances beyond the Solar System. Light years (ly) are used instead. Even though nothing moves faster than light, distances in the Universe are so vast that it can take years for the light to reach us.

Milky Way Galaxy

The spiral-shaped Milky Way Galaxy formed from one such dwarf galaxy. Its first stars died eventually, but their remains produced new generations of stars, including the star we know as the Sun.

MILKY WAY GALAXY

Light year

The distance that light travels in a year is called a light year. It is 9.46 million million km (5.88 million million miles). The most distant galaxies we see are about 13 billion light years away.

Wilkinson Microwave Anisotropy Probe (WMAP) spacecraft detected the dying heat of the early Universe

ANDROMEDA GALAXY

Back in time

It takes 2.5 million years for light to reach us from the Andromeda Galaxy. This means we see the galaxy as it was when light left it 2.5 million years ago. The furthest back we can look is to the dying heat of the Big Bang.

Expanding Universe

The Universe has been expanding since its start. We can measure how fast from the speeds at which galaxies are rushing away. The expansion slowed down until about 5–6 billion years ago, but then increased.

Elliptical
These ball-shaped galaxies include those that are round like a football, oval like a rugby ball, and others with shapes in between. Dwarf ellipticals are the most common type of galaxy.

Irregular
Galaxies with no regular shape or form are classed as irregulars. These relatively small galaxies are usually rich in gas and dust, with a high proportion of new and young stars.

Dazzling display

Barred spiral
Like spirals, the barred spirals are disc-shaped, but their arms wind out from the ends of a central bar-shaped region of stars. Stars in both types of spiral typically take a few hundred million years for one orbit.

Dark dust lane cuts across this active galaxy

Spiral
Disc-shaped galaxies with curving arms are classed as spirals. A central bulge consists of mainly older stars, and arms rich in bright young stars spiral out from it. Stars exist between the arms, but they are outshone by the brilliance of those in the arms.

Jet of material

Active galaxies
Some galaxies, such as Centaurus A, give off more light than is expected from their stars alone. It comes from material that circles around the supermassive black hole at the galaxy's centre before falling in. Bits of the material are fired out as jets from either side of the hole.

Galaxy shapes
All galaxies are one of four main shapes. These are spiral, barred spiral, elliptical, and irregular. The galaxies don't behave as solid objects; individual stars follow their own orbits around a galaxy's centre.

Blast-off! *Ooooh!* *Udderly brilliant* *Arrrr!* *What a whizzer*

GLITTERING GALAXIES

The Universe is thought to be home to at least 125 billion galaxies. Each consists of a huge number of stars, along with vast amounts of gas and dust, all held together by gravity. They come in a range of shapes and sizes, and differ in the number of stars they contain – from a few million to more than a trillion. Most, if not all, galaxies have a supermassive black hole at their centre.

TADPOLE GALAXY

Names and numbers
Galaxies are identified by catalogue numbers, which are combinations of letters and figures, and by their positions in the sky. Some galaxies also have names that describe what they look like, or are taken from the constellation they are in.

FRIED EGG GALAXY

Tadpole Galaxy
A long streamer of stars and gas extends from a spiral galaxy to form the shape of a tadpole. This odd form is the result of an encounter with another galaxy.

Fried Egg Galaxy
The yellow glow coming from this galaxy's centre resembles a fried egg. It is an active galaxy about a third of the width of the Milky Way Galaxy.

Just give them time...

Two spiral galaxies made of gas, dust, and stars have formed.

400 million years pass and the galaxies are closer together.

Another 250 million years pass and the galaxies merge to form an irregular galaxy.

It's all coming together!

Galaxy clusters
Instead of existing in isolation, galaxies are grouped in clusters. An individual cluster can contain up to a few thousand galaxies. Whatever the number, all clusters occupy a similar-sized spherical region of Space.

Galaxy formation
Billions of years ago, galaxies formed from the merging of groups of stars. These galaxies then interacted, and through collisions and mergers, their shapes, mass, and size changed.

Milky Way
The Sun and the night-time stars all belong to one galaxy, the Milky Way. It is a barred spiral containing about 500 billion stars and measuring 100,000 light years (ly) across, by 4,000 ly deep. Our Sun lies in one of the spiral arms about two-thirds of the distance from the centre to the edge. At the heart of the Milky Way is a supermassive black hole, called Sagittarius A*.

THE MILKY WAY DAIRY

Path of light
From our position inside the galaxy we see the Milky Way as a band of light across the night sky. The band is also known as the Milky Way.

Our cluster
The Milky Way belongs to a cluster of more than 40 galaxies known as the Local Group. Most are dwarf galaxies, orbiting the two biggest – the Milky Way and Andromeda galaxies.

We'll be here 'til the cows come home

About now then

Ready for the milk round?

Your churn!

Time for bed Daisy

COSMIC CAREERS FAIR

ASTRO LEGENDS

Arthur Eddington
In the 1920s, British astronomer Arthur Eddington showed that a star's energy comes from nuclear reactions within.

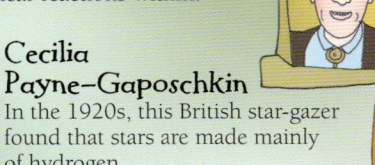

Fred Whipple
American astronomer Fred Whipple discovered six comets. In the 1950s, he explained that a comet is a dirty snowball.

Vera Rubin
Astronomers grew certain that dark matter exists after US astronomer Rubin showed its gravity affects how stars move inside galaxies.

Cecilia Payne-Gaposchkin
In the 1920s, this British star-gazer found that stars are made mainly of hydrogen.

Subrahmanyan Chandrasekhar
Born in India, Chandrasekhar is known for his work on stellar structure and the evolution of stars.

Fred Hoyle
British cosmologist Hoyle showed how elements are made in stars and coined the phrase "Big Bang".

Edwin Hubble
In the 1920s, the USA's Edwin Hubble discovered that the Universe is full of galaxies, and that it is expanding.

Computers
Astronomers use computers in a variety of ways, such as to control telescopes and spacecraft, to record, store, and analyse data, and to make detailed calculations that would otherwise take months. Computers are also used to simulate scenarios in Space, such as two galaxies colliding.

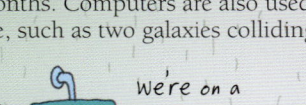

Spacecraft
Astronomers stay on Earth but send robotic craft to explore the Solar System at close range. On arrival at their destination, telescopes and other instruments on board the craft collect and record data. This is then relayed to the astronomers back on Earth.

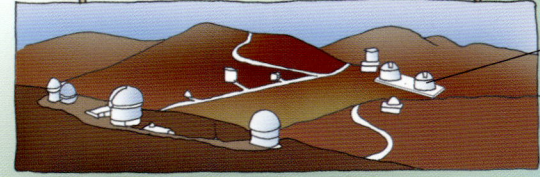

Observatories
Telescopes are housed in dome- or drum-shaped buildings. One or a group of these is called an observatory. The world's best observatories are located on the top of mountains, well away from city lights and where the air is thin, clear, and still.

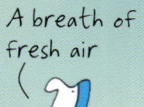

Domes stand several storeys high at Mauna Kea, Hawaii, home to some of Earth's largest telescopes

ASTRONOMER'S LIFE

Scientists who study the objects in the Universe are called astronomers. They study from Earth, relying on information travelling through Space. Objects are observed and data is collected, and an astronomer uses scientific and mathematical knowledge to find out more. A single astronomer doesn't study everything in the Universe but specializes in one aspect. Most work for a government organization, based at a laboratory, university, or observatory.

Astrophysicists
Many astronomers are astrophysicists concerned with the physical properties of objects. Astrophysicists can be grouped together as those interested in stars, galaxies, or Solar System objects.

Cosmologists
Astronomers studying the Universe as a whole are known as cosmologists. They are interested in how the Universe started, how it developed, and what it will be like in the future.

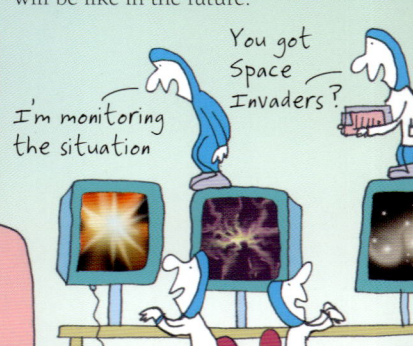

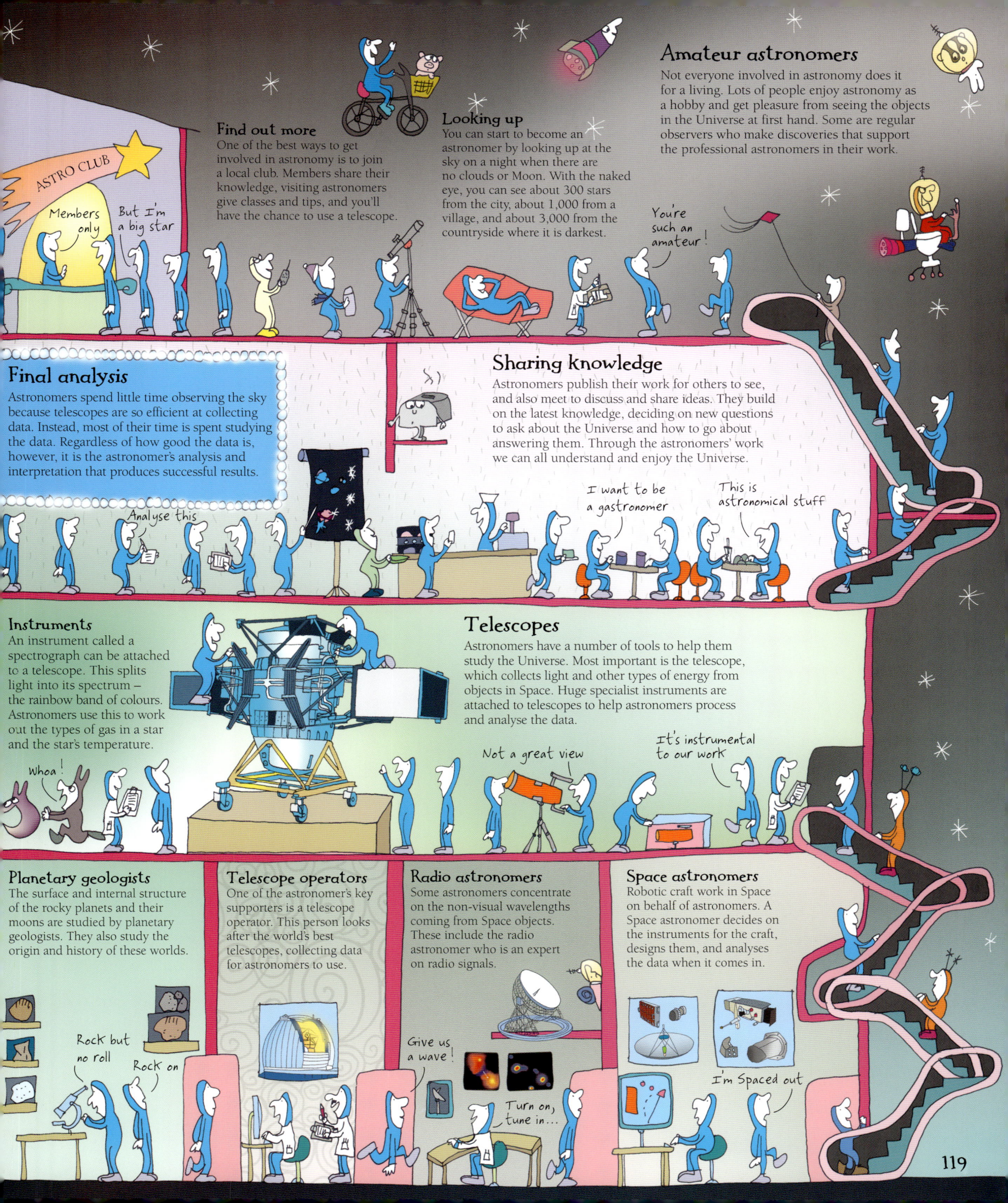

Find out more
One of the best ways to get involved in astronomy is to join a local club. Members share their knowledge, visiting astronomers give classes and tips, and you'll have the chance to use a telescope.

Looking up
You can start to become an astronomer by looking up at the sky on a night when there are no clouds or Moon. With the naked eye, you can see about 300 stars from the city, about 1,000 from a village, and about 3,000 from the countryside where it is darkest.

Amateur astronomers
Not everyone involved in astronomy does it for a living. Lots of people enjoy astronomy as a hobby and get pleasure from seeing the objects in the Universe at first hand. Some are regular observers who make discoveries that support the professional astronomers in their work.

Final analysis
Astronomers spend little time observing the sky because telescopes are so efficient at collecting data. Instead, most of their time is spent studying the data. Regardless of how good the data is, however, it is the astronomer's analysis and interpretation that produces successful results.

Sharing knowledge
Astronomers publish their work for others to see, and also meet to discuss and share ideas. They build on the latest knowledge, deciding on new questions to ask about the Universe and how to go about answering them. Through the astronomers' work we can all understand and enjoy the Universe.

Instruments
An instrument called a spectrograph can be attached to a telescope. This splits light into its spectrum – the rainbow band of colours. Astronomers use this to work out the types of gas in a star and the star's temperature.

Telescopes
Astronomers have a number of tools to help them study the Universe. Most important is the telescope, which collects light and other types of energy from objects in Space. Huge specialist instruments are attached to telescopes to help astronomers process and analyse the data.

Planetary geologists
The surface and internal structure of the rocky planets and their moons are studied by planetary geologists. They also study the origin and history of these worlds.

Telescope operators
One of the astronomer's key supporters is a telescope operator. This person looks after the world's best telescopes, collecting data for astronomers to use.

Radio astronomers
Some astronomers concentrate on the non-visual wavelengths coming from Space objects. These include the radio astronomer who is an expert on radio signals.

Space astronomers
Robotic craft work in Space on behalf of astronomers. A Space astronomer decides on the instruments for the craft, designs them, and analyses the data when it comes in.

EYE ON THE UNIVERSE

Astronomers use telescopes to look deep into the Universe. Like giant eyes, they collect light from objects and use it to produce images. Yet, telescopes are much better than eyes. They collect a lot more light, and produce magnified images. In addition to optical telescopes, which collect light, others collect different forms of energy. These reveal new aspects of familiar objects, and identify things that would otherwise remain undiscovered.

Telescope
A telescope has a main mirror (sometimes a lens) to collect light and focus it. A smaller mirror usually intercepts the focused beam of light and sends it into an instrument, a camera, or someone's eye.

Second mirror focuses light from main mirror onto third mirror

Light passes through telescope's open structure to main mirror

Main mirror
The bigger the main mirror, the more light it collects, enabling astronomers to see fainter and more distant objects. Large mirrors sag under their own weight, so small ones work together as one big mirror.

Third mirror sends light to instrument box

Mount
A telescope is supported on a mount, which allows it to move. Once on its target object, automatic controls keep it fixed on the object as Earth turns.

Main mirror made of 36 small mirrors is 10 m (33 ft) across

The view
A camera or spectrograph is positioned where the image would form. The light is recorded on an electronic chip and viewed on a computer.

Instrument box houses camera or spectrograph

Space energy
Light and other energy forms travel in waves of differing length. By collecting a range of these with special telescopes, we get a more complete view of the Universe. Not all the wavelengths reach Earth's surface. Shorter ones, such as X-rays, cannot penetrate Earth's atmosphere.

Gamma rays have the shortest wavelengths, and are emitted by supernovae

X-rays are released by stellar material falling into a black hole

Ultraviolet (UV) rays are given off very strongly by stars hotter than the Sun

Light rays come from stars, and sunlight is reflected by objects such as planets

Infrared rays are collected from cooler objects such as star-forming nebulae

Microwaves are short radio waves and are produced by the dying heat of the Big Bang

Radio waves are the longest, and have been used to discover otherwise invisible galaxies

120

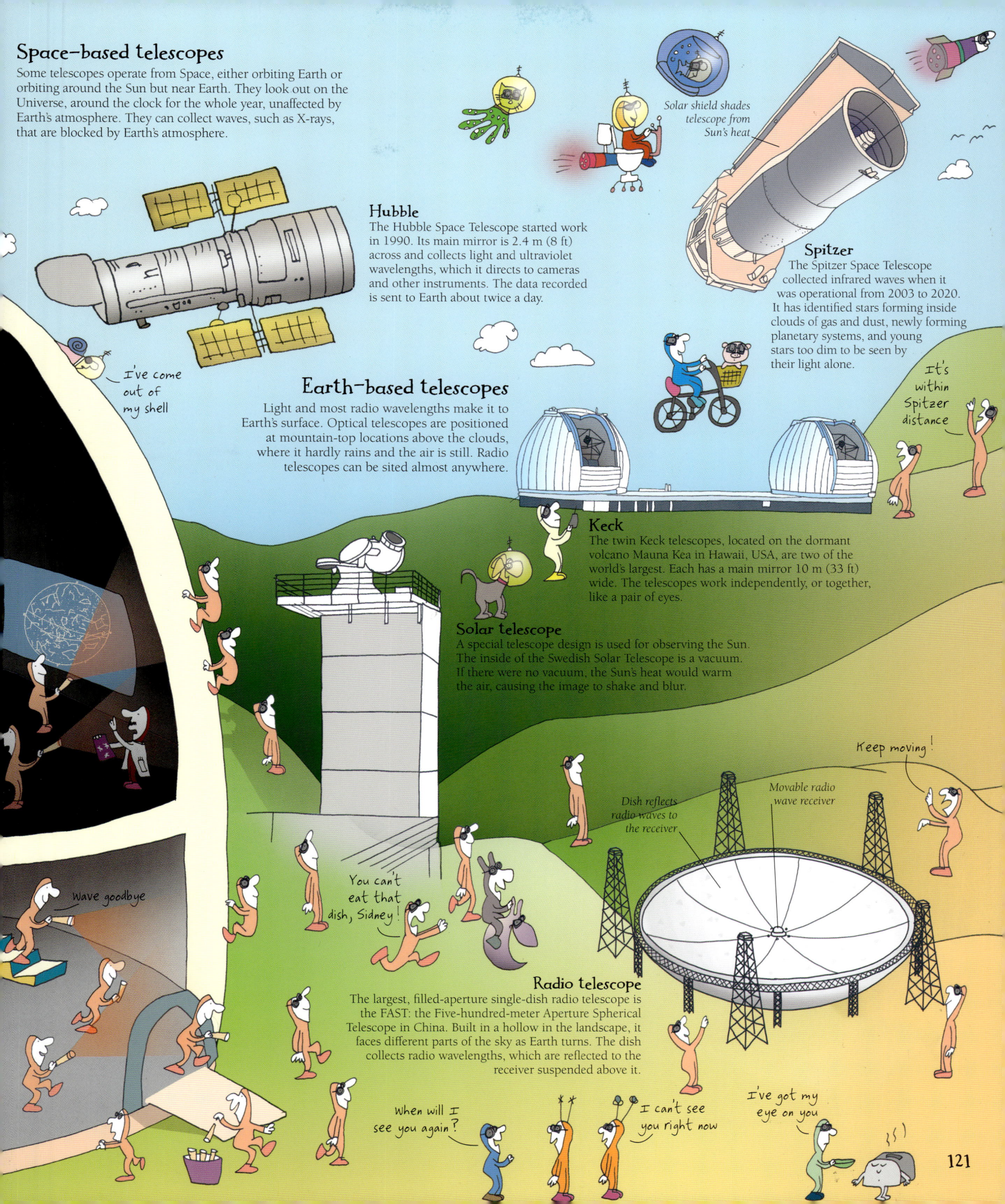

Space-based telescopes

Some telescopes operate from Space, either orbiting Earth or orbiting around the Sun but near Earth. They look out on the Universe, around the clock for the whole year, unaffected by Earth's atmosphere. They can collect waves, such as X-rays, that are blocked by Earth's atmosphere.

Hubble
The Hubble Space Telescope started work in 1990. Its main mirror is 2.4 m (8 ft) across and collects light and ultraviolet wavelengths, which it directs to cameras and other instruments. The data recorded is sent to Earth about twice a day.

Solar shield shades telescope from Sun's heat

Spitzer
The Spitzer Space Telescope collected infrared waves when it was operational from 2003 to 2020. It has identified stars forming inside clouds of gas and dust, newly forming planetary systems, and young stars too dim to be seen by their light alone.

Earth-based telescopes

Light and most radio wavelengths make it to Earth's surface. Optical telescopes are positioned at mountain-top locations above the clouds, where it hardly rains and the air is still. Radio telescopes can be sited almost anywhere.

Keck
The twin Keck telescopes, located on the dormant volcano Mauna Kea in Hawaii, USA, are two of the world's largest. Each has a main mirror 10 m (33 ft) wide. The telescopes work independently, or together, like a pair of eyes.

Solar telescope
A special telescope design is used for observing the Sun. The inside of the Swedish Solar Telescope is a vacuum. If there were no vacuum, the Sun's heat would warm the air, causing the image to shake and blur.

Dish reflects radio waves to the receiver

Movable radio wave receiver

Radio telescope
The largest, filled-aperture single-dish radio telescope is the FAST: the Five-hundred-meter Aperture Spherical Telescope in China. Built in a hollow in the landscape, it faces different parts of the sky as Earth turns. The dish collects radio wavelengths, which are reflected to the receiver suspended above it.

Living together

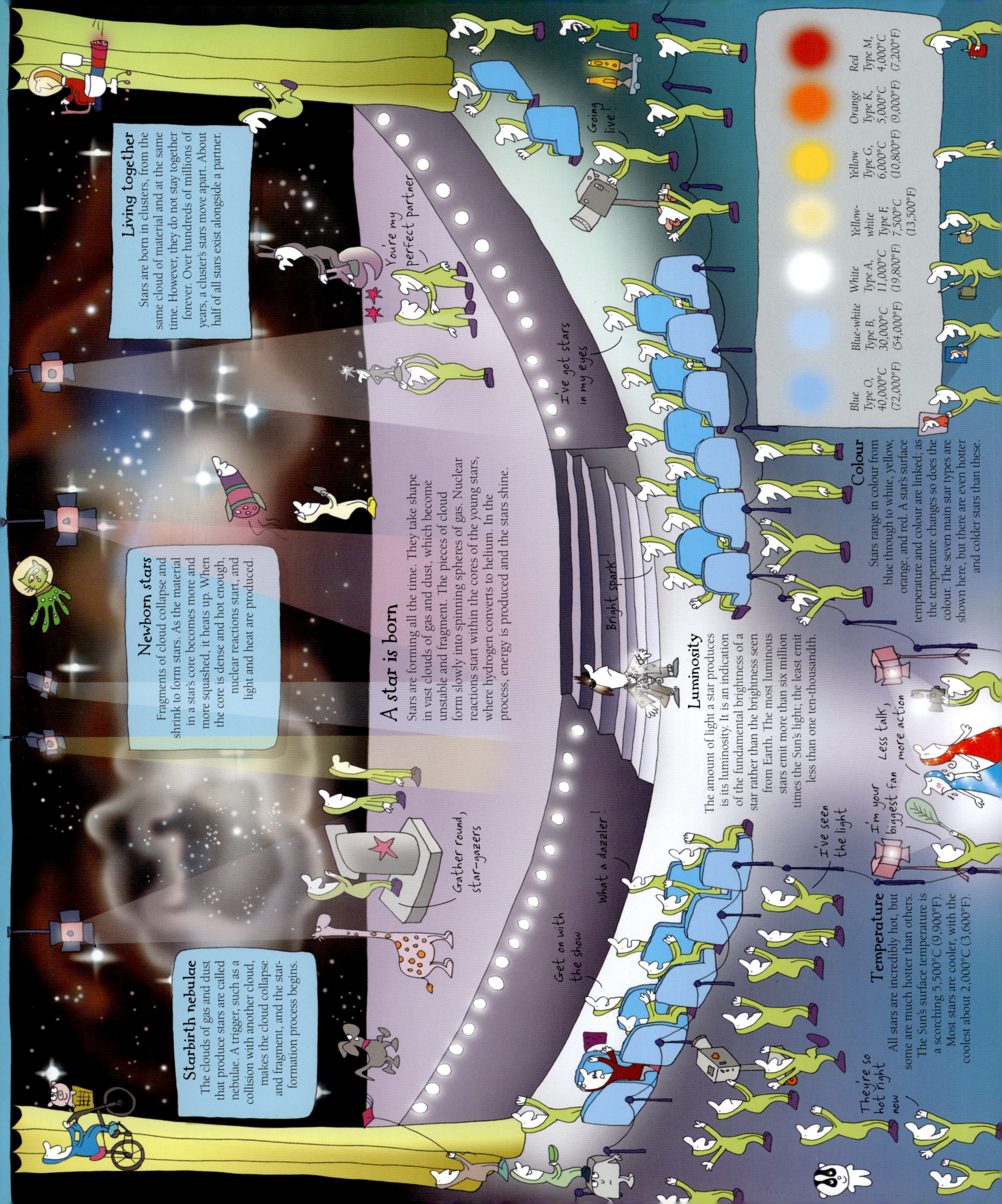

Stars are born in clusters, from the same cloud of material and at the same time. However, they do not stay together forever. Over hundreds of millions of years, a cluster's stars move apart. About half of all stars exist alongside a partner.

Newborn stars

Fragments of cloud collapse and shrink to form stars. As the material in a star's core becomes more and more squashed, it heats up. When the core is dense and hot enough, nuclear reactions start, and light and heat are produced.

Starbirth nebulae

The clouds of gas and dust that produce stars are called nebulae. A trigger, such as a collision with another cloud, makes the cloud collapse and fragment, and the star-formation process begins.

A star is born

Stars are forming all the time. They take shape in vast clouds of gas and dust. They become unstable and fragment. The pieces of cloud form slowly into spinning spheres of gas. Nuclear reactions start within the cores of the young stars, where hydrogen converts to helium. In the process, energy is produced and the stars shine.

Luminosity

The amount of light a star produces is its luminosity. It is an indication of the fundamental brightness of a star rather than the brightness seen from Earth. The most luminous stars emit more than six million times the Sun's light; the least emit less than one ten-thousandth.

Temperature

All stars are incredibly hot, but some are much hotter than others. The Sun's surface temperature is a scorching 5,500°C (9,900°F). Most stars are cooler, with the coolest about 2,000°C (3,600°F).

Colour

Stars range in colour from blue through to white, yellow, orange, and red. A star's surface temperature and colour are linked, as the temperature changes so does the colour. The seven main star types are shown here, but there are even hotter and colder stars than these.

Blue	Type O	40,000°C (72,000°F)
Blue-white	Type B	30,000°C (54,000°F)
White	Type A	11,000°C (19,800°F)
Yellow-white	Type F	7,500°C (13,500°F)
Yellow	Type G	6,000°C (10,800°F)
Orange	Type K	5,000°C (9,000°F)
Red	Type M	4,000°C (7,200°F)

STARS OF THE SHOW

All stars, except the Sun, are so far away that they appear as pinpoints of twinkling light to our eyes. They may look the same, but each star is unique and has its own characteristics. Stars differ in size, temperature, colour, luminosity, and mass. These attributes change as a star ages and moves from one stage of its life to the next. Of chief importance is mass – the amount of material a star is made of – because this determines the length and course of a star's life.

Gravity and pressure

A constant battle between gravity and pressure occurs inside stars. A star's gravity pulls its material into the centre, while the pressure of the central gas pushes the material out. The forces counterbalance each other and maintain the star's spherical shape.

Density

The size of a star is related to the density of its material. Two stars can be made of the same mass, but they can take up different volumes of space. When the material is spread out, the star is large, and when tightly packed, the star is much smaller.

Shape

Stars are spherical whatever their size and mass. They are not star-shaped but appear that way sometimes because of how their light passes through Earth's atmosphere. The light is bent and wobbled by bubbles of hot and cold air, giving the stars a pointed edge.

Mass

The amount of material that makes up the Sun is described as one solar mass. Other stars are measured in multiples or fractions of this. The most massive are about 100 times more massive, while the least are just one tenth of the Sun's mass.

Size

The mass of a star hardly changes during its life, but a star's size can vary greatly. The Sun is 1.4 million km (0.8 million miles) across. The largest stars are more than 1,000 times the Sun's width; the smallest are about one hundredth of it.

Star material

Stars are huge spinning globes of hot, glowing gas. They are mainly hydrogen and partly helium, together with small amounts of other elements. A star's gravity pulls the gas in and keeps it together. Much of this gas is squashed inside the star's core, where it produces energy, such as heat and light.

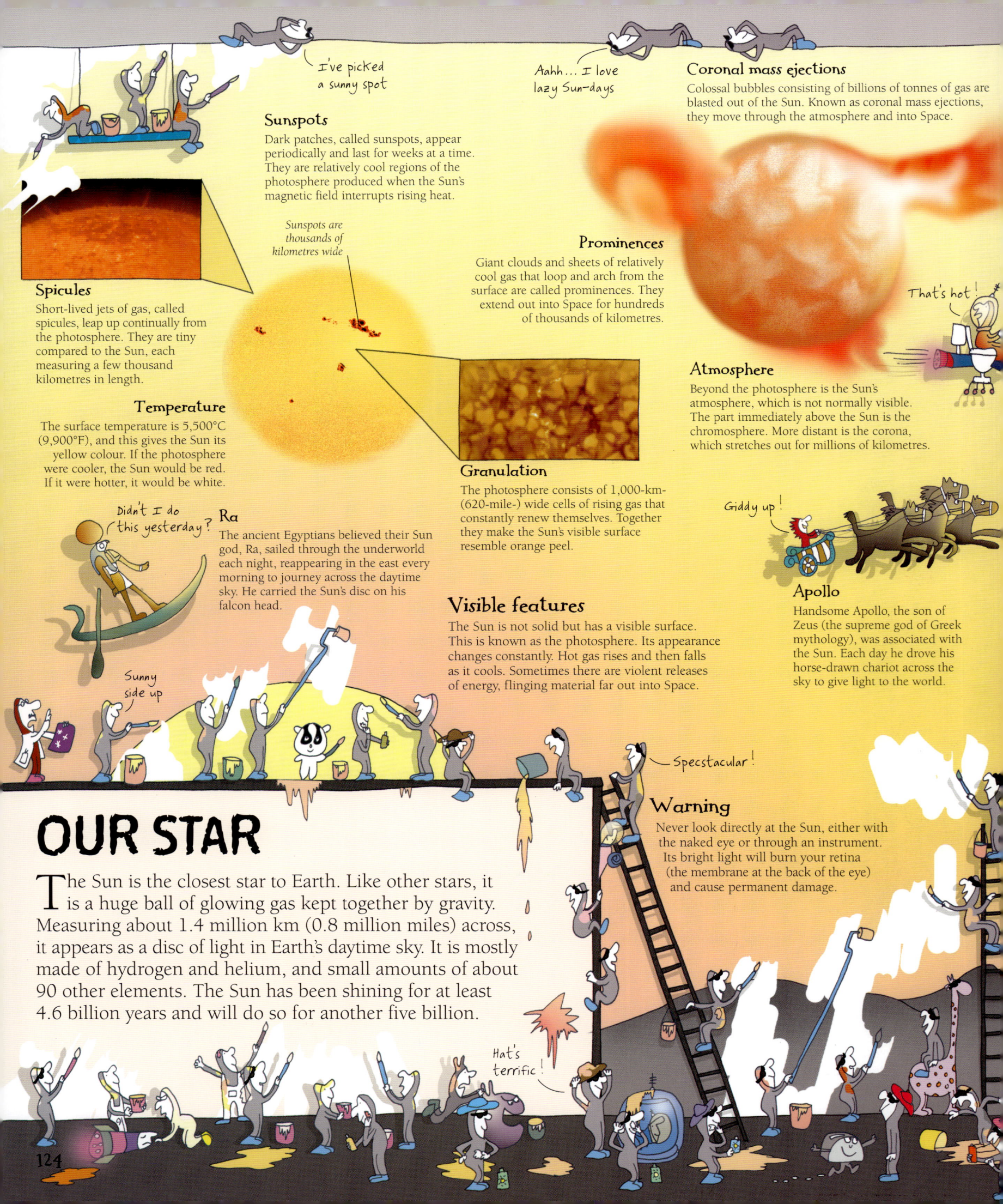

Sunspots
Dark patches, called sunspots, appear periodically and last for weeks at a time. They are relatively cool regions of the photosphere produced when the Sun's magnetic field interrupts rising heat.

Sunspots are thousands of kilometres wide

Prominences
Giant clouds and sheets of relatively cool gas that loop and arch from the surface are called prominences. They extend out into Space for hundreds of thousands of kilometres.

Coronal mass ejections
Colossal bubbles consisting of billions of tonnes of gas are blasted out of the Sun. Known as coronal mass ejections, they move through the atmosphere and into Space.

Spicules
Short-lived jets of gas, called spicules, leap up continually from the photosphere. They are tiny compared to the Sun, each measuring a few thousand kilometres in length.

Temperature
The surface temperature is 5,500°C (9,900°F), and this gives the Sun its yellow colour. If the photosphere were cooler, the Sun would be red. If it were hotter, it would be white.

Atmosphere
Beyond the photosphere is the Sun's atmosphere, which is not normally visible. The part immediately above the Sun is the chromosphere. More distant is the corona, which stretches out for millions of kilometres.

Ra
The ancient Egyptians believed their Sun god, Ra, sailed through the underworld each night, reappearing in the east every morning to journey across the daytime sky. He carried the Sun's disc on his falcon head.

Granulation
The photosphere consists of 1,000-km- (620-mile-) wide cells of rising gas that constantly renew themselves. Together they make the Sun's visible surface resemble orange peel.

Visible features
The Sun is not solid but has a visible surface. This is known as the photosphere. Its appearance changes constantly. Hot gas rises and then falls as it cools. Sometimes there are violent releases of energy, flinging material far out into Space.

Apollo
Handsome Apollo, the son of Zeus (the supreme god of Greek mythology), was associated with the Sun. Each day he drove his horse-drawn chariot across the sky to give light to the world.

OUR STAR

The Sun is the closest star to Earth. Like other stars, it is a huge ball of glowing gas kept together by gravity. Measuring about 1.4 million km (0.8 million miles) across, it appears as a disc of light in Earth's daytime sky. It is mostly made of hydrogen and helium, and small amounts of about 90 other elements. The Sun has been shining for at least 4.6 billion years and will do so for another five billion.

Warning
Never look directly at the Sun, either with the naked eye or through an instrument. Its bright light will burn your retina (the membrane at the back of the eye) and cause permanent damage.

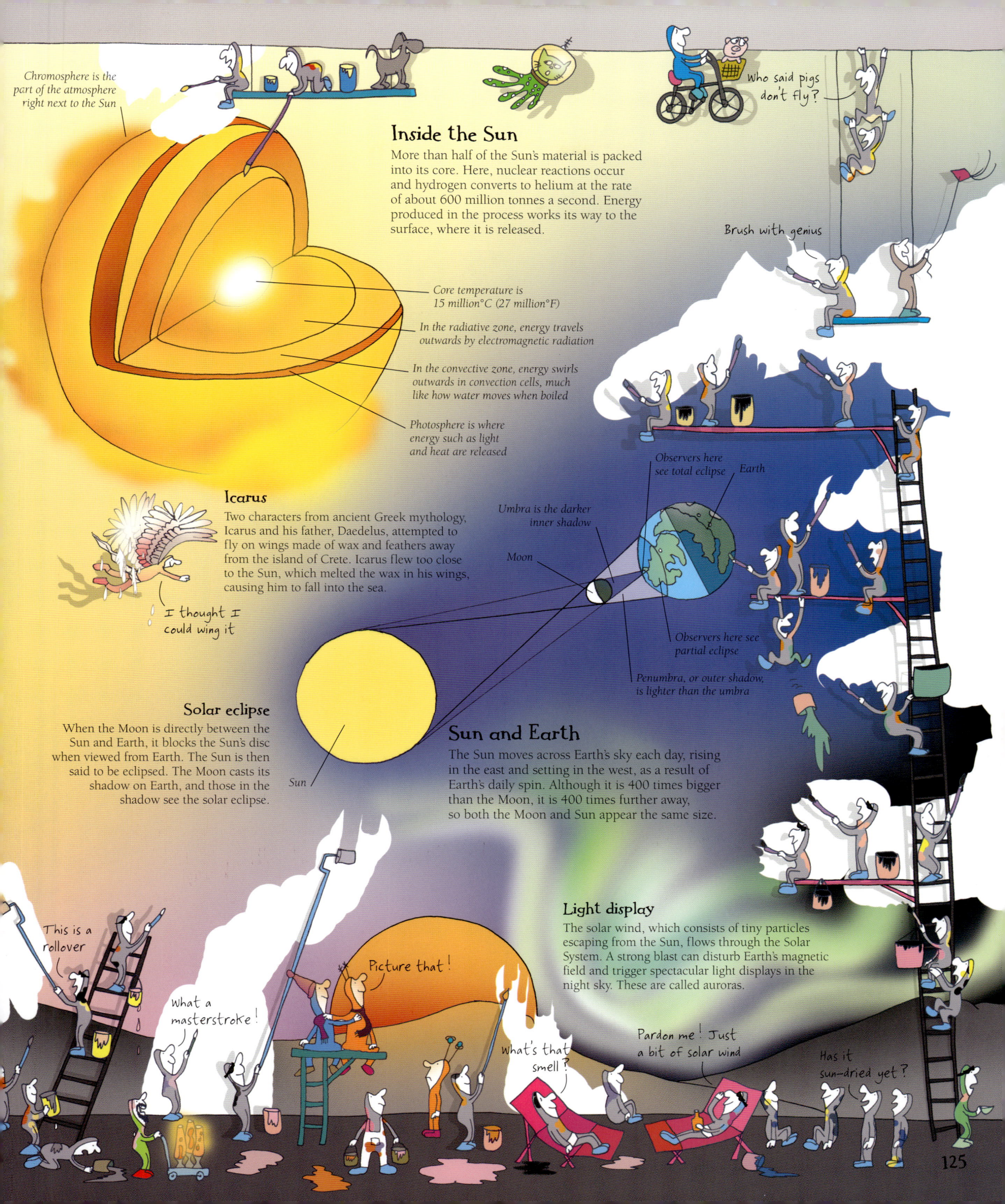

Chromosphere is the part of the atmosphere right next to the Sun

Inside the Sun

More than half of the Sun's material is packed into its core. Here, nuclear reactions occur and hydrogen converts to helium at the rate of about 600 million tonnes a second. Energy produced in the process works its way to the surface, where it is released.

Core temperature is 15 million°C (27 million°F)

In the radiative zone, energy travels outwards by electromagnetic radiation

In the convective zone, energy swirls outwards in convection cells, much like how water moves when boiled

Photosphere is where energy such as light and heat are released

Icarus

Two characters from ancient Greek mythology, Icarus and his father, Daedelus, attempted to fly on wings made of wax and feathers away from the island of Crete. Icarus flew too close to the Sun, which melted the wax in his wings, causing him to fall into the sea.

I thought I could wing it

Observers here see total eclipse

Earth

Umbra is the darker inner shadow

Moon

Observers here see partial eclipse

Penumbra, or outer shadow, is lighter than the umbra

Solar eclipse

When the Moon is directly between the Sun and Earth, it blocks the Sun's disc when viewed from Earth. The Sun is then said to be eclipsed. The Moon casts its shadow on Earth, and those in the shadow see the solar eclipse.

Sun

Sun and Earth

The Sun moves across Earth's sky each day, rising in the east and setting in the west, as a result of Earth's daily spin. Although it is 400 times bigger than the Moon, it is 400 times further away, so both the Moon and Sun appear the same size.

Light display

The solar wind, which consists of tiny particles escaping from the Sun, flows through the Solar System. A strong blast can disturb Earth's magnetic field and trigger spectacular light displays in the night sky. These are called auroras.

125

STARRY, STARRY NIGHT

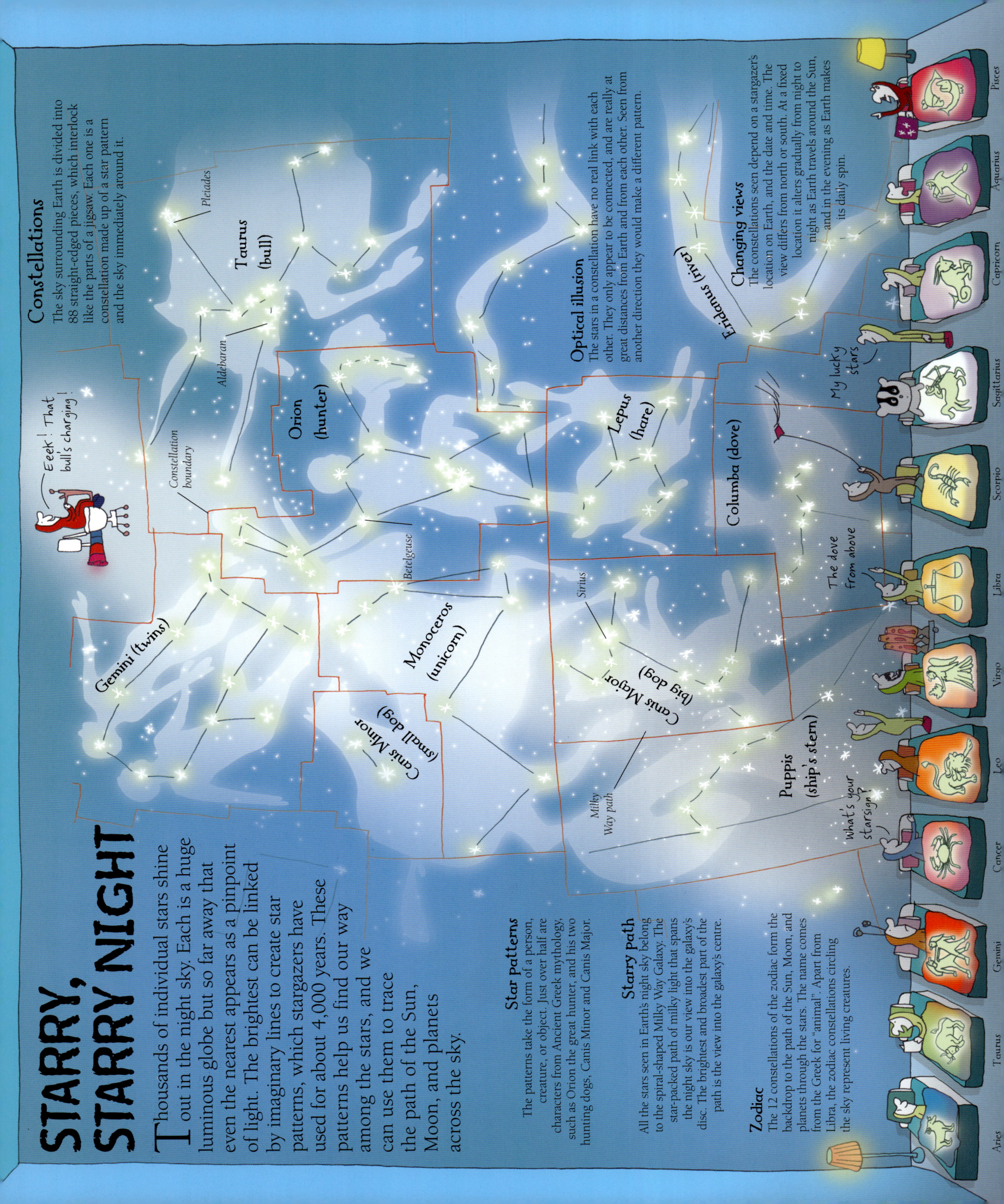

Thousands of individual stars shine out in the night sky. Each is a huge luminous globe but so far away that even the nearest appears as a pinpoint of light. The brightest can be linked by imaginary lines to create star patterns, which stargazers have used for about 4,000 years. These patterns help us find our way among the stars, and we can use them to trace the path of the Sun, Moon, and planets across the sky.

Star patterns
The patterns take the form of a person, creature, or object. Just over half are characters from Ancient Greek mythology, such as Orion the great hunter, and his two hunting dogs, Canis Minor and Canis Major.

Starry path
All the stars seen in Earth's night sky belong to the spiral-shaped Milky Way Galaxy. The star-packed path of milky light that spans the night sky is our view into the galaxy's disc. The brightest and broadest part of the path is the view into the galaxy's centre.

Zodiac
The 12 constellations of the zodiac form the backdrop to the path of the Sun, Moon, and planets through the stars. The name comes from the Greek for "animal". Apart from Libra, the zodiac constellations circling the sky represent living creatures.

Constellations
The sky surrounding Earth is divided into 88 straight-edged pieces, which interlock like the parts of a jigsaw. Each one is a constellation made up of a star pattern and the sky immediately around it.

Optical illusion
The stars in a constellation have no real link with each other. They only appear to be connected, and are really at great distances from Earth and from each other. Seen from another direction they would make a different pattern.

Changing views
The constellations seen depend on a stargazer's location on Earth, and the date and time. The view differs from north or south. At a fixed location it alters gradually from night to night as Earth travels around the Sun, and in the evening as Earth makes its daily spin.

Eeek! That bull's charging!

Gemini (twins)
Taurus (bull)
Pleiades
Aldebaran
Constellation boundary
Orion (hunter)
Betelgeuse
Monoceros (unicorn)
Canis Minor (small dog)
Canis Major (big dog)
Sirius
Milky Way path
Puppis (ship's stern)
Lepus (hare)
Columba (dove)
Eridanus (river)
The dove from above
My lucky stars
What's your star sign?

Aries · Taurus · Gemini · Cancer · Leo · Virgo · Libra · Scorpio · Sagittarius · Capricorn · Aquarius · Pisces

Name game

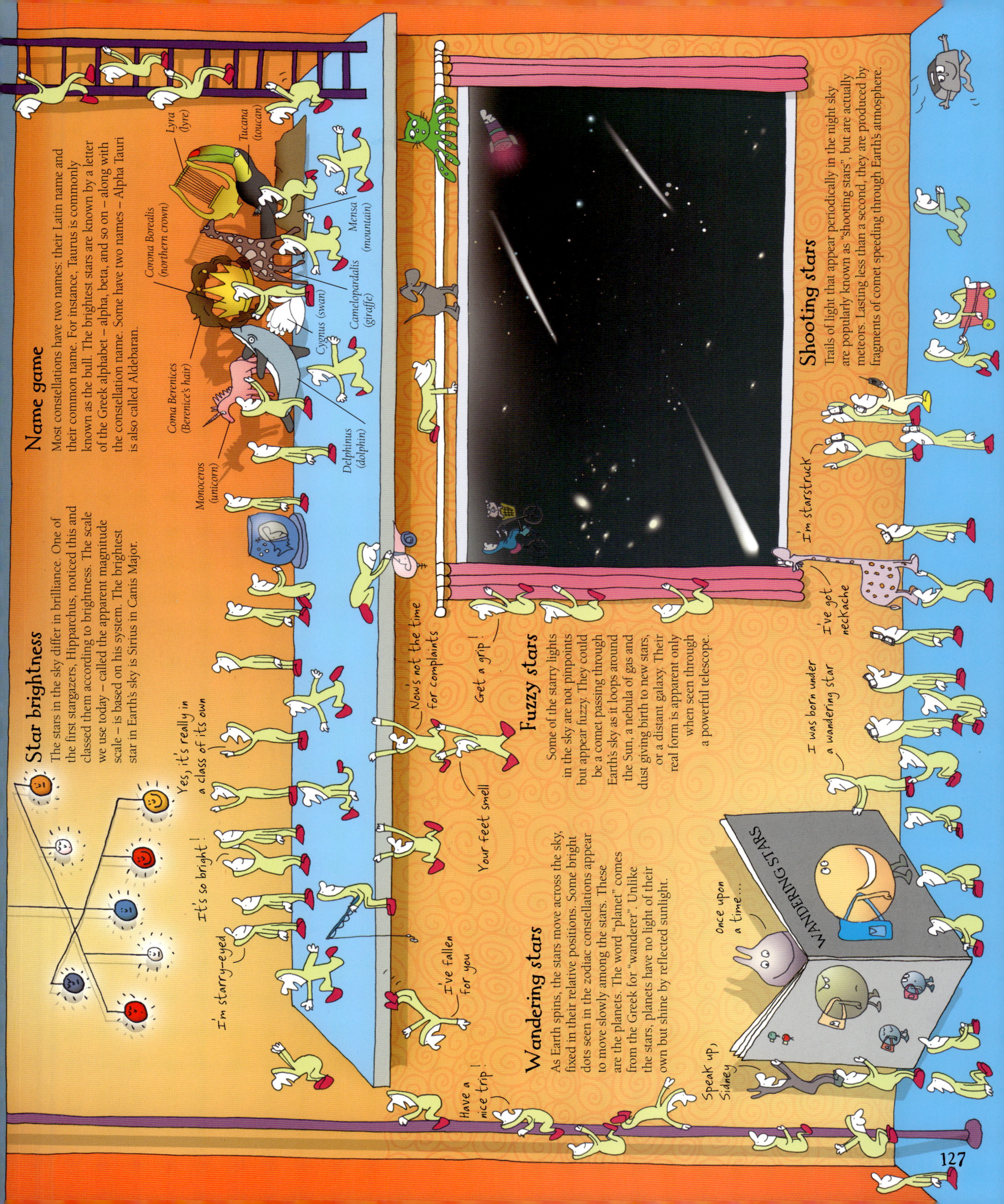

Most constellations have two names: their Latin name and their common name. For instance, Taurus is commonly known as the bull. The brightest stars are known by a letter of the Greek alphabet – alpha, beta, and so on – along with the constellation name. Some have two names – Alpha Tauri is also called Aldebaran.

Lyra (lyre)
Tucana (toucan)
Corona Borealis (northern crown)
Coma Berenices (Berenice's hair)
Cygnus (swan)
Camelopardalis (giraffe)
Mensa (mountain)
Delphinus (dolphin)
Monoceros (unicorn)

Star brightness

The stars in the sky differ in brilliance. One of the first stargazers, Hipparchus, noticed this and classed them according to brightness. The scale we use today – called the apparent magnitude scale – is based on his system. The brightest star in Earth's sky is Sirius in Canis Major.

Fuzzy stars

Some of the starry lights in the sky are not pinpoints but appear fuzzy. They could be a comet passing through Earth's sky as it loops around the Sun, a nebula of gas and dust giving birth to new stars, or a distant galaxy. Their real form is apparent only when seen through a powerful telescope.

Wandering stars

As Earth spins, the stars move across the sky, fixed in their relative positions. Some bright dots seen in the zodiac constellations appear to move slowly among the stars. These are the planets. The word "planet" comes from the Greek for "wanderer". Unlike the stars, planets have no light of their own but shine by reflected sunlight.

Shooting stars

Trails of light that appear periodically in the night sky are popularly known as "shooting stars", but are actually meteors. Lasting less than a second, they are produced by fragments of comet speeding through Earth's atmosphere.

127

RECYCLED UNIVERSE

Stars do not live forever, but they do have very long lives. Sun-like stars shine brightly for billions of years, while more massive ones last just a few million years. The mass of a star – the amount of material it is made of – not only determines the length of its life, but also how it dies. Most stars fade away, but the most massive end their lives abruptly. As stars die they shed material, which helps create a new generation of stars.

Death of Sun-like stars
The Sun and other stars made up of less than eight times the Sun's mass spend the longest part of their lives as main sequence stars. They shine brightly and steadily but change as they mature and die slowly.

Red giant
When the star's core has converted its hydrogen to helium, it collapses and the gas surrounding it is pushed out. The star becomes a red giant up to 100 times larger than before.

Planetary nebula
The star's core converts its helium into other elements. It becomes hotter and pushes off the outer star region. A planetary nebula (glowing shell of gas and dust) surrounds the dying star.

White dwarf
The star is now Earth-sized and no longer producing energy. It shines because of its stored energy. This is the final stage of its life. The white dwarf fades slowly and cools until it is a cold, dark cinder in Space.

Explosive end
Stars made of more than eight times the Sun's mass end their lives suddenly, in explosive fashion. Much of their star material is blasted into Space, but a core is left behind. What this is like depends on how much material it is made of.

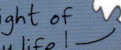

Black hole
A supernova core made of more than about three times the mass of the Sun does not stop collapsing at the neutron star stage. It continues to collapse, becoming so small and dense that it is a black hole in Space.

Supernova remnant
Material pushed off by the dying star is called a supernova remnant. It moves out from the explosion site and disperses slowly into Space.

Neutron star
If the core left behind by the supernova is between about 1.4 and 3 times the mass of the Sun, it collapses to form a neutron star. This is a city-sized sphere, which emits beams of energy that sweep across Space as it spins. A neutron star discovered by its beams is called a pulsar.

Supernova
When a massive star runs out of gas to convert, its core collapses and most of the star is blown off in a huge explosion, known as a supernova. The star goes very bright temporarily.

I am star stuff!
The Sun is mainly hydrogen and helium, but also includes small amounts of other elements. Earth formed close to the Sun from the same cloud of matter. Humans are material made from Earth's elements, so everything in our bodies was once in a star.

Star generations
Nuclear reactions inside the first stars produced new elements, which were dispersed when the stars died. This enriched material formed a new generation of stars, creating further amounts of new elements.

It's elementary
Most of the chemical elements in the Universe today, such as oxygen and carbon, were made by stars. Many were created by nuclear reactions inside stars, but others came from supernova explosions. The variety of elements Earth is made of came from stars.

First stars
When the Universe was young, the only chemical elements it contained were hydrogen and helium, so the first stars were formed from these two elements.

Stage 3
Dense clumps form in the clouds and collapse to form stars. The brilliant light of young stars clears parts of the clouds away and makes them glow.

Stage 2
In the mixed up material, clouds are drawn together by gravity. These clouds are huge, cold, and dark.

Stage 4
The stars are now in the prime of their lives. They shine steadily as nuclear reactions deep within them convert their hydrogen into helium and other elements.

Stage 1
Gas and dust is shed by stars nearing the ends of their lives. Over millions of years, it spreads out and mixes with thin hydrogen gas between the stars.

Stellar recycling
Material from dying stars, such as that pushed off when a supernova explodes, collects together as a vast cloud that will produce new stars. Successive generations of stars have been created in this way throughout the history of the Universe.

MEET THE FAMILY

Earth is part of a Space family called the Solar System, formed from a vast cloud of gas and dust about 4.6 billion years ago. It consists of the Sun and a number of objects orbiting around it. After the Sun, the most prominent family members are eight planets, but there are more smaller bodies. The planets were once thought to be unique, but we now know that other stars have planets orbiting around them, too.

Solar System
The four closest planets to the Sun are the rock and metal worlds of Mercury, Venus, Earth, and Mars. Beyond these are four planets known as the giants: Jupiter, Saturn, Uranus, and Neptune. Each planet and object in the system follows a path around the Sun, and one complete circuit of the Sun is called an orbit. As each object orbits, it also spins.

Sun
The largest and central member of the Solar System is the Sun. It is a star made of gas, and its gravity keeps the system together.

Jupiter
The largest planet and the fastest spinner is Jupiter. Like the other giants, it is mostly made of gas and liquid – the top of its thick gas atmosphere is what we see from Earth.

Neptune
The coldest planet and furthest from the Sun is Neptune. It has the longest orbit of all, completing one circuit every 165 years.

Earth
This rocky world is third out from the Sun. Earth is the only planet known to have liquid water and to support life.

Venus
Almost as large as Earth, Venus is the hottest and slowest-spinning planet. Beneath its unbroken layer of cloud is a surface of volcanic lava.

Mercury
Closest to the Sun and the smallest planet of all is Mercury. This grey, dry world covered by impact craters has the shortest orbit of just 88 days.

Uranus
Twice as far from the Sun than Saturn, Uranus is third largest of the giant planets. It takes 84 years to travel once around the Sun.

Mars
Next out from the Sun after Earth, Mars is the outermost rocky planet. It is a cold, dry world coloured rust-red by its soil.

Saturn
A complex system of rings surrounds Saturn, the second-largest planet and sixth out from the Sun.

Dwarf planets
These almost-round rocky balls orbit among other smaller objects. Pluto orbits in the Kuiper Belt of objects beyond Neptune.

Moons
More than 160 moons orbit the six outer planets. Jupiter's Ganymede is the largest. The smallest are irregular in shape.

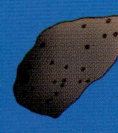

Asteroids
Billions of rocky bodies orbit the Sun between Mars and Jupiter. These are asteroids, unused material from when the planets formed.

Comets
Trillions of comets orbit beyond Neptune. When one of these gigantic dirty snowballs travels near the Sun, it grows gas and dust tails and a large head.

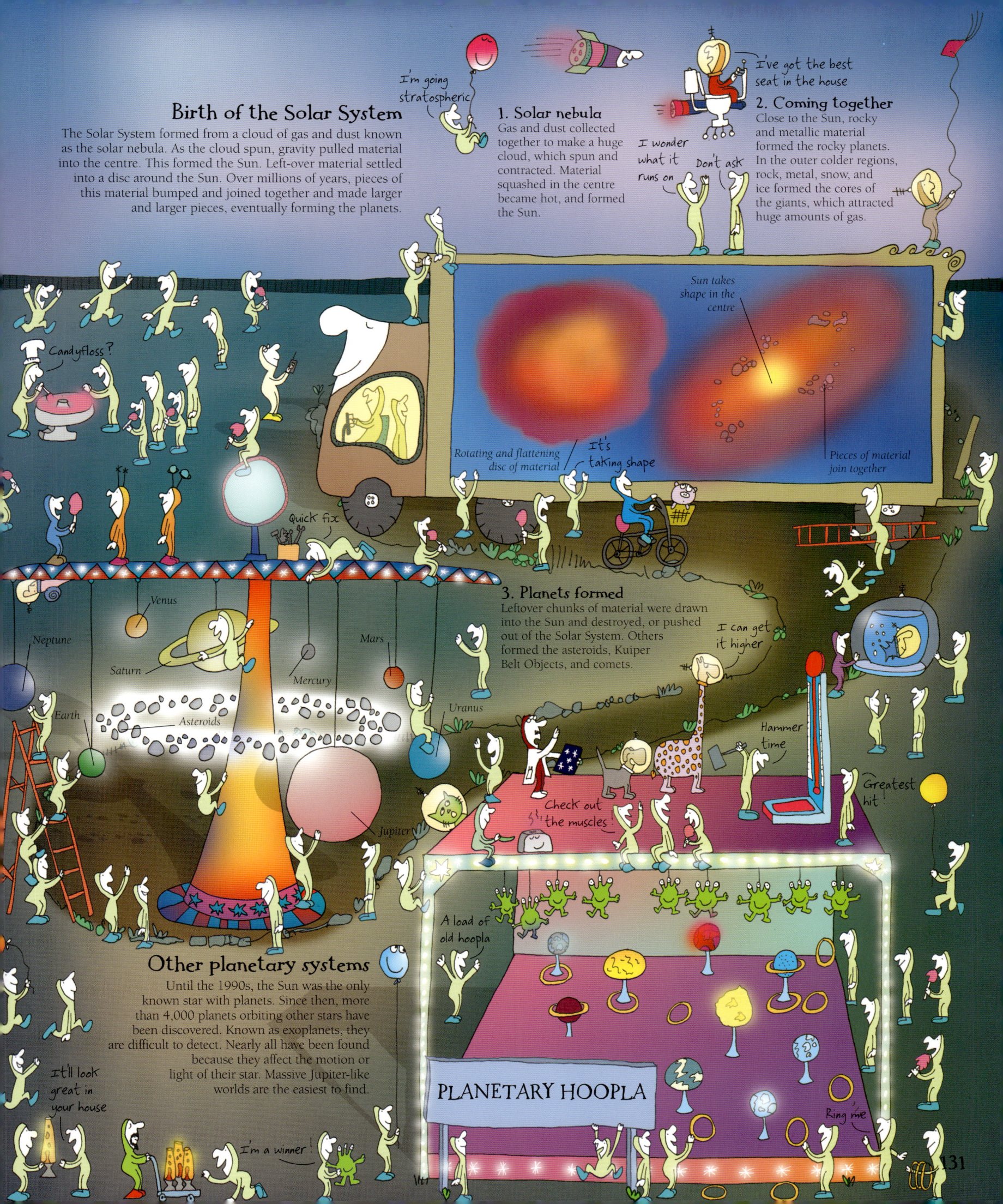

Birth of the Solar System

The Solar System formed from a cloud of gas and dust known as the solar nebula. As the cloud spun, gravity pulled material into the centre. This formed the Sun. Left-over material settled into a disc around the Sun. Over millions of years, pieces of this material bumped and joined together and made larger and larger pieces, eventually forming the planets.

1. Solar nebula
Gas and dust collected together to make a huge cloud, which spun and contracted. Material squashed in the centre became hot, and formed the Sun.

2. Coming together
Close to the Sun, rocky and metallic material formed the rocky planets. In the outer colder regions, rock, metal, snow, and ice formed the cores of the giants, which attracted huge amounts of gas.

3. Planets formed
Leftover chunks of material were drawn into the Sun and destroyed, or pushed out of the Solar System. Others formed the asteroids, Kuiper Belt Objects, and comets.

Other planetary systems
Until the 1990s, the Sun was the only known star with planets. Since then, more than 4,000 planets orbiting other stars have been discovered. Known as exoplanets, they are difficult to detect. Nearly all have been found because they affect the motion or light of their star. Massive Jupiter-like worlds are the easiest to find.

PLANETARY HOOPLA

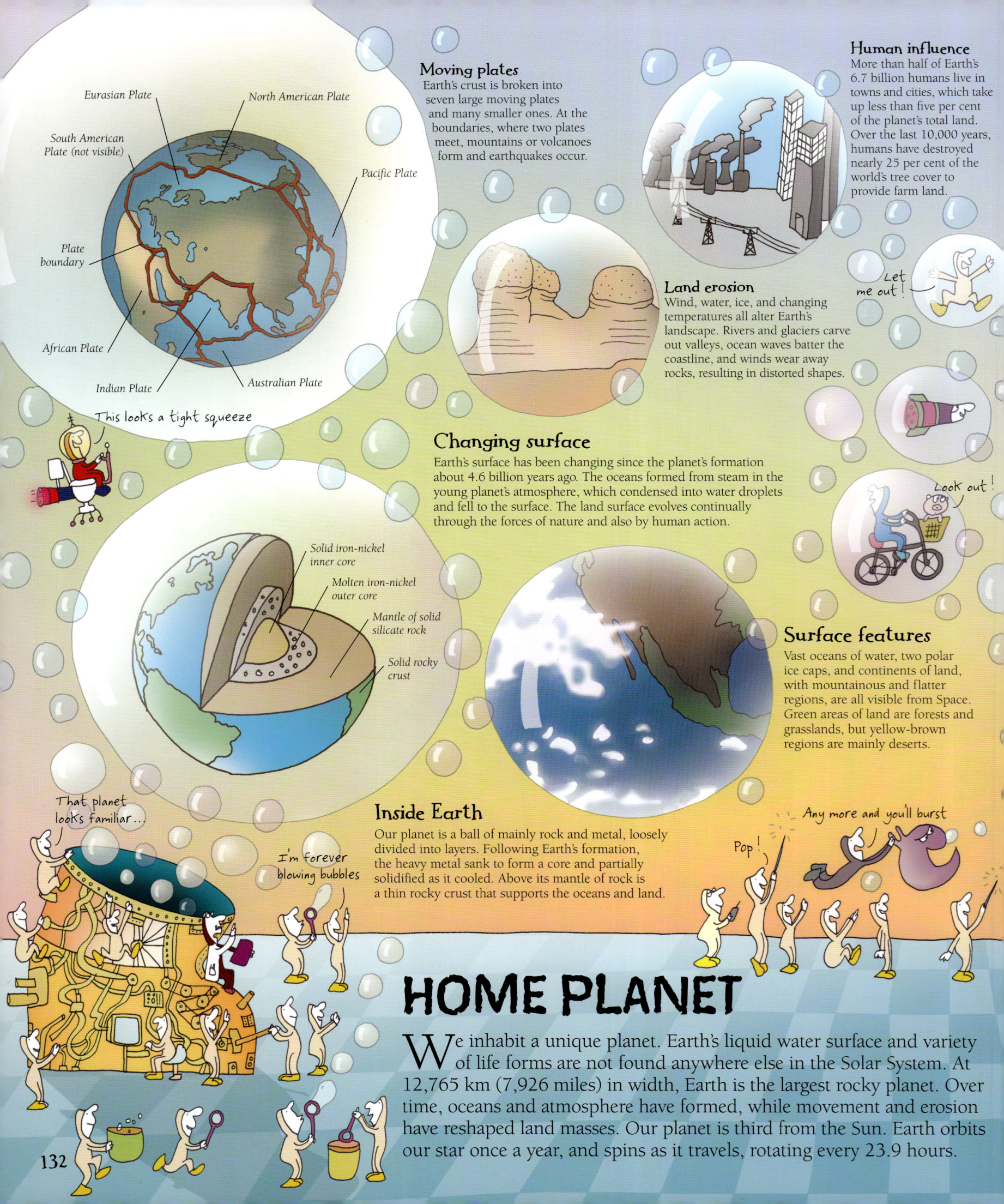

Moving plates
Earth's crust is broken into seven large moving plates and many smaller ones. At the boundaries, where two plates meet, mountains or volcanoes form and earthquakes occur.

Labels: Eurasian Plate, North American Plate, South American Plate (not visible), Pacific Plate, Plate boundary, African Plate, Indian Plate, Australian Plate

Human influence
More than half of Earth's 6.7 billion humans live in towns and cities, which take up less than five per cent of the planet's total land. Over the last 10,000 years, humans have destroyed nearly 25 per cent of the world's tree cover to provide farm land.

Land erosion
Wind, water, ice, and changing temperatures all alter Earth's landscape. Rivers and glaciers carve out valleys, ocean waves batter the coastline, and winds wear away rocks, resulting in distorted shapes.

Changing surface
Earth's surface has been changing since the planet's formation about 4.6 billion years ago. The oceans formed from steam in the young planet's atmosphere, which condensed into water droplets and fell to the surface. The land surface evolves continually through the forces of nature and also by human action.

Surface features
Vast oceans of water, two polar ice caps, and continents of land, with mountainous and flatter regions, are all visible from Space. Green areas of land are forests and grasslands, but yellow-brown regions are mainly deserts.

Labels: Solid iron-nickel inner core, Molten iron-nickel outer core, Mantle of solid silicate rock, Solid rocky crust

Inside Earth
Our planet is a ball of mainly rock and metal, loosely divided into layers. Following Earth's formation, the heavy metal sank to form a core and partially solidified as it cooled. Above its mantle of rock is a thin rocky crust that supports the oceans and land.

HOME PLANET

We inhabit a unique planet. Earth's liquid water surface and variety of life forms are not found anywhere else in the Solar System. At 12,765 km (7,926 miles) in width, Earth is the largest rocky planet. Over time, oceans and atmosphere have formed, while movement and erosion have reshaped land masses. Our planet is third from the Sun. Earth orbits our star once a year, and spins as it travels, rotating every 23.9 hours.

Water world

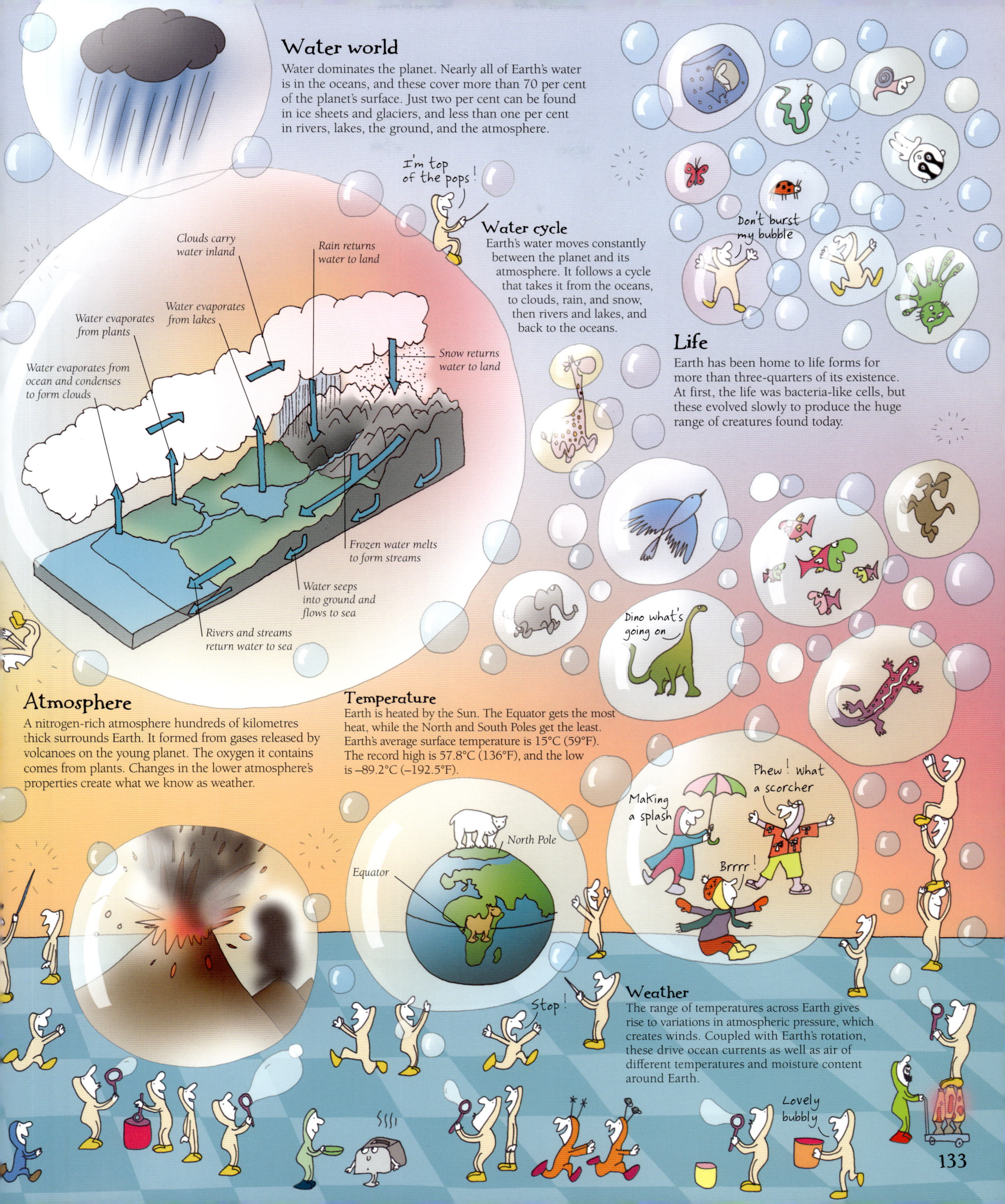

Water dominates the planet. Nearly all of Earth's water is in the oceans, and these cover more than 70 per cent of the planet's surface. Just two per cent can be found in ice sheets and glaciers, and less than one per cent in rivers, lakes, the ground, and the atmosphere.

Water cycle

Earth's water moves constantly between the planet and its atmosphere. It follows a cycle that takes it from the oceans, to clouds, rain, and snow, then rivers and lakes, and back to the oceans.

Clouds carry water inland

Rain returns water to land

Water evaporates from plants

Water evaporates from lakes

Snow returns water to land

Water evaporates from ocean and condenses to form clouds

Frozen water melts to form streams

Water seeps into ground and flows to sea

Rivers and streams return water to sea

Life

Earth has been home to life forms for more than three-quarters of its existence. At first, the life was bacteria-like cells, but these evolved slowly to produce the huge range of creatures found today.

Atmosphere

A nitrogen-rich atmosphere hundreds of kilometres thick surrounds Earth. It formed from gases released by volcanoes on the young planet. The oxygen it contains comes from plants. Changes in the lower atmosphere's properties create what we know as weather.

Temperature

Earth is heated by the Sun. The Equator gets the most heat, while the North and South Poles get the least. Earth's average surface temperature is 15°C (59°F). The record high is 57.8°C (136°F), and the low is −89.2°C (−192.5°F).

North Pole

Equator

Weather

The range of temperatures across Earth gives rise to variations in atmospheric pressure, which creates winds. Coupled with Earth's rotation, these drive ocean currents as well as air of different temperatures and moisture content around Earth.

BEST MATE MOON

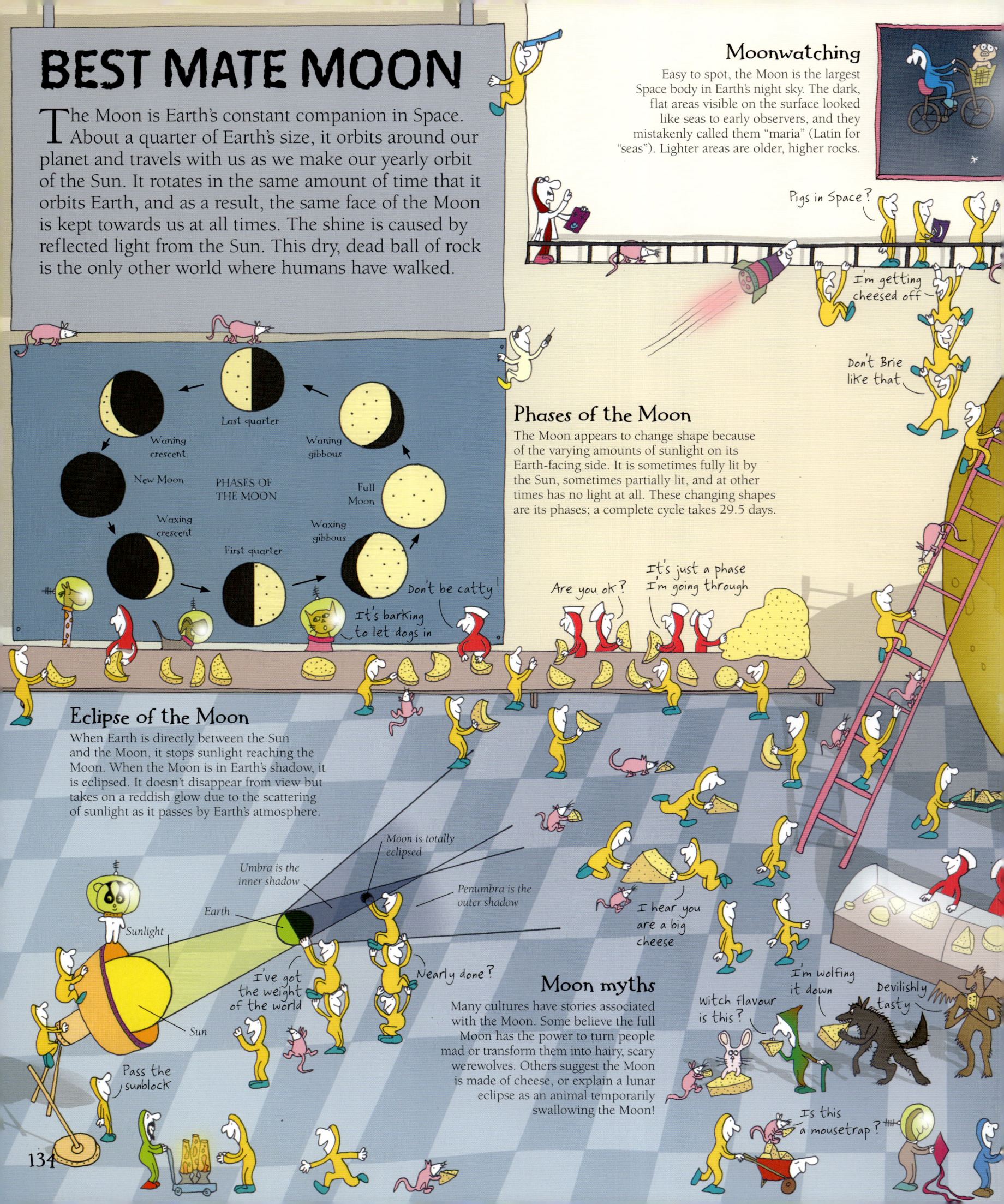

The Moon is Earth's constant companion in Space. About a quarter of Earth's size, it orbits around our planet and travels with us as we make our yearly orbit of the Sun. It rotates in the same amount of time that it orbits Earth, and as a result, the same face of the Moon is kept towards us at all times. The shine is caused by reflected light from the Sun. This dry, dead ball of rock is the only other world where humans have walked.

Moonwatching

Easy to spot, the Moon is the largest Space body in Earth's night sky. The dark, flat areas visible on the surface looked like seas to early observers, and they mistakenly called them "maria" (Latin for "seas"). Lighter areas are older, higher rocks.

Phases of the Moon

The Moon appears to change shape because of the varying amounts of sunlight on its Earth-facing side. It is sometimes fully lit by the Sun, sometimes partially lit, and at other times has no light at all. These changing shapes are its phases; a complete cycle takes 29.5 days.

PHASES OF THE MOON
- New Moon
- Waxing crescent
- First quarter
- Waxing gibbous
- Full Moon
- Waning gibbous
- Last quarter
- Waning crescent

Eclipse of the Moon

When Earth is directly between the Sun and the Moon, it stops sunlight reaching the Moon. When the Moon is in Earth's shadow, it is eclipsed. It doesn't disappear from view but takes on a reddish glow due to the scattering of sunlight as it passes by Earth's atmosphere.

- Sun
- Sunlight
- Earth
- Umbra is the inner shadow
- Penumbra is the outer shadow
- Moon is totally eclipsed

Moon myths

Many cultures have stories associated with the Moon. Some believe the full Moon has the power to turn people mad or transform them into hairy, scary werewolves. Others suggest the Moon is made of cheese, or explain a lunar eclipse as an animal temporarily swallowing the Moon!

134

Birth of the Moon

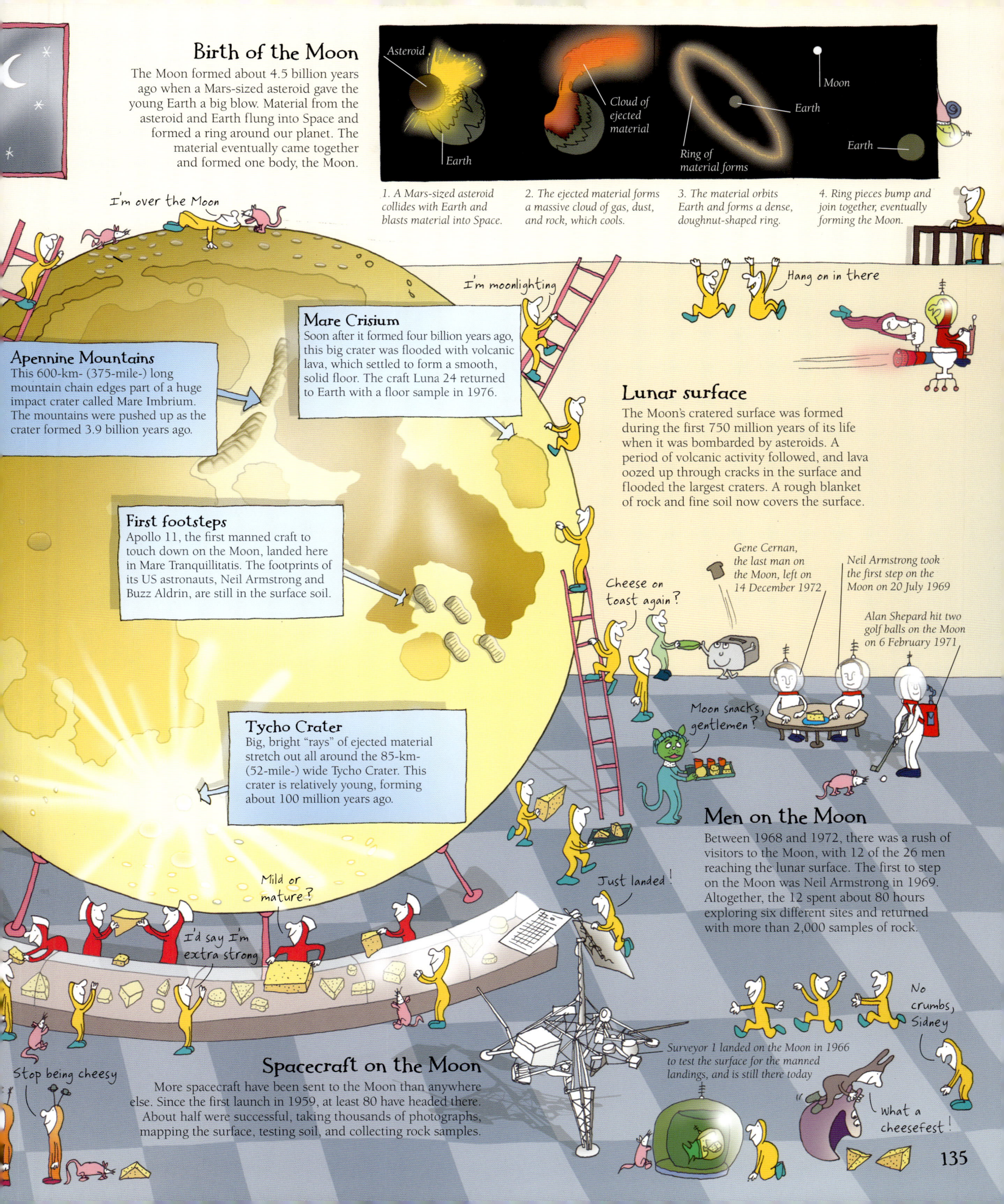

The Moon formed about 4.5 billion years ago when a Mars-sized asteroid gave the young Earth a big blow. Material from the asteroid and Earth flung into Space and formed a ring around our planet. The material eventually came together and formed one body, the Moon.

1. A Mars-sized asteroid collides with Earth and blasts material into Space.
2. The ejected material forms a massive cloud of gas, dust, and rock, which cools.
3. The material orbits Earth and forms a dense, doughnut-shaped ring.
4. Ring pieces bump and join together, eventually forming the Moon.

Apennine Mountains
This 600-km- (375-mile-) long mountain chain edges part of a huge impact crater called Mare Imbrium. The mountains were pushed up as the crater formed 3.9 billion years ago.

Mare Crisium
Soon after it formed four billion years ago, this big crater was flooded with volcanic lava, which settled to form a smooth, solid floor. The craft Luna 24 returned to Earth with a floor sample in 1976.

First footsteps
Apollo 11, the first manned craft to touch down on the Moon, landed here in Mare Tranquillitatis. The footprints of its US astronauts, Neil Armstrong and Buzz Aldrin, are still in the surface soil.

Tycho Crater
Big, bright "rays" of ejected material stretch out all around the 85-km- (52-mile-) wide Tycho Crater. This crater is relatively young, forming about 100 million years ago.

Lunar surface
The Moon's cratered surface was formed during the first 750 million years of its life when it was bombarded by asteroids. A period of volcanic activity followed, and lava oozed up through cracks in the surface and flooded the largest craters. A rough blanket of rock and fine soil now covers the surface.

Gene Cernan, the last man on the Moon, left on 14 December 1972

Neil Armstrong took the first step on the Moon on 20 July 1969

Alan Shepard hit two golf balls on the Moon on 6 February 1971

Men on the Moon
Between 1968 and 1972, there was a rush of visitors to the Moon, with 12 of the 26 men reaching the lunar surface. The first to step on the Moon was Neil Armstrong in 1969. Altogether, the 12 spent about 80 hours exploring six different sites and returned with more than 2,000 samples of rock.

Spacecraft on the Moon
More spacecraft have been sent to the Moon than anywhere else. Since the first launch in 1959, at least 80 have headed there. About half were successful, taking thousands of photographs, mapping the surface, testing soil, and collecting rock samples.

Surveyor 1 landed on the Moon in 1966 to test the surface for the manned landings, and is still there today

135

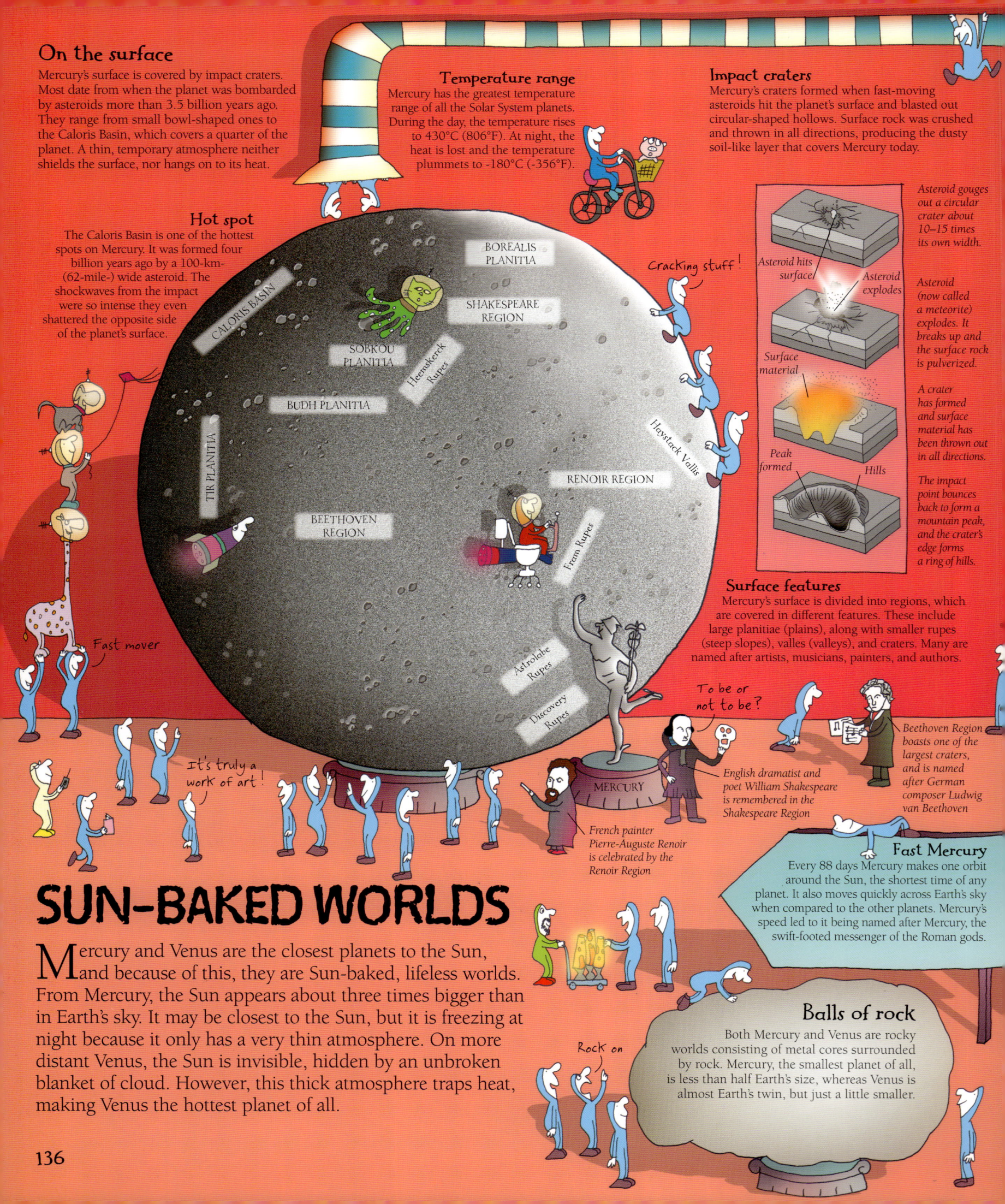

On the surface
Mercury's surface is covered by impact craters. Most date from when the planet was bombarded by asteroids more than 3.5 billion years ago. They range from small bowl-shaped ones to the Caloris Basin, which covers a quarter of the planet. A thin, temporary atmosphere neither shields the surface, nor hangs on to its heat.

Temperature range
Mercury has the greatest temperature range of all the Solar System planets. During the day, the temperature rises to 430°C (806°F). At night, the heat is lost and the temperature plummets to -180°C (-356°F).

Impact craters
Mercury's craters formed when fast-moving asteroids hit the planet's surface and blasted out circular-shaped hollows. Surface rock was crushed and thrown in all directions, producing the dusty soil-like layer that covers Mercury today.

Asteroid gouges out a circular crater about 10–15 times its own width.

Asteroid hits surface

Asteroid explodes

Asteroid (now called a meteorite) explodes. It breaks up and the surface rock is pulverized.

Surface material

A crater has formed and surface material has been thrown out in all directions.

Peak formed — Hills

The impact point bounces back to form a mountain peak, and the crater's edge forms a ring of hills.

Hot spot
The Caloris Basin is one of the hottest spots on Mercury. It was formed four billion years ago by a 100-km- (62-mile-) wide asteroid. The shockwaves from the impact were so intense they even shattered the opposite side of the planet's surface.

BOREALIS PLANITIA
SHAKESPEARE REGION
CALORIS BASIN
SOBKOU PLANITIA
Heemskerck Rupes
BUDH PLANITIA
Haystack Vallis
TIR PLANITIA
RENOIR REGION
BEETHOVEN REGION
Fram Rupes
Astrolabe Rupes
Discovery Rupes

Cracking stuff!

Fast mover

It's truly a work of art!

MERCURY

French painter Pierre-Auguste Renoir is celebrated by the Renoir Region

To be or not to be?

English dramatist and poet William Shakespeare is remembered in the Shakespeare Region

Surface features
Mercury's surface is divided into regions, which are covered in different features. These include large planitiae (plains), along with smaller rupes (steep slopes), valles (valleys), and craters. Many are named after artists, musicians, painters, and authors.

Beethoven Region boasts one of the largest craters, and is named after German composer Ludwig van Beethoven

Fast Mercury
Every 88 days Mercury makes one orbit around the Sun, the shortest time of any planet. It also moves quickly across Earth's sky when compared to the other planets. Mercury's speed led to it being named after Mercury, the swift-footed messenger of the Roman gods.

Rock on

Balls of rock
Both Mercury and Venus are rocky worlds consisting of metal cores surrounded by rock. Mercury, the smallest planet of all, is less than half Earth's size, whereas Venus is almost Earth's twin, but just a little smaller.

SUN-BAKED WORLDS

Mercury and Venus are the closest planets to the Sun, and because of this, they are Sun-baked, lifeless worlds. From Mercury, the Sun appears about three times bigger than in Earth's sky. It may be closest to the Sun, but it is freezing at night because it only has a very thin atmosphere. On more distant Venus, the Sun is invisible, hidden by an unbroken blanket of cloud. However, this thick atmosphere traps heat, making Venus the hottest planet of all.

Hot, hot, hot

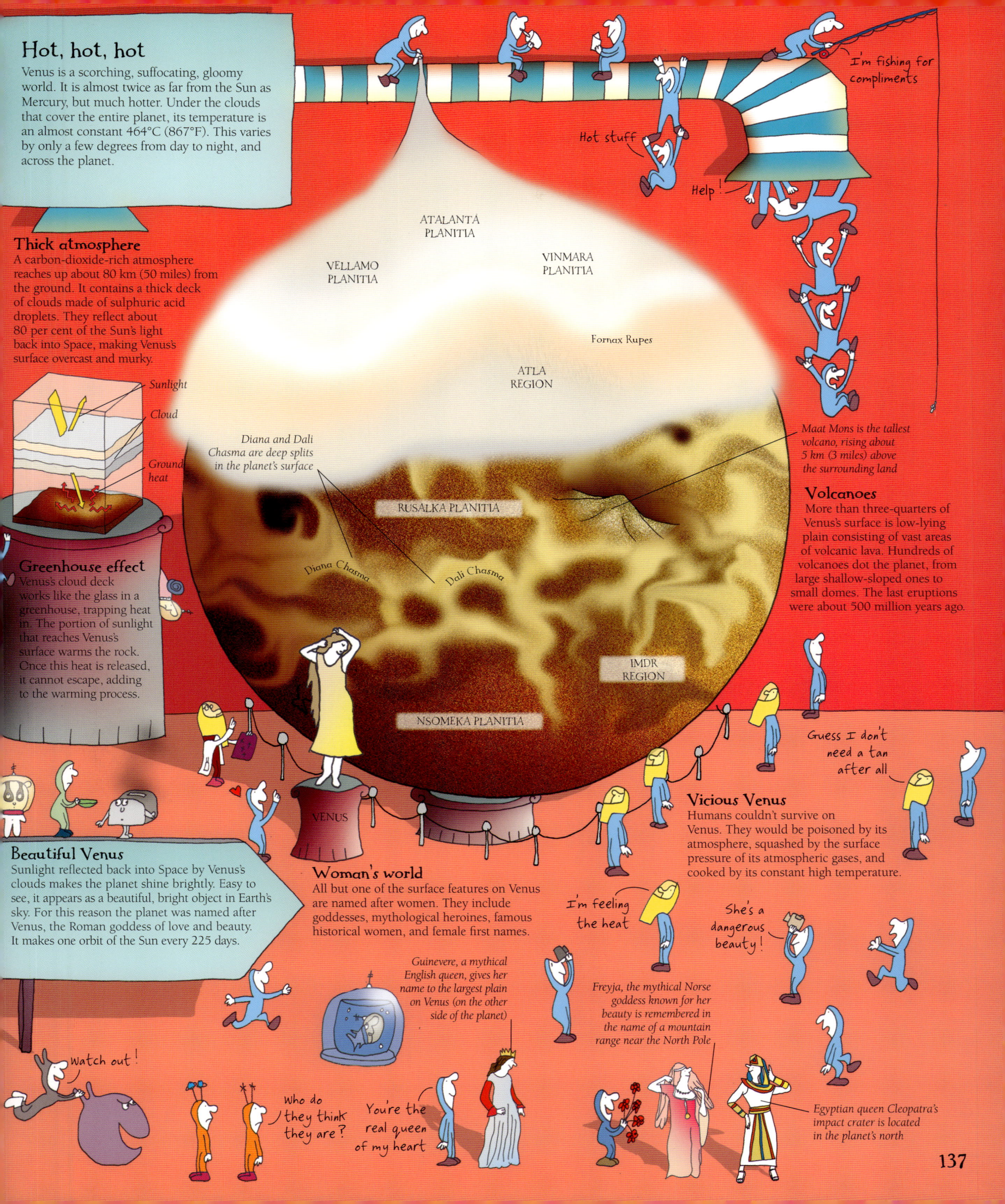

Venus is a scorching, suffocating, gloomy world. It is almost twice as far from the Sun as Mercury, but much hotter. Under the clouds that cover the entire planet, its temperature is an almost constant 464°C (867°F). This varies by only a few degrees from day to night, and across the planet.

Thick atmosphere

A carbon-dioxide-rich atmosphere reaches up about 80 km (50 miles) from the ground. It contains a thick deck of clouds made of sulphuric acid droplets. They reflect about 80 per cent of the Sun's light back into Space, making Venus's surface overcast and murky.

Greenhouse effect

Venus's cloud deck works like the glass in a greenhouse, trapping heat in. The portion of sunlight that reaches Venus's surface warms the rock. Once this heat is released, it cannot escape, adding to the warming process.

Beautiful Venus

Sunlight reflected back into Space by Venus's clouds makes the planet shine brightly. Easy to see, it appears as a beautiful, bright object in Earth's sky. For this reason the planet was named after Venus, the Roman goddess of love and beauty. It makes one orbit of the Sun every 225 days.

ATALANTA PLANITIA
VELLAMO PLANITIA
VINMARA PLANITIA
Fornax Rupes
ATLA REGION
Diana and Dali Chasma are deep splits in the planet's surface
RUSALKA PLANITIA
Diana Chasma
Dali Chasma
IMDR REGION
NSOMEKA PLANITIA
VENUS

Maat Mons is the tallest volcano, rising about 5 km (3 miles) above the surrounding land

Volcanoes

More than three-quarters of Venus's surface is low-lying plain consisting of vast areas of volcanic lava. Hundreds of volcanoes dot the planet, from large shallow-sloped ones to small domes. The last eruptions were about 500 million years ago.

Woman's world

All but one of the surface features on Venus are named after women. They include goddesses, mythological heroines, famous historical women, and female first names.

Guinevere, a mythical English queen, gives her name to the largest plain on Venus (on the other side of the planet)

Vicious Venus

Humans couldn't survive on Venus. They would be poisoned by its atmosphere, squashed by the surface pressure of its atmospheric gases, and cooked by its constant high temperature.

Freyja, the mythical Norse goddess known for her beauty is remembered in the name of a mountain range near the North Pole

Egyptian queen Cleopatra's impact crater is located in the planet's north

HOLIDAY ON MARS

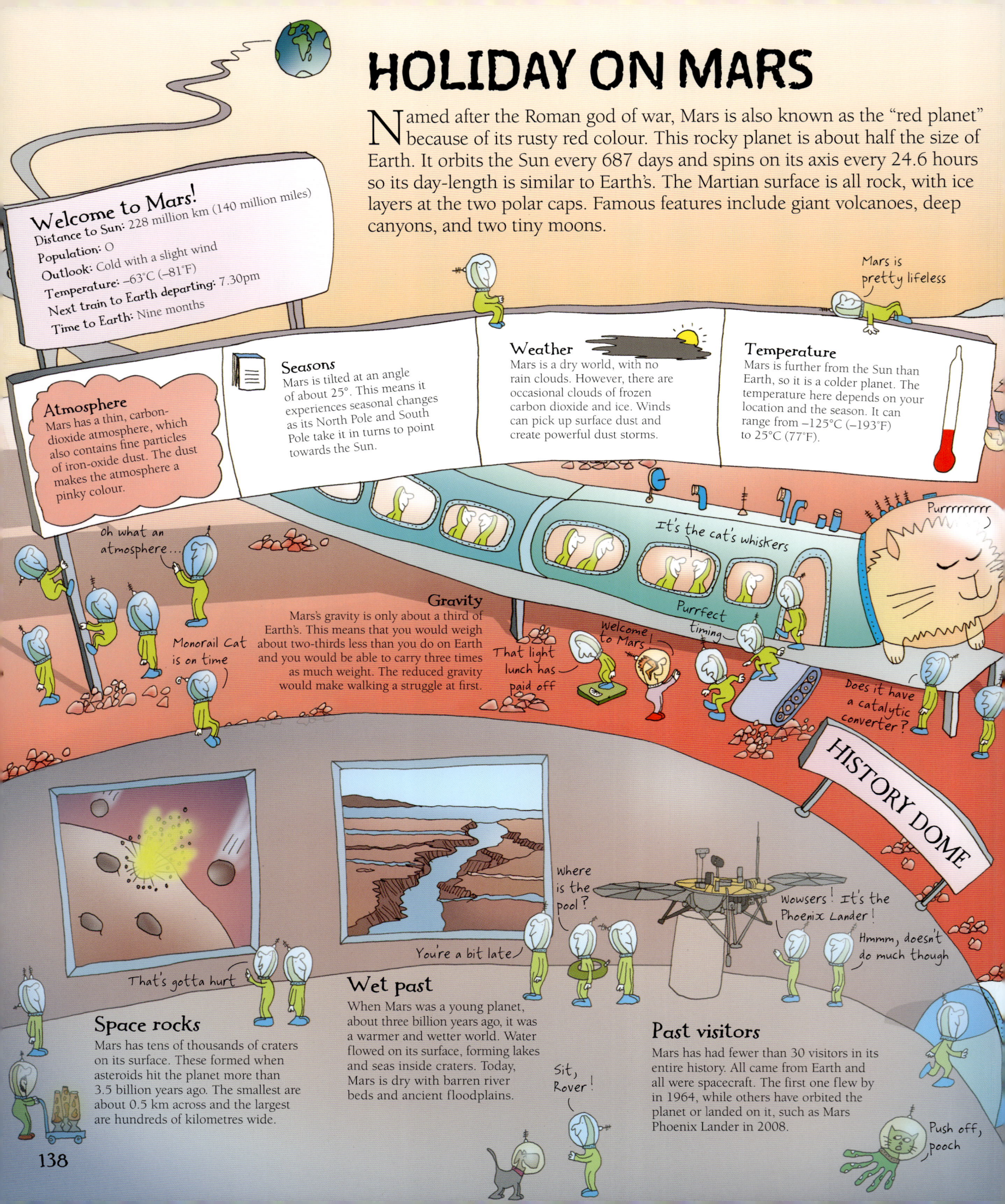

Named after the Roman god of war, Mars is also known as the "red planet" because of its rusty red colour. This rocky planet is about half the size of Earth. It orbits the Sun every 687 days and spins on its axis every 24.6 hours so its day-length is similar to Earth's. The Martian surface is all rock, with ice layers at the two polar caps. Famous features include giant volcanoes, deep canyons, and two tiny moons.

Welcome to Mars!
- **Distance to Sun:** 228 million km (140 million miles)
- **Population:** 0
- **Outlook:** Cold with a slight wind
- **Temperature:** −63°C (−81°F)
- **Next train to Earth departing:** 7.30pm
- **Time to Earth:** Nine months

Atmosphere
Mars has a thin, carbon-dioxide atmosphere, which also contains fine particles of iron-oxide dust. The dust makes the atmosphere a pinky colour.

Seasons
Mars is tilted at an angle of about 25°. This means it experiences seasonal changes as its North Pole and South Pole take it in turns to point towards the Sun.

Weather
Mars is a dry world, with no rain clouds. However, there are occasional clouds of frozen carbon dioxide and ice. Winds can pick up surface dust and create powerful dust storms.

Temperature
Mars is further from the Sun than Earth, so it is a colder planet. The temperature here depends on your location and the season. It can range from −125°C (−193°F) to 25°C (77°F).

Gravity
Mars's gravity is only about a third of Earth's. This means that you would weigh about two-thirds less than you do on Earth and you would be able to carry three times as much weight. The reduced gravity would make walking a struggle at first.

HISTORY DOME

Space rocks
Mars has tens of thousands of craters on its surface. These formed when asteroids hit the planet more than 3.5 billion years ago. The smallest are about 0.5 km across and the largest are hundreds of kilometres wide.

Wet past
When Mars was a young planet, about three billion years ago, it was a warmer and wetter world. Water flowed on its surface, forming lakes and seas inside craters. Today, Mars is dry with barren river beds and ancient floodplains.

Past visitors
Mars has had fewer than 30 visitors in its entire history. All came from Earth and all were spacecraft. The first one flew by in 1964, while others have orbited the planet or landed on it, such as Mars Phoenix Lander in 2008.

North Polar Cap

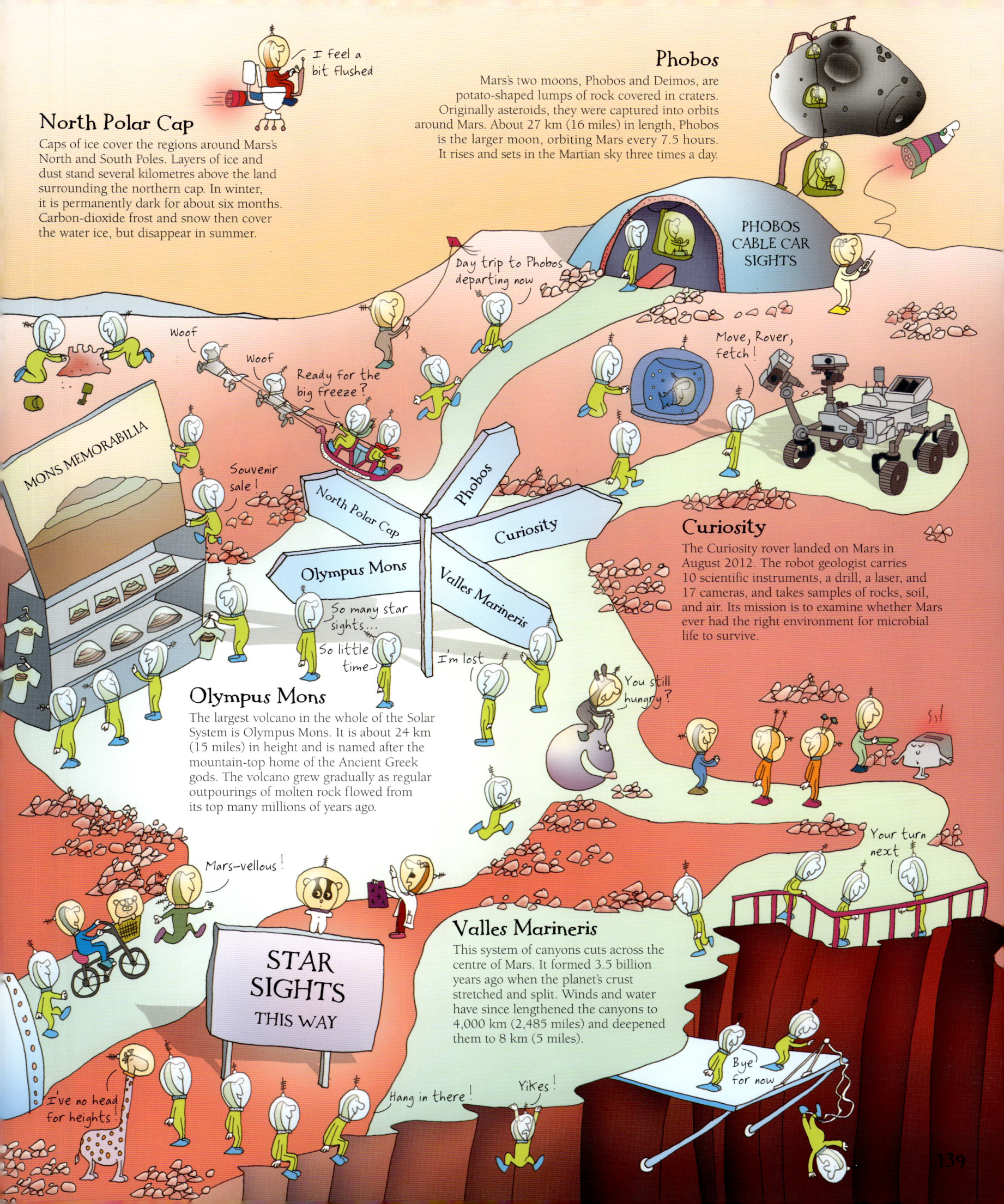

Caps of ice cover the regions around Mars's North and South Poles. Layers of ice and dust stand several kilometres above the land surrounding the northern cap. In winter, it is permanently dark for about six months. Carbon-dioxide frost and snow then cover the water ice, but disappear in summer.

Phobos

Mars's two moons, Phobos and Deimos, are potato-shaped lumps of rock covered in craters. Originally asteroids, they were captured into orbits around Mars. About 27 km (16 miles) in length, Phobos is the larger moon, orbiting Mars every 7.5 hours. It rises and sets in the Martian sky three times a day.

Curiosity

The Curiosity rover landed on Mars in August 2012. The robot geologist carries 10 scientific instruments, a drill, a laser, and 17 cameras, and takes samples of rocks, soil, and air. Its mission is to examine whether Mars ever had the right environment for microbial life to survive.

Olympus Mons

The largest volcano in the whole of the Solar System is Olympus Mons. It is about 24 km (15 miles) in height and is named after the mountain-top home of the Ancient Greek gods. The volcano grew gradually as regular outpourings of molten rock flowed from its top many millions of years ago.

Valles Marineris

This system of canyons cuts across the centre of Mars. It formed 3.5 billion years ago when the planet's crust stretched and split. Winds and water have since lengthened the canyons to 4,000 km (2,485 miles) and deepened them to 8 km (5 miles).

RING OF RUBBLE

Billions of asteroids orbit the Sun. These chunky rocks were left over when the planets were made. Each asteroid follows its own orbit, but most are found in a doughnut-shaped region of Space between the orbits of Mars and Jupiter. Together they make up the Asteroid Belt, also called the Main Belt. Asteroids, or pieces of them, have landed on Earth's surface. When this happens, they are known as meteorites.

NOW SHOWING: POPCORN IN SPACE!

Asteroid profile
Most asteroids are dry, dusty rocks, but some are made of metal, or a mix of rock and metal. Nearly all are irregular lumps with cratered surfaces. The largest is Ceres, which is 938 km (583 miles) across and is also classed as a dwarf planet.

CERES

Trojans

Ceres

Shape and size
Only eight asteroids are bigger than 300 km (186 miles) in width, and these are spherical. Of the irregular-shaped ones, such as Ida, 100,000 are more than 20 km (12 miles) across, and a billion are more than 2 km (1 mile).

IDA

Orbit and spin
Asteroids usually take between four and five years to orbit the Sun. Each one spins as it orbits, taking just a few hours for one complete spin.

Keep up!
Keep pedalling

DRIVE-IN SNACKS
Once you pop, you can't stop
Very pop-ular

Asteroid names
Of more than 1.1 million identified asteroids, 22,870 have been named. Astronomers who discover asteroids can name them. Most are named after people, such as the astronomers or their relatives, as well as writers, musicians, and fictional characters.

James Bond (fictional spy)
I spy...
Cheshirecat (the cat in Lewis Carroll's Alice in Wonderland)
Miaow for now
I'm the magic man
Mr Spock (the discoverer's cat was named after this Star Trek character)
Harrison, Lennon, McCartney, and Starr – members of 1960s music group The Beatles
Must be the Rolling Stones
Merlin (wizard of Arthurian legend)
Neigh he's not

Main Belt
More than 90 per cent of asteroids can be found in the Main Belt. They are the remains of a planet that failed to form. It would have been about four times as massive as Earth, but Jupiter's gravity stopped the material producing one object.

Beyond the belt
Some asteroids orbit the Sun outside the Main Belt. These include the Trojans, found in two groups along Jupiter's orbit, and near-Earth asteroids, which were once in the Main Belt but now follow orbits that bring them closer to Earth.

Jupiter
Trojans
Earth
Apollo
Eros
Mars
Sun
Ida

Trojans
There are several thousand Trojans, and they take 11.8 years to orbit the Sun once, the same length of time as Jupiter. They exist in two swarms: one is 60 degrees in front of Jupiter, the other is 60 degrees behind it.

Near-Earth asteroids
These asteroids follow orbits that cross or approach Earth's orbit. This means they can pass relatively close to Earth or, in rare cases, hit our planet. Apollo and Eros are both near-Earth asteroids.

COMING SOON: ASTEROID COLLISIONS!

CRATERING
Asteroid is less than 1/50,000th of size of larger asteroid
Crater forms

FRACTURING
Asteroid is 1/50,000th of size of larger asteroid
Asteroid fractures
Breaks into fragments
Forms ball of rubble

SHATTERING
Asteroid is more than 1/50,000th of size of larger asteroid
Larger asteroid shatters apart
Family of asteroids forms

Collisions
High-speed collisions occur between asteroids. Most involve a small asteroid forming an impact crater on a larger one. Asteroids can also fracture into pieces that come together again or shatter apart completely.

COMING SOON: DEATH OF THE DINOSAURS!

Fall to Earth
More than 170 craters exist on Earth where asteroids have smashed into the planet. Chicxulub, off the coast of Mexico, is a crater that formed 65 million years ago. Material thrown up by the impact affected the atmosphere, which some think led to the dinosaurs dying out.

Meteorites
About 3,000 pieces of asteroid, each weighing more than 1 kg (2 lb), fall on Earth's land or into its oceans every year. There are three main types: stony (making up 93 per cent of all meteorites), iron, and stony-iron.

Stony-iron meteorite
That's meteor-wrong!
Stone me!
Stony meteorite
We're on a rocky road
Watch your gnashers!
Slurp!
Iron meteorite
Rock on!

GIANT PLANETS

The four outer planets are the largest in the Solar System and are mostly made of gas and liquid. Jupiter, Saturn, Uranus, and Neptune are all ice-cold worlds far beyond Earth. Each has a ring system and a large family of moons. Jupiter and Saturn are called gas giants because of the great mass of hydrogen and helium they contain. Uranus and Neptune are known as ice giants.

Planetary profile
The density and temperature of the materials the planets are made of increases with depth. This affects the physical state of the material. For instance, Jupiter is mostly hydrogen. Below its atmosphere, the gas gradually becomes liquid, and deep down is like a molten metal.

Jupiter
This planet is the Solar System's record breaker. It is the biggest and most massive planet, and because it takes less than ten hours to rotate, it is also the fastest spinner. It is made of two and a half times the material of the other seven planets combined.

What a giant giant!

Jupiter is so huge that 11 Earths could fit across it, and 1,300 inside it

Great Red Spot, a giant storm bigger than Earth

Jupiter takes 12 years to travel once around the Sun

Saturn
None of the giants is a perfect sphere. They are all oblate like squashed balls – wider around their equators than from top to bottom. Saturn is the most oblate. It is also the least dense planet, and because of this, it would float if placed in water.

Saturn takes 29 years to orbit the Sun

Rings are made of thousands of individual ice pieces, each orbiting the planet

Stormy weather
All four giants have weather systems in their atmospheres, but Jupiter's is the most visible. The planet's fast spin helps pull its clouds into red-brown and white striped bands parallel to its equator. Spots on Jupiter's visible surface are giant weather storms.

Ring leader
All of the giants have rings, but Saturn's are the most extensive and spectacular. It has seven separate rings, each made of hundreds of ringlets. These are made of pieces of almost pure water ice ranging in size from dust grains to large boulders.

Families of moons
All but three of the moons that orbit Solar System planets orbit around a giant planet. Jupiter and Saturn have the largest families, with around 80 moons each. Jupiter's moon Ganymede is the largest moon – it is bigger than the planet Mercury.

Io, the most volcanic place in the Solar System

Galilean moons
Jupiter's four largest moons are known as the Galilean moons after the astronomer Galileo Galilei. Ganymede, Callisto, and Europa are icy, but Io is a volcanic world.

I cut a striking figure

It's Titanic!

Titan
Saturn's largest moon is Titan, and it is the only moon of any planet to have a substantial atmosphere. It is also the only moon that a spacecraft has landed on apart from Earth's Moon.

Shepherd moons
Each of the giants has irregularly-shaped moons ranging in size from a few to a few hundred kilometres across. These include some within Saturn's rings that shepherd the ring particles into position.

Gutterball

King of the gods
The biggest planet is named after Jupiter, king of the Roman gods and ruler of the heavens. He controlled storms, and all land struck by lightning was his.

I'm the greatest

Supreme ruler
Planet Saturn is named after the one-time ruler of all the Roman gods, who was overthrown by his son Jupiter.

BRAINWAVE BOWLING

Uranus
No planet is totally upright as it orbits the Sun, but none is as off-kilter as Uranus, which is tilted at an angle of 98 degrees. This is possibly the result of a collision with a large asteroid when Uranus was young. Its rings and moons circle its equator but appear to go round from top to bottom.

Blue colour of Uranus comes from methane gas in its atmosphere

Neptune
The coldest and most distant giant is Neptune. It is about 30 times further from the Sun than Earth, making the Sun appear 900 times dimmer. Neptune takes nearly 165 years to complete one orbit around the Sun. It has the fastest winds of any planet.

Neptune's equatorial winds blow at speeds up to 2,160 kph (1,340 mph)

Discoveries
Jupiter and Saturn have been known about since the first humans used their eyes to study the night sky, but Uranus and Neptune were discovered much more recently by astronomers using telescopes. Uranus was discovered in 1781 by William Herschel, and Johann Galle first spotted Neptune in 1846.

Miranda
Uranus has 27 moons, but the largest, Titania, is less than half the size of Earth's Moon. The fifth largest is Miranda, a strange-looking moon with landscape features from different time periods.

Miranda is 480 km (300 miles) across

Triton
Neptune has one main moon, Triton, and 12 smaller moons, four of which are within the planet's thin ring system. Distant Triton is a little closer to Neptune than the Moon is to Earth, and is a rocky world with an icy crust. It completes an orbit round Neptune in just under six days.

First god
In Roman mythology, Uranus was the first god, and god of the sky. He was father of Saturn, and grandfather of Jupiter.

Nautical Neptune
This planet is named after the Roman god of the seas. Neptune carries a three-pronged trident, and is also Jupiter's brother.

FROZEN WORLDS

There are trillions of comets in the freezing outer reaches of the Solar System. They are huge dirty snowballs that have remained unchanged since the Sun and planets formed 4.6 billion years ago. Occasionally, one travels closer to the Sun, and this changes its size and appearance. Many other small worlds of ice and rock live in a flattened ring beyond Neptune, known as the Kuiper Belt.

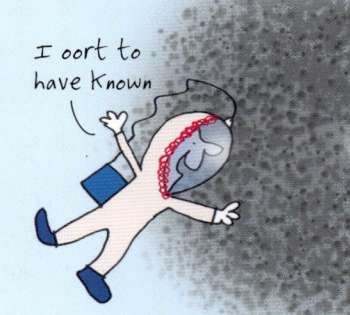

Comet characteristics
All comets consist of a giant snowball called a nucleus. Each is the width of a big city. Comets travelling close to the Sun become tens of thousands of times larger when they develop a vast head and tails.

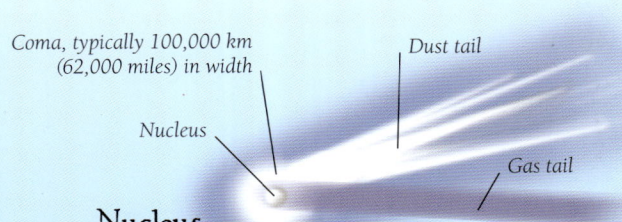

Coma, typically 100,000 km (62,000 miles) in width

Nucleus

Dust tail

Gas tail

Tails
Gas and dust released from the nucleus by the Sun's heat form two tails millions of kilometres long. The gas tail is straight and blue-white; the dust one is curved and white.

Nucleus
The nucleus is irregular in shape and is a mix of two-thirds snow and one-third rock dust. A thin layer of dust covers its surface.

Coma
A huge head called a coma is made of gas and dust. It forms when the Sun's heat turns the snow on the surface of the nucleus into gas, and loosens dust in the process.

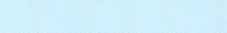

Oort Cloud
Comets follow independent orbits around the Sun. They do not travel in the same plane as the planets but in all directions. The vast majority orbit way beyond the planets and together make a large sphere of comets called the Oort Cloud.

Sun, planets, and Kuiper Belt in centre of Oort Cloud

Oort Cloud consists of trillions of comets

Comet names
New discoveries are usually named after the satellite, telescope, or person who spotted it. When two astronomers discover one comet independently, it is given both their names, for instance, Hale-Bopp. Occasionally three discoverers are included.

Great comets
Comet McNaught, 2007 – discovered 7 August 2006 by Scotsman Robert McNaught

Comet Hale-Bopp, 1997 – discovered 23 July 1995 by US astronomers Alan Hale and Thomas Bopp

Comet Hyakutake, 1996 – discovered 30 January 1996 by Japan's Yuji Hyakutake

Comet Bennett, 1970 – discovered 28 December 1969 by South African John Bennett

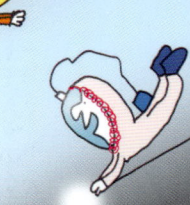

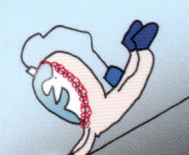

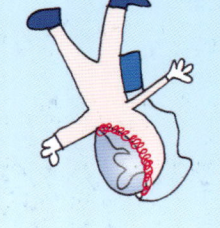

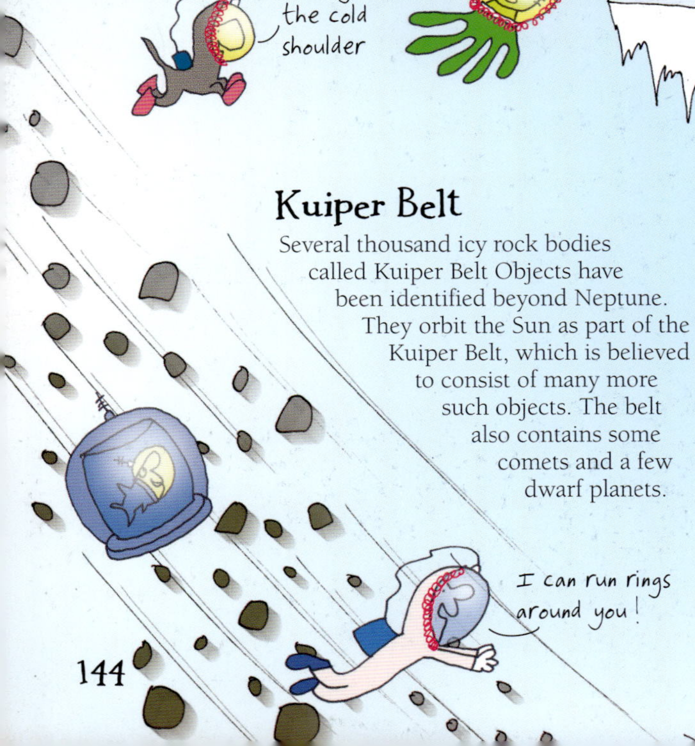

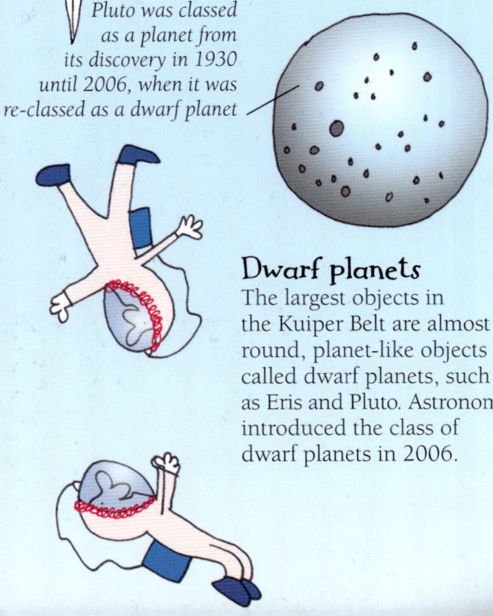

Kuiper Belt
Several thousand icy rock bodies called Kuiper Belt Objects have been identified beyond Neptune. They orbit the Sun as part of the Kuiper Belt, which is believed to consist of many more such objects. The belt also contains some comets and a few dwarf planets.

Pluto was classed as a planet from its discovery in 1930 until 2006, when it was re-classed as a dwarf planet

Dwarf planets
The largest objects in the Kuiper Belt are almost round, planet-like objects called dwarf planets, such as Eris and Pluto. Astronomers introduced the class of dwarf planets in 2006.

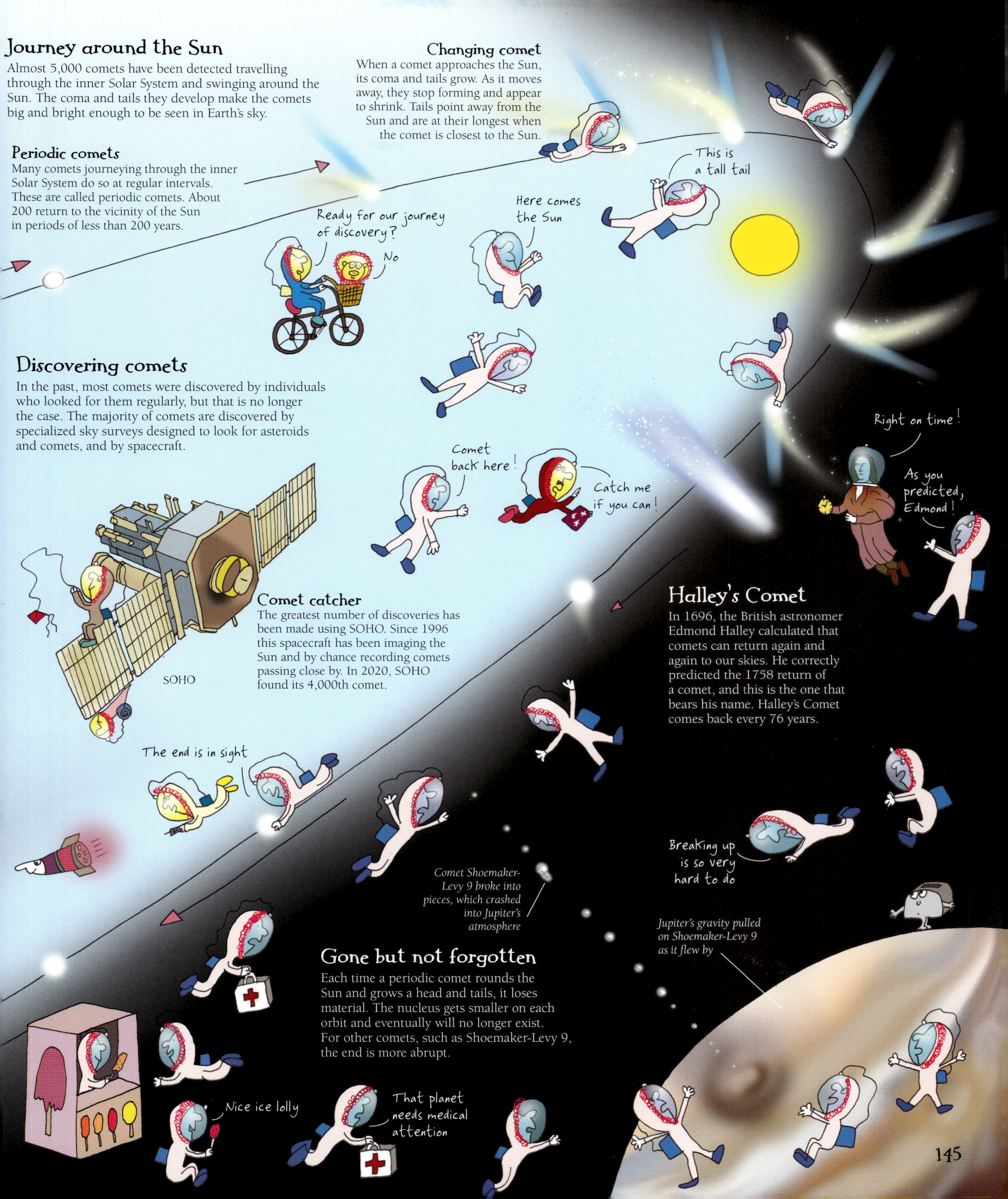

Journey around the Sun
Almost 5,000 comets have been detected travelling through the inner Solar System and swinging around the Sun. The coma and tails they develop make the comets big and bright enough to be seen in Earth's sky.

Periodic comets
Many comets journeying through the inner Solar System do so at regular intervals. These are called periodic comets. About 200 return to the vicinity of the Sun in periods of less than 200 years.

Changing comet
When a comet approaches the Sun, its coma and tails grow. As it moves away, they stop forming and appear to shrink. Tails point away from the Sun and are at their longest when the comet is closest to the Sun.

Discovering comets
In the past, most comets were discovered by individuals who looked for them regularly, but that is no longer the case. The majority of comets are discovered by specialized sky surveys designed to look for asteroids and comets, and by spacecraft.

Comet catcher
The greatest number of discoveries has been made using SOHO. Since 1996 this spacecraft has been imaging the Sun and by chance recording comets passing close by. In 2020, SOHO found its 4,000th comet.

Halley's Comet
In 1696, the British astronomer Edmond Halley calculated that comets can return again and again to our skies. He correctly predicted the 1758 return of a comet, and this is the one that bears his name. Halley's Comet comes back every 76 years.

Comet Shoemaker-Levy 9 broke into pieces, which crashed into Jupiter's atmosphere

Jupiter's gravity pulled on Shoemaker-Levy 9 as it flew by

Gone but not forgotten
Each time a periodic comet rounds the Sun and grows a head and tails, it loses material. The nucleus gets smaller on each orbit and eventually will no longer exist. For other comets, such as Shoemaker-Levy 9, the end is more abrupt.

145

Welcome to Space

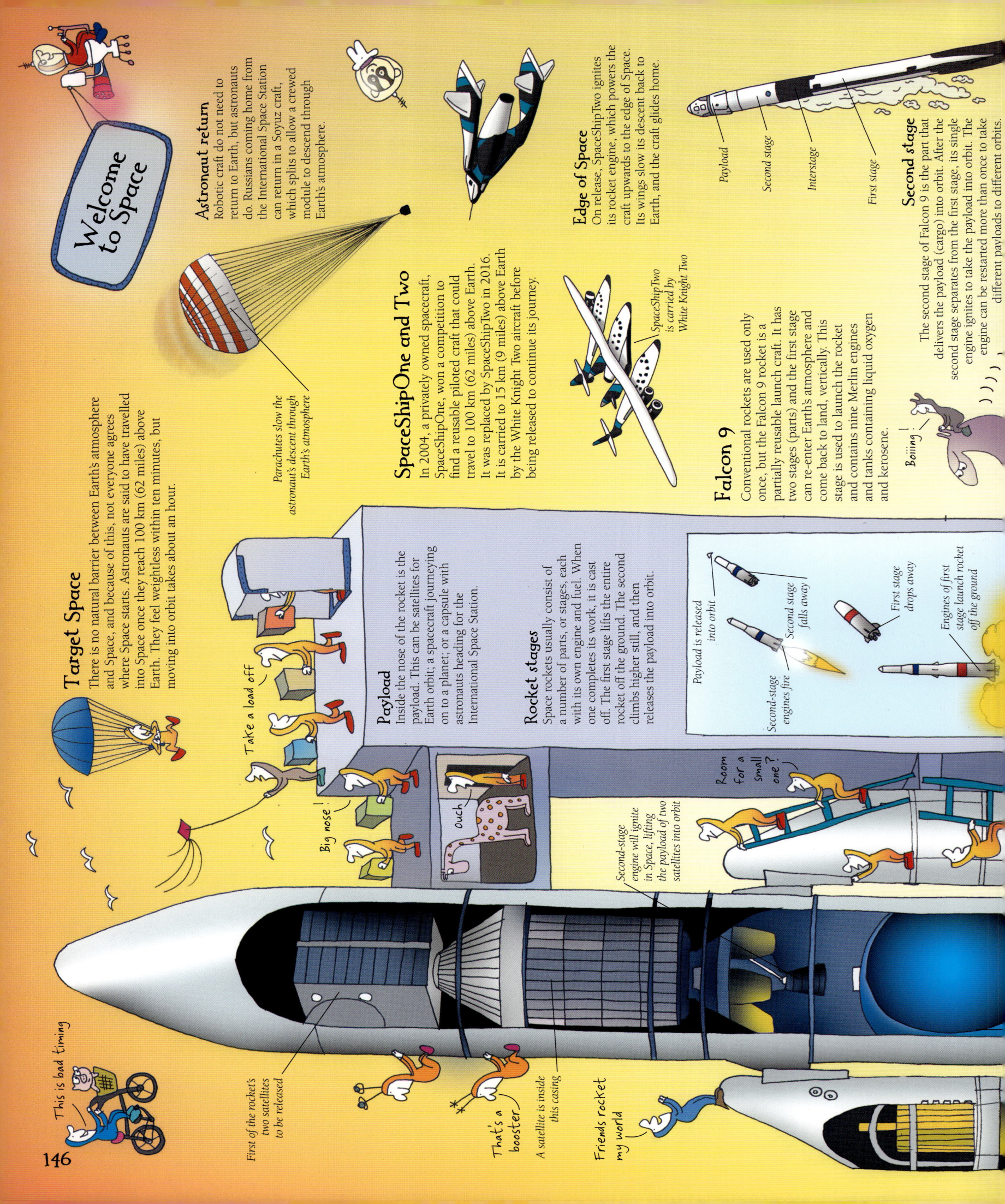

Target Space
There is no natural barrier between Earth's atmosphere and Space, and because of this, not everyone agrees where Space starts. Astronauts are said to have travelled into Space once they reach 100 km (62 miles) above Earth. They feel weightless within ten minutes, but moving into orbit takes about an hour.

Astronaut return
Robotic craft do not need to return to Earth, but astronauts do. Russians coming home from the International Space Station can return in a Soyuz craft, which splits to allow a crewed module to descend through Earth's atmosphere.

Parachutes slow the astronaut's descent through Earth's atmosphere

SpaceShipOne and Two
In 2004, a privately owned spacecraft, SpaceShipOne, won a competition to find a reusable piloted craft that could travel to 100 km (62 miles) above Earth. It was replaced by SpaceShipTwo in 2016. It is carried to 15 km (9 miles) above Earth by the White Knight Two aircraft before being released to continue its journey.

SpaceShipTwo is carried by White Knight Two

Edge of Space
On release, SpaceShipTwo ignites its rocket engine, which powers the craft upwards to the edge of Space. Its wings slow its descent back to Earth, and the craft glides home.

Falcon 9
Conventional rockets are used only once, but the Falcon 9 rocket is a partially reusable launch craft. It has two stages (parts) and the first stage can re-enter Earth's atmosphere and come back to land, vertically. This stage is used to launch the rocket and contains nine Merlin engines and tanks containing liquid oxygen and kerosene.

- Payload
- Second stage
- Interstage
- First stage

Second stage
The second stage of Falcon 9 is the part that delivers the payload (cargo) into orbit. After the second stage separates from the first stage, its single engine ignites to take the payload into orbit. The engine can be restarted more than once to take different payloads to different orbits.

Payload
Inside the nose of the rocket is the payload. This can be satellites for Earth orbit; a spacecraft journeying on to a planet; or a capsule with astronauts heading for the International Space Station.

Rocket stages
Space rockets usually consist of a number of parts, or stages, each with its own engine and fuel. When one completes its work, it is cast off. The first stage lifts the entire rocket off the ground. The second climbs higher still, and then releases the payload into orbit.

- Payload is released into orbit
- Second-stage engines fire
- Second stage falls away
- First stage drops away
- Engines of first stage launch rocket off the ground

Take a load off
Big nose!
ouch
Room for a small one?
Second-stage engine will ignite in Space, lifting the payload of two satellites into orbit
First of the rocket's two satellites to be released
That's a booster
A satellite is inside this casing
Friends rocket my world
This is bad timing
Boiiing!

146

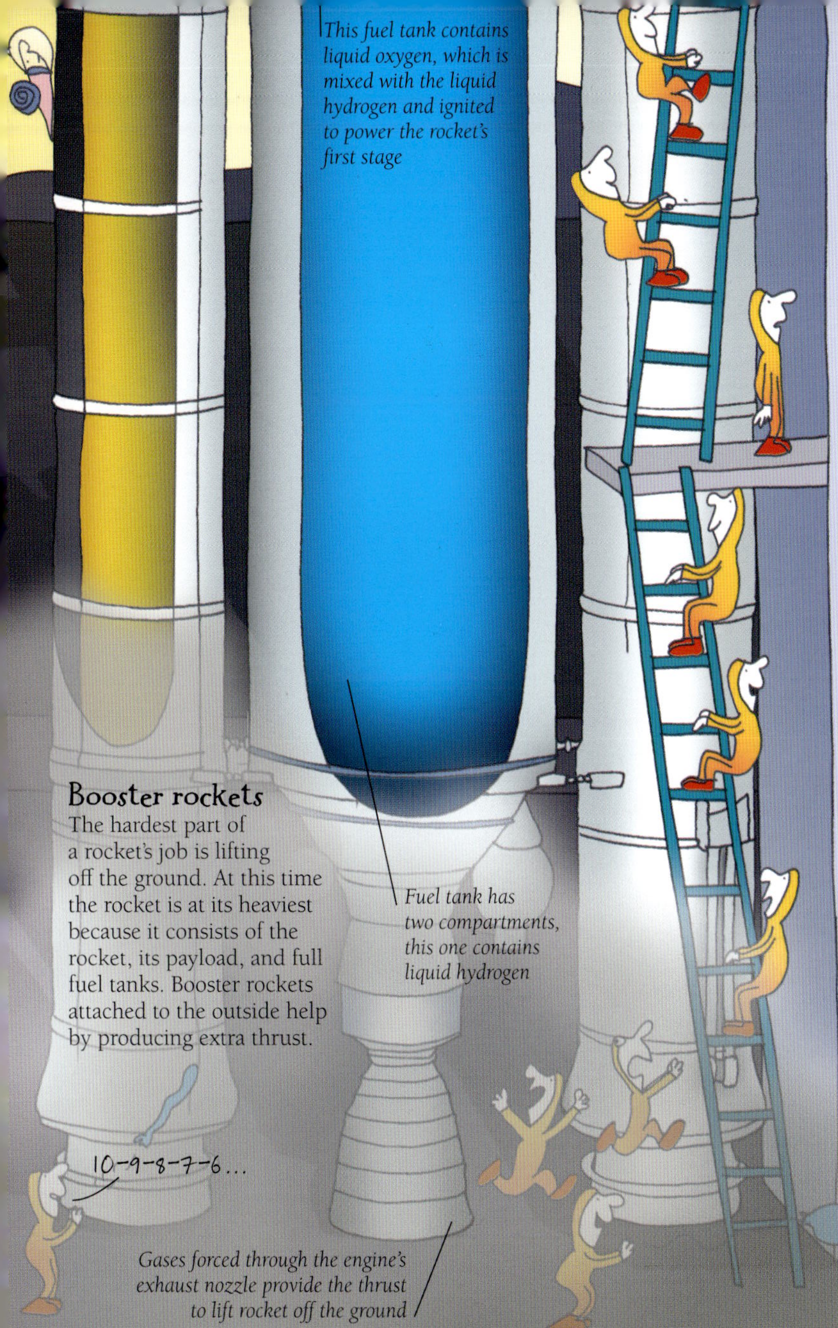

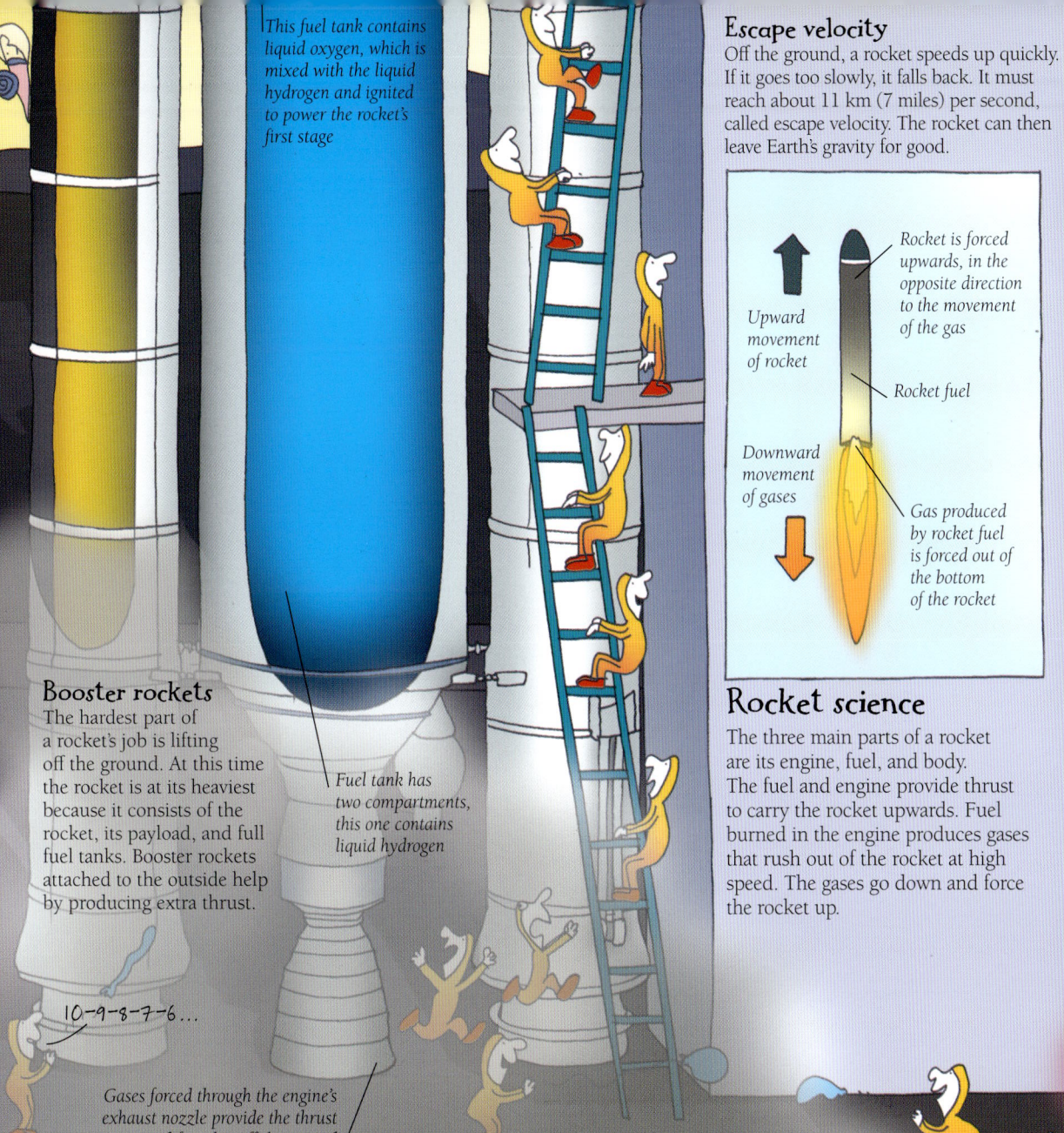

READY FOR LAUNCH

For anything to leave Earth and travel into Space, a rocket is required. The power of the rocket lifts it off the ground and achieves the necessary speed to get away from the pull of Earth's gravity. Within a short time the rocket's job is complete. It has delivered its cargo, known as the payload, into Space, and it is now the payload's turn to start work.

Booster rockets
The hardest part of a rocket's job is lifting off the ground. At this time the rocket is at its heaviest because it consists of the rocket, its payload, and full fuel tanks. Booster rockets attached to the outside help by producing extra thrust.

This fuel tank contains liquid oxygen, which is mixed with the liquid hydrogen and ignited to power the rocket's first stage

Fuel tank has two compartments, this one contains liquid hydrogen

Gases forced through the engine's exhaust nozzle provide the thrust to lift rocket off the ground

10–9–8–7–6…

Start the countdown

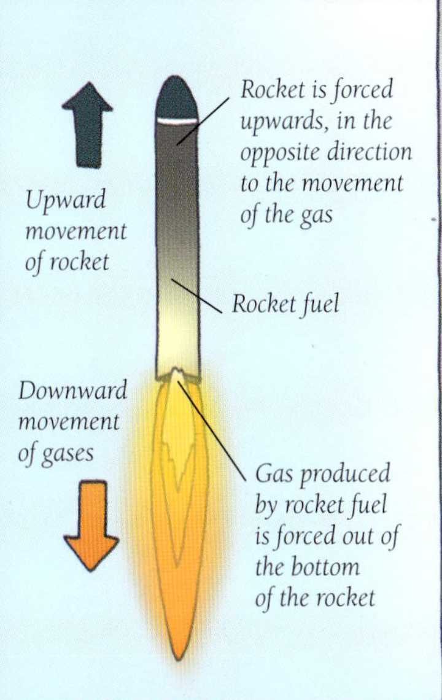

Rocket science
The three main parts of a rocket are its engine, fuel, and body. The fuel and engine provide thrust to carry the rocket upwards. Fuel burned in the engine produces gases that rush out of the rocket at high speed. The gases go down and force the rocket up.

Rocket is forced upwards, in the opposite direction to the movement of the gas

Rocket fuel

Gas produced by rocket fuel is forced out of the bottom of the rocket

Upward movement of rocket

Downward movement of gases

Escape velocity
Off the ground, a rocket speeds up quickly. If it goes too slowly, it falls back. It must reach about 11 km (7 miles) per second, called escape velocity. The rocket can then leave Earth's gravity for good.

Back home again
One of the main tasks of Falcon 9 is bringing astronauts to and from the International Space Station. Up to seven people can travel inside the Dragon capsule, which sits as the payload on the top of Falcon 9. Dragon has boosters for manoeuvering in space, and parachutes for slowing the descent when it comes back to Earth.

We've missed you!

Blast off
Rockets have been lifting off from Earth and heading for Space for more than 60 years. Today, about two rockets a week are launched, involving people from all around the world. Some nations launch rockets, but more send craft or astronauts into Space, or work as part of a global team monitoring a mission.

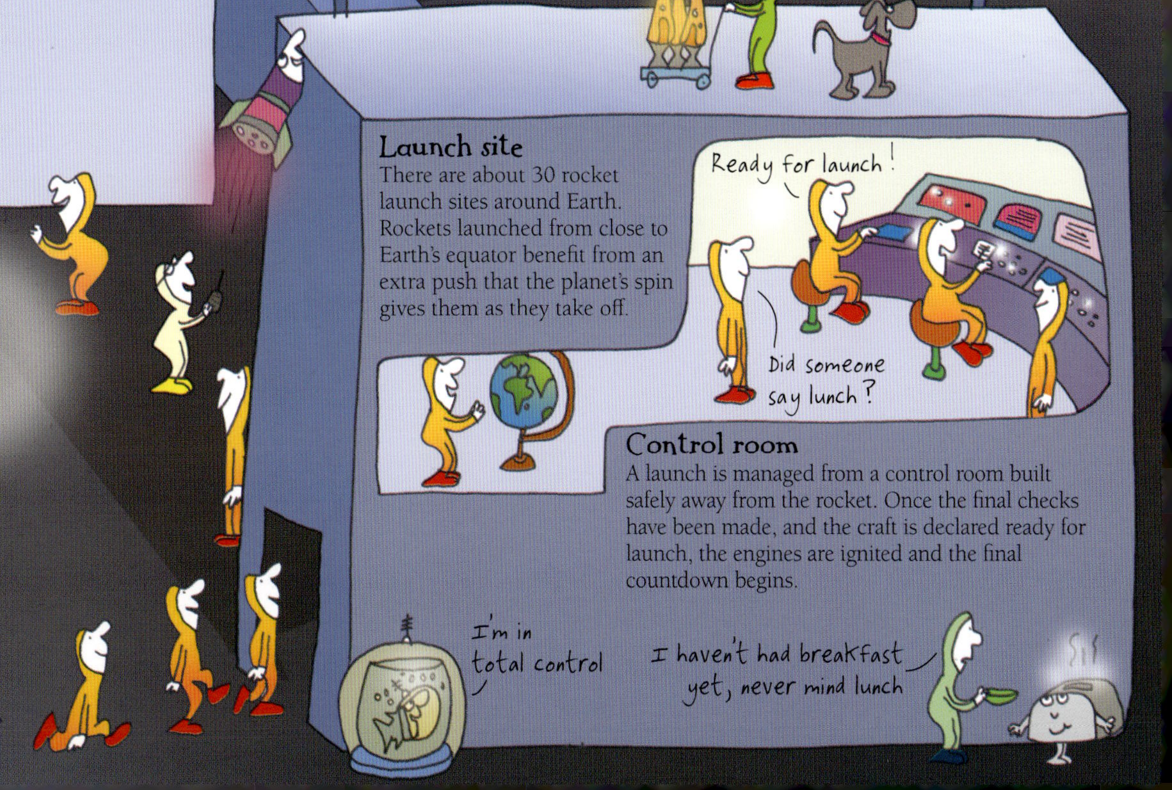

Launch site
There are about 30 rocket launch sites around Earth. Rockets launched from close to Earth's equator benefit from an extra push that the planet's spin gives them as they take off.

Ready for launch!

Did someone say lunch?

Control room
A launch is managed from a control room built safely away from the rocket. Once the final checks have been made, and the craft is declared ready for launch, the engines are ignited and the final countdown begins.

I'm in total control

I haven't had breakfast yet, never mind lunch

147

SPACE EXPLORERS SHOWROOM

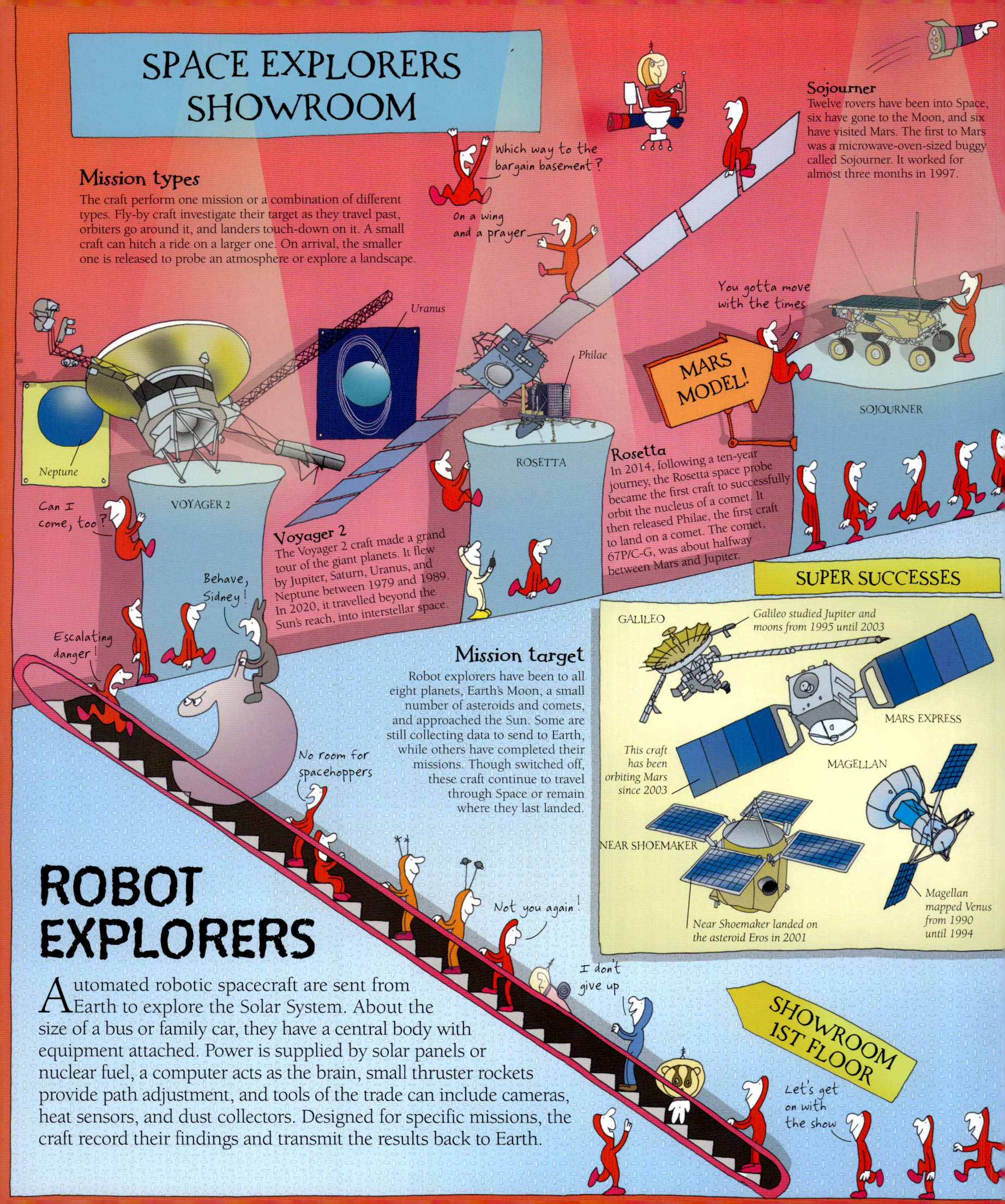

Mission types
The craft perform one mission or a combination of different types. Fly-by craft investigate their target as they travel past, orbiters go around it, and landers touch-down on it. A small craft can hitch a ride on a larger one. On arrival, the smaller one is released to probe an atmosphere or explore a landscape.

Sojourner
Twelve rovers have been into Space, six have gone to the Moon, and six have visited Mars. The first to Mars was a microwave-oven-sized buggy called Sojourner. It worked for almost three months in 1997.

Voyager 2
The Voyager 2 craft made a grand tour of the giant planets. It flew by Jupiter, Saturn, Uranus, and Neptune between 1979 and 1989. In 2020, it travelled beyond the Sun's reach, into interstellar space.

Rosetta
In 2014, following a ten-year journey, the Rosetta space probe became the first craft to successfully orbit the nucleus of a comet. It then released Philae, the first craft to land on a comet. The comet, 67P/C-G, was about halfway between Mars and Jupiter.

Mission target
Robot explorers have been to all eight planets, Earth's Moon, a small number of asteroids and comets, and approached the Sun. Some are still collecting data to send to Earth, while others have completed their missions. Though switched off, these craft continue to travel through Space or remain where they last landed.

SUPER SUCCESSES
- Galileo studied Jupiter and moons from 1995 until 2003
- This craft has been orbiting Mars since 2003 (MARS EXPRESS)
- Magellan mapped Venus from 1990 until 1994
- Near Shoemaker landed on the asteroid Eros in 2001

ROBOT EXPLORERS

Automated robotic spacecraft are sent from Earth to explore the Solar System. About the size of a bus or family car, they have a central body with equipment attached. Power is supplied by solar panels or nuclear fuel, a computer acts as the brain, small thruster rockets provide path adjustment, and tools of the trade can include cameras, heat sensors, and dust collectors. Designed for specific missions, the craft record their findings and transmit the results back to Earth.

SHOWROOM 1ST FLOOR

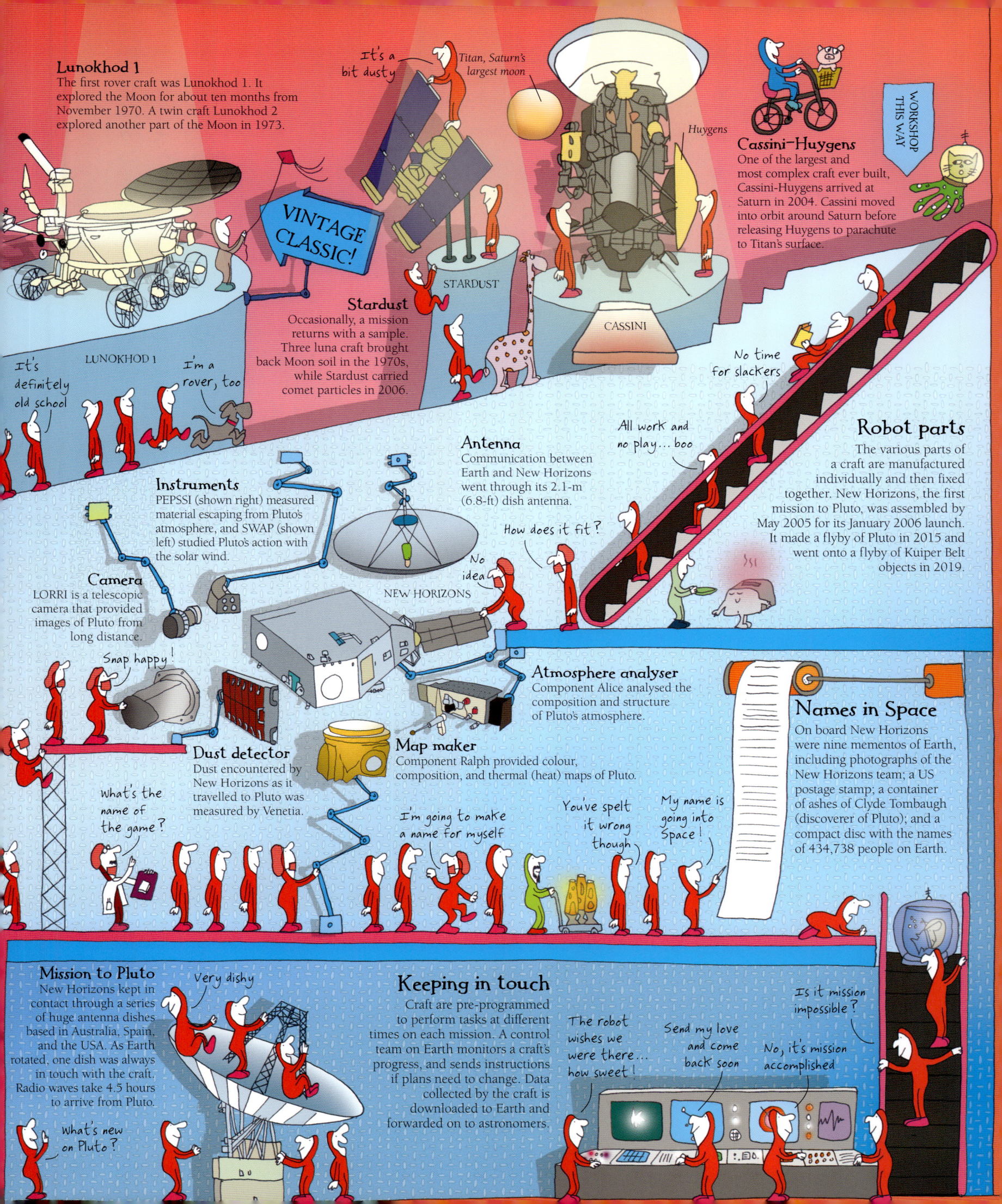

Lunokhod 1
The first rover craft was Lunokhod 1. It explored the Moon for about ten months from November 1970. A twin craft Lunokhod 2 explored another part of the Moon in 1973.

It's a bit dusty

Titan, Saturn's largest moon

Huygens

Cassini-Huygens
One of the largest and most complex craft ever built, Cassini-Huygens arrived at Saturn in 2004. Cassini moved into orbit around Saturn before releasing Huygens to parachute to Titan's surface.

WORKSHOP THIS WAY

VINTAGE CLASSIC!

STARDUST

CASSINI

Stardust
Occasionally, a mission returns with a sample. Three luna craft brought back Moon soil in the 1970s, while Stardust carried comet particles in 2006.

LUNOKHOD 1

It's definitely old school

I'm a rover, too

No time for slackers

All work and no play... boo

Robot parts
The various parts of a craft are manufactured individually and then fixed together. New Horizons, the first mission to Pluto, was assembled by May 2005 for its January 2006 launch. It made a flyby of Pluto in 2015 and went onto a flyby of Kuiper Belt objects in 2019.

Antenna
Communication between Earth and New Horizons went through its 2.1-m (6.8-ft) dish antenna.

Instruments
PEPSSI (shown right) measured material escaping from Pluto's atmosphere, and SWAP (shown left) studied Pluto's action with the solar wind.

How does it fit?

No idea

NEW HORIZONS

Camera
LORRI is a telescopic camera that provided images of Pluto from long distance.

Snap happy!

Atmosphere analyser
Component Alice analysed the composition and structure of Pluto's atmosphere.

Names in Space
On board New Horizons were nine mementos of Earth, including photographs of the New Horizons team; a US postage stamp; a container of ashes of Clyde Tombaugh (discoverer of Pluto); and a compact disc with the names of 434,738 people on Earth.

Dust detector
Dust encountered by New Horizons as it travelled to Pluto was measured by Venetia.

Map maker
Component Ralph provided colour, composition, and thermal (heat) maps of Pluto.

What's the name of the game?

I'm going to make a name for myself

You've spelt it wrong though

My name is going into Space!

Mission to Pluto
New Horizons kept in contact through a series of huge antenna dishes based in Australia, Spain, and the USA. As Earth rotated, one dish was always in touch with the craft. Radio waves take 4.5 hours to arrive from Pluto.

Very dishy

What's new on Pluto?

Keeping in touch
Craft are pre-programmed to perform tasks at different times on each mission. A control team on Earth monitors a craft's progress, and sends instructions if plans need to change. Data collected by the craft is downloaded to Earth and forwarded on to astronomers.

The robot wishes we were there... how sweet!

Send my love and come back soon

Is it mission impossible?

No, it's mission accomplished

SPACE SCHOOL

Space tourists

Seven private citizens have paid about $25 million each for a week's stay on the International Space Station. The first was US businessman Dennis Tito in 2001. Like him, the other Space tourists travelled there and back by Soyuz rocket. One of the tourists, Hungarian-born Charles Simonyi, returned for a second stay in 2009.

Ticket to ride

On 21 June 2004, SpaceShipOne made the first privately funded human spaceflight. The craft never flew commercially, but its successor (SpaceShipTwo) is taking bookings for tourist flights – if you have $250,000 to pay for it. The trip lasts about 2.5 hours, but only a few minutes of that is in Space.

Most time

Gennady Padalka has spent more time in Space than anyone else. The Russian made five individual missions between 1998 and 2015, and spent a total of 879 days in space.

Longest stay

The record for the longest single stay in Space is held by Russian Valeri Polaikov. He spent 437.7 days aboard the Mir Space station from 1994–5 during which he orbited Earth more than 7,000 times.

First spacewalk

Russia's Alexei Leonov was first to go outside a spacecraft. On 18 March 1965, while secured by a tether to Voskhod 2, he did a ten minute spacewalk. Today, astronauts have made more than 300 walks.

Man on the Moon

On 20 July 1969, US astronaut Neil Armstrong became the first person to walk on the Moon. He famously declared, "That's one small step for man, one giant leap for mankind".

First woman

Russian astronaut Valentina Tereshkova was the first woman in Space when she lifted-off aboard Vostok 6 on 16 June 1963 and orbited Earth 48 times. At least 50 females have been to Space since.

First in Space

The first human into Space was Yuri Gagarin. He travelled once around Earth in Vostok 1 on 12 April 1961. He took off from his own country, Russia, and landed back there 108 minutes later.

Hall of heroes

Most astronauts have travelled only as far as a few hundred kilometres above Earth. Only 26 people have been further: they went to the Moon and back, with 12 of them walking on its surface.

ASTRONAUTS WANTED

Around 570 men and women, from 41 nations, have left Earth and travelled into Space. These astronauts were selected by Space agencies who trained them for their missions. They were launched by either the USA, Russia, or China. This was the only way to get to Space until 2001, when tourists first had the opportunity to make a journey of a lifetime.

Space wardrobe

Three types of clothes are needed for a trip into Space. The launch and entry suit is worn for the journey to Space and back, a spacesuit is worn by an astronaut when outside the spacecraft, and casual clothes are worn inside.

Launch and entry suit
This one-piece suit with helmet and oxygen system is designed to protect the astronaut in an emergency. A harness with a parachute attached fits over the top.

Spacesuit
The white spacesuit provides an astronaut with their own Earth-like environment. It protects against the temperature extremes of Space, keeps the air pressure around the astronaut's body at the right level, and provides oxygen to breathe.

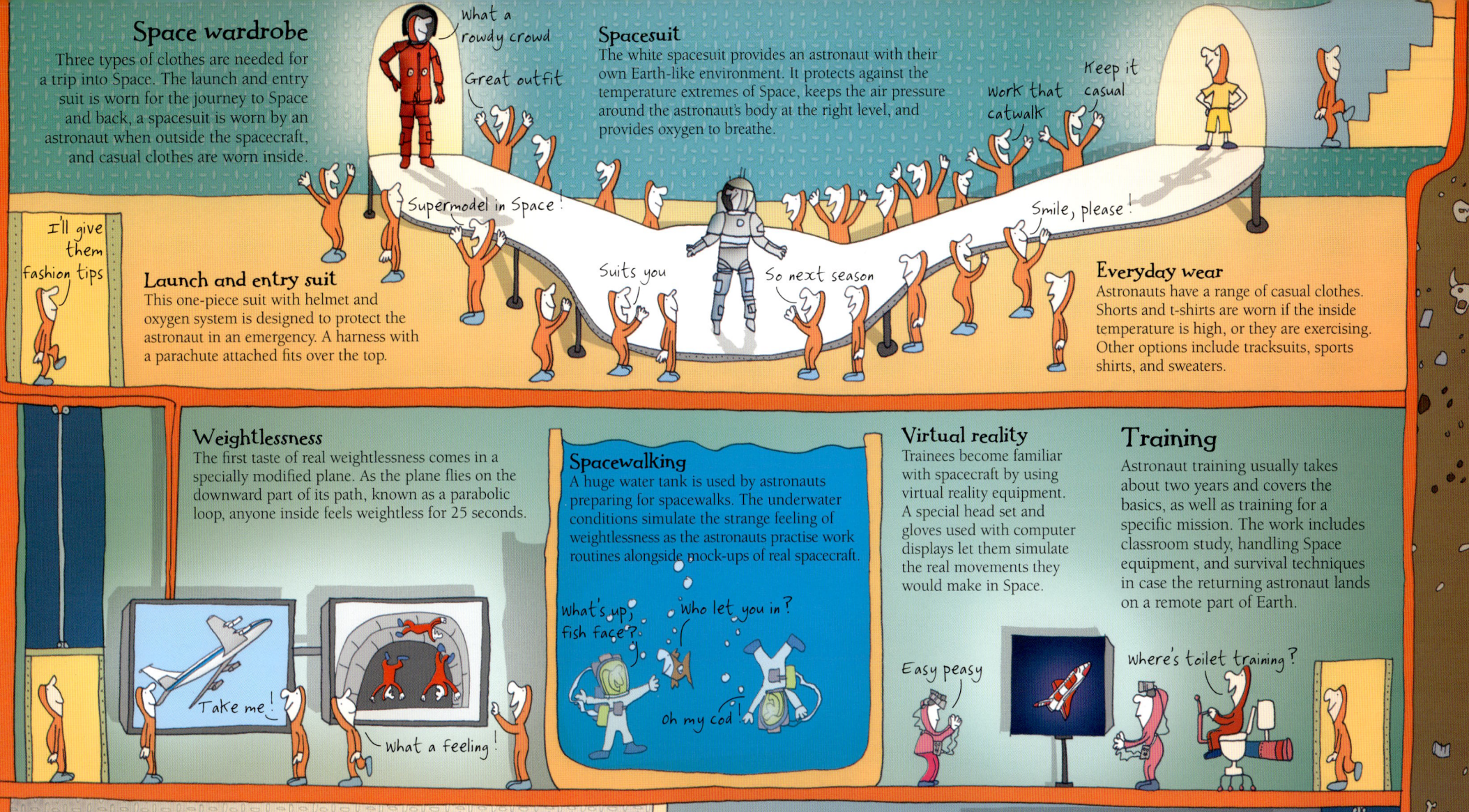

Everyday wear
Astronauts have a range of casual clothes. Shorts and t-shirts are worn if the inside temperature is high, or they are exercising. Other options include tracksuits, sports shirts, and sweaters.

Training

Astronaut training usually takes about two years and covers the basics, as well as training for a specific mission. The work includes classroom study, handling Space equipment, and survival techniques in case the returning astronaut lands in a remote part of Earth.

Weightlessness
The first taste of real weightlessness comes in a specially modified plane. As the plane flies on the downward part of its path, known as a parabolic loop, anyone inside feels weightless for 25 seconds.

Spacewalking
A huge water tank is used by astronauts preparing for spacewalks. The underwater conditions simulate the strange feeling of weightlessness as the astronauts practise work routines alongside mock-ups of real spacecraft.

Virtual reality
Trainees become familiar with spacecraft by using virtual reality equipment. A special head set and gloves used with computer displays let them simulate the real movements they would make in Space.

Job application

National Space agencies occasionally advertise for astronauts, though competition is fierce. When European astronauts were recruited in 2008, more than 8,400 people applied. Potential astronauts need outstanding ability in a scientific subject, as well as mental and physical fitness.

Astronaut requirements
Age: 27 to 37 years old
Height: 153–190 cm (60–75 in)
Language: Speak and read English
Education: University degree or equivalent in science-based subject
Health: Good, of normal weight, mentally sound
Personal qualities: Good reasoning, good memory, high motivation, flexibility, emotional stability
Extra assets: Flying experience

Home from home
The ISS provides everything that the astronauts need for everyday life. There is a galley-style kitchen, exercise equipment, and sleeping cabins. Lockers house their personal items, including clothes, books, and toiletries.

Space sick
Some astronauts experience Space sickness at the start of a trip. The headache and vomiting last only a day or two, but puffy eyes, a stuffy nose, and a slow heartbeat, which are the result of gravity not pulling on the body, affect everyone and last throughout the stay.

Space Station
The ISS consists of 18 major parts, launched separately and assembled in Space. The first parts were fitted together in 1998. It is about the size of a football pitch, and inside has the space of a five-bedroom house.

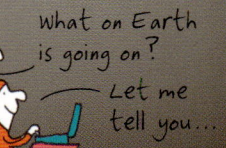

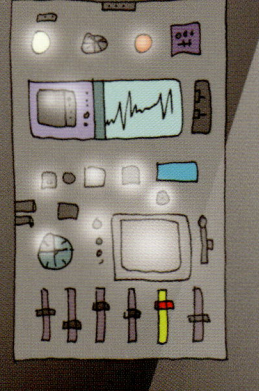

Solar panels on each side of the orbiter convert the Sun's energy to electrical power

Crew on board
Astronauts have lived on the station since the first three-person crew moved in on 2 November 2000 and stayed for 138 days. Crews consist of up to six astronauts at a time and include men and women from different nations.

LIVING IN SPACE

Astronauts live on board the International Space Station (ISS) about 390 km (240 miles) above Earth. This home and workplace orbits around our planet at 28,000 kph (17,500 mph), completing one circuit every 90 minutes. Astronauts are transported to and from the ISS by spacecraft that dock temporarily at the station. Days are spent building and maintaining the station, as well as carrying out scientific investigations. Crews usually stay for several months at a time.

Sleep tight
After a 16-hour working day, astronauts are ready for their eight hours of sleep. Their sleeping bags are fixed down so they do not float around. An eye-mask and ear plugs block out the light and noise of the station.

Keeping in shape

The astronauts follow an exercise routine for two hours a day to stay fit and healthy. The treadmill and bike not only exercise their muscles but also counteract the loss of calcium from their bones, as a result of the weightless conditions.

Mealtime

Favourite foods are chosen by astronauts before their departure and are incorporated into menus on a ten-day cycle. They have three meals a day, as well as extra snacks and drinks. The prepared and packaged food is re-hydrated and heated as needed.

Kibo: experiment laboratory

Destiny: experiment laboratory

Columbus: experiment laboratory

Unity: a connecting module, was the second part into Space

Canadarm2 jointed arm

Radiators control the station's temperature

Zarya: used for storage, was the first part into Space

Zvezda: includes the crew's living area

Space work

Weekdays are a routine of experiments and planning. Astronauts work in one of three laboratories – Destiny, Columbus, or Kibo. Experiments include testing their own bodies to learn how they are affected by Space. The results will help in the planning of future missions.

Spacewalk

Astronauts have made more than 235 spacewalks to install new parts of the station and carry out repairs. An individual is anchored to Canadarm2, a 17.6-m (55-ft) jointed arm that can move the full length of the station as they work.

Personal hygiene

Astronauts keep clean by having a daily sponge bath. There are two cloths each – one for washing and one for rinsing. They use one of the two toilets on board the station and clean their hair with rinse-less shampoo.

Spare time

At weekends, astronauts do household chores and relax. A favourite pastime is looking out of the window, but they also read, play games, take photographs, listen to music, watch films, and have races in the station.

ANYBODY OUT THERE?

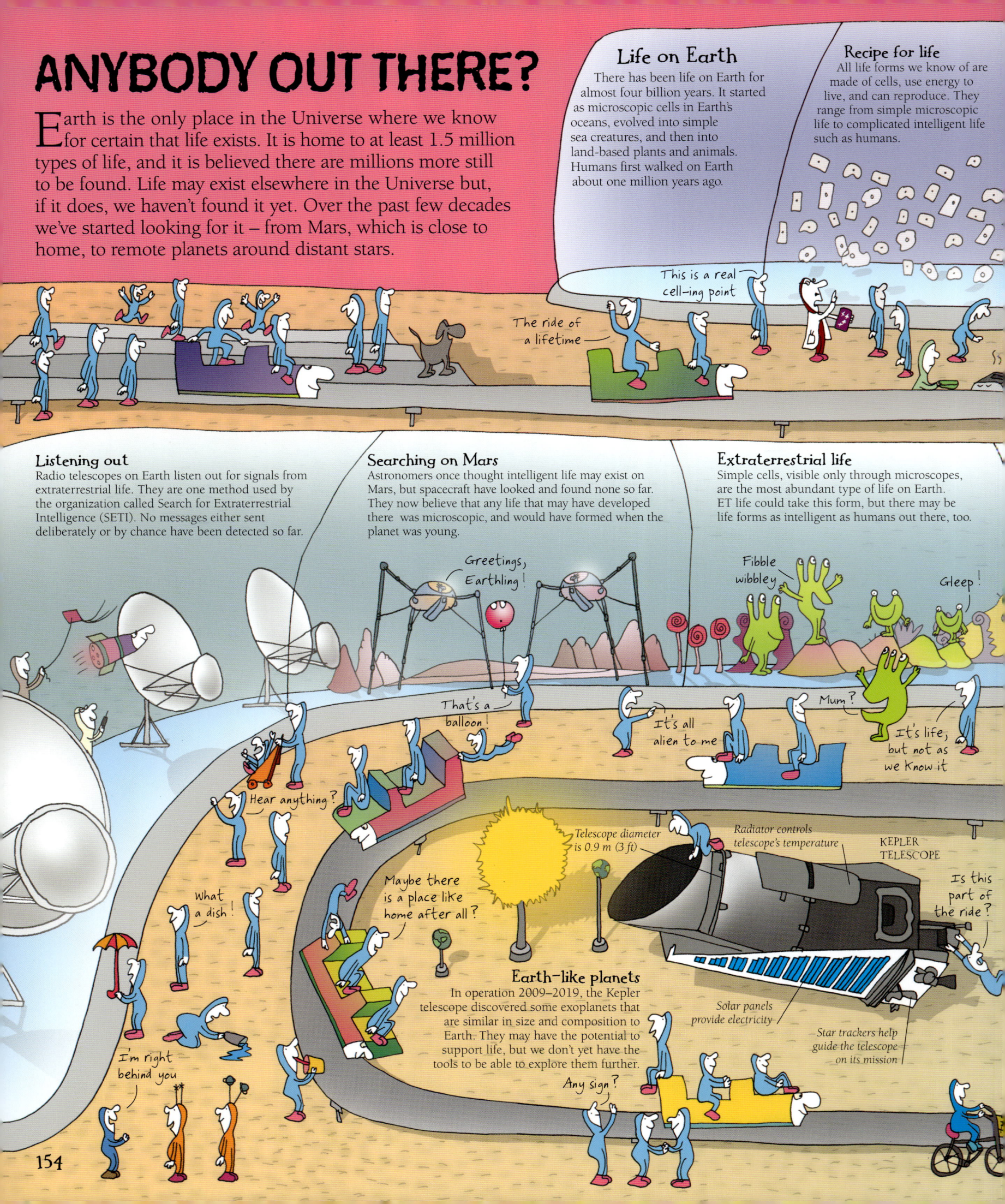

Earth is the only place in the Universe where we know for certain that life exists. It is home to at least 1.5 million types of life, and it is believed there are millions more still to be found. Life may exist elsewhere in the Universe but, if it does, we haven't found it yet. Over the past few decades we've started looking for it – from Mars, which is close to home, to remote planets around distant stars.

Life on Earth
There has been life on Earth for almost four billion years. It started as microscopic cells in Earth's oceans, evolved into simple sea creatures, and then into land-based plants and animals. Humans first walked on Earth about one million years ago.

Recipe for life
All life forms we know of are made of cells, use energy to live, and can reproduce. They range from simple microscopic life to complicated intelligent life such as humans.

Listening out
Radio telescopes on Earth listen out for signals from extraterrestrial life. They are one method used by the organization called Search for Extraterrestrial Intelligence (SETI). No messages either sent deliberately or by chance have been detected so far.

Searching on Mars
Astronomers once thought intelligent life may exist on Mars, but spacecraft have looked and found none so far. They now believe that any life that may have developed there was microscopic, and would have formed when the planet was young.

Extraterrestrial life
Simple cells, visible only through microscopes, are the most abundant type of life on Earth. ET life could take this form, but there may be life forms as intelligent as humans out there, too.

Earth-like planets
In operation 2009–2019, the Kepler telescope discovered some exoplanets that are similar in size and composition to Earth. They may have the potential to support life, but we don't yet have the tools to be able to explore them further.

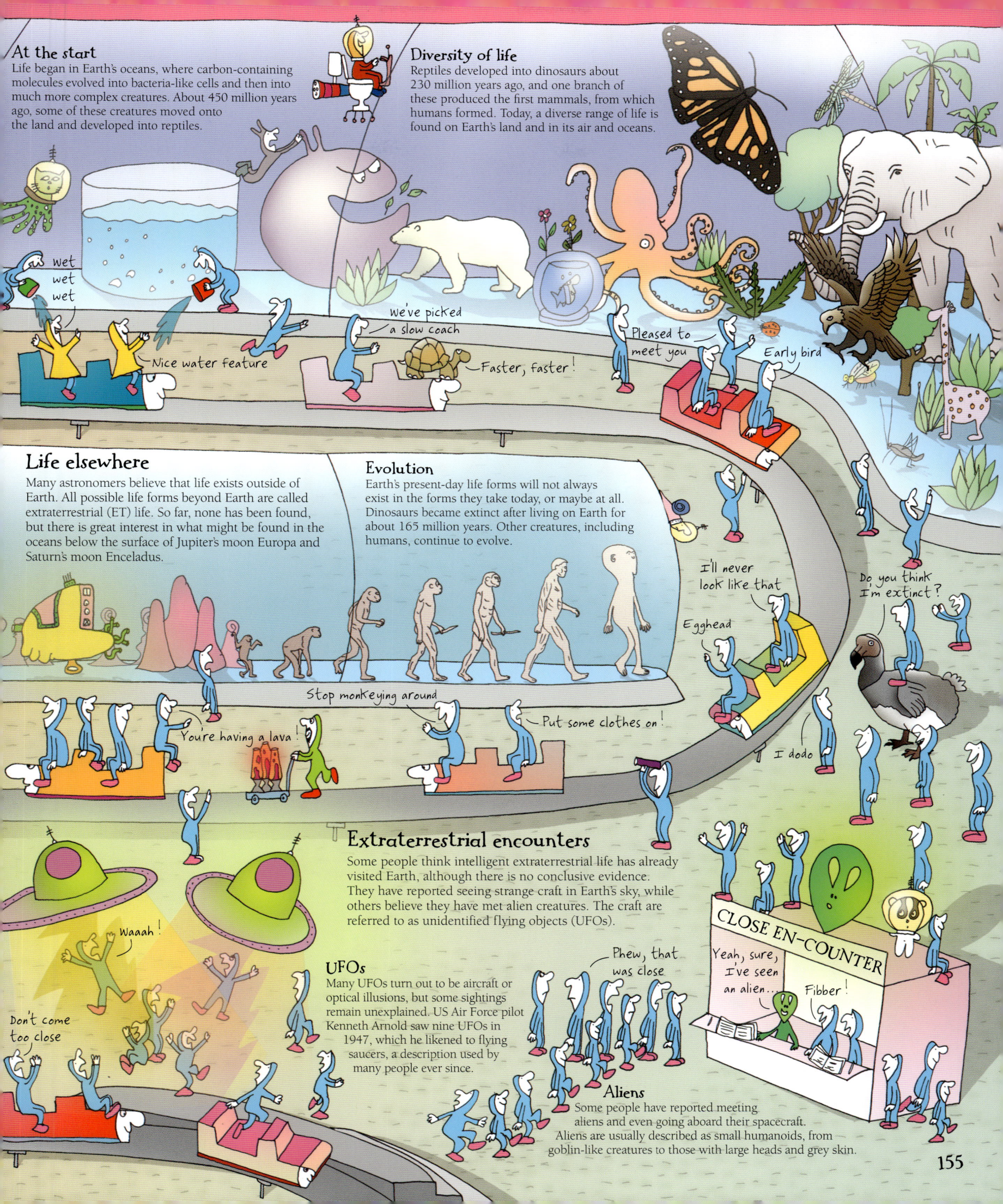

At the start
Life began in Earth's oceans, where carbon-containing molecules evolved into bacteria-like cells and then into much more complex creatures. About 450 million years ago, some of these creatures moved onto the land and developed into reptiles.

Diversity of life
Reptiles developed into dinosaurs about 230 million years ago, and one branch of these produced the first mammals, from which humans formed. Today, a diverse range of life is found on Earth's land and in its air and oceans.

Life elsewhere
Many astronomers believe that life exists outside of Earth. All possible life forms beyond Earth are called extraterrestrial (ET) life. So far, none has been found, but there is great interest in what might be found in the oceans below the surface of Jupiter's moon Europa and Saturn's moon Enceladus.

Evolution
Earth's present-day life forms will not always exist in the forms they take today, or maybe at all. Dinosaurs became extinct after living on Earth for about 165 million years. Other creatures, including humans, continue to evolve.

Extraterrestrial encounters
Some people think intelligent extraterrestrial life has already visited Earth, although there is no conclusive evidence. They have reported seeing strange craft in Earth's sky, while others believe they have met alien creatures. The craft are referred to as unidentified flying objects (UFOs).

UFOs
Many UFOs turn out to be aircraft or optical illusions, but some sightings remain unexplained. US Air Force pilot Kenneth Arnold saw nine UFOs in 1947, which he likened to flying saucers, a description used by many people ever since.

Aliens
Some people have reported meeting aliens and even going aboard their spacecraft. Aliens are usually described as small humanoids, from goblin-like creatures to those with large heads and grey skin.

155

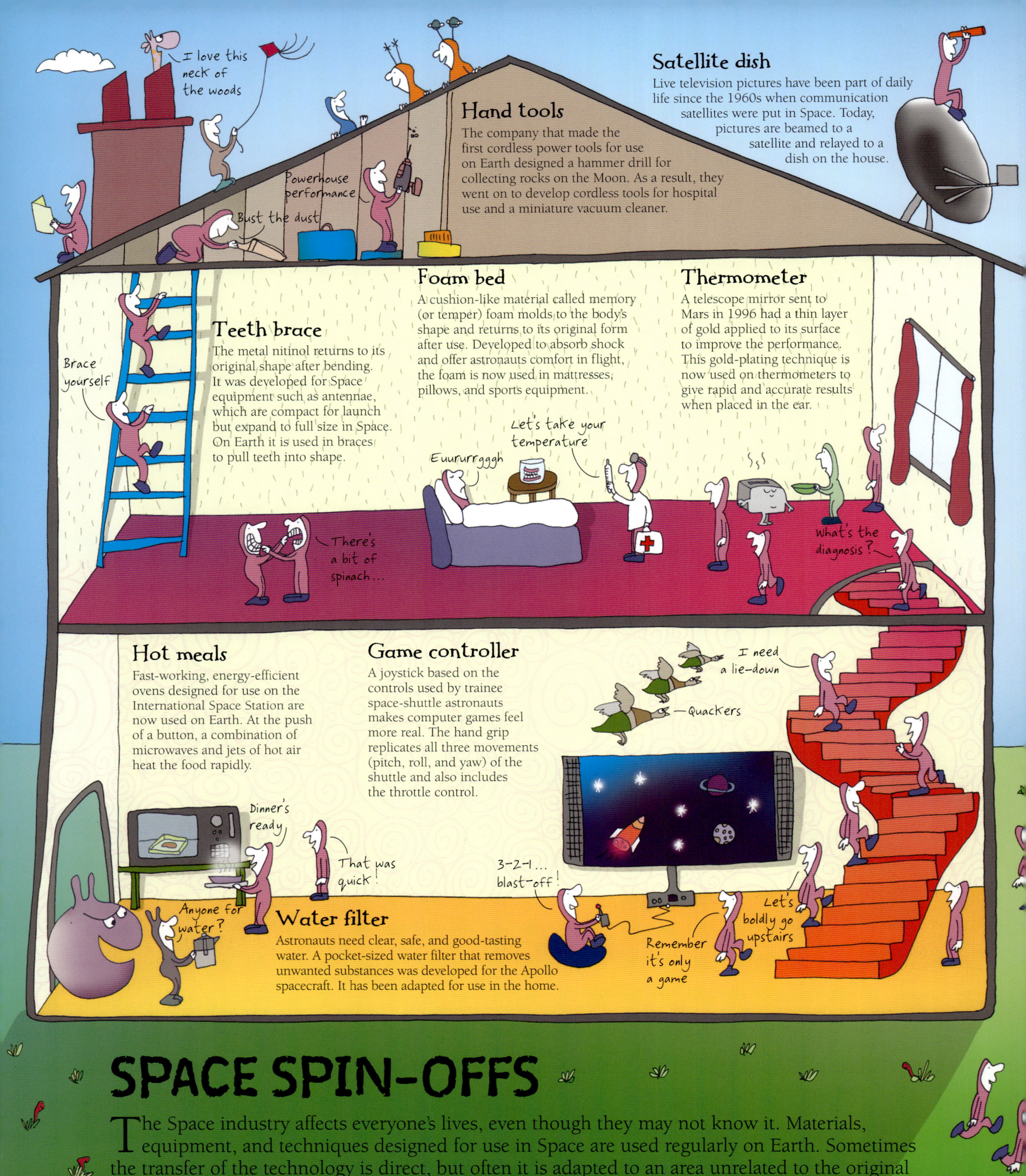

Satellite dish
Live television pictures have been part of daily life since the 1960s when communication satellites were put in Space. Today, pictures are beamed to a satellite and relayed to a dish on the house.

Hand tools
The company that made the first cordless power tools for use on Earth designed a hammer drill for collecting rocks on the Moon. As a result, they went on to develop cordless tools for hospital use and a miniature vacuum cleaner.

Foam bed
A cushion-like material called memory (or temper) foam molds to the body's shape and returns to its original form after use. Developed to absorb shock and offer astronauts comfort in flight, the foam is now used in mattresses, pillows, and sports equipment.

Thermometer
A telescope mirror sent to Mars in 1996 had a thin layer of gold applied to its surface to improve the performance. This gold-plating technique is now used on thermometers to give rapid and accurate results when placed in the ear.

Teeth brace
The metal nitinol returns to its original shape after bending. It was developed for Space equipment such as antennae, which are compact for launch but expand to full size in Space. On Earth it is used in braces to pull teeth into shape.

Hot meals
Fast-working, energy-efficient ovens designed for use on the International Space Station are now used on Earth. At the push of a button, a combination of microwaves and jets of hot air heat the food rapidly.

Game controller
A joystick based on the controls used by trainee space-shuttle astronauts makes computer games feel more real. The hand grip replicates all three movements (pitch, roll, and yaw) of the shuttle and also includes the throttle control.

Water filter
Astronauts need clear, safe, and good-tasting water. A pocket-sized water filter that removes unwanted substances was developed for the Apollo spacecraft. It has been adapted for use in the home.

SPACE SPIN-OFFS

The Space industry affects everyone's lives, even though they may not know it. Materials, equipment, and techniques designed for use in Space are used regularly on Earth. Sometimes the transfer of the technology is direct, but often it is adapted to an area unrelated to the original use. The benefits of the Space industry are enjoyed every day by all of us.

Hang-glider

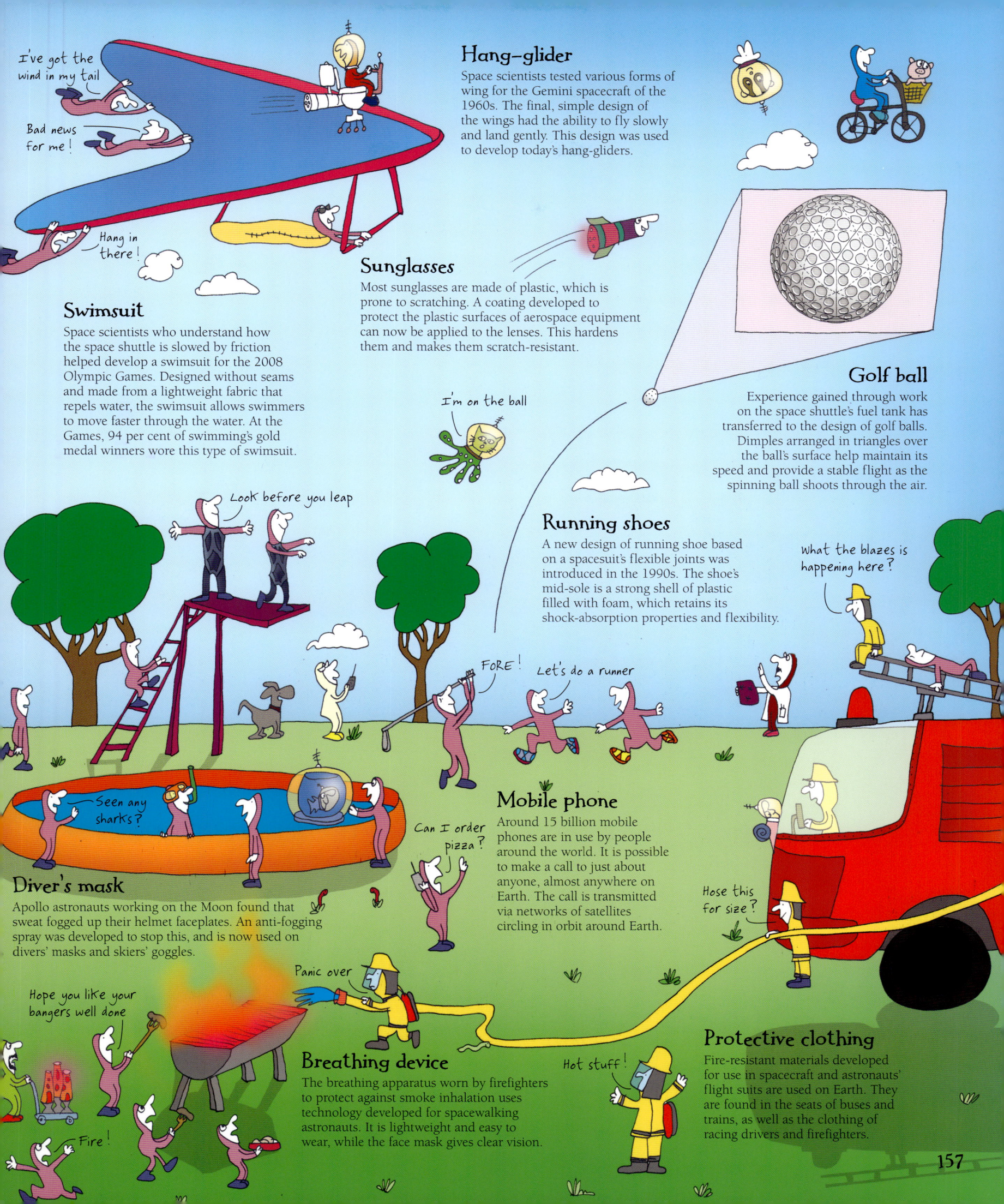

Space scientists tested various forms of wing for the Gemini spacecraft of the 1960s. The final, simple design of the wings had the ability to fly slowly and land gently. This design was used to develop today's hang-gliders.

Sunglasses

Most sunglasses are made of plastic, which is prone to scratching. A coating developed to protect the plastic surfaces of aerospace equipment can now be applied to the lenses. This hardens them and makes them scratch-resistant.

Swimsuit

Space scientists who understand how the space shuttle is slowed by friction helped develop a swimsuit for the 2008 Olympic Games. Designed without seams and made from a lightweight fabric that repels water, the swimsuit allows swimmers to move faster through the water. At the Games, 94 per cent of swimming's gold medal winners wore this type of swimsuit.

Golf ball

Experience gained through work on the space shuttle's fuel tank has transferred to the design of golf balls. Dimples arranged in triangles over the ball's surface help maintain its speed and provide a stable flight as the spinning ball shoots through the air.

Running shoes

A new design of running shoe based on a spacesuit's flexible joints was introduced in the 1990s. The shoe's mid-sole is a strong shell of plastic filled with foam, which retains its shock-absorption properties and flexibility.

Diver's mask

Apollo astronauts working on the Moon found that sweat fogged up their helmet faceplates. An anti-fogging spray was developed to stop this, and is now used on divers' masks and skiers' goggles.

Mobile phone

Around 15 billion mobile phones are in use by people around the world. It is possible to make a call to just about anyone, almost anywhere on Earth. The call is transmitted via networks of satellites circling in orbit around Earth.

Breathing device

The breathing apparatus worn by firefighters to protect against smoke inhalation uses technology developed for spacewalking astronauts. It is lightweight and easy to wear, while the face mask gives clear vision.

Protective clothing

Fire-resistant materials developed for use in spacecraft and astronauts' flight suits are used on Earth. They are found in the seats of buses and trains, as well as the clothing of racing drivers and firefighters.

TIME TRAVELLERS

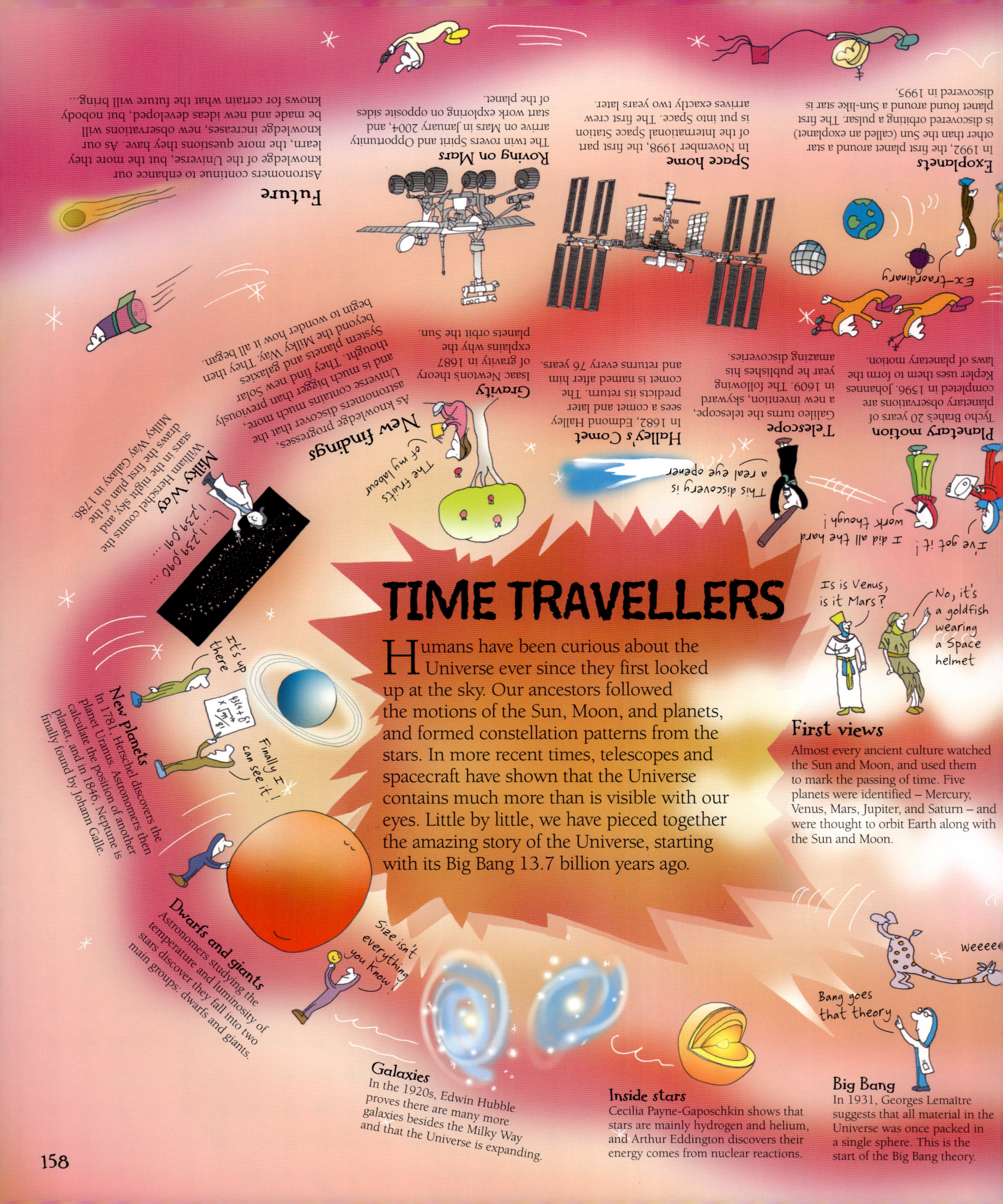

Humans have been curious about the Universe ever since they first looked up at the sky. Our ancestors followed the motions of the Sun, Moon, and planets, and formed constellation patterns from the stars. In more recent times, telescopes and spacecraft have shown that the Universe contains much more than is visible with our eyes. Little by little, we have pieced together the amazing story of the Universe, starting with its Big Bang 13.7 billion years ago.

First views
Almost every ancient culture watched the Sun and Moon, and used them to mark the passing of time. Five planets were identified – Mercury, Venus, Mars, Jupiter, and Saturn – and were thought to orbit Earth along with the Sun and Moon.

Big Bang
In 1931, Georges Lemaître suggests that all material in the Universe was once packed in a single sphere. This is the start of the Big Bang theory.

Inside stars
Cecilia Payne-Gaposchkin shows that stars are mainly hydrogen and helium, and Arthur Eddington discovers their energy comes from nuclear reactions.

Galaxies
In the 1920s, Edwin Hubble proves there are many more galaxies besides the Milky Way and that the Universe is expanding.

Dwarfs and giants
Astronomers studying the temperature and luminosity of stars discover they fall into two main groups: dwarfs and giants.

New planets
In 1781, Herschel discovers the planet Uranus. Astronomers then calculate the position of another planet, and in 1846 Neptune is finally found by Johann Galle.

Milky Way
William Herschel counts the stars in the night sky, and draws the first plan of the Milky Way Galaxy in 1786.

New findings
As knowledge progresses, astronomers discover that the Universe contains much more than previously thought. They find new Solar System planets and galaxies beyond the Milky Way. They then begin to wonder how it all began.

Gravity
Isaac Newton's theory of gravity in 1687 explains why the planets orbit the Sun.

Halley's Comet
In 1682, Edmond Halley sees a comet and later predicts its return. The comet is named after him and returns every 76 years.

Telescope
Galileo turns the telescope, a new invention, skyward in 1609. The following year he publishes his amazing discoveries.

Planetary motion
Tycho Brahe's 20 years of planetary observations are completed in 1596. Johannes Kepler uses them to form the laws of planetary motion.

Exoplanets
In 1992, the first planet around a star other than the Sun (called an exoplanet) is discovered orbiting a pulsar. The first planet found around a Sun-like star is discovered in 1995.

Space home
In November 1998, the first part of the International Space Station is put into Space. The first crew arrives exactly two years later.

Roving on Mars
The twin rovers Spirit and Opportunity arrive on Mars in January 2004, and start work exploring on opposite sides of the planet.

Future
Astronomers continue to enhance our knowledge of the Universe, but the more they learn, the more questions they have. As our knowledge increases, new observations will be made and new ideas developed, but nobody knows for certain what the future will bring.

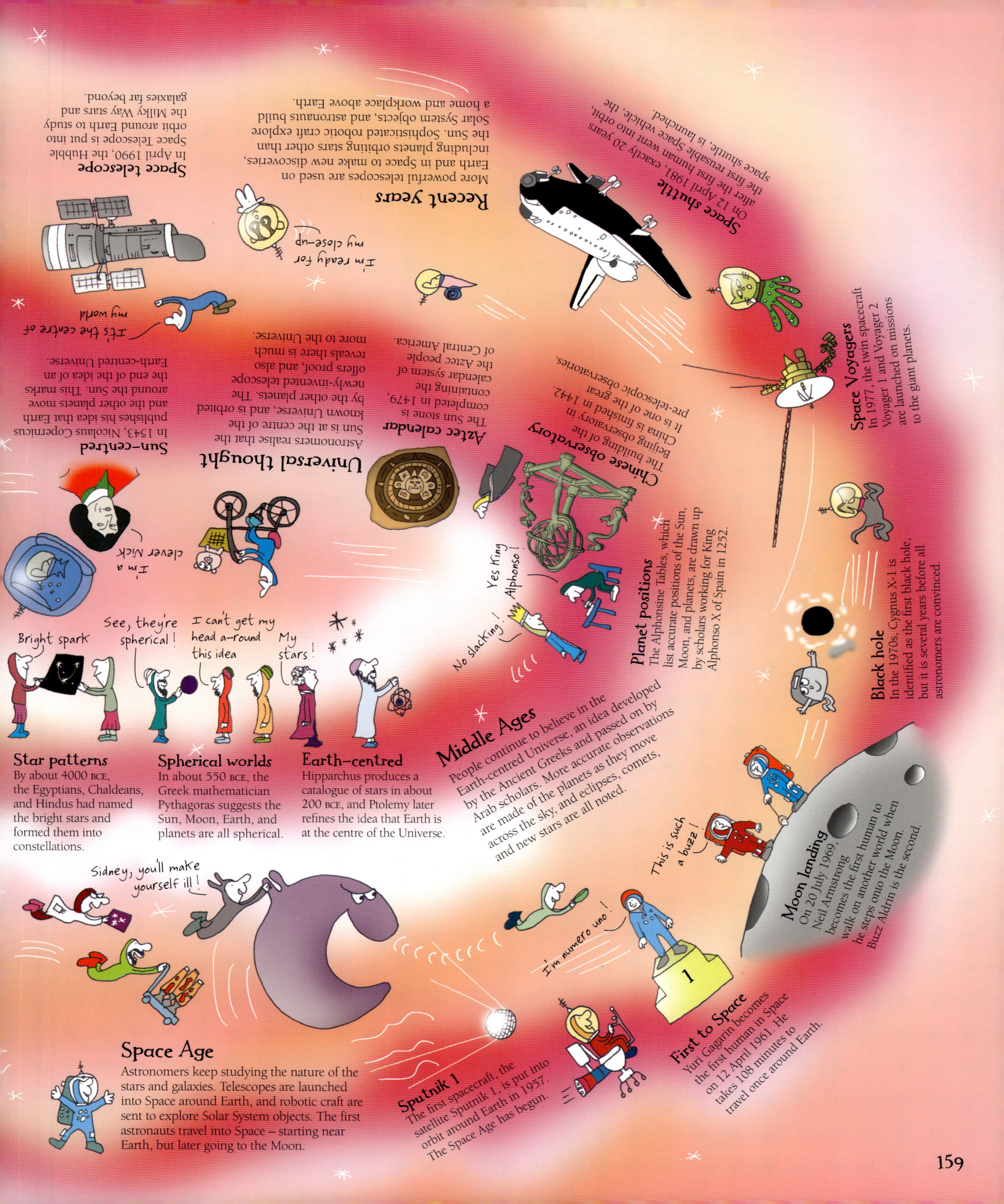

Space telescope
In April 1990, the Hubble Space Telescope is put into orbit around Earth to study the Milky Way stars and galaxies far beyond.

Recent years
More powerful telescopes are used on Earth and in space to make new discoveries, including planets orbiting stars other than the Sun. Sophisticated robotic craft explore Solar System objects, and astronauts build a home and workplace above Earth.

Space shuttle
On 12 April 1981, exactly 20 years after the first human went into orbit, the first reusable space vehicle, the space shuttle, is launched.

Space Voyagers
In 1977, the twin spacecraft Voyager 1 and Voyager 2 are launched on missions to the giant planets.

Sun-centred
In 1543, Nicolaus Copernicus publishes his idea that Earth and the other planets move around the Sun. This marks the end of the idea of an Earth-centred Universe.

Universal thought
Astronomers realise that the Sun is at the centre of the known Universe, and is orbited by the other planets. The newly-invented telescope offers proof, and also reveals there is much more to the Universe.

Aztec calendar
The Sun stone is completed in 1479, containing the calendar system of the Aztec people of Central America.

Chinese observatory
The building of the Beijing observatory in China is finished in 1442. It is one of the great pre-telescopic observatories.

Planet positions
The Alphonsine Tables, which list accurate positions of the Sun, Moon, and planets, are drawn up by scholars working for King Alphonso X of Spain in 1252.

Black hole
In the 1970s, Cygnus X-1 is identified as the first black hole, but it is several years before all astronomers are convinced.

Star patterns
By about 4000 BCE, the Egyptians, Chaldeans, and Hindus had named the bright stars and formed them into constellations.

Spherical worlds
In about 550 BCE, the Greek mathematician Pythagoras suggests the Sun, Moon, Earth, and planets are all spherical.

Earth-centred
Hipparchus produces a catalogue of stars in about 200 BCE, and Ptolemy later refines the idea that Earth is at the centre of the Universe.

Middle Ages
People continue to believe in the Earth-centred Universe, an idea developed by the Ancient Greeks and passed on by Arab scholars. More accurate observations are made of the planets as they move across the sky, and eclipses, comets, and new stars are all noted.

Moon landing
On 20 July 1969, Neil Armstrong becomes the first human to walk on another world when he steps onto the Moon. Buzz Aldrin is the second.

Space Age
Astronomers keep studying the nature of the stars and galaxies. Telescopes are launched into Space around Earth, and robotic craft are sent to explore Solar System objects. The first astronauts travel into Space – starting near Earth, but later going to the Moon.

Sputnik 1
The first spacecraft, the satellite Sputnik 1, is put into orbit around Earth in 1957. The Space Age has begun.

First to Space
Yuri Gagarin becomes the first human in Space on 12 April 1961. He takes 108 minutes to travel once around Earth.

159

FUTURE SPACE

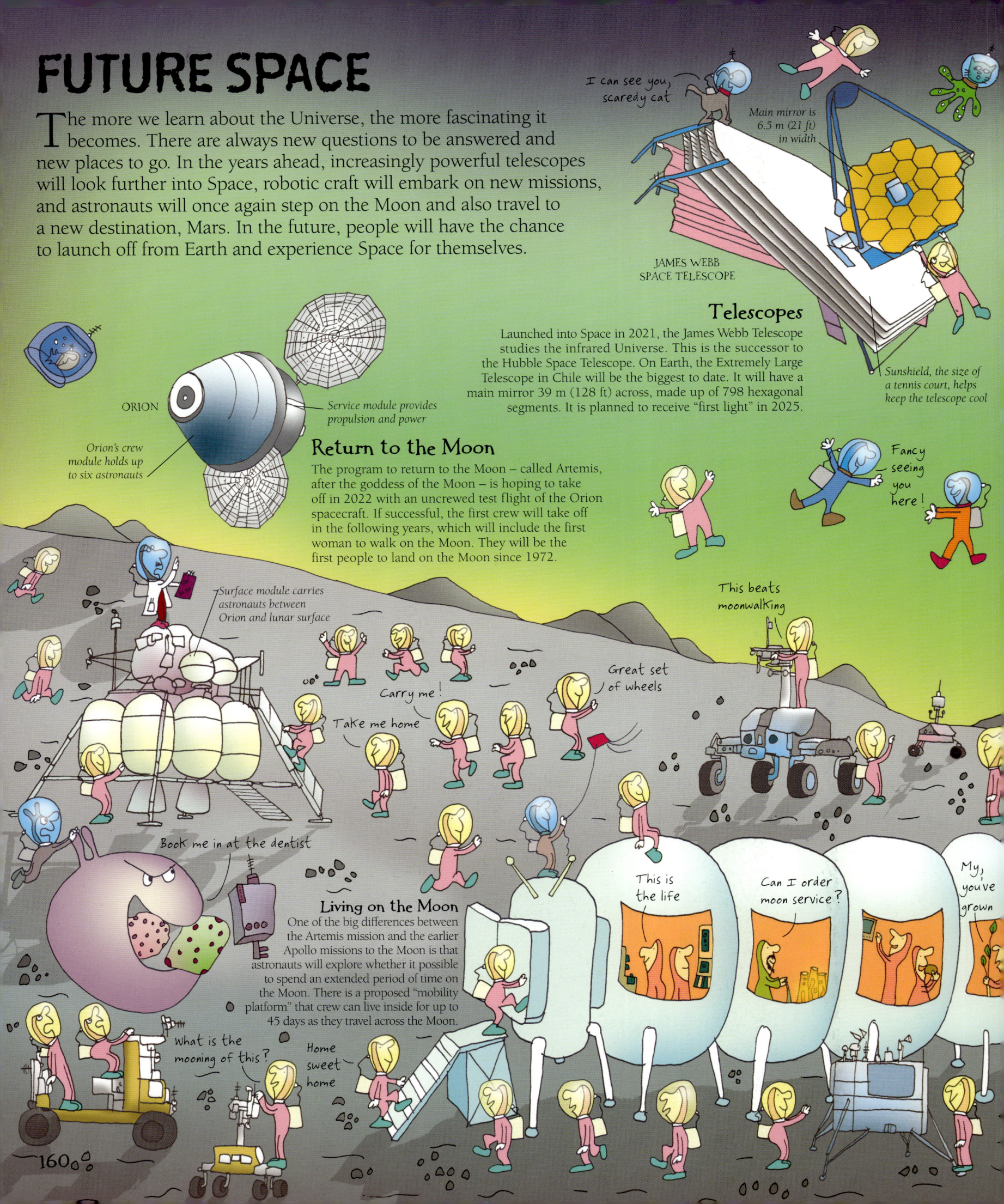

The more we learn about the Universe, the more fascinating it becomes. There are always new questions to be answered and new places to go. In the years ahead, increasingly powerful telescopes will look further into Space, robotic craft will embark on new missions, and astronauts will once again step on the Moon and also travel to a new destination, Mars. In the future, people will have the chance to launch off from Earth and experience Space for themselves.

JAMES WEBB SPACE TELESCOPE

Main mirror is 6.5 m (21 ft) in width

Sunshield, the size of a tennis court, helps keep the telescope cool

Telescopes

Launched into Space in 2021, the James Webb Telescope studies the infrared Universe. This is the successor to the Hubble Space Telescope. On Earth, the Extremely Large Telescope in Chile will be the biggest to date. It will have a main mirror 39 m (128 ft) across, made up of 798 hexagonal segments. It is planned to receive "first light" in 2025.

ORION

Orion's crew module holds up to six astronauts

Service module provides propulsion and power

Return to the Moon

The program to return to the Moon – called Artemis, after the goddess of the Moon – is hoping to take off in 2022 with an uncrewed test flight of the Orion spacecraft. If successful, the first crew will take off in the following years, which will include the first woman to walk on the Moon. They will be the first people to land on the Moon since 1972.

Surface module carries astronauts between Orion and lunar surface

Living on the Moon

One of the big differences between the Artemis mission and the earlier Apollo missions to the Moon is that astronauts will explore whether it possible to spend an extended period of time on the Moon. There is a proposed "mobility platform" that crew can live inside for up to 45 days as they travel across the Moon.

160

Searching in the dark

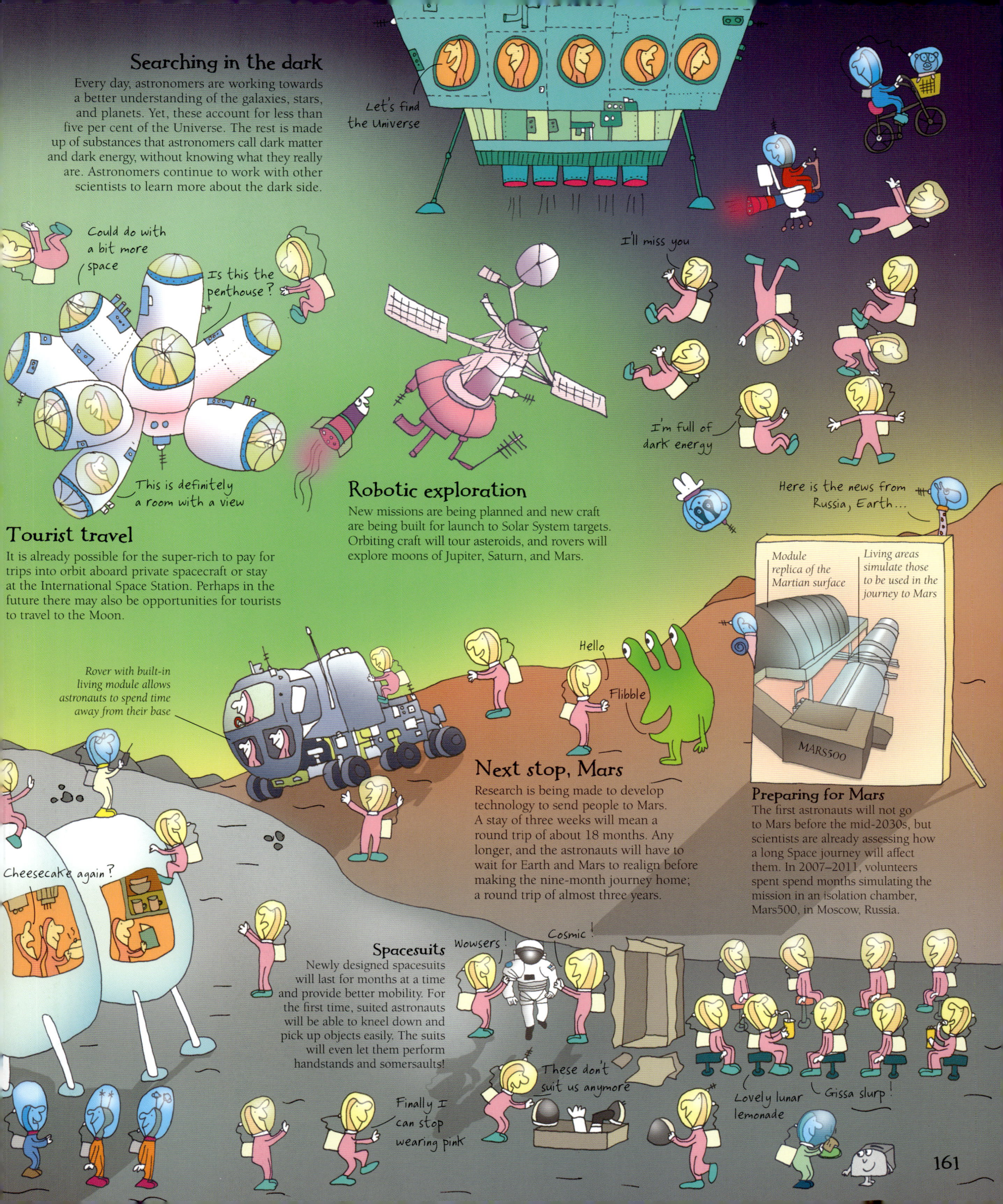

Every day, astronomers are working towards a better understanding of the galaxies, stars, and planets. Yet, these account for less than five per cent of the Universe. The rest is made up of substances that astronomers call dark matter and dark energy, without knowing what they really are. Astronomers continue to work with other scientists to learn more about the dark side.

Tourist travel

It is already possible for the super-rich to pay for trips into orbit aboard private spacecraft or stay at the International Space Station. Perhaps in the future there may also be opportunities for tourists to travel to the Moon.

Robotic exploration

New missions are being planned and new craft are being built for launch to Solar System targets. Orbiting craft will tour asteroids, and rovers will explore moons of Jupiter, Saturn, and Mars.

Next stop, Mars

Research is being made to develop technology to send people to Mars. A stay of three weeks will mean a round trip of about 18 months. Any longer, and the astronauts will have to wait for Earth and Mars to realign before making the nine-month journey home; a round trip of almost three years.

Preparing for Mars

The first astronauts will not go to Mars before the mid-2030s, but scientists are already assessing how a long Space journey will affect them. In 2007–2011, volunteers spent spend months simulating the mission in an isolation chamber, Mars500, in Moscow, Russia.

Module replica of the Martian surface

Living areas simulate those to be used in the journey to Mars

Spacesuits

Newly designed spacesuits will last for months at a time and provide better mobility. For the first time, suited astronauts will be able to kneel down and pick up objects easily. The suits will even let them perform handstands and somersaults!

Rover with built-in living module allows astronauts to spend time away from their base

161

Glossary

Acid
A compound containing hydrogen that splits up in water to produce positive hydrogen ions. Acids have a pH below 7.

Active galaxy
A galaxy that emits an exceptional amount of energy, much of which comes from a supermassive black hole in its centre.

Alien
A creature that originates from a world other than Earth.

Alkali
A base that dissolves in water, to create negatively charged hydroxide ions (OH-).

Alloy
A mixture of a metal and another substance.

Amplitude
The maximum height or depth of a wave, measured from a central point.

Antenna
An aerial in the shape of a rod, dish, or array for receiving or transmitting radio waves.

Apparent magnitude
A measure of the apparent brightness of a star when seen from Earth.

Asteroid
An object orbiting the Sun, usually between Mars and Jupiter, in a region called the asteroid belt. Asteroids are made of rock or metal.

Astronaut
The US term for a crew member of a spacecraft. It derives from two Greek words, *astron* (star) and *nautes* (sailor).

Astronomy
A branch of science that looks at the Universe, planets, and stars.

Astronomer
Someone who studies stars, planets, and other objects in space.

Atmosphere
The layer of gases held around a planet, moon, or star by its gravity.

Atom
The smallest part of an element that can exist and still have the characteristics of that element.

Aurora
A light display over a planet's polar regions produced when particles hit atoms in the planet's atmosphere, making the atmosphere glow.

Base
A compound that reacts with acid to form a salt. A base has a pH above 7.

Big Bang
The explosive event that created the Universe 13.7 billion years ago.

Biology
A branch of science concerned with the structure and behaviour of living organisms, such as plants and animals.

Black hole
A star or galaxy core that has collapsed in on itself. Black holes have gravity so strong that no matter, light, or other radiation can escape from them.

Bond
An attraction between atoms that holds them together as molecules.

Botany
The branch of biology concerned with plants.

Brightness
A measure of the light of a star. Astronomers measure brightness in two ways: as seen from Earth, and the amount of light a star emits.

Cape
A point or head of land, sticking out into the sea.

Catalyst
A substance that speeds up a chemical reaction without itself undergoing any change.

Cell
The basic unit in all living things. A cell may exist as an independent unit of life, or many can combine to form complex tissue, as in plants and animals.

Chemical reaction
A process that changes substances into new substances by breaking and making chemical bonds.

Chemistry
A branch of science concerned with the composition of substances and how they react with each other.

Chromosome
One of 46 thread-like packages of DNA found in the nucleus of body cells.

Circuit
A path through which an electric current can flow.

Cluster
A group of galaxies or stars held together by gravity.

Comet
An object made from ice, dust, and rocky particles, orbiting the Sun. Those travelling near the Sun develop a huge head and two tails.

Compound
A substance formed from two or more chemically bonded elements.

162

Conduction
The process by which heat or electricity passes through a substance.

Conductor
A substance that allows heat or electricity to pass through it easily.

Constellation
An imaginary pattern of stars and the region of sky around them. Earth's sky is divided into 88 different constellations.

Convection
The transfer of heat through a liquid or gas caused by warmer, less dense material rising, and cooler, more dense material falling.

Cosmologist
A person who studies the origin, evolution, and future of the Universe.

Crater
A bowl-shaped hollow on the surface of a planet or moon formed when an asteroid crashes into it.

Crystal
A solid substance with molecules arranged in a regular pattern.

Current
A flow of electrons.

Dark energy
A mysterious energy form that makes up 72 per cent of the Universe and is responsible for the acceleration of the expansion of the Universe.

Dark matter
Matter that does not emit energy but whose gravity affects its surroundings. It makes up 23 per cent of the Universe.

Density
A measure of how tightly the mass an object possesses is packed into its volume.

Dissolving
When a substance mixes into another substance completely, with every part of the mixture the same.

Distillation
A process for purifying or separating liquids by first boiling and then cooling the liquid.

DNA
Deoxyribonucleic acid. Long molecules found in the nucleus of body cells that carry the instructions needed to construct and operate that cell.

Dwarf galaxy
A small galaxy containing only a million to several billion stars.

Dwarf planet
An almost round body that orbits the Sun as part of a belt of objects.

Efficiency
A measure of how much energy is turned into useful work by a machine.

Electricity
The effect created by the movement or build-up of electrons.

Electrode
A conductor through which electricity enters or leaves something.

Electrolysis
A chemical reaction created by passing a current through an electrolyte.

Electrolyte
A compound that conducts electricity in electrochemical reactions.

Electromagnetic radiation
A range of energy waves that can travel through space. They include gamma rays, X-rays, ultraviolet, light, infrared, microwaves, and radio waves.

Electromagnetic spectrum
A group of energy-carrying waves arranged in order of increasing wavelength, including radio waves, microwaves, infrared waves, visible light, ultraviolet waves, X-rays, and gamma rays.

Electromagnetism
The relationship between electricity and magnetism.

Electron
A subatomic particle with a negative charge, found in orbits around an atom's nucleus.

Element
A substance that cannot be broken into any simpler substance by physical or chemical means.

Elliptical
Something shaped like an elongated circle.

Endothermic reaction
A reaction in which heat is taken in.

Energy
The ability of matter and radiation to do work. There are many forms of energy, and the unit for measuring energy is a joule (J).

Equation
A way of using symbols to represent how the reactants of a chemical reaction turn into the products. Each side of the equation must be balanced.

Equator
An imaginary line drawn around the middle of a planet, moon, or star, halfway between its north and south poles.

Exoplanet
A planet that orbits a star other than the Sun. Sometimes called an extrasolar planet.

Exothermic reaction
A reaction in which heat is given out.

Experiment
A scientific procedure carried out to test a hypothesis or prove a theory.

Extraterrestrial
Something or somebody that comes from somewhere other than Earth.

Fly-by
A close encounter made with a Solar System object by a spacecraft, which flies past without going into orbit.

Force
A push or a pull that changes the motion of an object. Force is measured in newtons (N).

Frequency
The number of waves passing a point each second, measured in hertz (Hz).

Friction
A force caused by one surface rubbing against another.

Fulcrum
The fixed turning point of a lever. Sometimes called a pivot.

Galaxy
An enormous grouping of stars, gas, and dust held together by gravity.

Gas
A state of matter with no definite shape or fixed volume. Particles in gasses have lots of kinetic energy.

Gene
One of the 25,000 instructions stored in the DNA inside a set of 23 pairs of human chromosomes.

Genetics
The branch of biology concerned with inherited characteristics between generations of plants and animals.

Giant planets
The four largest Solar System planets. In order of decreasing size and distance from the Sun, they are Jupiter, Saturn, Uranus, and Neptune.

Gravity
The force of attraction between two objects that have mass.

Helium
The second most abundant chemical element in the Universe.

Hydrogen
The lightest and most abundant chemical element in the Universe.

Hydrothermal vent
A crack in the ocean floor, where hot gases flow up from Earth's crust, heating the surrounding water.

Inertia
An object's resistance to any change in motion.

Inorganic chemistry
A field of chemistry that looks at substances that contain no carbon or only a very tiny amount of carbon.

Insulator
A material that is a poor conductor of heat or electricity.

Ion
An atom or group of atoms that has lost or gained electrons and so become electrically charged.

Kinetic energy
The energy a body has because of its motion.

Kuiper Belt Object
A rock and ice body orbiting the Sun within the Kuiper Belt, beyond the orbit of Neptune.

Lander
A spacecraft that lands on the surface of a planet, moon, asteroid, or comet.

Law
A statement of a scientific fact that says a certain thing will always happen under certain conditions, for example, Newton's laws of motion.

Lava
Molten rock released through a volcano on the surface of a planet or moon.

Lens
A piece of glass or plastic used to refract light. The centre of a convex lens curves towards you, and the centre of a concave lens bends away from you.

Lever
A simple machine consisting of a rigid bar turning around a fixed point called the fulcrum.

Light year
A unit of distance. One light year (ly) is the distance light travels in one year, which is 9.46 million million km (5.88 million million miles).

Liquid
A state of matter with no definite shape and fixed volume. Particles in liquids have more kinetic energy than in solids, but less than in gasses.

Longitude
A position to the east or west of a given point. Today, we measure longitude from a line running through Greenwich, England.

Luminosity
The total amount of energy emitted in one second by a star.

Lunar
Relating to the Moon. For example, the "lunar surface" is the surface of the Moon.

Machine
A device that changes one force into another to make work easier.

Magnetic field
An area around a magnet influenced by the magnet's force.

Main sequence
A stage in the lifetime of a star when the star shines by converting hydrogen into helium in its core. About 90 per cent of stars are main sequence stars.

Mare
A smooth plain of solidified lava on the Moon. (pl. maria)

Maroon
To leave someone behind during a sea voyage on an island or coast.

Mass
A measure of the amount of material (matter) a body is made of.

Mathematics
A branch of science concerned with the measurement, properties, and relationships of quantities and sets, using numbers and symbols.

Matter
Anything that has mass and fills space.

Mechanics
This area of physics looks at motion and the forces that produce it.

Meniscus
The curved surface of a liquid, caused by a variation in surface tension where the liquid touches the container.

Meteor
A short-lived streak of light produced by a small piece of a comet burning up in Earth's upper atmosphere.

Meteorite
Rock or metal from space that lands on the surface of a planet or moon.

Milky Way
The galaxy we live in. Also, the name given to the band of stars that crosses Earth's sky and which is our view into the galaxy.

Module
A complete unit of a spacecraft, for instance, the Zvezda module of the International Space Station.

Molecule
The smallest unit of an element or a compound that can exist and still have the properties of that element or compound, made of two or more bonded atoms.

Momentum
An object's tendency to keep moving, measured by multiplying its mass by its velocity.

Moon
A rock or rock-and-ice body, that orbits a planet or an asteroid.

NASA
The National Aeronautics and Space Administration, which was set up in 1958 by the US government to run their space exploration programme.

Natural elements
The 94 elements that make up all the matter on Earth.

Naturalist
A scientist who studies animals and plants.

Navigation
The science of finding a way from one place to another.

Nebula
A cloud of gas and dust in space. Some nebulae emit their own light, others shine by reflecting light, and those that block out light from background stars appear dark.

Neutral
A substance that is neither acid nor alkaline, such as water.

Neutron
A subatomic particle with no electric charge, found in an atom's nucleus.

Neutron star
A dense, compact star formed from the core of an exploding star. These stars are about the size of a city but have the same mass as the Sun.

Nuclear reaction
The process whereby elements inside a star produce other elements and energy is released. For example, hydrogen atoms fuse to produce helium, and energy such as heat and light is emitted in the process.

Nucleus
The body of a comet, the central part of a galaxy, or the central core of an atom. (pl. nuclei)

Nuclear physics
The branch of physics that studies and splits tiny particles called atoms.

Nuclear reaction
A reaction that splits apart or fuses together atomic nuclei.

Nucleus
The central part of an atom, containing protons and neutrons. The nucleus has a positive charge.

Oort Cloud
A sphere consisting of more than a trillion comets that surrounds the planetary part of the Solar System.

Orbit
The path that a natural or artificial body makes around another more massive body.

Orbiter
A spacecraft that orbits around a space body such as a planet or asteroid.

Organic chemistry
A field of chemistry concerned with substances that contain carbon, the substance vital to all living matter.

Organism
An individual form of life such as a single-celled bacterium, an animal, or a planet.

Peak
The highest point that a wave reaches.

Penumbra
The lighter, outer part of a shadow cast by a space body. Also, the lighter and warmer outer region of a dark, cool sunspot.

Periodic table
A table of all the elements that exist arranged in order of increasing atomic number. Elements with similar atomic structure are grouped in columns.

Petrochemical
A substance produced from petroleum or natural gas.

pH
The "power of Hydrogen": the measure of how acid or alkaline a substance is.

Pharmaceutical
A manufactured medicinal drug.

Photon
The particle responsible for electromagnetic energy.

Photosphere
The outer, visible layer of the Sun or another star.

Physics
A branch of science concerned with energy and forces. Physics looks at the very small (nuclear physics) to the science of the Universe.

Pilot
A skilled navigator.

Pitch
The high or low quality of a sound produced by its frequency.

Planet
A massive, round body that orbits a star and shines by reflecting the star's light.

Planetary nebula
An expanding nebula surrounding a mature star. This nebula is a colourful cloud of ejected gas and dust from the dying star.

Polar
Relating to the North and South Poles of an object.

Pole
One of the two opposite points on a magnet where the magnetic forces are strongest.

Polymer
A substance made from many identical molecules bonded together to form a long chain.

Potential energy
Energy stored for later use, for example, coal has potential energy, which can be converted to heat energy.

Power
The amount of work carried out in a certain time, measured in watts (W).

Pressure
The force felt when something presses against a surface.

Proton
A subatomic particle with a positive charge found in the nucleus of an atom.

Protostar
A very young star in the early stages of formation, before nuclear reactions start in its core.

Pulsar
A rapidly rotating neutron star from which brief pulses of energy are received as the star spins.

Radiation
Energy travelling as electromagnetic waves, such as light or heat.

Reactant
A substance that takes part in a chemical reaction, and is changed by the reaction.

Refraction
The bending of a beam of light as it passes from one substance into another, for example, from air to glass.

Resistance
The amount that a substance opposes the flow of an electric current.

Rocky planets
The four planets closest to the Sun and made of rock and/or metal. They are Mercury, Venus, Earth, and Mars.

Rover
A spacecraft that moves across the surface of a planet or moon.

Satellite
An artificial object orbiting Earth or another planetary body. Also, another name for a moon, or any Space object orbiting a much larger one.

Silicate
Rocky material containing the elements silicon, oxygen, and one or more other common elements. Most rocks on Earth are silicates.

Solar
Relating to the Sun. For example, the "solar temperature" is the temperature of the Sun.

Solar nebula
The spinning cloud of gas and dust that formed into the Solar System.

Solar System
The Sun and the objects that orbit it, including the planets and many smaller bodies.

Solar wind
A stream of particles emitted by the Sun.

Solid
A state of matter with a definite shape and fixed volume. Particles in solids have little kinetic energy.

Solute
A substance that dissolves to form a solution.

Solution
A mixture made by dissolving one substance in another. The particles of the substances are so evenly mixed that every part of the mixture is the same.

Solvent
A substance that dissolves other substances to form a solution.

Space probe
An unmanned spacecraft sent into space to study other planets and moons.

Spacewalk
An excursion by an astronaut outside a craft when in space.

Spectrograph
An instrument that splits energy, such as light, into its component wavelengths. This is then analysed to reveal an object's properties.

Spectrum
The rainbow band of colours that is produced when light is split.

Spices
The seeds, leaves, or bark of plants used to flavour food.

Static electricity
An effect caused by electrons building up in one place and creating an electric charge.

Star
A huge sphere of hot, luminous gas that generates energy by nuclear reactions.

Supercluster
A grouping of galaxy clusters held together by gravity.

Supergiant
An exceptionally large and luminous star.

Supernova
A massive star that explodes and leaves material behind, and whose core can become a neutron star, pulsar, or black hole. (pl. supernovae)

Suspension
A mixture containing particles too large to dissolve that are light enough to hang or float in the liquid or gas they are mixed with.

Synthetic
Created artificially rather than occurring naturally, for example, all the elements heavier than plutonium are synthetic.

Telegraphy
A way of transmitting signals or messages over long distances using, for example, flags, radio waves, or pulses of electric current.

Theory
An idea that explains why something happens as it does, for example, the Theory of Relativity.

Thermal
Relating to heat. A thermal map of an object shows the temperature across the surface of that object.

Trough
The lowest point that a wave reaches.

Tungsten
A metallic element, commonly used in incandescent light bulbs, that glows for a long time without melting or boiling away.

Umbra
The dark, inner shadow cast by a Space body. Also, the darker, cooler inner region of a sunspot.

Universe
Everything that exists – space and everything in it.

Vacuum
A space that is void of matter, including air.

Velocity
The speed and direction of an object.

Vibration
A repetitive movement back and forth or up and down.

Visible spectrum
The part of the electromagnetic spectrum that people can see as visible light.

Volume
The amount of space an object occupies.

Wavelength
The distance between two equivalent points on neighbouring waves.

Weightlessness
The sensation experienced by astronauts in Space because being in orbit is like constantly falling through Space.

Work
The amount of energy needed to perform a task, measured in joules (J).

X-rays
A type of radiation (energy in wave form) related to visible light and radio waves.

Zodiac
The band of 12 constellations that forms the background to the Sun, Moon, and planets as they move across the sky.

Zoology
The branch of biology that is concerned with animals.

Index

A

absolute zero 34, 59
acceleration 40, 41
acid rain 23
acids 22–23
active galaxies 116
Advanced Passenger Train 94
aircraft, supersonic 33
airliners 92, 93
airship 77
alchemy 58
Aldebaran 126, 127
Aldrin, Buzz 135, 159
aliens 155
alkalis 22
alloys 29
Alphonsine Tables 159
alternative energy
 sources 85
aluminium 13
ammonia 11, 23
amplitude 32
Andromeda Galaxy 115
anodes 52, 53
antennae 156
apatite 16
Apennine Mountains
 (Moon) 135
Apollo (asteroid) 141
Apollo 115 mission 135, 157
Apollo craft 135, 156
apparent magnitude 127, 58
Aperture Spherical Telescope 120
arc lights 80
Archimedes 70, 74
Arkwright, Richard 70, 75
Armstrong, Neil 135, 150, 159
Arnold, Kevin 155
Artemis 160
aspirin (acetylsalicylic
 acid) 28
assembly line 91
Asteroid Belt see also
 Main Belt
asteroids: 130, 131, 140–141
 collisions 141
 cratering 141
 fracturing 141
 Moon and 135
 names 140
 planetary impacts 136, 138,
 139, 141
 shattering 141
astronauts: 44, 146, 150–153, 159,
 future missions 160, 161
 inventions for 156–157
 living in Space 152–153
 training 151, 161
astronomers 118–119, 158, 159
 amateur 119
 and comets 144, 145
 future work 161
astronomy 9, 59
 telescopes 36
astrophysicists 118
astrophysics 9
Atanasoff, John 96
Atlantis Orbiter 146–147
atmosphere
 atmospheric pressure 133
 Earth's 133
 planets' 136, 137, 138
 Sun's 124–125
atomic bomb 107
atomic mass 12
atomic numbers 12
atoms 10–11, 114
 and electricity 48
 chemical reactions 19
 historical discoveries 58, 59
 in metals 29
 splitting 8, 59
attraction 46–47
auroras 47, 125
axe 62
axles 42
Ayres's aerial machine 78
Aztec calendar 159

B

Babbage, Charles 96
babies:
 disposable nappies 87
 mechanical patter 79
 rocking 78
Baekeland, Leo 63
Baekelite 63
Baird, John Logie 100, 101
ball-grinding machine 90
bar codes 107
Bardeen, John 96
Barnack, Oskar 68
bases 22–23
batteries: electric 52–53
 Leclanché cell 80
 Volta's pile 80
Bazalgette, Joseph 76
Beach, Chester 84
Beau de Rochas,
 Alphonse 91
Beek, Traugott 78
Beethoven Region 136
Bell, Alexander Graham
 71, 98
Bennett, Comet 144
Benz, Karl 88
Berliner, Emile 99
Berry, Clifford 96
Bessemer, Henry 95
Big Bang 114–115,
 118, 158
binary code 96, 97
binoculars 66
biochemistry 8
biology 8–9
black holes 45, 116,
 117, 128, 159
bleach 23
blood 23, 27
boats: motor boat 92
 rolling ball 79
 see also steamships
 warships
body temperature 34
Bohr, Niels 10
bombs 106
bonds 11, 21
booster rockets 147
Booth, Herbert 85
botany 8
Boulton, Matthew 72
bow and arrow 104
Bowser, Sylvanus J 90
Boyle, James 79
braces, teeth 156
Brahe, Tycho 158
Brattain, Walter 96
Braun, Ferdinand 100
Braun, Wernher von 106
breaking point 16
breathing devices 157
brightness 127
Brown, Harold 82
Brunel, Isambard
 Kingdom 76
Budding, Edwin 84
Budding, Hannibal
 Goodwin 67
building blocks 10–11
burning 18, 19, 28
Bushnell, David 105
Bushnell, Nolan 101
butter churn 78

C

calcite 16
calculating machines 96
calculus 58
Callisto 142
Caloris Basin 136
camcorders 69
camera obscura 66
cameras 66, 67, 68, 95
Canis Major 126, 127
Canis Minor 126
cannons 104
carbon 8, 13, 28
carbon dioxide 15, 28
cars: amphibious 94
 batteries 53
 diesel-engined 89
 electric 95
 fastest 88
 hybrid 88
 hydrogen-fuelled 52, 59
 petrol-driven 77, 88, 89
 rotary engines 89
 solar-powered 102
 steam-powered 76, 77
Cartwright, Edmond 74
Cassini-Huygens craft 149
catalysts 20
catalytic converters 20
catapult 104
cathedrals 58
cathode ray tube 100
cathodes 52, 53
cat's eyes 66
caustic soda 23
Cayley, Sir George 92
cells 54–55, 154
celluloid 68
Centaurus A 116
centrifuging 27
centripetal force 41
Ceres 140
CERN particle collider 58
Cernan, Gene 135
Chaldeans 159
Chandrasekhar,
 Subrahmanyan 118
Chappé, Claude 98
chariots 104
chemical energy 30
chemical equations 19
chemical reactions 18–21, 30
 electrochemical
 reactions 52–53
chemical symbols 12, 19
chemistry 8–9, 58
 in the home 28–29
 inorganic 9, 29
 organic 8, 28
Chicxulub Crater 141
China 159
Chindogo 79
chip and pin 101
chlorine 13
chromatography 27
chromosomes 54–55
Cinemascope 69
cinematography 68–69
circuits 50
Claude, Georges 81
cleaning 28
Cleopatra Crater 137
clock 63
cloning technology 102–3
clouds 133
clusters:
 galaxy 113, 117
 star 113, 122
 superclusters 113
Cochran, Josephine 71, 84
Cockerel, Christopher 93
codes 62
colloids 27
colour films 69
colours 39
comas 144
comets 130, 144–145
 discovery 118, 144, 145, 158
 formation 131
 historical observation
 of 158, 159
 missions to 145, 148, 149
 names 144
 nucleus 144

comets *continued*
  periodic 145
  Shoemaker-Levy 113 145
compact disc (CD) 100
compasses 47
compounds 11
compression 17
computer games 156
computer languages 62
computer-generated movies 69
computers 118, 71, 96, 47, 107
concave shape 36
concentration 20
Concorde 93
condensation 14
conduction and
conductors 35
  electrical 49
  lightning 48
  of heat 35
  superconductors 49
constellations 126–127, 159
contraction 34
consumer age 91
convection 35
convex shape 36
cooking 28
cooling 14, 25, 34
  superconductors 49
  water 24, 34
Cooper-Hewitt, Peter 81
Copernicus, Nicolaus 59, 159
copper 13, 21
cordless tools 156
corundum 16
cosmic microwave
  background radiation 114
cosmologists 118
cosmology 9
cotton gin 70
covalent bonds 11
cranes 42–43
craters:
  impact 136, 141
  Moon's 135
  on Earth 141
  planets' 136, 138
Cray, Seymour 96, 97
crossbows 104
crystals 16
Cugnot, Nicolas 76
Curie, Marie and Pierre 59
current, electrical 49
Curiosity rover 138
Cygnus X-1 black hole 159

D

Daguerre, Louis 67
Daimler, Gottlieb 88, 91, 92, 89
Dandini, Alessandro 79
Darby, Abraham 74
dark energy 115, 161
dark matter 58, 115, 118, 161
Davis, Jacob 86
Davis, Marion 87
Davy, Sir Humphrey 52, 80
De Forest, Lee 69, 99

Deimos 139
diamond 16
Dickson, William 68
diesel engine, 91, 92, 89
Diesel, Rudolf 91
digital camera 68
dinosaurs:
  evolution of 155
  extinction of 141, 155
Discovery Orbiter 146–147
dishwasher 71, 84
displacement 21
dissolving 26
distillation 27
divers' masks 157
DNA 54
Doppler effect 33
Drake, Edwin 90
Dunlop, John 90
dynamite 70, 105
Dyson, James 85

E

Earth 112, 129, 130, 132–133
  ancient beliefs about 159
  and asteroids 141
  and the Sun 125
  atmosphere 133
  belief in Earth-centred
    Universe 159
  core 132
  crust 132
  human influence 132
  life 112, 133, 154–155
  magnetic field 47, 59
  measurements 59
  surface 132
  temperature 34, 133
  water 25, 132, 133
  weather 133
Eastman, George 67
echoes 33
eclipses:
  historical observation of 159
  lunar 134
  solar 125
Eddington, Arthur 118, 158
Edison, Thomas 26, 68, 71, 81, 94, 98
efficiency 31
Egypt, Ancient 59, 124, 137, 159
Einstein, Albert 31, 45, 58, 59, 102
einsteinium 13
ejector seat 87
elastic band 86
elasticity 16
electric chair 82
electric drill 84
electric light 80, 82, 81
electric motor 70, 83
electricity 48–53, 77, 80–81
  alternating current 82, 81
  and energy 31, 50, 51
  circuits 50
  current 49
  conductors 49

electricity *continued*
  household devices 82–85
  insulators 49
  power generation 81
  resistance 49
  static 48
  supply 51
  used for heating 50
  used for lighting 29, 49, 50
electrochemical
  reactions 52–53
electrodes 52, 53
electrolysis 52–53
electrolytes 52, 53
electromagnetic radiation 120
electromagnetic
  spectrum 38–39
electromagnetism 51
electron microscope 64
electron orbits (shells) 12
electronics 96–102
electrons 10, 11
electroplating 53
elements 11, 12–13, 113, 114, 129
  natural 13
  radioactive 59
  synthetic 13, 58
emulsions 27
Endeavour Orbiter 146–147
endoscope 67
endothermic reactions 21
energy 30–31, 120
  as non-matter 15
  conversion of 31
  in chemical reactions 20, 21, 30
  kinetic 30, 34
  nuclear 51
  potential 30, 34
  renewable 31
  thermal 34, 35
  work 31, 42
Engelbart, Douglas 87
equations 19
Equator 133, 147
Eris 144
Eros 141
erosion 132
escalators 83–84
ethylene 28
Europa 142
evaporation 14
evolution 155
exoplanets 131, 158
exothermic reactions 21
expansion 17, 34
experiment 9, 59
explosions 21
explosives 105
extraterrestrial life 103, 154, 155
Extremely Large Telescope 160

F

factories 70, 75, 76
Falcon 9 146
falling 44
false teeth 86
Faraday, Michael 51, 70, 80, 83
Farnsworth, Philo T 100

Fein, Wilhelm 84
feldspar 16
Fessenden, Reginald 98
filtration 27
fire-resistant materials 157
firefighting equipment 157
Fisher, Alva 84
Fitch, Stephen 90
flight 92–62
  biggest aircraft 95
  bomber aircraft 106
  Concorde 38
  eagle-powered 78
  fighter aircraft 106
  hypersonic X-43 103
  jet aircraft 92, 93
  Maxim's flying
    machine 94
  navigation systems 107
  pedal-powered 78
  silent aircraft 102
  stealth aircraft 107
  steam-powered 77, 94, 95
flowers 39
Flowers, Tommy 96
fluorescent lighting 81
fluorite 16
flush toilet 63
fly-by craft 148
flying bedstead 93
flying saucers 155
flying shuttle 74
foam concrete 94
foam, memory 156
Focke, Heinrich 93
food: colourings 27
  energy from 31
food mixer 84
  ready-made meals 107
  sliced bread 87
  tinned 86, 107
force 40–41
  machines 42–43
Ford, Henry 91
four-stroke cycle 88
Fox Talbot, William 67
Franklin, Benjamin 9, 70, 82
frequency 32
Fresnel, Augustin 66
friction 41, 157
Fried Egg Galaxy 117
fruit 22
fuel: fossil fuels 28, 31, 51
  hydrogen as 52, 59
  oil distribution 27
fuel cells 102
fulcrums 43
future knowledge 158, 160–161

G

Gagarin, Yuri 150, 159
galaxies 113, 114–117, 158
  active 116
  distant 127
  dwarf 115
  formation 115, 117
  names and numbers 117
  shapes 116

169

galaxy clusters 113, 117
Galilean moons 142
Galileo craft 148
Galileo Galilei 64, 65, 158
Galle, Johann 158
gamma radiation 39
gamma rays 120
Ganymede 130, 142
Garnerin, André 94
gas lighting 80
gases 15, 17
  noble gases 13, 29
  propane 19
gears 43
  medieval crank 58
gelignite 105
Gemini constellation 126
Gemini craft 157
gene 54–55
generators 51
  electric 80, 31
  nuclear power 85
  steam turbines 77, 81
genetics 9
geologists: 119
  robot 139
germanium 12
giant planets 142–143, 148
Gifford, Henri 77
Gilbert, William 59
glaciers 132, 133
glass 29
gliders 92
global warming 93
Goddard, Robert 106
gods and goddesses 124, 137, 139
goggles, skiers' 157
gold 13
golf balls 157
Goodyear, Charles 90
Gorrie, John 84
gramophone 99
gravity 44–45, 59,
  113, 129, 158
  balanced forces 40
  discovery of 58
  of stars 123
  on Mars 138
  waves 58
  zero 44
Greece, Ancient 59
Greeks, Ancient 159
greenhouse effect 137
Gregory, James 65
grenades 105
Groof, Vincent de 95
Grosseteste, Robert 58
Grove, William 102
Guinevere Planitia 137
Gumper, Jake 90
Gutenberg, Johannes 62
gypsum 16

H

hairdryer, electric 84
Hale-Bopp, Comet 144
Halley's Comet 145, 158
hang-gliders 157

hardness 16
Hargreaves, James 75
Harrington, John 63
hats, self-raising 79
headphones 46
heart, artificial 87
heat and heating 34–35
  burning 18, 19, 28
  effect on matter 14
  effect on solvents 26
  electricity used for 50
  water 24, 25, 35
heating, electric fire 83
helicopter 93
helium 13, 114, 115
  in stars 123, 128, 129, 158
  in the Sun 124, 125, 129
Henson, William 95
Hero of Alexandria 74
Herschel, William 65, 158
Hertz, Heinrich 39
Higgs boson particle 58
Hindus, ancient 159
Hipparchus 127, 159
history 58–59
Holland, John Philip 105
holograms 99
Holt's ball-grinding
  machine 90
home movies 69
Honold, Gottlob 89
Hooke, Robert 65
Hoover 85
Hopper, Grace 62
hot-air balloon 92
hotel, Space 161
hovercraft 93
Howe, Elias 83
Hoyle, Fred 118
Hubble space telescope
  65, 121, 159, 160
Hubble, Edwin 118, 158
Hughes, David 98
Hughes, Howard 95
human beings 129, 132,
  154, 155
Hunley, Horace 95
Huygens, Christiaan 63
Hyakutake, Comet 144
Hyatt, John Wesley 68
hydrochloric acid 22
hydrogen 11, 12, 13, 114, 115
  and acidity 22
  as fuel for cars 52, 59
  in stars 123, 128, 129, 158
  in the Sun 124, 125, 129
hypothesis 9

I

ice 24, 25, 34
  in comets 144
  on Earth 132, 133
  on Mars 138, 139
Ida 140
implants 103
indicators 22
Industrial Revolution 75
inertia 40

inflation era 114
infrared radiation 38
inorganic chemistry 9, 29
integrated circuits 96, 97
internal combustion
  engine 77, 88, 90
International Space Station
  (ISS) 146, 152–153, 158, 160
  and space tourists 150
  meals 153, 156
  inventions 156–157
internet 101,107
Io 142
iron 18, 21, 46
  filings 46
  iron: extraction from ore 40
  smelting 74
iron, electric 82
  electrical 49
  heat 35
  ionic bonds 11
Islamic science 58

J

James Webb Space Telescope 160
Janssen, Hans 64
Jarvik, Robert 87
jeans 86
Jenney, William Le
  Baron 77
jet engine 71, 92, 93
Jobs, Steve 71, 96, 97
Johnson, Herbert 84
joining 21
Jouffroy d'Abbans,
  marquis de 76
Joule, James Prescott 59
joules 31
joysticks 156
Judson, Whitcomb 87
jukebox 85
Jump jet 93
Jupiter 130, 142, 148
  and asteroids 141
  comet impact 145
  future missions 161

K

Kay, John 74
Keck telescopes 121
Kelvin, Lord *see*
  Thomson, William
Kenji Kawakami 79
Kepler Telescope 154
Kepler, Johannes 158
kettle, electric 83
Kevlar 71
Kilby, Jack 96, 97
kinetic energy 30, 34
Kinetoscope 68
KitchenAid 84
Knight, Mattie 71
Korolev, Sergei 107
Kuiper Belt 130, 131,
  144, 149
Kwolek, Stephanie 71

L

Laënnec, René 63
landers 138, 148
lasers 99–100
  scalpel 67
lava 135
lavatory, flushing 63
law 9
lawnmower, electric 84
Leclanché, Georges 80
Leclanché battery 80
Leeuwenhoek, Antoni
  van 64
Leibniz, Gottried 58
Lemaître, Georges 158
lemon juice 22
Lenoir, Étienne 90
lenses 64–65, 36, 58
Leonardo da Vinci 70
Leonov, Alexei 150
levers 43
Levi Strauss 86
life 8–9, 15, 25
life preservers: suitcase
  lifejacket 79
  water suit 78
lift, steam-powered 77
light 36–37, 58
  bulbs 80, 81, 50
  characteristics 37
  chemical reactions 20
  colours 39
  electricity used for 29, 49, 50
  gases and 29
  rays 120
  reflection 36
  refraction 36
  speed of 37, 45, 59
  splitting 39
  visible spectrum 38
light years (ly) 115
lighthouses 66
lightning 9, 48
lightning conductor 70, 48, 82
Lippershey, Hans 65
liquids 14
  immiscible 27
Lo, Allen 95
load 42
locomotives: diesel 73
  electric 73
  Maglev 23
  steam 72, 73, 94
lodestone 46
Lumière, Louis and
  Auguste 68
luminosity 122
Luna 128 craft 135
Lunokhod 101, 149

M

machine tools 90
machines 42–43
  complex 43
  generators 51
  motors 51
  nanotechnology 59

Magellan craft 148
Magellan Telescope 160
magic lantern 68
magnetic domains 47
magnetic field 46, 47
magnetic resonance
 imaging (MRI) 49
magnets and magnetism 46–47
 electromagnets 51
 in generators 51
 in motors 51
Maiman, Theodore 99
Main Belt 140, 141
main sequence 58
mammals 155
Marconi, Guglielmo 71, 98
mare:
 Mare Crisium 135
 Mare Tranquillitatis 135
Mars 130, 138–139
 Mars Express 148
 Mars Phoenix Lander 138
 missions to 138
 possible life on 154
 robot explorers 139,
  148, 158
 sending men to 161
 telescope mirror 156
mass 44
 atomic 12
mass production 70,
 90, 91
materials 63
mathematics 9, 59
 calculus 58
Matheson's steam tram 78
matter 14–17, 114
Mauna Kea, Hawaii 121
Maxim, Hiram 94
Maybach, Wilhelm 88
McAdam, John 91
McNaught, Comet 144
mechanics 8
medical scanners 38, 49
medicines 28
Mendel, Gregor 9
Mendeleyev, Dmitri 12
meniscus 17
Mercury 130, 136
mercury: 13, 17
 thermometers 34
Merlin, Joseph 86
Mesopotamia 59
metallic bonds 11
metals 13
 alloys 29
meteorites 140, 141
meteors 127
microchips 96, 100, 97
microphone 98
microprocessors 96, 100,
 97, 103
microscope 36, 64, 65
microwaves 38, 58, 120
 background radiation 114
microwave oven 85
Middle Ages 159
military vehicles:
 Humvee 107
 tanks 106

milk 22
milk of magnesia 23
Milky Way Galaxy 113, 115,
 117, 126, 158
Mir Space station 150
Miranda 143
mirrors 36, 58
missiles: V-2 106
 ICBMs 107
 see also rockets
mixtures 26–27
 separating 27
mobile phone 100, 157
molecules 11, 14, 15, 16, 17:
 heat and 34
 in chemical reactions
  18–19, 20–21
 in water 24, 25
 nanotechnology 59
momentum 41
Montgolfier brothers 92
Moon (Earth's) 44, 134–135
 ancient cultures and 158
 and Space tourism 161
 birth 135
 collecting rocks on 156
 craters 135
 eclipse of 134
 historical study of 159
 living on 160
 missions to 135, 148, 149,
  150, 159, 160
 phases 134
moons (other planets')
 112, 130
 Jupiter 142
 Mars 139
 Neptune 143
 Saturn 142
 Uranus 143
Morse, Samuel 62
motion and movement
 40–41
 perpetual 43
 study of mechanics 8
 three laws of 40–41
motorbike 91
motors 51
mouse, computer 87
mousetrap 63
movie camera 68
movies 69
MP3 player 100
MRI scans see magnetic
 resonance imaging
Murdock, William 80
musical instruments 33
Muybridge, Eadweard 13
mythology:
 Ancient Egyptian 124
 Ancient Greek 124, 125,
  126, 139
 Ancient Roman 137, 138, 142, 143

N

nanotechnology 59, 102
NASA 68, 65, 107
Nasmyth, James 76

natural elements 13
Near Shoemaker craft 148
nebulae 113, 122, 127
 planetary 128
 solar 131
neodymium 46
neon signs 81
Neptune 130, 143, 148,
 158
neutral substances 22
neutralizing acids 23
neutron stars 128
neutrons 10, 48
New Horizons mission 149
Newcomen pump 75
Newcomen, Thomas 75
Newton, Isaac 40, 58,
 65, 158
newtons 31, 40
Niepce, Nicéphore 66
Nims, Jerry 95
nitinol 156
nitrogen 13
nitroglycerine 105
Nobel, Alfred 70, 105
noble gases 13, 29
non-matter 15
North Pole 47
Northern Lights 47
Noyce, Robert 96, 97
nuclear energy 51
nuclear fission 58, 59
nuclear fusion 59
nuclear physics 8
nuclear power 85, 103
nuclear reactions 31, 39,
 125, 129
nucleus 8, 10
 comet's 144

O

observation 9
observatories 118
 Chinese 159
oceans 25, 132, 133,
 155
oil 27, 28
oil wells 90
Olympus Mons 139
Oort Cloud 144
Oppenheimer, Robert 107
optical fibres 29
Orbiters 146–147, 148
orbits 130, 44
 asteroids' 140, 141
 comets' 144
 Moon's 134
 planets' 136, 138, 143
organic chemistry 8, 28,
Orion constellation 126
Orion craft 160, 161
Ørsted, Hans Christian 51
Otis, Elisha 77
Otto, Nikolaus 91
ovens: electric 83
 microwave 85
 energy-efficient 156
oxygen 11, 133

P

Pabst, Hans Joachim 93
Padalka, Gennady 150
Panhard Levessor 89
paper bags 71
parachutes 94, 95
Parsons, Charles 76,
 77, 81
particle collider 58
particles: charged 48
 light 37
 subatomic 10, 59, 58
Pascal, Blaise 96
patents 62, 63
Pauling, Linus 11, 58
payloads 146, 147
Payne-Gaposchkin,
 Cecilia 118, 158
peaks 32
penumbra 37
periodic comets 145
periodic table 12–13, 59
perpetual motion 43
Perry, Stephen 86
petrol pump 90
pH scale 22–23
pharmaceuticals 28
Philae craft 148
Phobos 139
phone signals 38
phonograph 98
phosphorous 13
photography 66, 67, 20, 36
photons 37, 38
 in auroras 47
photosphere 125
physical sciences 8
physics 8, 59
Pierce, John 101
pitch 32
planetary geologists 119
planetary motion, laws
 of 158
planetary nebulae 128
planetary remains 112
planets 44, 59, 112, 127,
 130–131, 136–139
 ancient cultures and
  158, 159
 distant 112
 dwarf 112, 130, 144
 Earth-like 154
 exoplanets 131, 158
 giant 142–143, 148
 historical study of 158, 159
 moons 112, 130, 139, 142, 143
 rings 142
 shape 142
plastics 63
pliers 43
Pluto 130, 144
 mission to 149
pneumatic tyre 63, 90, 89
poles 46, 47
poles (polar regions):
 on Earth 133
 on Mars 138, 139
Poliakov, Valeri 150
polymers 28

171

polythene 28
potential energy 30, 34
Poulsen, Valdemar 99
power 31
power station, Pearl
   Street (New York) 81
power stations 51, 59
pressure 15, 123
printing press 62
prisms 39
propane gas 19
protons 10, 11, 48
protostars 112
Ptolemy 59, 159
pulleys 42–43
pulsars 128
pumps:
   Archimedes screw 74
   steam-powered 72, 74, 75
Pythagoras 159

Q

quantum theory 59
quartz 16

R

Ra (sun god) 124
radar 38, 99
radiation 35
   background 114
   electromagnetic 120, 38–39
radio 71, 98–99
   car radios 89
   transistor radios 99
   see also telegraph
radio astronomers 119
radio telescopes 121, 154
radio waves 120, 121, 38
radioactivity 59
railways 72, 94
rain 133, 25
   acid rain 23
rainbows 39, 58
ramps 42
razor, electric 85
Reber, Grote 65
recording 33
red giants 128
reflection 36
refraction 36
refrigerator 84
relativity 45, 58
Renaissance 59
Reno, Jesse 84
Renoir region 136
reptiles 155
repulsion 46
resistance 49
rivers 132, 133
roads 90, 91
robots 101, 103, 59
rockets 146–147
   gunpowder 104
   launch sites 147
   liquid-fuelled 106, 107
   see also missiles
Rohwedder, Otto Frederick 87

roller skates 86
robot explorers 139,
   148–149, 159, 161
Romans 59
Rømer, Ole 59
Röntgen, Wilhelm 59
Rosetta craft 148
rovers 138
Rowlands, Henry 78
rubber: elastic band 86
   synthetic 107
   vulcanization of 90
Rubin, Vera 118
Ruska, Ernst 64
rust 18
Rutherford, Ernest 58

S

safety pin 86
salicylic acid 28
salt 11
satellite communications 46
satellite dishes 156
satellites 157
Saturn 130, 142
   missions to 148, 149, 161
Savery, Thomas 74
Schick, Col. Jacob 85
science: branches 8–9
   future 58–59
   history 58–59
   method 9
   theoretical 58
screw propulsion:
   steamships 76
screws 42
Search for Extraterrestrial
   Intelligence (SETI) 154
Seely, Henry 82
semaphore 98
sewage system 76
sewing machines 83
shadows 37
Shakespeare Region 136
Shaw, Percy 66
Shepard, Alan 135
shepherd moons 142
Shockley, William 96
shoes, running 157
shooting stars 127
showers, pedal-powered 25
Siemens, Werner von 73
Sikorsky, Igor 93
silicates 59
silicon 12
silver 13
Sinclair, Clive 95
Singer, Isaac 83
Sirius 126, 127
skating 41
skyscrapers 77
smelting, iron ore 74
snow 133
   comets made of 144
   on Mars 139
soap 23, 28
Sobrero, Ascanio 105
sodium 11, 12

SOHO 145
Sojourner rover 148
solar cars 102
solar energy 85
solar nebulae 131
Solar System: 44, 59,
   112, 115, 130–131
   comets in 145
   search for life in 155
   see also planets, Sun
solar wind 125
solids 14
   non-crystalline 16
solutes 26
solutions: 26
   concentrated 20
   saturated 26
solvents 25, 26
sounds and sound
   waves 32–33
Southern Lights 47
Soyuz craft 146, 150
Space 44–45, 58
Space astronomers 119
Space shuttle 146–147, 157, 159
   replacement of 160
Space sickness 152
Space technology
   spin-offs 156–157
space tourism hotels 102
Space walks 150, 151, 153, 157
Space, definition of 146
spacecraft 118, 159
   and comets 145, 148, 149
   fly-by 148
   landers 138, 148
   Mars missions 138, 139, 148, 158
   Moon missions 135, 148, 149,
      150, 159, 160
   orbiters 146–147, 148
   payload 146
   private 146, 150
   robot explorers 139,
      148–149, 159, 161
   rockets 146–147
   Titan mission 142
SpaceShipOne 146, 150
SpaceShip Two 146, 150
spacesuits 151, 157
   future 161
Spangler, James 85
spark plugs 89
spectacles 66
spectrographs 119, 120
spectrum, visible
   38–39
speed of light 37, 45, 59
speed of sound 33
Spencer, Percy Lebaron
   58, 85
spinning 41
spinning frame 70, 75
spinning wheel 74
Spirit rover 139, 158
Spitzer Space Telescope 121
splitting 21
   atoms 8, 59
   light 39
Spruce Goose 95
Sputnik 1 satellite 159

Stanley Steamer 77
star clusters 113, 122
Stardust craft 149
stars 45, 112–113, 115, 118,
   122–123
   ancient cultures and 159
   birth 112, 122, 129
   brightness 127
   colour 122
   constellations 126–127, 159
   death 113, 128, 129
   density 123
   dwarfs and giants 128, 158
   gas 123
   gravity and pressure 123
   historical study of 158, 159
   luminosity 122
   mass 123
   maturing 113, 128
   neutron 128
   protostars 112
   shape 123
   shooting 127
   size 123
   temperature 122
starter motor 89
static electricity 48
steam 24–25, 35
steam engines:
   beam engine 72
   cars 76, 77
   flying machine 40
   locomotives 72, 73, 40
   tram 78
   turbine 76, 77, 81
steam hammer 76
steam power 72–23, 34, 90
steamships 76
   rocking saloon 95
   steam-turbine powered 22
   see also boats, warships
steel 46
Stephenson Robert 72
Stephenson, George 73
stethoscope 63
Stonehenge 59
street lights 80
Strite, Charles 84
subatomic particles 10, 59, 58
sublimation 15
submarines: nuclear 107
   pedal-power 105
sulphuric acid 22, 53
Sun 34, 44, 59, 113, 115,
   124–125, 128, 129
   ancient cultures and 158
   atmosphere 124–125
   centre of Solar System 130
   core and energy 125
   coronal mass ejections 124
   danger of looking at 124
   eclipse of 125
   effect on comets 145
   effect on the Moon 134
   formation 131
   granulation 124
   prominences 124
   spicules 124
   telescope for 121
   temperature 124

Sun gods, ancient 124
sunburn 39
Sundback, Gideon 87
sunglasses 157
sunspots 124
supercomputer 97
superconductors 49
supergiants 59
supernova remnants 128
supernovae 128, 129
supersonic flight 33
surface tension 17
Surveyor 1 spacecraft 135
suspensions 26–27
Swan, Joseph 80
swapping 21
Swedish Solar Telescope 121
swimsuits 157
synthetic elements 13, 58

T

Tadpole Galaxy 117
talc 16
talkies 69
tape recorder 99
Taurus constellation 126, 127
Technicolor 69
technology, adaptation
 of 156–157
telegraph: electric
 see also radio
 telegraphy 71, 98
telephone 71, 98
 mobile phones 100
telephone signals 38
telescope 64, 65, 36,
 119, 120–121, 143
 Aperture Spherical 120
 future 160
 history of 158, 159
 Space-based 121, 159, 160
telescope mirror 156
telescope operators 119
television 100–1
television signals 38
Telstar 101
temperature 20, 24–25,
 26, 34–35
 Earth's 133
 planets' 136, 137, 138
 see also cooling heating
 stars' 122
 Sun's 124
Tereshkova, Valentina 150
theoretical science 58
theory 9
thermal, definition of 59
thermometer 34, 156
Thompson, Robert 90
Thomson, William
 (Lord Kelvin) 59
tides 44
time 45
time travel 59, 102
tinned food 86, 107
Titan 142, 149
Titania 143
Tito, Dennis 150

toaster, pop-up 84
tomatoes 22
Tombaugh, Clive 149
tongs 43
tools: machine 90
toothpaste 23
topaz 16
torpedoes 95, 105
tourism, Space 150, 161
toys, electric 82
traffic lights 87
transformers 51
transistor 96, 99
transport 88–93
Trevithick, Richard 72, 94
triode valve 99
Trippel, Hans 94
Triton 143
Trojans 141
troughs 32
turret lathe 90
Tycho Crater 135

U

UFOs (unidentified
 flying objects) 155
ultraviolet radiation 39
ultraviolet rays 120
umbra 37
Universe 112–113, 161
 ancient beliefs about 159
 creation of 114–115
 expansion 115, 118
 historical study of 158–159
uniwheel 79
uranium 12
Uranus 130, 143, 148, 158

V

vacuum cleaners 85
Valles Marineris 139
Velodouche 79
Venus (goddess) 137
Venus (planet) 130, 136-137
video games 101
virtual reality 151
viscosity 17
visible spectrum 38
volcanoes:
 on Earth 132
 on Mars 138, 139
 on the Moon 135
 on Venus 137
Volta, Alessandro 80, 53
voltage 51
Voskhod 2 craft 150
Vostok craft 150
Voyager craft 148, 159
vulcanization 90

W

Wankel, Felix 89
warships:
 aircraft carriers 106
 battleships 106

warships *continued*
 man o' war 105
 see also boats, steamships
 triremes 104
 washing machine 84
water 113, 132, 133, 24 25
 and electrolysis 52
 and temperature 24, 25, 34, 35
 as compound 11
 chemical equation 19
 molecular structure 24
 pH level 22
 properties 17
 salt water 34, 52
 sound in 33
water cycle 133
water filters 156
waterwheels 58, 74
Watson-Watt, Robert 99
Watt, James 72
wavelength 32, 120
waves:
 electromagnetic 38–39
 gravitational 58
 light 37
 sound 32–33
weak bonds 11
weather 133
 on Jupiter 142
 on Mars 138
weaving, looms 74
wedges 43
weight 44
weightlessness 146, 151
Westinghouse, George 82, 81
wheel 42–43, 63, 90
 automobile wheels 89
wheelbarrows 43, 58
Whipple, Fred 118
white dwarfs 128
 Kepler 154
White Knight Two 146
Whitehead, Robert 105
Whitney, Eli 70
Whittle, Frank 71, 92
Wilkinson Microwave
 Anisotropy Probe
 (WMAP) 115
winds: 133, 138, 143
 solar 125
wireless 98
work: energy 31, 42
 machines 42–43
Wozniak, Steve 71, 96, 97
Wright, Wilbur and
 Orville 92

X

x-rays 39, 59, 120, 121

Z

Zelenka, Thomas 79
zero gravity 44
zip fastener 87
zodiac 126, 127
zoetrope 67
zoology 8

Acknowledgements

Dorling Kindersley would like to thank Jackie Brind for the original indexes and Jenny Finch for naming Sidney Spacehopper.
No Brainwaves were harmed during the making of this book.

All images © Dorling Kindersley

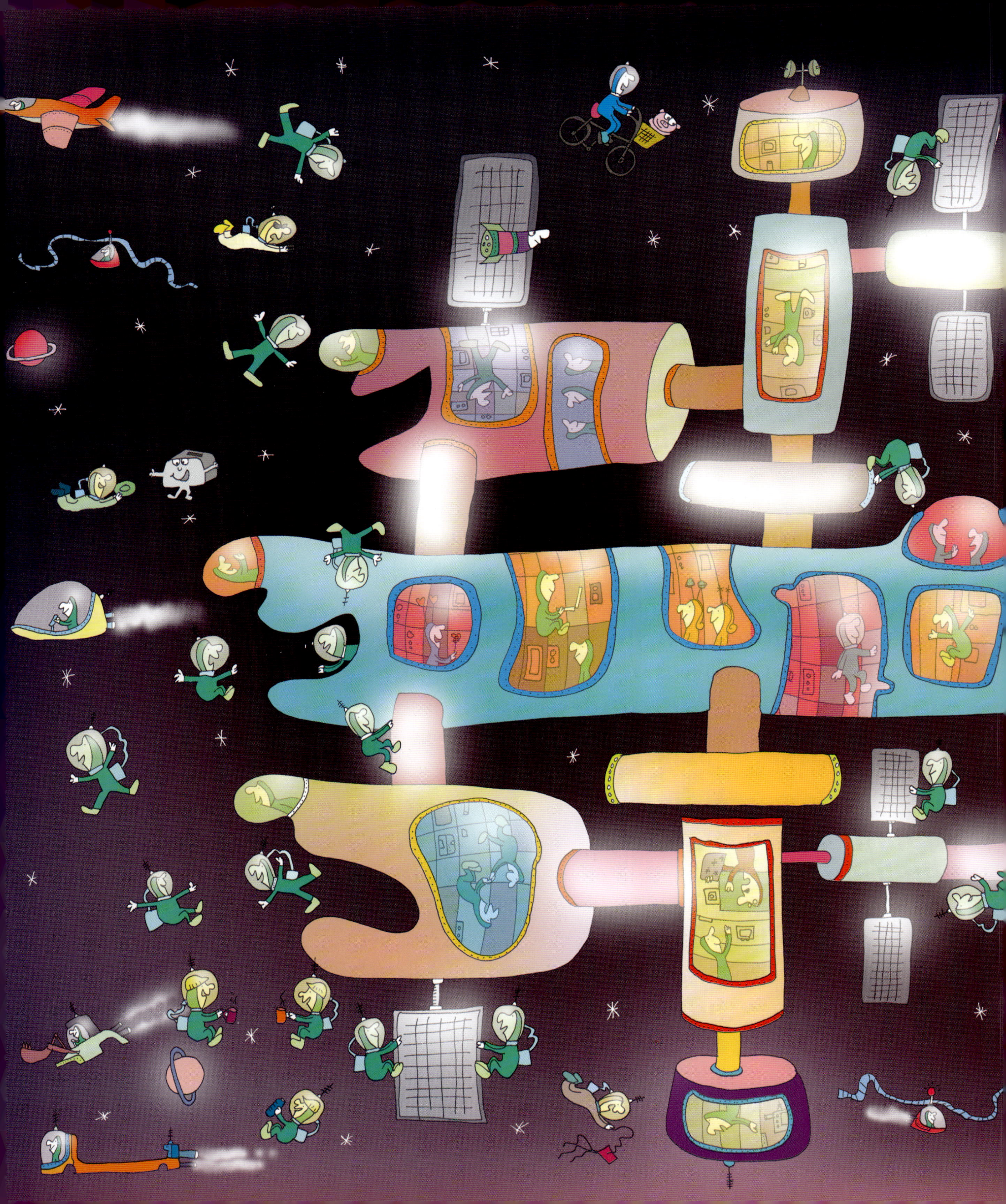

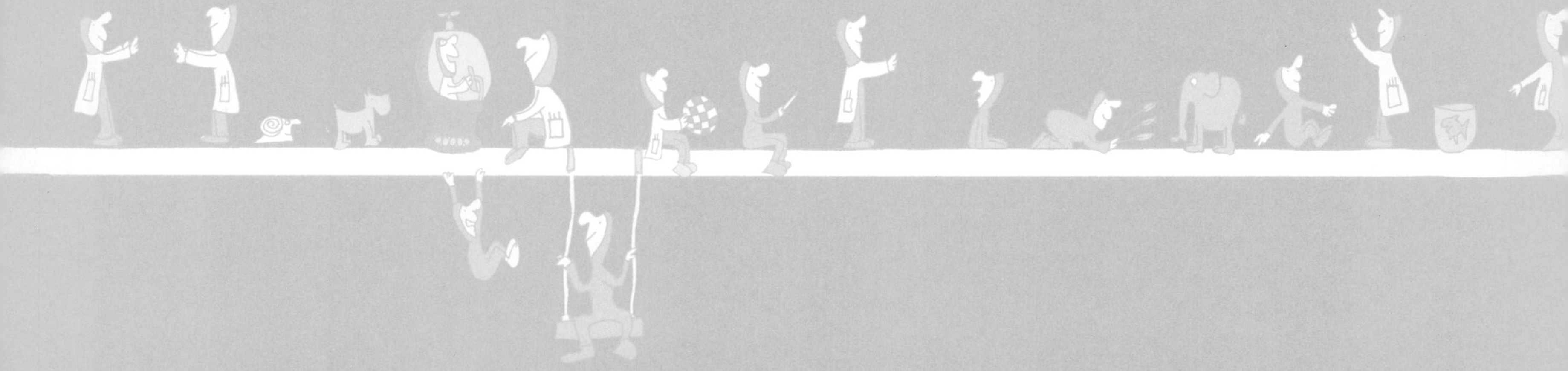